MW00612580

The New Durkheim

The New Durkheim

IVAN STRENSKI

RUTGERS UNIVERSITY PRESS

NEW BRUNSWICK, NEW JERSEY, AND LONDON

To

Antoine, Bob, Bill, Don, Ed, George, Jeff, Jennifer, Jerry, Jim, John,
Louis, Marcel, Mark, Philippe, Richard, Robert, Sue, Terry,
Werner, Viktor, and Willie

"I cannot divorce myself from the work of a school. If there is any
individuality, it is immersed within voluntary anonymity. Perhaps
what characterises my scientific career . . . is the feeling of working
together as a team, and the conviction that collaborating with
others is a drive against isolation and the pretentious search for
originality." (Marcel Mauss, "An Intellectual Self-Portrait")

LIBRARY OF CONGRESS CATALOGING-IN-PUBLICATION DATA

Strenski, Ivan.
  The new Durkheim / Ivan Strenski.
    p.   cm.
  Includes bibliographical references and index.
  ISBN-13: 978-0-8135-3893-8 (hardcover : alk. paper)
  ISBN-13: 978-0-8135-3894-5 (pbk. : alk. paper)
  1. Religion and sociology.   2. Durkheim, Emile, 1858–1917.   I. Title.
  BL60.S77 2006
  306.6—dc22

                                                    2005035672

A British Cataloging-in-Publication record for this book is available
from the British Library.

Copyright © 2006 by Ivan Strenski
All rights reserved

No part of this book may be reproduced or utilized in any form or by any means,
electronic or mechanical, or by any information storage and retrieval system,
without written permission from the publisher. Please contact Rutgers University
Press, 100 Joyce Kilmer Avenue, Piscataway, NJ 08854–8099. The only exception to
this prohibition is "fair use" as defined by U.S. copyright law.

Manufactured in the United States of America

CONTENTS

PART ONE
Introduction

1   So Much More Durkheim   3

PART TWO
Turning the Philosophical Ground

2   Durkheim, Hamelin, and the "French Hegel"

3   The Ironies of *Fin-de-Siècle* Rebellions against
Historicism and Empiricism in the École Pratique des
Hautes Études, Fifth Section   66

PART THREE
The Vagaries of Religious Belonging

4   Durkheim, Judaism, and the Afterlife   87

5   Zionism, Brahminism, and the Embodied Sacred:
What Durkheimians Owe to Sylvain Lévi   118

6   The Rise of Ritual and the Hegemony of Myth:
Sylvain Lévi, the Durkheimians, and Max Müller   134

7   Durkheim, Hubert, and the Clerical Modernist
Discourse on Symbolism   158

PART FOUR
Institutions and Other Afflictions

8   Durkheim, Disciplinarity, and the "Sciences Religieuses"   181

9   Liberal Protestant Theology and/or "Science Religieuse"   203

10 The Durkheimians and the Protestants in the
École Pratique, Fifth Section: The Dark Side   216

PART FIVE
Politics and Pedagogy Today

11 Durkheim Sings: Teaching the "New Durkheim"
on Religion   229

12 Christians, Durkheimians, and Other Animals   249

13 Sacrifice, Gift, and the Social Logic of Muslim
"Human Bombers"   270

14 A Durkheimian Text in Turkey: Ziya Gökalp,
Hüseyin Nail Kubali, and Muslim Civil Society   303

Notes   337
References   349
Index   367

PART ONE

Introduction

229-30

[handwritten margin notes:]

229-30
au. Stud. Toronto
(1970s? (ref. for reductive)
cliche ~ Durk.,
"New Durk." attrib. to Lukes 1974
au. moves to relig. Studies —
(similar to lib. theol. ~ 1900)

polemic vs. P. Singer ~ Chr. ~~~ vs animal rights
rather forcest arg ~ medieval, Chr. emph. Community
à la Durk;
∴ community w. animals
is Chr. tradth,
∴ Durk. helps move
Chr. to animal lib.!

1

So Much More Durkheim

While known commonly, and almost exclusively so, as the first "sociologist," Émile Durkheim is coming increasingly to be seen as far more than that. A new appreciation of Durkheim, extending well beyond traditional academic boundaries, has been under way for more than three decades and has now accomplished a good deal of what it originally set out to do. This revived appreciation of Durkheim and Durkheimian thought has emerged from several centers of activity in Europe and North America, primarily from scholars in the humanities and human sciences, such as history, philosophy, religious studies, and continental *sociologie*. In large part, this new look at Durkheim is soundly historicist. It takes its impetus from the desire to uncover the nature of the Durkheimian intellectual project in terms of his original intentions, and insofar as these aims were worked out in the particular historical context of Durkheim's own time and place. As such, this historicist re-examination of Durkheimian thought encouraged thickly contextualized readings of Durkheimian texts, emphasizing the desire to understand the authorial intentions of Durkheim and his fellows. This collection of my own essays aims to assemble some samples of these new "historicist" studies of Durkheimian social thought, especially about religion.

While the spirit of this new Durkheimian scholarship has been collaborative and collegial, the success of this new scholarship was impelled by the original efforts of three small clusters of individuals and their enabling institutions.

The first major intellectual impetus to the modern Durkheim revival was Steven Lukes's monumental *Émile Durkheim: His Life and Work* (Lukes 1972). Although a philosopher by training, Lukes produced a still widely used and now classic work of richly contextualized intellectual history. This systematic and massive survey of the entire biography of Durkheim situated his writings both within their European historical settings and in terms of Durkheim's intentions for realizing certain of his scientific and political projects. At the same time, Lukes established the first coherent and consistent bibliography of Durkheim's work. This has greatly facilitated all subsequent Durkheimian scholarship by establishing a regular system of classification and enumeration for the Durkheim bibliography that has become the accepted consensus scheme for Durkheim scholars worldwide. On the heels of Lukes's work, early efforts at providing exhaustive bibliographies of Durkheim and the Durkheimian school were undertaken, notably, by Yash Nandan in the 1970s and 1980s (Nandan 1977; 1980).

Lukes's book attracted—and continues to attract—attention in part because his historical work exceeded in quality the generally patchy or relatively shallow intellectual histories of Durkheim up to that time. Lukes worked not only from the major texts of Durkheim, but also from a variety of heretofore unexploited archival materials, interviews, and obscure publications previously not taken into account. Thanks to the new perspective that some of these data gave Lukes, he was able to depart with confidence from the so-called "presentist" and theoretical readings of Durkheim, wherein Durkheim's writings were seen primarily from the viewpoint of their utility in bolstering present-day theoretical preoccupations in the social sciences. Biographical materials afforded Lukes the beginnings of a new perspective on Durkheim. Lukes thus was able to place far more emphasis upon trying to clarify what *Durkheim*'s overall purposes and intentions were in proposing his theories than had been previously possible. Lukes did so in a spirit of inquiry that considered the full range of Durkheim's intentions, their complexities and interactions. How did Durkheim's theories fit within the projects that he pursued in his institutional and political life? For Lukes, Durkheim's thought was not purely theoretical, but also political and ethical at the same time. To understand Durkheim and his thought, one had to see how this complex mix of intentions was resolved in particular cases. As a person of democratic socialist leanings himself, Lukes took special delight in rectifying some of the misconceptions surrounding Durkheim's life and character foisted upon him by conservative thinkers like Robert Nisbet (Nisbet 1966).

What also differentiated Lukes's approach from what was typical of the time was his, at least relative, detachment from whether or not Durkheim's thinking facilitated any particular form of theorizing in our own day. This contrasted fundamentally with classics of an earlier era such as Talcott Parsons's *The Structure of Social Action*. Parsons interpreted Durkheim's thought as a kind of "anticipation" of a theoretical orientation that he himself sought to establish in sociology (Parsons 1937). Insofar as Parsons informed his study with history, he did so in order to provide historical legitimacy for his own constructive theoretical efforts. He argued that a clear underlying direction in the thought of Durkheim (and other major social theorists) could be detected, and that it could be put to use for current social theorizing. In a similar vein, Jeffrey C. Alexander, himself somewhat straddling the line between Parsons's presentism and Lukes's historicism, published a most formidable successor to Parsons's book. His four-volume *Theoretical Logic in Sociology* provided a powerful example of constructive sociologizing aided by a commendable degree of history. Nonetheless, for all Alexander's serious dedication to history, both he and Parsons still remained committed first and foremost to building a theory of society (Alexander 1982a; 1982b; 1983; 1984; Parsons 1937).

A second source of the present reassessment of Durkheim and Durkheimian social thought may be traced to the last years of the 1960s and to the efforts of Philippe Besnard and Victor Karady at the Maison des Sciences de l'Homme in Paris. They instigated and supervised a series of projects anthologizing, editing, and publishing the primary sources—many heretofore unavailable—of Durkheim, Maurice Halbwachs, Marcel Mauss, and others close to the original Durkheimian circle (Karady 1968; 1975). Besnard's *The Sociological Domain* also deserves mention for collecting the individual contributions of a dozen or so scholars who devoted themselves to exposing the many ways the followers of Durkheim made independent contributions to the development of social thought in the Durkheimian style beyond Durkheim himself (Besnard 1983). In Paris, Besnard has for many years been a generous and attentive host and an invaluable guide to visiting scholars seeking to make their way through the maze of Durkheimian research in France. He thus functioned to provide an essential point of reference and intellectual contact for all who passed through the capital; his office likewise created a modest archive of unpublished "Durkheimiana" and a center for the dissemination of research on the Durkheimians from its location in the École des Hautes Études en Sciences Sociales. An excellent example of the fruitfulness of collaboration with Besnard are the achievements of Québec sociologist Marcel Fournier. On his own, Fournier published a massive intellectual biography of Marcel Mauss, and together with Besnard, edited and published a volume of Durkheim's letters to Mauss (Besnard & Fournier 1998; Fournier 1994).

Third, the immense contributions of England's W.S.F. Pickering put him alongside others at the top of any list of main figures in the Durkheim revival. Pickering has been a tireless and productive promoter of scholarship reassessing Durkheim and Durkheimian work. Not only has Pickering authored and edited several key anthologies of Durkheim's work, he has also produced a major work on *Durkheim's Sociology of Religion* (Pickering 1975; 1984; 1993; 2000). In the English-speaking world, Pickering has been the hub of publishing, collaborative research and conference organizing in connection with his foundation of Oxford's British Centre for Durkheimian Studies. These efforts have resulted in several volumes of collected essays on Durkheimian themes, edited primarily with Willie Watts Miller (Allen et al. 1998; Martins & Pickering 1994; Pickering 2000). Pickering also founded the journal *Durkheimian Studies/Études Durkheimiennes,* which is now jointly edited with Miller and has sponsored occasional publication and translations into English of short works by Henri Hubert, Marcel Mauss, and others under the auspices of the British Centre of Durkheimian Studies.

Benefiting from the collaborative work of both English and Continental institutional centers, North American Durkheimians have contributed substantially to the Durkheim revival as well, although mostly as individuals. Operating for the most part under the rubric of the history of science, some of the most influential early essays historicizing Durkheim's scholarship come from the pen of two American scholars, W. Paul Vogt and Robert Alun Jones (Jones 1975; 1981a; 1981b; 1984; Jones & Vogt 1984; Vogt 1983a; 1983b). Jones is responsible, as well, for rigorous use and defense of the historicist method first developed by the Cambridge intellectual historian, Quentin Skinner (Jones 1977; Skinner 1969). He has recently published a major work on the development of Durkheim's sociological realism (Jones 1999). In terms of institution building, about the only effort matching what the Europeans have done is "The Durkheim Pages" website, built and maintained by Jones at the University of Illinois Artificial Intelligence Center for the Humanities (http://www.relst.uiuc.edu/durkheim). There, one can access a wealth of information, such as on-line versions of Durkheim's texts, bibliographies, discussions, news of conferences, and so on. For my part, I have gained much from the articulations of the historicist method that Jones adapted from Skinner and from the original research Jones has contributed to all those interested in understanding Durkheim and the Durkheimians. My three Durkheimian books—*Durkheim and the Jews of France* (1997), *Contesting Sacrifice* (2002), and *Theology and the First Theory of Sacrifice* (2003)—owe tremendous debts to Jones, and indeed to Besnard, Pickering, and other members of the new Durkheimian *équipe* as models of the practice of intellectual history. The essays in the present collection reflect that same indebtedness.

In many ways, a palpable sense of a new Durkheimian *équipe* is thus alive today, thanks mainly to the efforts of these generous and devoted colleagues. Meeting in periodic international and regional conferences and communicating through the journal are those one might see as making up this new *équipe*. A partial list of such a new and international *équipe* would include, in addition to those just mentioned, Neil J. Allen, John I. Brooks III, Mark Cladis, James Clifford, D. Egashira, Marcel Fournier, Michael Gane, Werner Gephardt, Terry Godlove, Robert Alun Jones, Josep R. Llobera, Jennifer Mergy, Laurent Mucchielli, Dénes Némedi, Don Nielson, Giovanni Paoletti, William Ramp, Tristram Reilly, Susan Stedman Jones, Michele Richman, Warren Schmaus, Ivan Strenski, Kenneth Thompson, Edward Tiryakian, and others. Also active in encouraging the work of these Durkheimian scholars were two friendly family members of Durkheim's Etienne Halphen, Durkheim's grandson, and Claudette Raphaël Kennedy, a granddaughter of Céline Durkheim, an elder sister of Émile Durkheim. The anthropologist, Maurice Bloch, son to Mrs. Kennedy from her first marriage to Pierre Bloch, has also participated actively in conferences held under the auspices of the British Centre for Durkheimian Studies.

While the deepest and broadest growth of the Durkheim revival stems from the humanities—from intellectual history, philosophy, religious studies, history of science, the Continental *sciences humaines*, and such—a notable Durkheimian revival of its own has also taken root in mainline American sociology. Besides the work of sociologists like Alexander, who ought to be recognized for his early promotion of Durkheimian studies, sociologist Mustafa Emirbayer has recently attained a kind of prominence in sociology for a series of articles and a book virtually announcing a reassessment of Durkheim that the humanists would find recognizable (Alexander 1988). Emirbayer has argued that Durkheim should be seen as a distinctive "sociologist of modernity," a figure who deployed discourses particularly salient for the social problems of our own time (Emirbayer 2003). His seminal essays of 1996, "Useful Durkheim" and "Durkheim's Contribution to the Sociological Analysis of History," signaled Emirbayer's larger program of introducing a different kind of Durkheim to mainline American sociology (Emirbayer 1996a; 1996b). For instance, Emirbayer emphasized many of the themes prominent in the work of Durkheim revivers in the humanities, and which also appear in this book. These would include special attention to themes such as the critical place of the work of the later Durkheim, the so-called "religious" Durkheim, to "social life as a network of relations and transactions" (Emirbayer 1996b, 110), to "Durkheim's turn to cultural analysis . . . of the internal complexity and causal significance of cultural structures" (Emirbayer 1996b, 115), to his "causal assessment of 'ritual process' and 'the sacred'"(Emirbayer 1996b, 113), to Durkheim's anticipation of discussions of the conditions of civil society (Emirbayer 1996b, 110, 116; Emirbayer 2003, chs. 8, 9), and finally to Durkheim as analyst of historical phenomena, reprising in part the often overlooked, nearly half-century old, article of Robert Bellah's on the relation of Durkheimian work to the historical sciences (Bellah 1959; Emirbayer 1996a). Before moving on, some points about these parallel movements in reassessing Durkheim might be noted.

To readers outside the academic fields of sociology or history of the human sciences, it might seem odd that Emirbayer operates in almost total ignorance of—in the sense of apparently being either deliberately or accidentally both *unaware of* and *uninterested in*—the work of reassessing Durkheim done by Besnard, Fournier, Jones, Pickering, Vogt, and others whom I label the "humanists." Save for insignificant citations of Steven Lukes or Mark Cladis, Emirbayer cites none of the figures I have mentioned in the Durkheim revival in the humanities. At least three points can be made about this observation. First, like many members of particular academic disciplines, far too many mainline American sociologists, like others within their own disciplinary confines, seem to operate in a universe of their own. Even when it comes to sociology, for too many mainline American sociologists, Bellah, Nielsen, Tiryakian and a few others excepted, "sociology" means *American* sociology, with virtually no account being taken of work done in Europe (with the partial exception of Great Britain), or at least in languages other than English. As a result, sociology originating outside of North America is virtually non-existent. The same cannot be said for the humanist Durkheimians, who consist of a broadly international array of scholars, including such distinguished figures as Edward Tiryakian. Second, as an exchange between historian Robert Alun Jones and sociologist Dean Gerstein showed, a deep gap still divides historians from sociologists as to how the history of the great social theorists is to be written (Jones 1984). Insofar, then, as the humanists pursue an historicist line of inquiry, and tend to play down mainline American sociology's interest in theory construction, this mutual "ignoring" of each other's work on Durkheim will continue.

For my part, I have tried to bridge these disciplinary gaps by citing and celebrating the work of Emirbayer—for instance, in my treatment of Durkheim and civil society—even if I share with my humanist colleagues a general lack of enthusiasm for constructing grand social theories—as Emirbayer puts it: "new horizons of inquiry" (Emirbayer 2003, 2). Nonetheless, let a thousand theories bloom and contend! But, so too let historical research continue without being saddled with the job of bolstering the plausibility of some social theory. Theories ought to stand or fall on their own merits—not on whether or not Durkheim, for example, had the same ideas in mind or not. Having said this, it is then all the more remarkable that, despite their different, sometimes antagonistic, origins and purposes, both humanist and American sociologist revivers of Durkheim agree so much on the kind of Durkheim they wish to bring to the attention of readers today.

I. Philosophy in a Different Key

Ironically, we can give a plausible answer to the question of why this larger image of Durkheim is not better known only by appealing to the historical intentions of Durkheim that sociological theorists often pass over (Jones 1984). Thus, one reason Emirbayer has had to labor to revive and reclaim Durkheim for sociology is that Durkheim sometimes hardly seems like a sociologist at all—and certainly not like a recognizable representative of mainstream American sociology! If anything, Durkheim's background fitted him out for a career in academic philosophy, which in his day was a far more capacious field than so-called "professional" philosophy is today. No wonder American sociologists have looked elsewhere for theoretical guidance.

Worse yet, much of the kind of "philosophy" that Durkheim knew resembled nothing so much as wide-ranging new disciplines of our own time such as "humanities" or "cultural studies." Witness, for example, the extraordinary range of interests encompassed by some of the philosophers and co-workers linked in various ways with Durkheim. Lucien Lévy-Bruhl was celebrated as an historian on French and German Neo-Kantian philosophy long before his books on the science of morals, primitive thought, the "savage" mind, and such (Lévy-Bruhl 1966a; 1966b). Charles Renouvier, similarly, not only served as France's leading interpreter of the highly technical philosophy of Immanuel Kant, but also wrote a book on the science of morals, and works of political advice for devotees of the republic, as well as analyses of systems of government and general critical essays on culture and religion (Renouvier 1848; 1851; 1912; 1918). Célestin Bouglé functioned as an unofficial cultural ambassador to the United States in the 1930s, and delivered a notable address to the Teachers College at Columbia University on the general culture of French philosophy (Bouglé 1938). Although first an historian, then a philosopher, one of Durkheim's inner circle, Henri Hubert, was not only a talented graphic artist, art historian, and museum curator, but also a published field archeologist and folklorist. During the First World War, he was credited with designing "caterpillar" tracks for use on French battle tanks; after the war, he advised the French government on the restoration of cultural monuments in the territories recovered from Germany, all projects demonstrating Hubert's orientation to a broadly encompassing study of material culture (Drouin 1929, 49–50). A philosopher and historian of religion by training, Marcel Mauss trafficked not only in the *avant-garde* world of the emergent surrealist movement in Paris, but also in bolshevik, then later socialist, politics and economics at the turn of the century (Clifford 1988). His enormously influential work on gift exchange alone would place Mauss among the leading interdisciplinary and cross-cultural leaders of modern humanities and cultural studies (Davis 2000; Derrida 1991; 1995; Mauss 1967; Titmuss 1971). The Durkheimian circle thus

burst the bounds of anything that might be contained within the confines of academic philosophy. It was therefore even further from the kind of "sociology" that would be embraced by members of the American sociological guild.

Given the wide-ranging nature of this culture of philosophy of Durkheim's day, it would not be surprising to learn that Durkheim too was accomplished in fields not usually identified with professional philosophy. Like a Renouvier or a Lévy-Bruhl, Durkheim was accordingly also an historian and theorist of pedagogy, moral education, and morals, a student of traditional societies, a writer of patriotic tracts during World War I, a prominent defender of Dreyfus, a champion of charitable relief efforts to Jews fleeing the Russian pogroms of the early twentieth century, and a lifelong, although thoroughly eclectic and radical, philosopher. Durkheim was, in short, cast in the same tradition of French public intellectuals that we know well today in the careers of such ideologically diverse notables as Claude Lévi-Strauss, Bernard Henri-Lévi, Tzvetan Todorov, Jean-Paul Sartre, and others. As we will see, Durkheim pioneered the study of religious ritual life and the comparative study of the world's religions, and in doing so was an active agent of social reform and religious change in his own milieu. The present collection of essays represents an attempt to cast new light on this wide-ranging "new Durkheim"—the public intellectual, the practitioner of "cultural studies" well before the term was coined in its present-day sense—and thus one who was "far more" than the mainline professional sociologist, even the sociologist of religion. This collection aims then to showcase some of the new Durkheim both engaged in religion—if only on occasion to distance himself from it—and the Durkheim who launched, I am prepared to argue, the most fruitful tradition of the study of religion to this date.

2. Biographical Guideposts

Can we perhaps trace Durkheim's interests in religion to the details of his biography, given that attitudes to religion are frequently linked to upbringing and significant moments in one's personal life? Or do we need to look elsewhere? There has been much speculation and heated debate, for example, about the genesis of Durkheim's interest in religion, given the highly charged nature of Durkheim's Jewish origins (Strenski 1997; Tiryakian 1979). While the entire debate over Durkheim's Jewishness and its possible relation to his interests in religion cannot be rehearsed here, the proposition should be addressed if only to argue that it remains dubious. As a teenager, Durkheim had already abandoned Jewish religious practice. In doing so, he thus rejected the clerical calling to the rabbinate that had been prepared for him as the eldest son in a family with a long history of rabbinic service. Thus, one finds it hard to justify Durkheim's interest in religion by reference to the childhood Judaism that he cast aside.

What seems more critical to the formation of Durkheim's young mind, however, was Durkheim's choice to pursue higher education in the national capital and at its elite institutions, and thus to seek out a national and universal identity in place of local provincial and religious particularist identifications. To wit, a year or so after his alienation from Judaism had reached crisis levels, Durkheim left his home in Epinal for what was a formative new life in Paris. In the capital, Durkheim attended one of the classical *collèges* designed to prepare applicants for entry into the exclusive École Normale Supérieure, where the cream of France's elite secular secondary school teachers were trained. Durkheim succeeded in gaining entrance there, training primarily as a philosopher.

These years at the École Normale Supérieure (1879–1882) gave the new life that Durkheim had fashioned for himself a definite shape. Among his classmates were future national (and world) luminaries such as the philosopher, Henri Bergson, and the great statesman, the socialist Jean Jaurès. Among instructors, Durkheim was greatly influenced by the "scientific" history of Gabriel Monod and even more perhaps by the historian of Roman religion and domestic rituals, Numa Denis Fustel de Coulanges. Among philosophers, the neo-Kantian, Émile Boutroux, guided Durkheim to his conception of the existence of different levels of being, such as social life. Reinforcing Boutroux's influence was Alfred Espinas. A major figure in the "eclectic" tradition of philosophy and social thought in France, Espinas was dean of the Faculty of Letters at the University of Bordeaux when Durkheim was appointed there. Durkheim credited Espinas with his conviction that social life was not only distinctive, as Boutroux had argued, but that it was also governed by laws that were independent of the laws of biology and personal psychology. Such diverse intellectual influences made Durkheim's nurture at the École Normale Supérieure far richer than what is usually encompassed by academic philosophy.

Among others forming Durkheim's mind from outside the circle of his instructors at the École Normale Supérieure was the Neo-Kantian republican philosopher and theologian, Charles Renouvier. Durkheim's understanding of Kant as well as his passion for a science of morality probably derive from Renouvier. More than that, Renouvier's political liberalism, especially its affirmation of the sacredness of the individual human person, seem a major source of Durkheim's inclinations towards a "religion of humanity." Guided in large part by the values of Renouvier, and enhanced by his close friendship in Bordeaux with the neo-Hegelian Renouvierian, Octave Hamelin, Durkheim articulated a form of humanistic liberalism that remained with him throughout his life. Like other French progressives of his era, Durkheim's affinity for Hegelian revisions of Neo-Kantianism recalled not only Hamelin, but also such notables as the legendary promoter of left-wing Hegelianism, socialist organizer, and chief librarian at the École Normale Supérieure from 1888 to 1926, Lucien Herr. Over against the dual extremes of utilitarian individualism and materialism, on the one side, and collectivist socialism and pantheist spiritualism, on the other, Durkheim sought to integrate an unruly French egoism with a broad, but concrete, communalism. Durkheim's public defense of Captain Alfred Dreyfus, articulated in terms of the French republic's collective valuation of the *individual* as a sacred being, captured what has aptly been called the eclectic "social individualism" at the core of his values. Individuals are formed by participation in social groups, by being nurtured within the bosom of society. The individual is therefore not an abstract, atomized unit, but a being in living relationship with its social context. We will see more of this shortly when we take up Durkheim's relation to the religion of humanity popular in his day among his intellectual peers.

Durkheim went directly from the École Normale Supérieure to a career teaching philosophy at a series of provincial *lycées*. In 1887, after a short government-sponsored tour of German universities (1885–1886), Durkheim took a position especially created for him in social science and pedagogy at the University of Bordeaux. He remained there for fifteen fruitful years until 1902, producing the first books for which he would subsequently gain widespread fame: *The Division of Labor in Society, Suicide,* and *The Rules of Sociological Method.* In Bordeaux, Durkheim also began to develop an interest in ethnological topics, such as totemism, and also religion. Durkheim lived the final fifteen years of his life in Paris, where he succeeded Ferdinand Buisson in the chair of the Science of Education at the Sorbonne. He likewise continued the work he had already begun in Bordeaux organizing the review annual, *L'Année Sociologique,* and pursuing his work on pedagogy, religion, and social science. In the capital, he also produced the work for which he is justly most famous, *The Elementary Forms of the Religious Life* (1912). He died on the eve of the end of the First World War, considerably wounded in spirit by the battlefield death of his son, André, but writing what he considered would be his masterpiece, a book to have been entitled *La Morale.*

Given the importance of academic philosophy both to Durkheim's formal education and to his intellectual outlook, I have devoted the essays of the first part of this collection, "Turning the Philosophical Ground," to Durkheim's philosophical nurture and its innovations. In Chapter One, "Durkheim, Hamelin, and the French Hegel," I seek to place Durkheim within the tradition of left-wing neo-Hegelian renovators of Kant. His grounding in this philosophical base explains many of the features of Durkheim's thought: his drive to make philosophy "concrete" or empirical; his synthetic, some would say "eclectic" style; his concern with themes like altruism, duty, sacrifice, and so on; his understanding that the philosophy in question was more than just an academic pursuit, but involved a "culture" and politics as well. Chapter Two, "The Ironies of *Fin-de-Siècle* Rebellions against Historicism and Empiricism in the École Pratique des Hautes Études, Fifth Section," shows how Durkheim breaks out—if only partly—of the positivism that marked his earlier conception of the nature of science, and thus out of an easy reduction of religion to society.

3. Religion≡Society or Society≡Religion?

By beginning this collection with a series of essays on philosophy, I am proposing a definite narrative line in the chronological educational development of Durkheim's mind. The formative youthful encounter with philosophy at the École Normale Supérieure laid a foundation for what followed, even if Durkheim's mature career represents his deliberate attempts to break free from the agendas and methods of the mainstream of French academic philosophy—to "turn the philosophical ground"—as this section's subtitle implies. At least one signature expression of this early Durkheimian philosophical mind is the famous (or infamous) identification of religion and society. In some ways, this identity bears many of the features of a meta-physical claim about the deep nature of religion and its elements, such as god. Underneath appearances or "*meta*-physics," Durkheim seems to be say-ing, the real nature of religious symbols hides the reality of society—itself a metaphysical entity as well.

How Durkheim came to this interest in religion, as I have noted, remains a mystery. William Robertson Smith's great book, *Lectures on the Religion of the Semites,* is frequently, and with good reason, cited for its influence upon Durkheim's turn both to the study of simple societies and religion. Durkheim's first two major books, *The Division of Labor in Society* (1893) and *Suicide* (1897) dealt with social problems of so-called "advanced" industrial societies, while his masterpiece in the study of religion, *The Elementary Forms of the Religious Life* (1912), explored so-called "primitive" ritual and reli-gion, and dealt with topics such as the sacred, totem, tabu, sacrifice, ordeals, myth, and symbolism—all set among the aboriginal folk of Australia. These were not the interests one might have expected from an author concerned mostly with the problems of the industrial society. Yet, in a way, a continu-ity may be discerned at least from *Suicide* to the *Elementary Forms* despite general agreement among scholars that in about 1895, Durkheim shifted interests to religion, and to the so-called "primitive" societies, because he felt that they held secrets useful to modern societies. The social reformer in Durkheim sensed that the social malaises afflicting the France of his day could be remedied by learning the lessons of the secure and viable social orders of traditional societies. How, given the threat of war with Germany or with the fissiparous individualism bred by modern urban life (the political anarchism of the day was also a concern), could modern societies hope to maintain sufficient cohesion to survive and thrive? Durkheim reasoned that the secrets of social integration and coherence were there to be learnt in the *elementary forms of social life* in the societies of so-called "primitive" peoples, where coherence and well-regulated order was the norm.

There, nothing was more elementary, more fundamental, than tradi-tional religious life—the myths, rituals, ordeals, secret societies, and dynamic collective life. If one could isolate and identify the "elementary" religious institutions, practices, and mechanisms that "primitive societies" employed to secure their own coherence, then perhaps modern folk could either create

or retrieve these aspects of a social technology of order and coherence for
their own use? *The Elementary Forms* answered this question by proposing
that aboriginal Australian religious life of elaborate sacrificial ritual might
provide a model for the France of its day, and indeed every modern society.
A spiritual core of devotion and social generosity was needed to bind people
to each other into a coherent whole even in the advanced industrial societies of our day. Therefore as ritual animal sacrifice was required in traditional societies, so also would the civic sacrifice of duty and devotion to
country be needed to insure France's integrity. This was Durkheim's way
of asserting the importance of the "society≡religion" side of the religion/
society identity, since in the various social forms that one might observe in
traditional societies, there was concealed a moral bond, secured by a
spiritual "glue."

Despite this, too many readers fail to see Durkheim as asserting
the "religious" quality of the inner bonds holding society together—the
"society≡religion" identity—on a par with the "religion≡society" one. They
have got hopelessly stuck on one reading of Durkheim's identification
of religion and society as the sociological reductionism of religion to society. While Durkheim does indeed believe that religion and society are
"identical"—"religion≡society"—identity relations are more complex than
one thinks. Identities can be read in two ways—with either member being
taken as the logical subject. Thus, when we say that twin A of a pair of
identical twins is "identical" with twin B, we are also saying that twin B is
identical with twin A—both "A≡B" and "B≡A." We are thus saying that it
does not matter to the nature of the relation of A to B which end of the
identity is read or expressed first. Sentences are linear, and thus have to
start from a beginning, then go to the end and stop! We have to start some-
where in making the assertion of identity, but that starting point is arbitrary. In the same way, when Durkheim claims that religion and society
are "identical"—"religion≡society" and "society ≡religion"—this is to make
claims that can be read from different starting points as well—as "religion≡
society" or as "society≡religion." First is the familiar reductionist one that
"religion≡society"—that religion has a *social* nature. But this is also to
open the door to another claim—perhaps reductionist in the opposite direction—namely "society≡religion"—or that society has a *religious* nature.
Subjects and predicates merely swap places in the sentence. The desire to

demonstrate the fruitfulness of the research fostered by taking a serious look at *both* articulations of Durkheim's "religion≡society"/"society≡religion" identity drives the essays in this collection. Indeed, I believe reading this identity as "society≡religion" has been neglected and that it in fact has proved to be far the more fruitful way of reading Durkheim's thought on the relation of religion to society than the narrow focus on the Durkheimian sociological "reduction" of religion as "religion≡society." So, this reductionist reading of Durkheim first needs to be explained, and the contrast to it accordingly put into perspective with the alternative reading I shall try to exploit in these essays.

Just what is this Durkheimian sociological reductionism? And, how is it connected to its non-reductionist alternative? I take it that there are at least two aspects to the reductionist reading of the "religion≡society" identity—I shall call them the "hard" and "soft" reductionisms.

4. Durkheimian Reductionism, "Hard" and "Soft"

Commonly regarded as the most important feature of Durkheim's thought about religion—doubtless because of the apologetic anxieties it both excites and stirs—is Durkheim's "hard" sociological reduction of religion. This takes the form of a kind of metaphysical claim itself that all talk of god can be reduced to talk about society. It is to assert that when religious people speak of god, they are really referring to the religious feelings excited by their membership in a religious fellowship or group. Thus, when recent news reports tell us of the success of massed religious rallies—revival meetings, Billy Graham Crusades for Christ, the Shi'ite Islamic religious delirium characteristic of Ashura, Promise Keepers gatherings that pack immense football stadiums, the fervor of thousands upon thousands of pious Muslims circumambulating Mecca's Ka'aba at the Hajj, the zest of religious enthusiasm in the new "Mega Churches" such as The Harvest and Vineyard—the Durkheimian hard "reductionist" hears all they need to hear. All talk of god was really about and derived from our social experience. The religious experience of "spirit" is explainable in terms of the dynamics of crowd-induced enthusiasms in rituals. Further, the "religious" experiences that form the core of these groups is not only generated by the dynamics of crowd behavior, but is really about the "crowd" itself. Although believers *[handwritten margin notes: "here are overturn hist. ED (because he wants a diff. interp ~ rely"]*

do not recognize it, their beliefs do not reflect or correspond to the existence of anything real outside the human realm, such as a "god."

As atheists, it is true that the Durkheimians asserted these claims about the real social identity of religion on dogmatic grounds. They did not believe an experience of god or spirit was rationally defensible, and therefore possible, because gods or spirits either did not exist or were beyond the cognitive abilities of humans to experience.

As for Durkheim's "soft" sociological reduction of religion, I mean that Durkheim both highlights the studies of religious social groupings and that he "socializes" the study of religion by bringing a sociological apperception to what might be thought otherwise to be individual matters. Thus, a soft sociological reduction of religion turns attention to the collective, group, or institutional functions and contexts of religion. In this way, Durkheim has spurred the study of religious communities such as monastic groups, charismatics, local cults, "world" religions, ritual associations, ethnic and national religions, institutions such as the church, synagogue, and so on. Further, insofar as his work concerned matters that seemed individual in nature, such as philosophical doctrines, psychological states, or theological dogmas, Durkheim wished to cast a social light upon them, indeed to show how they were dependent upon their social location for much of their form and content. How, for example, might the early Christian belief in the visitations of the Holy Spirit be related to the effervescent vitality of the young community and its avid ritual life? How and why was the notion and experience of the "sacred" so widely deployed in the religions of the world, and why was it so often linked with the practices and identities of religious communities? One thinks in particular of Mary Douglas's work on the relation of ritual pollution beliefs to the social structures of the groups holding such beliefs (Douglas 1970; Douglas 1973). Projects like these show a fruitfulness that far overwhelms the results of the crude Durkheimian "hard" reductionism of religion to society, even if it is in terms of "hard" reductionism that Durkheim's work on religion is usually sold.

5. Society's Religious Heart

Just as there was *more* to Durkheim than his sociological work—his pedagogical, philosophical and ethical studies, etc.—there is also *more* to the identity between religion and society than its reductionist side, especially more than the "hard." As I have already mentioned, identities are funny things—actually something like "two-way streets" in the world of logic. Thus, to identify religion and society *may* mean (and it does so mean for Durkheim) that religion is *really* about society; it also means that society *is* religious!

But what Durkheim meant by this is not what a good number of others within his milieu proposed. They wanted to found fully-fledged religions of humanity. Thus, in appreciating what Durkheim's "religion≡ society" meant when "society" was made subject of the identity we need to resist seeing this positing of a religious character to society as asserting a crude (or even refined) worship of society. Durkheim's sense of the "religiousness" of society needs to be located with considerable care, so that it not be confused with the advocacy of a neo-religion, replete with its full-scale rituals, clerical hierarchy, and such, that some of his peers enthusiastically sought to do. In the non-reductionist sense of the "religion≡society" identity that I shall discuss in this book, I am not asserting that Durkheim was some literal sort of prophet or priest of a new religion. He was, nonetheless, trying to bring out the non-material, ideal, or cultural—"religious"—quality of human sociability. Thus, as early as 1883–84, in his *Cours de philosophie* at the Lycée at Sens, Durkheim asserts that society itself possesses an explicitly "spiritual"—religious—value:

> Nothing is wider off the mark than the mistaken accusation of materialism which has been leveled against us. Quite the contrary: from the point of view of our position, if one is to call the distinctive property of the individual representational life spirituality, then one should say that social life is defined by its hyperspirituality. By this we mean that all the constituent attributes of mental life are found in it, but elevated to a very much higher power and in such a manner as to constitute something entirely new. (Durkheim 1974, 34)

This spiritualism extends even to the soul since, for Durkheim, the "soul" was simply the presence of society in us. "Soul" was just a shorthand for speaking of the values and socially formed consciences that society had imbued in us. Even more radically Durkheim resorted to an objective idealism and projects the mind everywhere in nature: The "mind finds itself in all degrees, only more or less rudimentary: everything lives, everything is animated, everything thinks" (Durkheim 1884, 498).

Significantly, late in life he speaks in the same "spiritualist" voice as he did in 1883–84. In 1914, Durkheim developed the idea of the spiritual or "religious" nature of society with specific application to the possible reality of religion when he addressed a joint meeting of progressives—the Union of Free Thinkers and Free Believers—on the theme, "Religious Sentiments at the Present Time." Some of these folk were religious liberals, while others were agnostics or atheists. But both groups met in the spirit of openness to dialogue with their opposites. Durkheim had words for both groups, and positioned himself squarely *between* them—as a free thinker with a sense of the reality of religion, but not with any conviction about the literal truth of theistic claims. First, taking the side of the free thinker agnostics or atheists, Durkheim dismissed any sort of nostalgia for theism or a belief in a transcendent god: "Ladies and gentlemen, here is an idea that we absolutely have to get used to; it is that humanity is left on this earth to its own devices and can only count on itself to direct its destiny. . . . At first sight it can disturb the man who is used to imagining as superhuman the forces he leans on" (Durkheim 1975a, 187). This unsentimental atheism will be discussed at length in Chapter Four. There I note that Durkheim does not yield to the temptation to return to his religious roots, even at learning of the death of his son, André. In a letter to the philosopher Xavier Léon, dated 20 April 1916, Durkheim announces his disaffection with traditional religion unambiguously:

> "It is truly incredible that the therapeutic of moral grief should still be as Epicurus described it. I am not aware that anything new has since been said on this subject. It is inconceivable that this should be the great human malady and that almost nothing should have been done to treat it. Of course I know that the religions are there, and that their practices are rich in experience that is unconscious and full of accumulated wisdom. But their wisdom is crude and empirical; nothing resembling ritual practices has been of use to me or seems effective to me." (Lukes 1972, 556)

Yet, for all of Durkheim's atheism, he did not mean to reduce human reality to the motion of atoms and a materialist conception of humanity.

Accordingly, again speaking to the Union of Free Thinkers and Free Believers, Durkheim argues that human beings possess their own perhaps autonomous value. Durkheim shows himself to be, in fact, a kind of "humanist." "If, however, he succeeds in convincing himself that humanity alone can furnish the support he needs, is there not something highly comforting in this prospect, since the resources he is clamouring for are so readily available, so close to hand . . . ?" (Durkheim 1975a, 187). Reaffirming this celebration of the reality of the human realm, Durkheim applies its lessons to religion, in a way that grants religion a reality—but without transcendental validity—not unlike that he grants to the human realm. Speaking of the reality of religion, Durkheim specifically lectured the free thinkers about its palpable power:

> Indeed religion is not only a system of ideas, it is above all a system of forces. The man who lives according to religion is not only one who visualizes the world in a certain way, who knows what others do not, he is above all a man who feels within himself a power of which he is not normally conscious, a power which is absent when he is not in a religious state. The religious life implies the existence of very special forces . . . ; in the words of the well-known phrase, let it suffice to say that these are the forces which move mountains. (Durkheim 1975a, 182)

It is, thus, with parts of Durkheim's thought like these that I have tried to contend—that part of Durkheim's thought that seeks to bring out the ideal, religious, value-laden aspects of human social life as things of their own worth attention in their own right.

6.   Durkheim's Uniquely Unsentimental Religion of Humanity

An instructive example of Durkheim's emphasis upon the social, ideal, religious, or value-laden content *inside* human life was his analysis of the human individual, and individualism itself, inspired by the debates of the Dreyfus Affair. Durkheim's pronouncements in the Dreyfus Affair publicized the fact that he believed that the human individual was a "sacred being," and thus that human reality was special in some way, as I have already indicated that Durkheim believed. This regard for the individual as "sacred," is, of course, a core idea of the "religion of humanity" (Durkheim 1898; Durkheim 1975a; Durkheim 1975b; Durkheim 1975c). And, because it is, its assertion can mislead readers in understanding Durkheim's own conception of a religion of humanity, and by extension, what he meant when he asserted that society had a moral, religious, or ideal nature.

Thus, as an expression of Durkheim's own "religious" orientation, his notion of the religion of humanity needs carefully to be qualified. And, since Durkheim's belief in the sacredness of the individual is perhaps the only religion to which he might be said to have subscribed, I can think of no better way to illustrate in its fullest form what Durkheim's sense of the religiousness of society—the "society≡religion" identity—might mean, than by reflecting briefly on how Durkheim understood the religious sense of the human individual. Although Durkheim's religion of the human individual is not the main preoccupation of the collection of essays in this volume, simply letting its lessons register will give the most convincing lie possible to the view of Durkheim as a simple sociological reductionist. He was, as I should like to insist upon saying, *much more.*

Durkheim's most famous articulation of a religion of humanity came in his passionate defense of the sacredness of the human individual, made in the context of the defense of Captain Dreyfus. Durkheim asserted therefore that individualism was the religion of humanity—indeed, the "religion of today" as Durkheim says.

> The human person, whose definition serves as the touchstone according to which good must be distinguished from evil, is considered as sacred. . . . It has something of that transcendent majesty which the churches of all times have given to their Gods. It is conceived as being invested with that mysterious property which creates an empty space around holy objects, which keeps them away from profane contacts and which draws them away from ordinary life. . . . Man is, at the same time, both believer and God. (Durkheim 1898, 62)

While Durkheim sounds *traditionally* "religious" here, he turns out to be much less so than he appears to be. Durkheim was often linked with Auguste Comte, because of their common use of the neologism, "sociology." This naturally caused some of Durkheim's contemporaries to imagine that he too sought to found an neo-Catholic style religion of humanity in Comtean style—a movement that actually built churches and held services. Further, given Durkheim's strong republican political views, one might also have imagined that he would be partial to some revival of the neo-religious festivals of the Revolution and along with them, neo-religious versions of Roman Catholic liturgy and belief. So, while few observers of the cultural scene in Durkheim's day would have been surprised to learn that Durkheim had defended Dreyfus in terms typical of a "religion of humanity," Durkheim's religion of humanity is not to be confused with more literally conceived examples of this neo-religious movement in late nineteenth and early twentieth century France. Nothing of a Comtean sect seems evident among Durkheim's ambitions—even though we find a talk of spirit and spiritualism nonetheless. Reading Durkheim for his religious sensibilities does not therefore require us to think of him in the manner of a traditionally religious person or founder of a religious cult. What Durkheim was essentially trying to do in this aspect of his thought was to bring out the spiritual, ideal, or religious dimensions of social life—the "society≡religion" connection.

This is why the notable condemnation of late nineteenth and early twentieth century religions of humanity, written by a Roman Catholic priest, Dom Besse, is wrong as far as Durkheim was concerned. Besse took aim at a host of humanists—Durkheim, the Reinachs, the Sabatiers, and the Roman Catholic modernists—and he lumped them all together (wrongly, I believe). Entitled *Les religions laiques: un romanticisme religieux,* Besse's book sarcastically attacked the religious sincerity of the spiritual sensibility of these well-meaning folk as soppy religious romanticism (Besse 1913). For Besse, these proponents of a religion of humanity were simply unable to stomach the indigestible irrationality and mystery of real religion. So, these religious humanists preferred in its place a sentimental nostalgia for religion, enriched with the metaphors and images of religion in the service of something higher and altogether different.

To give Besse his due, Durkheim did believe that religion was possible without the mysticism and surrender of the critical intellect. As he put it in "Individualism and the Intellectuals," "This cult of man has for its first dogma the autonomy of reason and for its first rite freedom of thought." But this is not the same as the red-blooded religions of humanity that some of Durkheim's fellow humanists proposed. Indeed, by comparison with others similarly dedicated to the religion of humanity, Durkheim's humanist piety seems rather modest. Compare, for example, the assertions of neo-idealist philosopher (and one-time member of the Durkheimian *équipe*) Dominique Parodi:

> . . . for the thinking man, religious feeling is . . . the feeling of vitality: to take a religious viewpoint is to identify and commune with the life of the world in order to feel it like a heartbeat, in order to feel the effect of being alive, not only in our puny individual life, but in the great life of the All, in order to harmonize our aspirations and thoughts with the rhythm of the universal breath—in a word, in order to feel one with the world, grounded in it, and aware of it in us. In this sense, even a strictly atheistic philosophy, completely denying divine personality, creation, or personal immortality, could be essentially religious as long as it could feel and think of the universe as a whole—as long as it could identify itself in mind and heart with universal necessity. (Parodi 1913, 524)

Typical as well of this fervor was Ferdinand Buisson, whom Durkheim would succeed in the chair of "Science of Education" at the Sorbonne. Humanism was "the" religion, even perhaps more truly religious than the "religions":

> "There is only one religion; there has ever been but one under the numberless forms corresponding to the different ages of human civilisation. This is the religion of goodness: or to analyse it more deeply, the religion of the spirit aspiring to fulfill its function of spirit . . . Religion, which is nothing else than the instinct and urge of humanity pursuing its destiny; religion, which man draws out of the depths of himself, and which he represents to himself as coming to him from the deep of heaven." (Besse 1913, 51)

It is hard indeed to imagine Durkheim saying anything of the same ilk as Buisson and Parodi. Both classic expressions of the religion of humanity take "religion" far more literally than Durkheim did. Thus, despite the calumnies of Besse, we seem justified in believing in the sincerity of Durkheim's religion of humanity only as far as it involved the sacredness of the human individual. Durkheim's religion of humanity then embraces the sense I have tried to give to his non-reductionist understanding of the "religion≡society" identity. Among other things, Durkheim contributes a sort of "religious" appreciation of our understanding of society. Thus he reads the religion/society identity as a way of saying that all social forms contained a spiritual or normative—"religious"—aspect to them—the "society≡ religion" formula. Every kind of "society" or human group, whether family, tribe, nation, trade union, and so on, was not therefore just an agglomeration of particulars, but a unit of humanity linked together by the common values that at once constitute it and that it holds sacred. So, on this reading of the god/society identity, the Durkheimians were asserting the "godly" quality of social reality. It is this side of the god/society identity that fits with the deeply held Durkheimian views of the importance of religion and of its primacy in time and agency among other social institutions. Materialists therefore attacked the Durkheimians for insisting upon the place of norms, values, consensus, beliefs, and other intangibles—"spiritual" factors—in the make-up of human reality.

This spiritual quality of Durkheim's work explains why even in his own time, Durkheim's theories were seen as alternatives to the economistic materialism of Marxism, even though they were fully social and scientific in ambition. Indeed, Durkheim actually provides an alternative both to Marxian economistic materialism and to the abstract individualist interpretations of human life that Marx attacked as well. Like Marx, Durkheim challenged the conventional wisdom of our entrenched abstract individualism, and pushes us to seek the underlying social constraints and causes that shape the way people act—whether this be their religious behavior or anything else. Social and cultural constraints are thus paramount in Durkheim's view, and as such seem more subtle, complex, and diverse than Marx's economism would allow. Thus, today, when the socio-cultural dimensions conditioning economic life itself are gaining new appreciation, Durkheim's emphasis upon the role of religion and kindred socio-cultural factors in social formation will become more compelling as well.

I have given special attention to this "society≡religion" strand in Durkheim's thought in the second part of the essays that follow, "The

Vagaries of Religious Belonging." There, I discuss the religious aspects of Durkheim's thought itself, that aspect of his thought typically ignored by those who would see Durkheim only in the narrowest sociological terms. These include Durkheim's ideas about the afterlife and the immortality of the soul in Chapter Four, "Durkheim, Judaism, and the Afterlife"; Chapter Five, "Zionism, Brahminism, and the Embodied Sacred," where we encounter Durkheimian reflections on the ideal of a non-spiritual and therefore embodied conception of the sacred; Chapter Seven, "Durkheim, Hubert, and the Clerical Modernist Discourse on Symbolism," where I recount a large part of the relation of Durkheim and the Durkheimians in conversations about the nature and future of religion with the religious liberals of his day, primarily those called the religious Modernists; and Chapter Six, "The Rise of Ritual and the Hegemony of Myth: Sylvain Lévi, the Durkheimians, and Max-Müller," where the Durkheimians rehabilitate the dignity of ritual in religion.

7. Agonies of Institutional Life

The third part of this book, "Institutions and Their Religious Afflictions," the penultimate division of the collection, engages in something of a Durkheimian analysis of Durkheim's work on religion. The essays in this part, after all, deal with the institutional setting of his ambitions for the study of religion in places like Paris's École Pratique des Hautes Études, Fifth Section. I refer to "religious afflictions" in Durkheim's efforts to engage the key institutions of the study of religion in France because so much of his relation with the main figures of the Fifth Section was characterized by struggle and rejection. Chapter Eight, "Durkheim, Disciplinarity, and 'Sciences Religieuses,'" charts the institutional structure of the study of religion in France in the Fifth Section and how the Durkheimians made their way into it. Chapter Nine, "Liberal Protestant Theology and/or 'Science Religieuse'?" focuses on the particular relation to the scientific study of history in the Fifth Section. Chapter Ten, "The Durkheimians and the Protestants in the École Pratique, Fifth Section: The Dark Side" emphasizes the agonistic, often personal nature of the struggles between the Durkheimians and the French Liberal Protestants.

8. Durkheimian Teamwork

One final aspect of the social circumstances of Durkheim's career needs to be underlined—Durkheim's scholarship was the work of a team, a long-lived and intense collaboration with his fellow workers. Readers will, therefore, note that in the essays making up this collection I often do not distinguish—at least sharply—the thought of Durkheim from that of his closest collaborators, Henri Hubert and Marcel Mauss. This is primarily because, on the whole, there is either no distinction or one is impossible to make with any degree of accuracy. The thoughts of these three were too intricately entangled with one another. From all we know, Durkheim, Hubert, and Mauss worked together intensively in what was one of the most remarkably complete cases of collaborative scholarship in the human sciences. Furthermore, this is the way that Durkheim wanted it. Although Durkheim's years in Bordeaux were happy and productive, Durkheim's move to Paris in 1902 facilitated—in very large part by his nephew, Marcel Mauss, and Mauss's close collaborator, Henri Hubert—the tight collaboration established among the three. Hubert and Mauss also recruited members for what arguably was Durkheim's most important "work," that lively and extravagantly talented team of co-workers, the Durkheimian *équipe*. This remarkable community not only absorbed and deployed Durkheimian ideas for generations but also shaped a good deal of what and how Durkheim himself would think and write.

As historians of religion themselves, Hubert and Mauss, for example, made significant contributions to Durkheim's articulation of the central notion of sacrifice in *The Elementary Forms*. Both Hubert and Mauss were as enthusiastic about religion as Durkheim. Moreover, they seem to have been so quite independently of Durkheim's urgings, and prior to their association with him. Before the work of *L'Année sociologique* had begun, Hubert and Mauss had trained extensively in the history of religions; Durkheim had not. Hubert and Mauss even directed the *Année* sections on *sociologie religieuse*; Durkheim never did. Mauss alone wrote 206 reviews on religious topics in the *Année*'s first series; Durkheim managed fifty. While Durkheim published virtually nothing substantial on religion between his 1899 "De la définition de phénomènes religieux" and the 1912 *Elementary Forms*, Hubert and Mauss, singly or in collaboration, produced studies on magic, the papal states, prayer, sacrifice, and time. In 1904 Hubert wrote his "Introduction à la traduction française" to P. D. Chantepie de la Saussaye's *Manuel d'histoire des religions*, which was recognized by Henri Berr as a manifesto for the Durkheimian program of religious studies. While Hubert taught twelve of his seventeen courses between 1901 and 1912 on religion, and Mauss taught twenty of twenty-three in roughly the same period, Durkheim taught only one! When we consider the creation of the *Elementary Forms*, we should not forget that Mauss had always been interested in ethnography and "primitive religions"; Durkheim displayed an interest in these fields only after the arrival of Mauss in Bordeaux in 1895. Mauss collaborated with Durkheim in *Primitive Classification,* a work generally acknowledged as formulating ideas later developed by *Elementary Forms*; Condominas also claims Mauss's inaugural lecture at Hautes Études not only retraces elements of his introduction to *Sacrifice*, but that Durkheim repeats "presque textuellement" Mauss's position in the *Elementary Forms*. Durkheim was thus not "unique" in the *équipe* in his devotion to religious studies, nor is it clear that he was in many areas its prime mover.

9. Durkheimian Social Policy and Pedagogy Today

The final part of this collection consists in a set of applications of Durkheimian theory to contemporary political and social problems, as well as a treatment of pedagogical difficulties in teaching Durkheim. Chapter Eleven, "Durkheim Sings: Teaching the 'New Durkheim' on Religion," argues for an emphasis upon Durkheim as developed in this book. Because I believe this "New Durkheim" is more interesting in light of current intellectual interests in the study of culture and values, I believe this approach also provides a more attractive way to expose students to the entire range of Durkheim's works and to Durkheimian themes in general. Chapter Twelve, "Christians, Durkheimians, and Other Animals," first examines the reputation of Christianity for encouraging insensitivity to animal rights, then contrasts this to a newly recovered late medieval—and "Durkheimian" *avant la lettre*—Christian theology affirming a common social bond between humans and other animals. Chapter Thirteen, "Sacrifice, Gift, and the Social Logic of Muslim 'Human Bombers'" employs Durkheimian gift and sacrifice theories to offer a novel interpretation of the logic of so-called "suicide" bombings in today's Middle East. Chapter Fourteen, "A Durkheimian Text in Turkey," consists of two main parts. First, I consider the historical role of Durkheimian social theory in Turkish nationalist Ziya Gökalp's articulation of the statist ideology adopted by Kemal Atatürk. Second, I offer an account of attempts by later-day—but equally Durkheimian—Turkish dissidents of Kemalism, who attempted to offer a theory of resistance to statism in modern-day Turkey, based on Durkheim's notion of intermediary institutions ("civil society"), articulated in his posthumous *Professional Ethics and Civic Morals.*

Past reluctance to identify and elaborate on the implications of the emotionally moving aspects of Durkheim's work seem grounded in a needless fear of seeming "unprofessional." This strikes me as simple intellectual timidity. It is to straitjacket the thought of Durkheim and ourselves in the heavily starched white coats of pseudoscience, when we should be trying critically to take up the implications of what one of the greatest of all modern thinkers has written. The aim of my teaching the Durkheimian corpus and the purpose of this collection of essays are to offer a bold assertion of the power and fecundity of a humanist reading of Durkheim, of the interdisciplinary Durkheim, the Durkheim of history, philosophy, pedagogy, anthropology, and the study of religion, a Durkheim of rigorous and critical intellect, and one, at the same time, of vision and spirit.

PART TWO

Turning the Philosophical Ground

2

Durkheim, Hamelin, and
the "French Hegel"

I shall argue that Durkheim's mature social thought shows heretofore unrecognized similarities with the thought of Octave Hamelin (1856–1907), and together with Hamelin, to a specific strain of Hegelianism then being explored by democratic socialists in Durkheim's France. Commentators have long noted the close relations between Hamelin and Durkheim, typically without declaring what these were; similarly tantalizing but loose talk has circulated about Durkheim's Hegelianism, with just as little intellectual content or historical location. I hope to go some way in remedying our lack of historical knowledge about Durkheim's intellectual orientation, and in doing so suggest that Durkheim was in ways even more Hegelian than at least the acknowledged leading French Hegelian thinker of his day, Octave Hamelin.

I. Durkheim and the "General Culture" of Philosophy

To pay attention to Durkheim's place among the philosophers is really to recapture something of the view of Durkheim's contemporaries. "Philosophy" meant something more in Durkheim's time than our "technical" or "professional" philosophy; it meant inquiry into perennial human problems, more like what passes as the humanities on the contemporary academic scene. We also know Durkheimian sociology was a broad and capacious

Reprinted from *Réflexions historiques/Historical Reflections* 16 (2–3) (1989): 135–70, by permission of the editor.

enterprise of crosscultural and interdisciplinary character (Strenski 1987b). This indicates more than recognition of Durkheim's academic training and interest in moral philosophy and epistemology, established from the time of his *agrégation* in philosophy at the École Normale Supérieure and his reports on the teaching of philosophy in Germany in 1887. It testifies to the great breadth of the domain of philosophical discourse in Durkheim's France—a breadth of discourse which Durkheim himself could exploit to hold "conversation" with such diverse figures as Auguste Comte, Theodule Ribot, Georges Sorel, Herbert Spencer, Wilhelm Wundt, or even the "economists," Schmoller and Wagner (Durkheim 1887). What is more, philosophy was also part of a way of life, a "culture" as well as a matter of thought.[1] It included what one of Durkheim's closest collaborators, Célestin Bouglé, called a self-conscious (French) conception of *culture générale* (Bouglé 1938), or even what Durkheim called *la culture philosophique* (Durkheim 1906, v).

Despite its broad range, this general culture of philosophical discourse was dominated from the center by university-based academic philosophy. It is Victor Karady's view that at least in its early phases, Durkheimian sociology came to take an important place *within* this field of academic philosophy. Karady also suggests that the agendas of this academic philosophy exerted strong influence over the early life of Durkheimian sociology—so much so that one can speak of academic philosophy determining the structure of early Durkheimian sociology itself (Karady 1983, 77). Karady thus speaks of "sociology's entrenchment in philosophy" (Karady 1983, 79), of the "enduring philosophical bondage of early sociology" (Karady 1983, 78). The intellectual dominance of philosophy was similarly reinforced by Durkheim's practice of recruiting members of the original *équipe* from the young *agrégées* in philosophy. Whatever Durkheim's original *équipe* was, it was not, as often assumed, a "group of sociologists Durkheim brought together in 1898" (Coser 1971, 164). Most of the original *équipe* had taken the highest possible degree in philosophy (Karady 1983, 79). Those not so trained seemed pressed to show competence in philosophical discourse all the same (Hubert 1905).

2.   Hegel to Hamelin to Durkheim?

In light of Durkheim's close relation to philosophy, it is only natural to inquire about connections with Durkheim's friend and colleague, the

philosopher Octave Hamelin. Contemporary philosophical commentators of
the late nineteenth and early twentieth centuries frequently claim a close
affinity between the thought of Durkheim and Hamelin. René Le Senne even
asserts that Hamelin influenced Durkheim's distinction of sacred and profane in his masterpiece, *The Elementary Forms of the Religious Life* (Senne 1927).
But interestingly enough, the trail from Durkheim to Hegel leads us as much
through Hamelin as it does directly from Durkheim to Hegel. Hamelin is best
known for a posthumously published work based on his doctoral thesis, *Essai
sur les éléments principaux de la représentation* (Hamelin 1907). Hamelin's chef-
d'oeuvre argued for (1) the primacy of *représentations*, (2) the status of "relation" as the "simplest law of things," leading to (3) the dialectic resolution
of oppositions. The *Essai* also taught personalism and an equally radical
absolute idealism, one in which *représentations* in turn would have a major
place. For Hamelin, nothing exists or is conceivable outside thought (Parodi
1922: 187–88). Among his other major works are the historical and theoretical
works, *Le Système de Descartes* (1911), *Le Système d'Aristotle* (1920), *Le Système de
Renouvier* (1927) (Hamelin 1927). He wrote numerous articles, among them
essays on induction, education, Stoic logic, opposition in the thought of
Aristotle, the origins of Spinozism, the will, liberty, and certainty.[2]

The intellectual influence of Hegelian philosophy upon Hamelin and
other rationalists was widely recognized in its time. Yet, it remains true that
it was greatly overshadowed in our minds and in reality by the spectacular
intrusion of Hegelian thought into France in the 1930s (Rawlinson 1917,
92). Names like Hyppolite and Kojève are well-known to students and historians of French philosophy today, while virtually nothing could be said
about Hamelin (Kelly 1981; Poster 1973). Making things more difficult for us
is the fact that although the commentators of Hamelin's day are unani-
mous about the fact of his debt to Hegelian thought, they are obscure
about its precise meaning. For example, we get little help from contemporary commentators who cite Hamelin as single-handedly responsible for
the rediscovery of Hegel in turn-of-the-century France, but add no sup-
porting details (Parodi 1919a, 433). Although another commentator speaks
of Hamelin "supplementing the doctrines of Renouvier by those of Hegel,"
particulars are again not listed (Gunn 1922, 71). Even though no less a figure than Bruschwicg claims that Hamelin wanted to "demonstrate Charles
Renouvier's doctrine with Hegel's," he leaves it at that (Theau 1977, 41).

Arnaud Dandieu only vaguely describes what he means in saying that Hamelin synthesized the thought of Hegel with that of Descartes (Dandieu 1931, 77). Hamelin is said to have played a principal part in reversing the decline in the fortunes of Hegelian thought, which followed on the decline of the influence of Victor Cousin earlier in the nineteenth century, but again what this means remains unclear (Dandieu 1931, 77).

But put into the historical and comparative perspective of Hamelin's Neo-Kantian German brethren, claims about Hamelin's debt to Hegel grow in clarity—even if Hamelin's rediscovery of Hegel was not German in its inspirations.[3] Hamelin's program resembles the better known Baden (idealist) reaction to the German "back to Kant" movement of the same period. Paradoxically, Hegelian influence runs strong there in such key representatives of the German movement as Ernst Cassirer (Strenski 1987a, 26–28). Hamelin's masterpiece of absolute idealism, *Essai sur les éléments principaux de la representation*, is viewed as an Hegelian work, written in deliberate opposition to Bergson (Parodi 1919b, 432). Carrying this comparison further, the *Essai* is said to play *ésprit* and values to Bergson's *élan*, independently mirroring Cassirer's assertion of the superiority of neo-Hegelian *Geist* over the *Leben* of the irrationalist philosophies of life (Strenski 1987a, 30–32). Part of my job will be to determine just how "Hegelian" Hamelin's thought really is, especially as it relates to Durkheimian thought.

Thus we return to Durkheim. Hamelin was central to the neo-Hegelian movement of synthesis and reform. But his contemporaries held, and I concur, that Durkheim also moved in these same neo-Hegelian circles. I am thus arguing nothing less than that Durkheim was indeed part of this new appropriation of Hegel associated heretofore *only* with Hamelin. Thus we should take care how we describe this relation. A simple one-way influence of Hamelin the "philosopher" upon Durkheim the "sociologist" will not do. Durkheim shared many of the neo-Hegelian moral, epistemological, and metaphysical views which were connected with Hamelin—but which in fact seem to derive just as plausibly and independently from Hegel.[4] Hamelin and Durkheim were in a way two philosophical thinkers who took divergent paths from shared neo-Hegelian beginnings.[5] Thus, this paper is not making an argument for the "influence" of one upon the other so much as their joint participation in a common intellectual effort that can reasonably be called philosophical.

2.1.   *Hamelin and the Culture of Renouvier's "Ésprit Philosophique"*

Durkheim and Hamelin apparently met each other while colleagues at the University of Bordeaux in 1886. The two young instructors were united in a "noble and most confidential friendship" which was to last until Hamelin's death in 1907.[6] Just as Durkheim's appointment at Bordeaux came partly as a result of official Republican political influence, Hamelin's was said to have been "dictated to the minister [of public instruction] by reasons of [neo-critical] doctrine" (Dauriac 1909, 488). Lukes tells us that after the conviction and *châtiment* of Dreyfus in 1894, they jointly founded a local chapter of La Jeunesse Laïque (Lukes 1972, 358). Durkheim and Hamelin were thus apparently drawn to each other by their mutual interests in the common moral and philosophical vision informed by the work of the neo-critical philosopher, Charles Renouvier.[7] Georges Davy tells us Durkheim's "Renouvierism was . . . kept up quite late and accentuated again when he made the acquaintance at Bordeaux of that other Renouvierist, Hamelin, who became for him such a great friend" (Davy 1919, 186). Known variously as a Neo-Kantian or neo-critical philosopher, Renouvier's rationalism dominated liberal republican thought so thoroughly that he is and was commonly regarded as the official philosopher of the Third Republic. Renouvier worked primarily in the areas of epistemology, politics, and morals.[8] Of his twenty-one books the most interesting to us are his manuals of government and citizenship, a difficult and uncompromising anti-utilitarian moral treatise, *Science de la morale*, a revision of Kant, *Critique de la doctrine de Kant*, and a statement of his idea of person as the culmination of the categories, *Le Personnalisme*.[9] His reputation for critical thinking was apparently well earned, since his contemporaries referred to him as the "French Hume" (Theau 1977, 43). This epithet may be doubly well-earned given Renouvier's phenomenalist reworking of some Kantian notions. He rejects the *Ding an sich*, for instance. Further, he critically reread Kant to eliminate the transcendental aesthetic and the traditional organization of the categories (Turlot 1976, 68). But this reputation also meant, for someone like Hamelin, that Renouvier was altogether too empiricist (Dauriac 1909, 485).

To a superficial observer, Hamelin's thought looks much like that of Charles Renouvier's. In broad terms, Hamelin continued Renouvier's personalism and commitment to free will. Likewise, authors like Steven Collins have called attention to Hamelin's treatment of the Kantian categories in the novel style of Renouvier (also found in Durkheim). Intellectual relations between Hamelin and Renouvier were likewise always strong and always recognized as being so by their contemporaries (Andler 1932, 86). Even in his attempts to accentuate their differences, one of Hamelin's former students, Lionel Dauriac, observed that even if Charles Renouvier did not satisfy all of Hamelin's philosophical appetites, he satisfied them more than anyone else (Dauriac 1909, 485). Yet notwithstanding the fact that he was regarded as Renouvier's successor, Hamelin did not simply recite the lessons of his great mentor.

Much the same can be said for Durkheim and his relation to Charles Renouvier. Lukes lays out an impressive list of Renouvier's ideas which can be traced throughout Durkheim's thought. These include items that seem to reflect Renouvier's Kantianism in Durkheim's thought: his concern for morality, for the dignity of the human person and justice, rather than utility, and his pursuit of *a priori* categories of thought. Further, there are aspects of Renouvier's thinking which seem to originate elsewhere: his interest in the scientific study of morality, his belief in the importance of social solidarity and practical means of enhancing it through voluntary associations, his political liberalism, and the idea that the categories of thought might vary from society to society (Lukes 1972, 54–57). But, as we will see, Durkheim also takes his own route in certain cases, following a line more readily associated with the same Hegelian trends of thought Hamelin follows.

Hamelin's relation to Durkheim even went beyond the great man himself. It extended to Durkheim's nephew, closest collaborator, and major representative of Durkheimian thought after the master's death, Marcel Mauss. It is widely known that Durkheim and Mauss worked closely together. Indeed, the more we learn about the inner workings of the Durkheimian *équipe*, the harder it is to assign separate origins to various features of Durkheimian thought. Now Hamelin needs to be given special attention because of his special relation to Mauss. At Bordeaux, for example, it is well known that Mauss studied closely under his uncle. But what is not generally known is that Mauss was perhaps as much Hamelin's student, too. Mauss credits Hamelin with having imparted to him nothing less than what is commonly regarded among scholars of the Durkheim school as perhaps his chief intellectual gift—his *ésprit philosophique*.[10] Precisely what this meant in all details lies beyond the scope of this paper. However, N. J. Allen anticipates part of my main argument by calling attention to Mauss's philosophical interest in the human person: "Mauss himself inclined to the view of Hegel and Hamelin that the truest and most fundamental categories appeared late in human history"—such as the idea of the individual human person (Allen 1985, 40). The two men remained close, even after Durkheim moved on to Paris. Indeed, partly because of the relation with Mauss and Lucien Herr (historian of philosophy, socialist activist, and head librarian at the École Normale Supérieure), Hamelin was well known and regarded by the circles in which Durkheim and his *équipe* moved. This apparently was true even to the extent of personal matters. We possess letters between Mauss and Hamelin dealing with quite mundane affairs, such as one from Mauss in 1901, where Mauss even offers to make the personal arrangements for Hamelin's visit to Paris.[11] After his many years at Bordeaux, Hamelin took up his chair at the Sorbonne and the École Normale Supérieure in 1905. But in September 1907, after having reached the summit of his academic aspirations, Hamelin was struck down. He died, the victim of a failed attempt to save two seaside swimmers from drowning. A mighty wave swept him out to sea during the rescue attempt, and he perished (Durkheim 1906, v).

Since then Hamelin's death has become the stuff of moral parable, connected with a chivalrous, yet thoroughly discredited, *fin de siècle* moral and philosophical idealism. According to conventional French wisdom, wiser generations, like our own, have replaced moral idealism and altruism with (according to taste) a more "realistic" or cynical morality of practical self-interest. School children learn the lessons of hardheaded practicality from the example of the "folly" of Hamelin's life and accidental death.

What interests me is that Durkheim wrote an obituary for the purpose of honoring his old friend. That Durkheim should write an *hommage* at all was remarkable, since during his entire life, Durkheim wrote only four obituaries.[12] Yet, testifying to the common cultural mind formed by Renouvier's public philosophy, Durkheim was stirred to the task by the death of Hamelin. Durkheim felt Hamelin had not received his due in the routine notice published by *Le Temps* at the time of his death. It was but a mere "summary mention," says Durkheim; so he volunteered his own tribute to Hamelin to the Paris daily to set the record straight. The rhetoric of Renouvieran civic sacrifice and heroism dominates Durkheim's obituary. Among other things, Durkheim says Hamelin died nobly. He died a sacrificial "victim"—much as he lived—in selfless but meaningful devotion to others.[13] Only Hamelin's "devotion" to his students prevented him from acquiring the professional peer recognition his academic achievements merited. Significantly, Durkheim argued that this spirit of "self-sacrifice" was anything but futile. Perhaps thinking of his own efforts with *L'Année sociologique*, Durkheim notes that Hamelin's *dévouement* constituted a form of moral investment in creating an entire generation of philosophers—a sacrifice required to insure an enduring place for Hamelin's thought in the philosophical world of his own time (Durkheim 1907). We will return to these themes when we discuss Hamelin's moral philosophy.

3.   Durkheim, Hamelin, and the Socialist Hegel

In the face of the virtual absence of citations to Hegel in Durkheim's (and Hamelin's) work, why should it be plausible that Hegelian thought played a significant role in forming Durkheim's thought toward the end of the nineteenth century? Durkheim's thought *seems* to—and doubtless does— echo that of many possible thinkers. Why, for example, are not the well-known influences of Comte and Saint Simon sufficient? Such a possibility should not be ruled out, although what we have is apparently a case of overdetermination. It is a matter of historical controversy itself to what degree even these French thinkers and their followers owed debts to Hegel (D'Hondt 1971). Comte and Hegel, for instance, both read and knew each other's work (D'Hondt 1971, 17–8); Hegel frequented the *salon* of Rachel Varnhagen where St. Simonian ideas flourished (D'Hondt 1971, 20). This is one reason why I have preferred the term "Hegelian," instead of naming Hegel himself.

Yet, there is more. Durkheim moved in intellectual circles where we know Hegel was being read and interpreted anew, yet where not much could be made of it publicly. Because of what Michael Kelly called the "conspiracy of silence" about the influence of Hegel in France (after 1870), we will perhaps never know its precise story (Kelly 1982, 16). In France (after 1870), interest in Hegel was *toujours secret* for many of the same patriotic

reasons other prominent German thinkers received scant public recognition from French scholars working to recover national pride after the *déba-*
cle at Sedan (D'Hondt 1971, 19). Kelly notes that even the teaching of Hegel
was proscribed in France after the Franco-Prussian war (Kelly 1981, 37).
Durkheim's silence about Hegel would then fall into the same pattern of
his well-known silences about the work of both Marx and Weber—and this
when he knew well the details of the German intellectual scene from quite
early in his career.

The effect of the "secrecy" of Hegel's influence in Durkheim's day is
compounded by its own failure to make a lasting impact on the intellectual
scene—at least with the exception of Durkheim. Both at its inception and
in its maturity, bad political luck plagued moderate Hegelianism. Thus,
while it is true that Hamelin led a rediscovery of Hegel among philosophers in French universities, the major influx of Hegelian thought into
France during our period came through the democratic socialist movement (Parodi 1919b, 433). But because of the fiercely right-wing nationalist
mood of the 1890's, socialists had to keep their admiration for Hegel under
wraps. Bad enough that Hegel was seen as a Prussian thinker, much less a
German; Hegel still had the reputation of being a statist at a time when statism favored the interests of the right in France. Thus beyond difficulties in
bringing this moderate Hegelian socialism to birth, intensified war hyste-
ria, acute class strife, and the tragic death of its major theoretician, Jean
Jaurès, in 1914, nipped moderate socialism before it had a chance to flower.
Thus was the fate of the moderate Hegel sealed. The Hegel of the 1930's
would be a very different animal, and so also would be the international
political "jungle" where Stalinism and Hitlerism stalked each other across
a radically divided Europe. Yet Hamelin, too, was part of the socialist recep-
tion of Hegel. He was first of all personally acquainted with such key play-
ers in the socialist Hegelian camp as Lucien Herr.[14] There is evidence of
Hamelin's progressive political and moral commitment from the days when
Hamelin and Durkheim did Dreyfusard politics at Bordeaux. And, as we
will see, he advocated a "socialist" morality in the early 1880's while a young
colleague of Durkheim's on the faculty of the university at Bordeaux.
Another, more theoretical, part of Hamelin's socialism was to have seen
Hegel both as an individualist and ameliorist, a coat cut to fit the cloth of
the Third Republic's reforming liberalism (Turlot 1976, 56). Thus even the

intention of Hamelin's appropriation of Hegel may have been at least partly political or social, even if Hamelin's Hegelian publications are primarily in the field of metaphysics.

What needs emphasis here, then, are the *living* intellectual forces agent in the formation of Durkheim's thought, rather than the *texts* he may have read. Durkheim surely read the Hegelian metaphysics and epistemology associated with Hamelin; he also shared the political thoughtworld of Hegelian political and social thinking with prominent neo-Hegelians, like Jean Jaurès and the librarian of the École Normale Supèrieure, Lucien Herr.[15] They ran courses in the world of action parallel—but again not identical—to that which Durkheim would run in the world of politics and academic sociology. On different fronts, Octave Hamelin, Charles Andler, Lucien Herr, and Jean Jaurès each actively advanced what I shall call the "second wave" of Hegelian influence into France. And, although Durkheim never says so, it seems impossible that he himself could have remained aloof from the sweep and surge of what to him must have been a most agreeable flow of notions.

Thus Durkheim's participation in an Hegelian thought-world common to a Hamelin, Jaurès, or Herr reveals a side of Durkheim usually not much appreciated today. Here is Durkheim not only working within the ambit of *avant garde* rationalist philosophy, but also a "philosophy" driven by the essentially religious agenda peculiar to Hegelian thought: this is "philosophy" which paints in bold cosmological strokes across the vast canvas of the history of humanity, setting out an evolutionary vision of what the human future might be. This is Durkheim in the context of a kind of "philosophy" which is, at the same time, a kind of religion in its own right, shared in ways with Jaurès, Herr, and others—the neo-Hegelian religion of humanity.[16] First let us fill out the details of Hegel's fortunes in France, and see just what character it had in the late 1890's when Durkheim and Hamelin would have been susceptible to influence of Hegelian thought.

3.1.   *Two Images of Hegel in France: Before and After 1870*

In political terms, before 1870, Hegel enjoyed a glamorous image among social progressives. His thought was seen inspiring social revolution in favor of human liberty; his role as Prussian state philosopher was played down. In the Comtesse de Gasparin's romantic novel *L'Hégélien*, the novel's dashing namesake, the captain of a revolutionary regiment, makes a hurried appearance. In reply to questions from a French countess eager to understand his cause, we learn of the Hegelian captain's noble ideals in a "sort of profession of socialist faith" (D'Hondt 1971, 23). "Bread for everybody! And, joy and leisure too! Let no one any longer be counted among the earth's disinherited; nor let some wallow in opulence while others go hungry; harvests should ripen for the benefit of all; and everybody should have silk furniture and a life of ease!" (D'Hondt 1971, 23). To French progressives, Hegel was their "German-born brother," socialist, and rebel (D'Hondt 1971, 22). Even before 1830, Hegel had enjoyed a certain vogue among philosophers such as Auguste Comte and Victor Cousin. There, partisans of the enlightenment rallied to Hegel because Hegel was seen as an anti-clerical and atheist enemy of orthodox piety. Hegel was also seen as a pantheist because of his doctrine of absolute spirit. This was understood as meaning very roughly that "God is everything; everything is God." Yet interpreters of this formula tended to read it with the opposite of what is usually taken to be its main emphasis: "everything is God" is emphasized and "God is everything" is played down. For these pantheists this meant that things thought mundane were in fact shot through with divinity—"everything is God." Interestingly enough, these pantheists were among the first socialists in France.

From the first third of the nineteenth century, French Hegelian socialists—many of whom were Saint-Simonians—emphasized links between socialism and pantheism. Others went so far as to assert that "Communism is the politics of pantheism" (D'Hondt 1971, 14). Thus, when they learned of left-wing Hegelian pantheism, the Saint-Simonians recognized something of their own beliefs. Significantly, after making his proto-socialist profession of faith, the gallant Hegelian captain of Madame de Gasparin's romantic novel casually tells his French countess, "Je suis Dieu." Contemporary commentators even said that Hegelianism was really a "second saint-simonianism": "the same pantheism" (D'Hondt 1971, 23). Especially important in this pantheism of the "second saint-simonianism" was how it entailed the belief in the sacredness of humanity. In Hegelianism, the Saint-Simonians found not only the "same pantheism," but also "the same 'incarnation' of God in man, the same divinization of man" (D'Hondt 1971, 15).

This emphasis upon the "everything is God" side of the pantheist identity betrays an important and persistent nuance of socialist pantheism. It was often not so much the mystical oneness of all things in an absolute that captured the socialist imagination, but rather its humanism. Since "everything is God," so too is humanity. Later, of course, with Marx this will become the inerrant savior class—the proletariat. In 1842, Alexandre Weil spoke of a pantheism amounting to an incarnation of God in humanity—a "*panthéisme personnificateur*" (D'Hondt 1971, 12). For these Hegelian and Saint-Simonian pantheists, ordinary humanity in itself had dignity, indeed, divinity. Although coming much later, toward the end of the century, this idea of an indwelling divinity may be why a French (at least partly Hegelian) humanist socialist like Jaurès was at one and the same time a life-long pantheist (Tresmontant 1960). Kolakowski goes as far as to claim "metaphysical pantheism" led Jaurès "to embrace socialism and that he never departed from it in later years" (Kolakowski 1981, 123). For Jaurès, pantheism entailed the dignity of human beings, and thus the central theses of the religion of humanity. Paraphrasing Jaurès, Kolakowski notes that the great socialist borrows his idea of Being from Parmenides and Hegel. Among the many things Jaurès says in his philosophical works, he believes that "the evolution of Being comprises everything." And further, "That unity is God, of whom it may be said that he is above the world, but also in a sense that he *is* the world: he is the self in every self, the truth in every truth, the consciousness in every consciousness" (Kolakowski 1981, 122). Jaurès, then, like other Hegelian socialists, based his adherence to the religion of humanity upon a pantheism which was historically derived from Hegel, or at least logically related to his major tenets.

As if to confirm his broadly Hegelian sympathies, Hamelin also trafficked in the more exotic domains of spiritualism common to left-Hegelian pantheists such as Jaurès. Although he remained a theist, Hamelin tended toward a mystical pantheism, where God was seen as immanent in the world system (Theau 1977, 44). This is in sharp contrast to his mentor, Charles Renouvier, who remained a dualist. For Renouvier, God was external to the world. Further putting distance between himself and his pantheist-tending colleagues, Renouvier deepened his commitment to traditional religion. No longer able to abide the illiberalism emanating from the Vatican, he was one of the few prominent Roman Catholic intellectuals who converted to Protestantism. Along with his personal conversion, Renouvier wrote a massive seven-volume theological work which sought to provide the intellectual justification for the national conversion of France to Protestantism (Renouvier 1963, 7 vols.).

Such links, however, between progressivist French socialist thought and Hegelianism were rare after 1870. They weakened with the decline of Saint-Simonianism and the French-German rivalries of the last third of the nineteenth century. Thus, before 1870 in France, there seems to have been no *right* Hegelian movement to speak of. Yet after 1870, critics of Hegel could only "see" him as a right-wing Prussian apologist for authoritarian militarism. Hegel was proscribed in French academic institutions. Interestingly enough, Charles Renouvier was among the leaders of this successful campaign against Hegel, arguing against the consensus of the early half of the century that Hegel's absolute objective idealism and authoritarian politics were intrinsically connected. Significantly, as we will see, this link was implicitly rejected by republican Octave Hamelin's development of an absolute idealism inspired by Hegel.

Hegel's reputation was not, however, to be reformed until near the end of the century. Once again, this work of reclaiming Hegel for the forces of progressive humanism was accomplished by French socialists. Jean Jaurès wrote his Latin thesis on the origins of German socialism in the thought of Luther, Kant, Fichte, and *Hegel*. There Jaurès spoke of Hegelian socialism as a socialism of morals (Kelly 1981, 39). Another familiar of Durkheim's, Charles Andler, came to similar conclusions in his own doctoral dissertation on the origins of German state socialism. His argument in favor of the power of representations over institutions points forward toward Durkheim's own view along these lines and backward to Hegel's personal view. In a letter to Niethammer, 28 October 1808, Hegel wrote "Once the realm of representation is revolutionized, actuality cannot hold out" (Toews 1980, 56). But major public rehabilitation of the political reputation of Hegel came as late as 1893 in Lucien Herr's remarkable "Hegel" article in the *Grande Encyclopédie*.

3.2. *Lucien Herr's Hegel: Liberty, Person, and "Possibility"*

An Alsatian like Andler and Durkheim, Herr was by training a Germanist. He was particularly grieved about the division of progressive forces into

French and German camps. Much like Andler and Jaurès, he sought throughout his life to reforge an alliance of French and German intellectuals against their common ideological enemy (Meyer 1977, 236). The first step in this project was to counter the Marxists by rehabilitating Hegel. He tried to set the record straight in his very influential "Hegel" article in the *Grande Encyclopédie* (Kelly 1981, 38). Herr's article fits the style of a contribution to a general encyclopedia: it introduces Hegel's thought according to its great divisions—phenomenology, logic, nature, and spirit; moreover, surveys the life and letters of the great man. But Herr's motive in his summary article is clearly apologetic: Hegel is a kind of Enlightenment *philosophe*, and champion of liberty. Without denying at least the scandal of appearances, for the benefit of French progressives, Herr tries to excuse the Prussian authoritarianism attributed to Hegel's political acts and thought: it was true that Hegelian philosophy "was official and imposed doctrine, and he himself had no scruples about the use of the civil authority of the State against dissidents. But it is not quite accurate to say that *he*, willingly and servilely, put his thought at the service of Prussian authoritarianism" (Herr nd, 998).

True, Herr admits, Hegel thought that the bureaucratic authoritarian Prussian monarchy seemed best adapted to his own system's political conceptions. Likewise in *The Philosophy of Right*, Hegel appeals to state intervention against liberal political disturbances. Then, late in life, he also opposed the English Reform Bill. But Herr pleads that although these views may make Hegel seem unsavory, Hegel must be judged against the backdrop of the "terror that the July Revolution inspired in him" and within the context of the logic of his entire philosophy and personality—not just a phrase or two, or even an entire book (Herr nd, 998). And, having duly admitted the man's shortcomings, Herr strikes the keynote for what we are tempted to call a "hymn for Hegel"—changing, as it were, the tune carried by political progressives since it was intoned thirty years earlier by a fellow Republican, Charles Renouvier. Dealing directly with the *ad hominems*, Herr begins:

> Nothing authorizes us to attribute these intemperate manifestations of his doctrine and his psychological nature to illiberal and personal motives. . . . Everything that his works teach us about him, everything we are told about him—after his period of juvenile romantic enthusiasm for the revolution of 1789—everything reveals

to us a man of simple and steady temperament. He stayed all his life the good-natured and upright Swabian, a regular and tenacious worker, a man of pure intellectuality, without superficiality, a man of powerful inner imagination, without charm or sympathy, a *Bürger* of modest and tame virtues, and above all, a civil servant, a friend of strength and order, realist and respectful. His inventive and systematizing powers allowed him to interpret and rationally to justify these native tendencies and sentimental prejudices. He was, more than anyone perhaps, one of those people who are "all of a piece" and who never give up anything of their true nature. (Herr nd, 998)

With Hegel's character now redeemed, Herr goes on to bring out the libertarian spirit of Hegel's thought as he perceived it.

3.3. *Herr's Hegel and Durkheim*

Partly because Durkheim himself belonged to the same progressive milieu as Herr, Jaurès, and others, partly because he was attracted (although never officially enrolled) by this kind of socialism, these aspects of Hegel's thought also have strong Durkheimian echoes. They mark Hegel as a progressive son of the Enlightenment, as a thinker formidable for his "intellectualism and critical idealism"; on top of what we know of his relation of Hamelin, they mark Durkheim once more, and for different reasons, as a thinker of the same spiritual affiliation as (at least a left wing) Hegel (Herr nd, 1002). For Herr, a deep underlying spiritual and libertarian vein seems to undermine the *étatiste* reputation of Hegelian thought. Right or wrong, Herr believes, in the end, the evolution of the state will show itself as "nothing but the history of the successive progress of the consciousness of liberty" (Herr nd, 1000). Durkheim's vision of the individual as end and highest product of human social evolution too urges that society gives birth to the individual as it grows more and more complex. In this light, Charles Andler's observation that "Hegelian teaching remains quite visible in the premier lineaments of a sociology where truth is always identified with liberty," sounds a note of confirmation (Andler 1932, 67).

Those who have thus far accepted my analysis of parallels between Durkheim[17] and Hamelin will not be surprised to learn that Hamelin's scheme of dialectic, like Herr's, culminates in the concrete individual human person, rather than in the Absolute (Berger 1968, 90). It is the view of Steven Collins that even without Herr's personalist reading of Hegel, such a focus on the concrete human individual person is profoundly Hegelian. Says Collins, "the universal *Geist* is not a separate, transcendent reality but is immanent in the process of its own self-realization through empirically individual embodiments" (Collins 1985, 79, n71). Further, Hegel's central vision is summed up, to Herr's satisfaction, in the slogan recently embraced by the prominent Durkheimian Louis Dumont: "The real is the rational; the rational is the real" (Dumont 1970, 138). This is first to make an idealist act of faith in the power of representations—familiar enough to present readers and to students of the late Durkheim: "nothing is produced which is not the end of the progressive realization of the idea." Second, Hegel lets Herr, the "possibilist" socialist, make an idealist's act of faith in Progress—something also central to Durkheim's late nineteenth-century viewpoint: "the eternal procedure of the realizing of the idea is unique and necessary, and cannot be accomplished in any other way" (Herr nd, 1002). But lest the powerful surge of reason seem to validate revolutionary fanaticism, Herr notes, like Durkheim, that evolution owes debts to the past, and even while transcending the past does not destroy it. Rather, the present fulfills the past, as Durkheim argued:

> Indeed what do we even mean when we talk of contemporary man, the man of our times? It is simply the agglomeration of those characteristic traits whereby today's Frenchman can be identified and distinguished from the Frenchman of former times. But this cannot really give us a picture of the whole of modern man; for in each one of us, in differing degrees, is contained the person we were yesterday, and indeed in the nature of things it is even true that our past personae predominate, since the present is necessarily insignificant when compared with the long period of the past because of which we have emerged in the form we have today. It is just that we don't directly feel the influence of these past selves precisely because they are so deeply rooted within us. (Durkheim 1977, 11)

Indeed, if not going far enough to come down hard in favor of the undying reality of the past, Durkheim dissolves the present: "the truth is that the present . . . is by itself nothing; it is no more than an extrapolation of the past, from which it cannot be severed without losing the greater part of its significance" (Durkheim 1977, 15).

Like their German Social Democrat brethren across the Rhine, Bernstein and even philosopher Ernst Cassirer, French democratic socialist Hegelians like Jaurès and Herr sought an evolutionary socialism typically in express opposition to the revolutionary forms of socialism of the time connected with the syndicalism of Georges Sorel. That they may have failed to capture the allegiance of their hour of history is less important for us than that we understand what they tried to do (Fabiani 1988, 82–83). All four thinkers moved in the same intellectual orbits around the as yet unknown Hegelian "sun." Durkheim, Hamelin, and the "possibilist" socialists like Jaurès shared common attitudes towards critical oppositions: they liked resolving them by conciliation.

4. Three Ways to Renovate Rationalism

Now these positive correlations between the thought of philosophers like Durkheim and Hamelin, on the one side, and socialist thinkers like Andler, Herr, and Jaurès, on the other, should persuade most readers of the existence of some kind of Hegelian current of thought flowing through the progressive culture of the late 1890s. Yet to trace the outlines of its unique Hegelian shape we will need to hold up the image of the work of Charles Renouvier (1815–1903) for contrast. This is especially so for Durkheim and Hamelin since both are on record as indebted to the work of the great Neo-Kantian philosopher of the Third Republic. In this way we will be in a position to judge both the distinct *differences* Hegelian thought made to Durkheim and Hamelin, as well as what it reinforced or "overdetermined." We have noted general similarities in the thought of these three men already. Let us see how they match up in greater detail.

4.1. *Ethics: Altruism and/or Duty*

In terms of their ethics, it is not surprising that Durkheim, Hamelin and Renouvier should be anti-utilitarian. But at the same time, it is surprising to learn that they were significantly critical of Kant as well.[18] Each of these renovators of rationalism sought in his own way to assert an ethic which, unlike that of Kant and the utilitarians, was based on material notions of justice and human sympathy, rather than on a formal notion of duty. Their ethics were also social in nature rather than individualist. In this they traced the broad outlines of Hegel's own criticisms of Kant's moral theory (Taylor 1975, 376).

Taking Durkheim first, consider the following example of these general positions. Despite the Kantian ring to much of Durkheim's talk of obligation and duty, Ernest Wallwork has shown that Durkheim expressly opposed Kant by making altruism an ideal of human morality. For Durkheim, Kant's categorical imperative cannot serve as a standard for morality because it may lead to ethical egoism. What, asks Durkheim in effect, logically prevents the categorical imperative from being universalized into the maxim of "I'm all right, Jack"—the maxim that individuals should simply look after themselves (Wallwork 1985, 88)?

What is more, for Durkheim, Kant's view that morality never involves using persons as means leads both to logical and moral absurdities. Kant's categorical imperative would forbid people from using themselves as a "means" to the happiness of others—as in the case of self-sacrifice or altruistic behavior.[19] But Durkheim held that sacrificing oneself for others is the *ultimate* justification for moral standards, as we have seen in his obituary for Hamelin. Indeed, Durkheim believed that doing an act for another and at some personal cost to oneself is both a necessary and sufficient condition for constituting an act as moral (Wallwork 1985, 89). This is so despite the fact that Durkheim accepts that such perfect self-sacrifice is an "ideal," "that we can approach indefinitely without ever realizing" it (Durkheim 1960, 329). When we try to live it in reality, self-sacrificing altruism thus throws up an "antinomy" between the "joy" of release from egoism together with the "pain" of the real loss of pleasure—an "antinomy . . . so deep and so radical that it can never be completely resolved" (Durkheim 1960, 328).[20]

It was apparently Renouvier who taught Durkheim that sympathy and love for humanity should govern justice—not Kantian duty (Gunn 1922, 232; Renouvier 1918, 165, 206). Although Renouvier felt altruism was an ideal, like Durkheim, he felt it was difficult to realize in reality. Thus, self-sacrifice was the stuff of sanctity; obligation better fit the life of the citizen (Gunn 1922, 239). Renouvier also undercuts the egocentrism of the Kantian principle of duty by allowing no "radical difference between the duty toward oneself and towards others" (Hamelin 1927, 383). Yet in the end, he remained an ethical individualist because he granted the individual human person priority over the claims of others: one needs a self, so to speak, in order even to give up oneself (Gunn 1922, 237). As a personalist, but also sympathetic to socialism, Hamelin balanced the interests of the individual against those of society (Hamelin 1927, 382–83). In his study of Renouvier, Hamelin could be even more personalist than the Protestant convert, Renouvier. Hamelin took issue with his mentor's view that there was no "radical difference" between the duty toward oneself and towards others. "Duty toward oneself," argued Hamelin, "is always subject to an appeal by a better informed conscience"—namely one's own (Hamelin 1927, 382). Despite his own heroic death, Hamelin also notes with approval Renouvier's individualist view that the obligation of altruism is incumbent only upon the saint; ordinary people are only expected to adhere to their obligations (Gunn 1922, 239).

4.2.   *The Individual under Socialism*

Yet, while Hamelin celebrates his own personalism, he does so from a socialist perspective in the style of other French left-Hegelian socialists like Lucien Herr, Charles Andler, and Jean Jaurès. Renouvier, by contrast, tended to be anti-socialist and more the bourgeois individualist (Hamelin 1927, 401). Hamelin tells us of sympathies for a kind of socialism, and for the simultaneous distaste for the "altogether too individualist" character of Kant's idea of "right" (*droit*) (Hamelin nd). Although he rejected what he called "absolute socialism" for moral reasons, "our conception of justice," says Hamelin, "is eminently socialist. . . . Social things always encompass a relation with something other than oneself! Although this is not to deny that justice resides in the moral agent, this goodness only realizes itself in being practised in relation with someone else" (Hamelin 1907, 451; Hamelin nd). Hamelin accordingly deplores Kant's moral formalism, and prefers a morality in which humanity "ought to be a concrete and positive end" and in which our "social duty [is a] goal of human behavior"[21] (Hamelin nd). This is different, of course, from Hegel's objection to Kant's moral formalism, which Hegel simply finds empty of any useful content (Taylor 1975, 375). Yet Hegel's view that the idea of freedom can fill up the Kantian moral void at least seems consistent with Hamelin's celebration of humanity, which after all, is spelled out in terms of liberty. Thus, although these three thinkers diverge, their differences do not seem to matter much regarding their views on that perennial problem of modern social philosophy, the relationship between individual and group. Like Hegel before them, Renouvier, Hamelin, and Durkheim advanced a social individualism: the individual is sacred, but realizes fulfillment only in solidarity with others (Collins 1985, 58; Taylor 1975, 375). Each combined his social outlook with an equally vital personalism. Even Renouvier, the most individualist of the three, believes that the essential meaning of justice emerges in interpersonal relations. Both Renouvier and Hamelin held relation to be first and fundamental among the categories (Gunn 1922, 69). Therefore, despite differences, I think we can then see how Durkheim and Hamelin, especially, took their places along with other philosophers seeking to rethink the received heritage of Kantian ethics, in relation to the socializing tendencies of left Hegelian French democratic socialists such as Herr, Jaurès, and Andler. For his part, Renouvier, although a renovator of Kant in his own way, seemed to keep clearer of the socializing tendencies that accompanied Hegelian thought into the late 1890s.

4.3. *Morality and History: "Concreteness" and Cultural Relativism*

Related to these views of the relation of individual to society was an historicist idea of the person, which in turn raised the question of the relativity of morals to cultural context. Steven Collins observes that like the Durkheimians, Renouvier and Hamelin, too, saw the categories of thought as historically developed and conditioned, "person" among them (Collins 1985, 58). For them, the person was an embodied, concrete individual, and thus one's idea of person could change as historical conditions changed (Gunn 1922, 69). These are recognized stock-in-trade Hegelian notions as well. For Hegel, the moral life is called *Sittlichkeit*. Charles Taylor takes this to mean "moral obligation I have to an ongoing community of which I am a part" (Taylor 1975, 376). Edward Westermarck, the ethical relativist, was quick to cite Hegel's authority for such positions. Westermarck quotes Hegel to the effect that " 'the wisest men of antiquity have given judgment that wisdom and virtue consist in living agreeably to the Ethos of one's people' " (Westermarck 1960, 29). Together with its etymological associations with the German word for customs (*Sitten*), we are thus immediately plunged into the discourse of cultural and moral relativism characteristic of Durkheimian thought (Lukes 1972, 89; Taylor 1975, 376).

Yet how far Durkheim, Renouvier, and Hamelin took the historicist dimension of Hegelian thought differed. This is to say that there was a range of opinion about just how the Hegelian project of historicizing morality was to be taken. One way the philosophers of this time expressed their interests in history and ethics was by speaking of making moral philosophy more "concrete." Just what this meant was not always clear. But the quest for concreteness indicated such trends of ethical theory as Durkheim's moral relativism, his sociology itself, science of morals or sociology of knowledge—all efforts to make dependent upon empirical conditions what had hithertofore been thought timeless matters of speculation.[22] What confuses the reader, however, is that such unlikely candidates as Hamelin's absolute idealism were included in this movement. One contemporary critic said Hamelin's idealism "pursues the concrete everywhere" (Parodi 1919b, 449). What this means we will see shortly. For now, we should note that Hamelin at least *thought* he had heeded the call to greater concreteness. But as an absolute idealist, he never went as far as Durkheim in the direction of radical moral relativism, and not at all toward empirical treatments of moral judgment. Consider the examples of Hamelin's approach to morals in historical context.

In terms of their relative "concreteness," Hamelin's approach to morals seems midway between Durkheim's and Renouvier's. This is to say that, although each of these three philosophers paid at least lip service to the social location of moral norms, they differed with respect to how much weight to give the *concrete* social milieu in the moral judgment.

Thus Hamelin wrote that Renouvier should be congratulated for integrating "morality and history—without being confused for one another—indeed far from that" (Hamelin 1927, 399). Hamelin apparently had in mind the way he himself dealt with morals by locating ethical inquiry in a comparative historical context. In his various lecture courses on morals, Hamelin showed the kind of acquaintance with cross-cultural comparison from ethnography and history of religions we usually associate only with historians of religions themselves or with the Durkheimians. In his lectures on Quatrefages's *Universality of Moral and Religious Sentiments*, Hamelin shows sophistication about the diversity of moral systems, ranging from the Amerindians, "fetishism," and Hottentots to the Buddhists. With a familiarity we might associate with Durkheim, Hamelin discusses Lubbock's *Origins of Civilization*, but judges it deficient in treatment of tribal cultures.[23]

Unhappily, in Hamelin's view, Renouvier does not go far enough in his quest for concreteness. The connections made between ethics and history are too general; specific relations are called for, says Hamelin (Hamelin 1927). Thus, in the end, Renouvier's *morale* suffers from being a "pure *morale*" (Hamelin 1927, 356–58). Despite Renouvier's claims to reconcile ethics and society, his morale implies an "isolated moral agent," even though no such thing exists in reality (Hamelin 1927, 358). Hamelin claims that for Renouvier ethics is like geometry, which although "pure" in itself, *may* be applied "in history" (Hamelin 1927, 356). The "complications born of history are discarded" in making ethical judgments, he concludes about his great mentor (Hamelin 1927, 381).

But although Hamelin likes the greater concreteness history brings morality, he stops short of moral relativism. He really prefers the way Renouvier preserves the (at least relative) autonomy of moral judgment. In Hamelin's eyes, for Renouvier, "morality and history . . . are reconciled enough so that one sees how they influence one another. [But] an historical study of morality and ethics would be possible without ethics being absorbed into history." Despite the worst historical conditions, then, Hamelin affirms his rationalist faith that man remains a "moral animal," never losing the ability to seek the good (Hamelin 1927, 400). Hamelin is thus equally critical about Durkheim but from the opposite pole: Durkheim's attitude to morals is, in a way, too concrete. Hamelin completely rejects Durkheim's moral relativism; he likewise rejects the notion which lies at the basis of Durkheim's science of morals, that morality has an "empirical foundation." Hamelin holds instead a theory of obligation in which it is reason itself which presents itself as obligatory (Hamelin 1907, 450).

Yet even while objecting to the perceived direction of Durkheim's thought and applauding a degree of Renouvier's belief in the autonomy of moral judgment, Hamelin (confusedly) affirms the social nature of human life, including human moral life. "Man is—he cannot be other than a social being . . . man has always been society [since] the social is not . . . a mere accessory and efflorescence of individual [but] a milieu and necessary cradle as well. It is a prolonging of the external world on which the individual depends, as he depends on the world in general. [Therefore] part of moral fact seems social" (Hamelin 1907, 451). But this does not make Hamelin radical in his treatment of the relation of society and moral judgment. For him, Durkheim goes much too far in making ethics a dependent feature of social life. "Maybe social obligation was first felt as external—but once obligation is felt, it is something other than social," says Hamelin. Quite simply, Hamelin believes that "moral facts are not simple social facts" (Hamelin 1907, 451).

Thus, we can see here that while these three closely related thinkers agree (with Hegel) that morality should be historicized, only Durkheim really pushes the relation to anything like radical Hegelian lengths. Hamelin comes closest to Durkheim, and takes up second position, leaving Renouvier in the rear. Nonetheless, their endeavors do show once again how Durkheim and Hamelin were playing in the league of Hegelian renovators of Kantian thought—who at least felt they needed to tip their hats in the direction of morality as Hegelian *Sittlichkeit.*

5. Reconciliation and Opposition

Renouvier differed most from Durkheim and Hamelin regarding the attitudes of the latter two thinkers toward contradiction and opposition. Let us first consider the way Hamelin distinguished himself from Renouvier by adapting Hegelian attitudes toward opposition.

For Renouvier contradictions were final; when presented with logical opposition, one had to choose one or the other (Theau 1977, 44). And, there things stopped. Thus the law of contradiction became basic to Renouvier's logic. Hamelin, like Hegel, saw oppositions as the beginning of ontological movement. Unlike Renouvier, he felt that contradictions were reconcilable by the use of dialectic (Gunn 1922, 67). Hamelin recognized "as a fundamental law of all thought the necessary correlation in the mind of opposed notions." Mind never poses an idea without posing its opposite. Hamelin believed these oppositions could be resolved, sometimes into third terms; or they were "correlated" or integrated. However one might reconcile them, they were not left as contradictions opposed to one another in the manner of Renouvier, or even left magically to be *aufgehebt* as emphasized by later radical readings of Hegel. Hamelin wanted a dialectic of "correlative contraries which are complementary" (Cornu 1968, 156). In consequence, Hamelin was committed to the importance of the concept of "relation," so much so that he made the classic idealist move of "constituting things with relations" (Parodi 1919b, 435). He saw in relation the simplest law of things (Parodi 1919b, 434).

A fine example of this conciliatory style of dealing with oppositions applied to public affairs can be found, as we might expect, in Jean Jaurès. The great socialist made a reputation in his time for just this kind of political logic of correlation and conciliation. Jaurès was a model of political optimism. He believed that differing interests could be worked out between social combatants, and that full-scale class war was avoidable. Leszek Kolakowski warns that this often gave Jaurès the look of the "Pangloss of socialism" (Kolakowski 1981, 117). And, when we look more closely at this "universal conciliator" (Kolakowski 1981, 115), we see that Jaurès attempted to overcome many of the same oppositions as Durkheim and the other renovators of rationalism—science and religion, idealism and materialism, the individual and society, spirit and matter. In general terms, then, the practical drift of Hamelin's abstract statements on the reconciliation of oppositions is hard to catch. As we noted in contrast with the position of Charles Renouvier, Hamelin thought contradictions were more apparent than real. Thus, if one thought about them sufficiently, one could reconcile them to one another—although not always in a balanced way.

5.1. *Hamelin "Reconciles" Science to Philosophy*

Now both Durkheim and Hamelin seem to practice Hegelian reconciliation by trying to resolve the classic opposition of science and philosophy. However differently they may interpret the task of reconciliation, as we will see, they are nonetheless under its sway. For them, science and philosophy are said not to be absolutely opposed; rather, they actually show an underlying unity. In a way, the game both Hamelin and Durkheim play in these strategies of reconciliation, as we will see, may remind one of Jaurès, the (Hegelian) "Pangloss of socialism."

As a kind of Pangloss of idealism, Hamelin believes one transcends what is assumed an unbridgeable opposition without negating either pole. Rather, we eliminate serious difference by understanding each pole anew from a novel perspective. On the question of the progress of knowledge, Hamelin argues in the same vein. The common view is that the progress displayed by the sciences casts philosophy's concern for perennial (and thus perennially *unsolved*) problems in an inferior light. Hamelin's answer to this invidious comparison is, on the one hand, to show how "scientific" philosophy really is, and on the other, how historical and human a thing science is.

A classic claim to autonomy by the sciences is that they work and think cumulatively and collaboratively; philosophy, like all the "arts," is a virtuoso operation where one "discovery" follows another along no particular progressive line. But Hamelin argued that collective research and writing are not the exclusive province of the sciences; nor is virtuoso individual research restricted to philosophy (Hamelin 1957, 153–54). Both have elements of each. The sciences are not removed from the personal and historical realms. Far from being truths anonymously delivered from the heavens, most of the great theories are, after all, personal products of known creators: Galileo, Lagrange, D'Alembert, and so on. We also have reason to doubt the unqualified progressive nature of science—consider how scientific theories, once ruled out of favor, subsequently are revived. The optics of Fresnel, says Hamelin, represents a return to Descartes, after being out of favor for a time. Lastly, it should not be forgotten that the great philosophers have made contributions to our cognitive sophistication. The understanding of innate ideas advanced by Kant is a clear improvement over the first groping attempts to formulate these notions by, say, Descartes. Thus philosophy has had its part in the development of science and therefore is not irreconcilably opposed to it. It would not surprise students of the philosophy of science, then, that Fernand Turlot notes Hamelin's influence on the philosopher of science Henri Poincaré (Turlot 1976, 249). Therefore, in true Hegelian style, Hamelin believed that at the heart of the reality of science lies an opposition which gives it life.

5.2. *Durkheim "Reconciles" Philosophy to the Science of Society*

It is generally not appreciated that the later Durkheim's work coincides, as he says, with plans to "renew" philosophy by applying its problematic to "concrete" societies (Durkheim 1982a, 237). It was Durkheim's belief that making philosophy particular and *empirical* made it no *less* philosophical—especially since this new philosophy took on all the great perennial questions of the old, while locating them in particular societies. Staying close to philosophy, sociology continued to deal with perennial problems set by

Kantian *philosophy*, such as the origin and nature of the categories of thought, religion, morality, and so on. Thus, for example, Durkheim's quarrel with the Kantians is not over the fundamental problematic, but over the nature of the origins of the categories? "For these [Kantian] philosophers categories shape reality beforehand, while for us they sum it up. According to them they are the natural law of thought: for us they are the product of human artifice. Yet from both viewpoints they express synthetically thought and reality" (Durkheim 1982a, 240).

Contemporary commentator André Lalande claims Durkheim "holds to what he calls a *spiritualism of fact*" (Lalande 1906). In this way, sociology enables us, Durkheim said, to "philosophize about things rather than words. One may even go so far as to say that sociological reflection is called upon to take up an extension, in a natural progression, in the form of philosophical thinking" (Durkheim 1982b, 239). Thus, Durkheim tried as hard to "sociologize" certain philosophical categories as to do a special kind of philosophy fashionable in his time. Another way of putting it would be to say that Durkheim and the "philosophers" were in a way divided by positions taken *within* the traditional field of academic philosophy. Crudely put, they disagree over whether "natural" innatism or social innatism tells the truth about the origins of categories. In this way, Durkheim continued to participate anew in the "conciliatory" styles of thinking prevalent in the neo-Hegelian philosophical world of his day, but from the perspective of this renewed "philosophy" that he called "sociology."

Thus, although Durkheim and Hamelin drew different conclusions from their attempts to reconcile science and philosophy, it seems that Durkheim and Hamelin were reaching for the similar goal of "reconciliation." Hamelin may have been trying to show that philosophy and science were already like each other, and that, implicitly, philosophy was just as good as science. Durkheim, however, attempted a reconciliation of philosophy to science by creating a sociology which he believed is in fact a renewal of philosophy. In effect, Durkheim wanted to show how his "sociology" was better at doing philosophy's job than (traditional) philosophy itself. Yet in going the route of "reconciliation"—if only rhetorically—both Hamelin and Durkheim take their places alongside Jaurès and the other "conciliatory" Hegelian renovators of rationalism.

6. The Rhetoric of Reconciling Ideal and Real

Another domain where this rhetoric of reconciliation dominates the intellectual agenda of Durkheim and Hamelin is the so-called relation of the ideal and the real. Few other areas of Durkheim's thought could be more important to the characterization of that thought than the synthesis he sought to articulate between the "ideal" and the "real." The same could be said for Hamelin.

We already know that Hamelin made a name of distinction for himself as an absolute idealist. Likewise we also know that Durkheim was widely regarded, wrongly in my view, as just as much the idealist. The reality is, however, far more complex—and more interesting to boot. It remains true that Hamelin's idealism is absolute, and thus that he does not really achieve, as we have seen, the balanced conciliation of opposites promised in the Hegelian program. Yet, interestingly enough, Durkheim *does* seem to be truer to the Hegelian spirit of making the spiritual concrete than does a recognized Hegelian such as Hamelin. Durkheim does after all reconcile philosophy with science by producing a sociology which genuinely borrows from both speculative and empirical realms. Hamelin, by contrast, continues to fight a rearguard battle for the autonomy of philosophy even as he tries to show how science is a little like philosophy and philosophy a little like science. Then Durkheim seems more serious about the Hegelian vision of morality as relative to historical and cultural than Hamelin, who once again wants to raise the rationalist flag for the autonomy of moral judgment. If I am correct in believing Durkheim even more Hegelian than a recognized Hegelian like Hamelin, then we should see this borne out as well in their attitude toward reconciling spirit and matter in the anthropological realm. Let us first look at Hamelin.

6.1. *Hamelin's Descartes: Occasionalism Is Semi-Idealism*

Here no better case can be chosen to demonstrate my contention than Hamelin's approach to overcoming opposition in his treatment of Cartesian dualism. Then we can go on to examine Durkheim's approach to a parallel problem at the center of his thought. After a tortuous exegesis of Descartes's view of the relation of mind and body, Hamelin concluded that Descartes's resolution of the mind-body opposition was idealist. This is unexpected because Descartes is usually regarded a dualist about mind and body—something Hamelin knows full well.

Hamelin's first move is to argue that Descartes was not a pure dualist, but at least occasionalist about the relation of mind and body. Thus, Hamelin provisionally accepted that Descartes gave reality to both material and ideal factors, and that the two principles possessed complementary powers. Material substance seems superior to thinking substance because thought depends on the real world for its objects of representation. Yet thinking substance is better known because it is available to us by direct introspection. Thus, at first the two are reconciled to each other because each has distinct advantages over the other. But then Hamelin goes further to chart their interaction. After having noted their interdependence, Hamelin declares for the superiority of thought to non-thought, and converts occasionalism into a halfway house *en route* to absolute idealism. Since thought can represent nonthought, thought is thus the "measure of reality." Thought can duplicate non-thinking substance by its powers of representation, and thus the two principles are reconciled to each other, but with thought in a superior position—as philosophy was with respect to science as we saw earlier. Thus, for all his talk about reconciling oppositions, as he does in his theory of morals, Hamelin seems simply to prefer one opposite over the other—even if he delays the final verdict. There is little of an Hegelian dialectic here, and rather more of a Berkeleyan idealist assertion of thought. As Charles Taylor puts it, Hegelian idealism is not one which "would resolve dualism by affirming spirit alone" (Taylor 1975, 241).

6.2. *Durkheim: Ideas Related to Things*

Now Durkheim operates to overcome oppositions as well, but in a different, I think more Hegelian, way: Durkheim holds onto the tensions between opposites without lapsing into either an easy idealism or materialism. Consider the example of the synthesis between concepts or *représentations* versus concrete societies, Durkheim's resolution of the opposition of collective representations and social morphology. There the formula, the mature Durkheimian synthesis, finds collective representations and social morphology existing in a *dialectical* relation to one another. In *The Elementary Forms* (1912), Durkheim says,

> Care must be taken not to see our theory of religion as a simple revival of historical materialism: this would show a complete misunderstanding of our ideas. . . . Certainly, we regard it as obvious that social life depends on its substratum and bears its marks, just as the mental life of the individual depends on the brain and in fact on the whole organism. The *conscience collective* is something more than a simple epiphenomenon of its morphological base. . . . In order to obtain [the *conscience collective*] . . . a synthesis *sui generis* of particular consciences is necessary. The effect of this synthesis is to produce a whole world of sentiments, ideas, images which once created obey the laws appropriate to them. (Pickering 1975, 152)

Or, put in order to stress the interdependence of ideal and material factors, Durkheim says,

> The ideal society does not stand outside the real society: it is part of it. Far from being torn between two opposite poles, we cannot be part of the one without being part of the other. A society is not simply constituted by a mass of individuals who compose it, by the territory they occupy, by the things they use and actions they perform, but above all by the idea it has about itself. (Pickering 1975, 151)

We might add that this does not represent a sudden "deathbed" or merely personal conversion. Durkheim had already made this view explicit in "Individual and Collective Representations" (1898) (Durkheim 1974,1–34). There the formula is that collective representations (in this case, myth) are "partially autonomous realities with their own way of life." Myth is "not directly related to the particular feature of the social morphology" (Durkheim 1974, 31). This formula also governs the approach of Durkheim's closest theoretical collaborators in the *Année sociologique*, Henri Hubert and Marcel Mauss, in their discussions of myth (Strenski 1985, 354–71). It is late Durkheimian dogma.

Readers beware: although related to the claim that collective representations are *active* in society—often taken as the only sense of later Durkheim's "idealism"—this synthesis cannot be reduced to it. Collective representations are reconciled with, but *without being reduced to,* the social substratum. Likewise, this is *not* simply to claim that collective representations are taken by the mature Durkheim to be proper elements for explaining social phenomena. *Both* ideal and material factors in society are to be seen together as elements accounting for the dynamic of life in society (Robertson 1984, 195). What distinguished Durkheim's mature sociology was not a simple conversion to the view that *représentations* were substantial, where previously they may have been shadows of social morphology. What distinguished Durkheim's mature sociology was the subsequent view that *both* representations *and* things mattered, and that they mattered *together*. I am claiming that this move was taken *within,* and not in spite of, neo-idealist philosophical movements of Durkheim's last days.

6.3.   *Durkheim, Hamelin, and the* Fin-de-Siècle *Hegel*

The dialectic scheme of resolving oppositions practiced by both Durkheim and Hamelin was no more a mere logical technique than it was for Hegel himself. It embodied an attitude toward social oppositions, as well, such as the conflict between individual and society, perennial in the modern world—and especially acute in the world Durkheim and Hamelin cohabited. Both men, it will be recalled, were very early participants in Dreyfusard organizations. Social conflict afflicted France in ever more acute ways just before the First World War, especially the rise of the militant worker movement and a new nationalism.

In Durkheim's day, however, Cartesianism was the principal ideology of progressive French liberals. But Cartesianism had two fatal drawbacks: first, Cartesian individualism was asocial, and thus unable to represent collective interests to either trade unionists or nationalists. Second, despite Hamelin's tortured attempts to turn Cartesian occasionalism into a step on the way to absolute idealism, Descartes was still seen as a dualist. Thus. Cartesian occasionalism did not provide a useful model for conceiving or resolving the seemingly intractable social contradictions of the day. Occasionalism just stated an opposition, and left it at that. Another model of dealing with social contradictions was needed. Now, just at this time, as we have seen, democratic socialists sympathetic to Durkheim's sociological thinking were prominent in a *fin-de-siècle* introduction of Hegelian thinking. I have argued that this *fin-de-siècle* Hegelian milieu was material in the formation of Durkheimian thought. Although Hegelian thinking was anticipated by Comte and Saint Simon among others, it at least reinforced the renovations of French rationalism realized in part by Octave Hamelin and Durkheim himself. Thus, whether because Durkheim was influenced by Hamelin's Hegelianism or because, like Hamelin, he synthesized Hegel and Renouvier independently, I have argued that we should think of Durkheim as part of this *fin-de-siècle* Hegelian renovation of French rationalism.

7. Politics and the "French Hegel"

In this light, it would be well to conclude by considering how my analysis suggests a re-reading of Durkheim's relation to Third Republic liberalism and the philosophy of Neo-Kantian Charles Renouvier. It has been customary to see Durkheim and Renouvier in abiding accord as intellectual moving spirits within the Third Republic. But this affinity may well have been concentrated in its period of maximum or exclusive effect as well as in particular domains of Durkheim's life and thought. Moreover, it may not account for distinctive features of the later Durkheim in the way that appeals to Renouvier's renovators—in particular, Hamelin. Although Renouvier's influence runs deep in Durkheim and persists throughout the course of his whole life, it seems free of serious rationalist competitors only in the earlier part of Durkheim's career—say at least before the years of the Dreyfus Affair. Then and throughout the Affair, the issue was still how the republic might be saved. From the last third of the nineteenth century, Renouvier's visionary teaching plotted out a strategy for the future for the Third Republic: he asserted the freedom and sacredness of the individual within the framework of a necessary dependence and solidarity with others; he mapped out a theory of secular republican education and economic social justice; he fixed morality in the center of any political plan, and the scientific study of morality, therefore, at the center of republican deliberations about morality in the modern state. Thus, Renouvier's influence on Durkheim seems concentrated on what we might call the earlier Durkheim—Durkheim the social moralist. But after the Affair, the rationalist influences in Durkheim's thought take a turn more identifiable with the "correlative" efforts of Octave Hamelin.

By 1906 or so, by the time the Third Republic had solidified its gains against Army and Church, the legitimacy or *salvation* of the republic was not the issue. Questions were raised rather about the Third Republic's moral mediocrity, its struggles with "irrationalist" ideologies and a radicalized working class. It came under attack from monarchists, radical republicans, and the socialists (Scott 1951). These new problems raised questions only partly addressed by Renouvier. What would be the Third Republic's positive ideological direction, and what would drive it toward those ends—Bergsonian *élan vital*, Marxian class struggle, Sorelian "myth," or Durkheimian and neo-rationalist "ideals"?

Along with this shift in the political culture of the years after Dreyfus, the agendas and approaches of philosophers in this time seem to have shifted as well. Indeed, we have seen with Cartesianism that the political and philosophical dimensions of thought in this epoch cannot easily or even profitably be separated. The partisans of "life" and action, "irrationalist" thinkers like Bergson and James, the *Action Française*, and the Catholic revivers were as "philosophical" as they were political. They were likewise ascendant in the period only a few years after Dreyfus had been pardoned and Church officially separated from State. Put in negative terms, in the years after the pardon of Dreyfus, the Third Republic faced a series of challenges to *reconcile* newly mobilized and empowered cultural and political opponents: the republic needed to heal the wounds opened up between republic and religion caused by the very success of its drive for secular legitimacy. It likewise needed to attend to the divisions of class and to conciliate labor unrest, which had flared up violently in the early years of the century. But the partisans of the rationalist Charles Renouvier took action at the same time. As renovators of rationalism, they were especially active in Durkheim's last years. Chief among this new generation of anti-Bergsonian renovators of Renouvier was Hamelin. I have suggested that as the philosophical rationalists shifted their ground in the early years of the century in connection with both political and philosophical changes, so along with them did Durkheim.

If I am correct in emphasizing the location of Durkheim's mature synthesis within the complex of cultural and philosophical politics of the new idealism of the renovators of Renouvier, this should not surprise: he was one of them. Although I do not overestimate the degree of real continuity in Durkheim's thought, the Durkheim of *Division of Labor* really did give way to a kind of "idealist" renovation in *The Elementary Forms* and the essays on collective representations, pragmatism, and values. I submit that Hamelin and Durkheim ran much of the same intellectual and political course together as renovators of Renouvier. Understanding them this way puts Durkheim's mature thought into the new light of the new "dialectical idealism" governing the theoretical logic of his mature synthesis. Thus, although commentators have frequently, but tentatively, called attention to "Hegelian" elements of Durkheim's thought, what they really "saw" there was Hamelin's liberal, republican transformations of Hegel.

Acknowledgments

Part of the research on this subject was made possible by a 1988 Travel to Collections grant from the National Endowment for the Humanities. I should also like to thank the staff of the Bibliothèque Victor Cousin for their kindly assistance, and Professor Antoine Faivre of École Pratique des Hautes Études, Fifth Section for his intellectual support and hospitality on my stay in Paris.

3

The Ironies of *Fin-de-Siècle* Rebellions against Historicism and Empiricism in the École Pratique des Hautes Études, Fifth Section

In its various manifestations, transformations, and exaggerations as "positivism," "inductivism," "historicism," and so on, the "end of empiricism" has been announced with regularity since the *fin-de-siècle* (Novick 1988, chs. 5–9). These days, especially from self-designated "postmodernist" or "poststructuralist" thinkers, we also are given to believe that these many-faceted and various "revolts" against empiricism have settled scores once and for all. But are these revolutions in fact truly so final as the portentous claims of the poststructuralists would have us believe? I shall argue that they are not, and indeed that the adoption of either an empiricist epistemological style or, for want of better terms, a constructivist or rationalist one, is more a matter of polemic strategy than deep principles.

Especially as known to me in its *fin-de-siècle* French incarnation, the study of religion is as rich a resource and as lively a venue for such fundamental epistemological discussions as any branch of the humanities and human sciences. What interests me is both the frequent failure of epistemological promise to live up to practice, and somewhat more disconcertingly, to live up to other of its own promises. Some prominent students of religion have, I submit, taken the lead in declaring the death of empiricist styles of inquiry only to resuscitate them for their own use. I want to focus

Reprinted from *"Religion in the Making": The Emergence of the Sciences of Religion* (eds.) Arie L. Molendijk and Peter Prels (Leiden: Brill, 1998), with permission of Brill Academic Publishers.

on historical examples of such crossings back and forth by major figures in the study of religion in France of the *fin-de-siècle*. Here, I will consider beliefs about the role of the mind in concept formation in connection with an empiricist style of doing history, what is called *histoire historisante*. Jean Réville of the École Pratique des Hautes Études led a short-lived attempt to displace the reigning *histoire historisante* in the history of religions in France. Alongside Jean Réville opposing *histoire historisante*, but at a considerable ideological distance from him, were the great sociologist, Émile Durkheim, and two of his closest confederates, Henri Hubert and Marcel Mauss—the latter pair also at the time both members of the faculty of the Fifth Section. I feel that these episodes in the history of the study of religion can best be dramatized as adding up to a thwarted revolution. The anti-historicist thrust led by Jean Réville did not survive his death. And, in the absence of other significant support for Jean Réville's views, the old *histoire historisante* resumed its virtual monopoly within the Fifth Section, continuing there to this day. Similarly, although the Durkheimians also stood in part for an anti-empiricist approach to the study of religion, their inconsistency regarding its thoroughgoing execution has left a legacy of confusion as to what a Durkheimian history of religions might have been or still might be. Why did these revolutions fail, and what lessons are to be learned from this episode in the history of the study of religion?

I want to argue that there is a rationality in the failure of these revolutions and in the inconsistency of these rebellions against empiricism and historicism. It is nothing less than the rationality of getting one's own way, of seeing one's views prevail. Thus, the movement from a study of religion which assumes its concepts are "discovered"—given in the data—to one in which one assumes that concepts must be "invented" seems an historically contingent movement itself and thus based on certain sometimes extra-intellectual interests. So, as well, is the counter movement against the ideal of a study of religion in which basic concepts are believed to be inventions. Above all, the movement back and forth across these boundaries of episte-mological value embodies a strategy for advancing a polemic. We are then perhaps all, on occasion, empiricists—when, that is, we want to claim that our ideas are supported by the way things are or when we want to hold up constructed notions to the withering criticism of the empirical facts. Similarly, we move to constructing data when we want to advance new notions against those thought to be natural and given. Viewing concepts as "invented" then may represent inquiry in its critical mode, inquiry in which we contest the status of concepts considered "natural" or taken for granted by those who speak of them as "discovered"—as brute "facts." Inventors of concepts often have in mind replacing those felt to be "there" or "discovered" with others fit for other purposes. Empiricism, though, represents that moment of inquiry where arguments are advanced on the basis of the "facts." Often as not, empiricists use the tactic of an appeal to "facts" critically too—in particular to expose what they took to be the illegitimate "imposition" of ideas onto data.

In this swing of epistemological styles at least one lesson can, I think, be learned: interests influence whether or not we adopt an empiricist mode, or whether we challenge it. The choice of adopting one position or another is then itself historically conditioned; it is contingent upon interests and circumstances. The relativity of epistemological stances accounts in part for why the same thinkers can be considered conceptual rebels at one point in their careers and conceptual conservatives at others without fundamentally changing their beliefs. I want to show not only how Durkheim and the Durkheimians fell into this pattern, but how some of Durkheim's contemporaries prominent in the study of religion in France did as well.

I.   Empiricism and Historicism in Maurice Vernes's *Study of Religion*

First, let us consider the vicissitudes of an empiricist style of doing history often simply called "historicism"—something which Fritz Ringer has conveniently termed a "hyper-empiricism" (Keylor 1975, 9). The term "historicism" can be problematic, since it is employed to name a sprawling array of styles of writing history, including the history of religions. I want however to use the term quite narrowly to translate what the French call—ever since historian Henri Berr named it so—the *histoire historisante*. For the French, "historicism" in this sense names a so-called "scientific" history, an "objective" history, one governed by critical and empirical guidelines. As such, the ideal of history was to confine itself to "knowledge" as imagined by empiricism—as based ultimately on sense experience. Theological claims, statements of transcendental belief, speculations, imaginings, and even interpretations lay outside the proper bounds of an *histoire historisante*. The historian's mind is essentially passive with respect to the data, because real-ity impresses its characteristics upon the mind. The data speak for them-selves. Theories, beliefs, or concepts, then, are secondary and derived directly as copies of the world. As William R. Keylor sums up, *histoire historisante* held the "belief that the facts of history are essentially self-explanatory and do not require the mediation of preliminary hypotheses, interpretative theories, or operational definitions. From this epistemologi-cal assumption, it follows that the historian's principal function is to locate, accumulate, collocate, and authenticate historical documents, and that such procedures constitute a scientific approach to the study of history" (Keylor 1975, 3).

An object lesson in the practice of such an historicist history of religions is the work of Maurice Vernes. Founder of the distinguished *Revue de l'histoire des religions*, Liberal Protestant Vernes was well informed about what such canons of scholarship demanded of historians. They demanded loyalty to ideals of objectivity and scientific detachment, spelled out as aversion to theology and devotion to the rigors of systematic inquiry—the so-called *méthode historique*. In his short survey of the history of Israel, Vernes described his method accordingly: "This little volume, written by a Protestant who remains attached to the tradition of his church and to Christianity, embodies an ambition: that by means of the respectful and truly *objective* way in which the facts have been presented, it will be just as useful to Catholics, Protestants and Jews as to the unchurched. This is a book of *history*, and as such excludes *theological doctrine*" (Vernes 1891, vii). Beyond these three marks—objectivity, "historical method," and aversion to theology—Vernes and others of his ilk had a distinct "aversion" to the intrusions into historical narrative of what they called "philosophy" (Réville 1886, 357). Like that of other historians of his generation, the work of Vernes was in part defined in reaction to historical system builders such as Hegel, Vico, or Comte. Above all, Vernes wanted to exclude all such elaborate world "systems" from imposing their grand schemes onto history writing (Strenski 1991, 109–27).

So paralyzed by empiricist caution was Vernes, however, that he even opposed more modest "impositions" than the extravagant speculative schemes of a Hegel and the others. No "mental constructs" or models would be permitted. Nothing would be allowed to be called "history" which, as he put it, failed to emerge from the "facts" (Goblet d'Alviella 1885, 174). Thus, Vernes's attacks against "philosophy" in history were simply assertions of the privileged place of an empiricist value of the historical methodology in accounting for the origin of historical concepts and entities. On its other side, this was to reject the legitimate place of prior presuppositions or models in writing historical narrative. Vernes's aversion to "philosophy" in effect thwarted what could have been an independent, French hermeneutic history of religions. And, in general, French history did not fully recover from similar attacks by the historicist French academic establishment until Raymond Aron's work of 1938 (Aron 1961; Keylor 1975). And one could argue that the history of religions as written in the Fifth Section has still not done so. Academic posts in history of religions in France which featured interpretive or theoretical approaches had then to be made outside the "religious sciences" or Fifth Section, and instead sought refuge among members of the *Annales* movement and in the Sixth Section.

Given his resistance to so-called "philosophical constructs" in history, Vernes wrote nothing remotely theoretical on, say, such a magnet for theoretical thinking and speculative thinking as ritual sacrifice. Significantly, Vernes always wrote about "sacrifices" in the plural, instead, for instance, as "sacrifice" as such. This betrays both the depth of Vernes's reservations about making general theoretical claims, and also his reluctance to posit the existence of an *institution* called "sacrifice." All we have in effect are impressions and particulars. To say we have "sacrifice" is to step over the line into speculation about the existence of cultural species. Vernes did not therefore feel that he needed to take responsibility for any such concept of "sacrifice"—even at the level of a model or scientific "object" of the same name. Typical of this hyper-empiricist way of writing history of religions, his discussions of sacrifice plodded along dutifully and described discrete situations, but without conceptual commitment or theoretical comment of any kind. No mention of Robertson Smith, Tylor, or Frazer darkened the pages on "sacrifices" written by Vernes. None of this, of course, inoculated Vernes against doing his own (unwitting) theoretical thinking and conceptualization: it merely found him taking as "natural" and given those concepts of sacrifice which others had invented. Vernes thus wrote with appreciation of Wellhausen's conception of sacrifice as a festive meal, but without seeming to realize that this notion represented a major and controversial conceptual innovation of the period? That Wellhausen's notion of sacrifice committed Vernes to some concept or interpretive model of sacrifice seems utterly to have escaped him. This inconsistency did not, however, escape the notice of Vernes's critic and colleague and coreligionist, Jean Réville (Réville 1886, 60, 346–63, 357–60).

2. A Brief Retreat from *Histoire Historisante* in the Fifth Section

One therefore seeks in vain for theoretical or even theological readings of descriptions of ritual sacrifices issuing from the pen of Maurice Vernes. Unlike his peers, Robertson Smith or Albert Réville, Vernes strove to maintain a kind of scientific chastity. He neither denounced nor celebrated sacrificial practices. Indeed, he did not even question them—even in the face of the scandal of human sacrifice in ancient Israel. The same cannot be said for Vernes's notable Liberal Protestant colleagues in the Fifth Section and elsewhere, such as the Révilles, Albert and Jean, or the Belgian, Eugène, le Comte Goblet d'Alviella. When they discussed sacrifice, they did so as *theological* critics, not as loyalists to the *histoire historisante*—even though it was these French Liberal Protestants and their intellectual forebears who had pioneered this discipline in France in order to reform the study of religion there against the religious and theological hegemony of the Catholics. Perhaps confident now of having defeated their age-old foe, our latter-day Liberal Protestant historians of religion could launch their own attempts to achieve theological domination and thus to criticize the empiricist histories of religion produced by Vernes. They dismissed his work as being mere catalogues of facts, exercises in "rigorous sifting" and "scrupulous" verification of data—just, of course, what Vernes wanted them to be, and just what we would expect from a writer who behaved as if his mind was little more than a mirror of the world around it (Goblet d'Alviella 1885, 170–78; Réville 1886, 349, 357). Our Liberal Protestant historians of religion had other work to do—theology. In a remarkable admission of his transparently theological motives pressing an evolutionist program for the study of religion Jean Réville said that to deny evolution in religion as Vernes had done would have had the intolerable result of placing all religions into the same developmental class (Réville 1903, 432). In short, if the confusing facts of religious life—no clear indication of progress—did not fit the theological theory of progressive evolution toward fulfillment in a kind of Liberal Protestantism, so much the worse for the facts!

In their will to interpret the data, the Liberal Protestants were part of a larger movement of impatience with and rebellion against the established historicism Vernes represented. The first move toward such an interpretive history was sponsored by the historian and intellectual entrepreneur, Henri Berr. He opposed his *histoire de synthèse* explicitly to the reigning *histoire historisante* of the academic establishment. Significant for us, Berr was in communion with the Liberal Protestants of the Fifth Section whom we have just been discussing, especially with Jean Réville (Réville 1907, 200). Berr commissioned a report on the first international congress of the history of religions (1900) from Jean Réville for the inaugural number of *Revue de synthèse historique*. In this little piece Réville showed himself committed to an interpretive history, reminiscent in ways of Dilthey—even if he could not quite let go of the *histoire historisante* (Réville 1900, 211–13). Typical of Jean Réville's turn toward his ideals of *histoire de synthèse*, he asserted that the "historian has not finished his task until, with the aid of the testimonies which he has preserved, he reconstitutes their exact tenor" (Réville 1907, 202). To Jean Réville, the task of this frankly speculative reconstructing of the frame of mind of religious folk lays a special burden upon the historian, and calls forth, quite literally, a kind of "methodological Methodism" or "Rousseauism." As if reclaiming part of the vital Methodist heritage of French Protestantism itself, Réville said that although he did not denigrate the many studies of religion done "from outside," one must now seek "the human soul" so that one can "find the underlying and true explanation of religious phenomena in the imagination, heart, reason, conscience, instincts and passions" (Réville 1907, 203). A Catholic commenting on this address was somewhat puzzled by the new Jean Réville who emerged there, and called attention to Réville's supposed methodological "eclecticism" (Collomp 1912, 523). To his mind, Jean Réville tried at once to adhere to the erudition of the *école historique*, while simultaneously heading off into the unknown territory of Berr's *histoire synthètique* (Réville 1899, 412). Whether the two could be married remained an open question.

In loosening the grip of "scientific" history, however, Jean Réville also relaxed other restrictions on academic inquiry insisted upon both by the constitution of the Fifth Section and by Vernes's historical practice. Jean

Réville accordingly announced the project of launching scientific theology (Réville 1899, 412). Thus, in about 1900, an influential party within the Fifth Section were poised to break the monopoly of the *histoire historisante* of Vernes and others, and in effect to launch a study of religion informed by both theological and hermeneutic styles of inquiry. Due, however, to the sudden deaths of both Albert Réville and Jean Réville only months apart, and stifled by the growing influence of theological neo-orthodoxy, this early attempt at an interpretive study of religion—as well as a new ecumenical liberal theological effort—was stillborn. We will never know what would have become of Jean Réville's alternative to Vernes's hyper-empiricist study of religion. What we do know is that despite his forecasts and hopes, by most accounts, the character of the study of religion typical of the Fifth Section remains substantially, with some exceptions, close to the pattern established in the last century by Vernes, and thus in effect as historicist as Vernes might have wished it. Almost before the first "end" of historicism in the study of religion could be declared, it became a thing of the past.

Let me conclude this discussion of history writing in noting two delicious ironies attending the debates between Vernes and the Liberal Protestant establishment in the Fifth Section.

First, Vernes's suspicions of interpretive history led him to some surprisingly contemporary conclusions. This should give us pause in judging the merits of Vernes's empiricism, despite its unfashionable quality. Vernes's empiricism led him, for instance, to challenge the most hallowed and widely accepted "fact" about religion of his day—the evolutionism, in particular the theological evolutionism—of his Liberal Protestant brethren. Vernes argued against evolution in religion, because to him it was a straightforward speculative imposition, a virtual religious prejudice of its own. It only "reflects the ideological preferences of the historian," said Vernes (La Planche 1991, 93). This evolutionism was "not at all historical," Vernes declared flatly, meaning that it failed to meet tests of empirical confirmation against the facts (La Planche 1991, 93). In any religion, at any particular time, one could, Vernes argued, *simultaneously* find features of religion which were supposed to be lodged in discrete stages of temporal development. Does not one find a kind of polytheism in the cult of the saints and blessed virgin among Catholics— but *at the same time* as one also must admit Catholicism's indubitable monotheism? Or, does not any polytheist, when focussed on a particular deity, at that moment, and thus *simultaneously*, not enter the spiritual frame of mind of the monotheist (Goblet d'Alviella 1885, 173)? So, where, then, is the clear bright line of evolutionary progress in religion that all of Vernes's Liberal Protestant colleagues felt was so obvious a "fact" of religious life? Again, as Vernes himself charged, the belief in evolution prevalent among the historians of religion of the Fifth Section only "reflects the ideological preferences of the historian." Because it was thus aimed at undermining progressive theological histories proffered by the Liberal Protestants, the *histoire historisante* of Vernes was naturally enough contested by them. The Liberal Protestant leadership of the Fifth Section and Faculty of Theology, in particular Albert and Jean Réville and *doyen* of the Protestant Faculty Frédéric Lichtenberger, led the charge in a polemic against Vernes (Lichtenberger 1889). The Révilles sought to re-theologize the study of religion in France over against the noncommittal *histoire historisante* more to Vernes's liking.

Second, I would like to bring out a final irony. Even though the Liberal Protestants were open to a more interpretive history of religions, as we have seen, they advanced their view on the basis of the very *empirical givenness* of religious evolution which they—at least Jean Réville—sought to transcend! For these incipient rebels against empiricism, then, religious data were here seen as having an objective shape dictated by the nature of religious progress. Comte Goblet d'Alviella, accordingly, pronounced on the "quasi-certitude" of religious evolution (Goblet d'Alviella 1885, 173). By thus embracing empiricism, historians of religion like Goblet d'Alviella then re-entered Vernes's house by the back door, so to speak, just as they thought that in criticizing his empiricism, they had slammed the "front door" on him and his empiricism as they left. Whatever its drawbacks, then, when used critically, Vernes's demanding empiricism could cut through the cobwebs of received opinion which its purveyors never would have imagined were interpretations of data.

3. Back and Forth with the Durkheimians: Historicism and Constructivism

The Durkheimians also perfected the slippery art of playing both empiricist and rationalist styles of inquiry off against each other. The result was confusion about just where they stood on the nature and origin of categories of inquiry. That the Durkheimians are confused is easy to show. Typical of this confusion are the words of two of Durkheim's closest co-workers, Henri

Hubert and Marcel Mauss. Echoing Durkheim's 1898 critique of *histoire historisante*, they nonetheless start immediately down the slippery slope to confusion: "Sociology in no way implies a disdain for facts, . . . it does not recoil from particulars, but . . . phenomena are intellectually significant only when grouped according to types and to laws" (Durkheim 1980, 49). What is this but the Durkheimians telling us they want to have things both ways? We revere objective "facts," they affirm, but we want the liberty as intelligent subjects to decide which facts count and which do not! W. Paul Vogt wittily observed that such inconsistency was occasionally costly: "At least, the Durkheimians' tendency to say that they based themselves solely on the facts, while basing themselves mostly on good reasoning about the facts, led now and then to some embarrassing slips" (Vogt 1983, 189).

In their empiricist moments, we find Hubert saying that the classification of "religious systems" is "demanded by the nature of things" (Hubert 1904, 219), or, for instance, that the "unity" of sacrifice is "real" (Hubert & Mauss 1964, 13). Such language belongs to the discourse of concept formation proper to empiricism, and is taken for granted by a practice of history writing which seeks to bring all claims to the bar of human sense experience. The human mind simply takes in what is already there in nature. Facts are objective, independent of our perceptions, interests, and strategies. No leaps of faith beyond empirical common sense observation are required. Statements such as these doubtless led Durkheimian Robert Hertz to assert that Hubert and Mauss's *Sacrifice* was, for example, an exemplary work of "wholesome inductive method, equally removed from pure erudition and arbitrary speculation" (Hertz 1909, 219).

Another example of Hubert and Mauss's empiricist style finds them saying that the existence of totemism and polytheism indicates the existence of "natural groups of facts . . . [and] essential common traits." I think we would generally recognize this as a statement of an empiricist stance regarding the origin of concepts, typical of the epistemological stance of the *histoire historisante.* The job of such historians is not to inject their own theories, interpretations, or speculations into what is "given" in the brute facts of history. Their job is to reflect what the world outside the historian is—to "ask the natives," so to speak.

But for all their fine words in favor of such empiricist values of concept formation in their putatively scientific study of religion, the Durkheimians also claimed that the basic categories of the study of religion were *a priori* The mind constructed data; its categories made facts what they were. Describing his life's work, Hubert says "In the analysis of religious facts, it is representations which preside over their development, and which regulate logic. We have retrieved [*dégagé*] the idea of the sacred, and we have retrieved it as a category of the implicit mental operations within religious facts. Our originality consists in this study of the categories of collective thought" (Hubert 1979, 206).

Basic categories of the study of religion needed to be *constructed* as an essential part of a program of scientific research. Accordingly, in an introduction to a section of Volume 9 (1906) of the *Année sociologique* called "Nomenclature," Marcel Mauss discusses under what conditions the term "taboo" might be added to a scientific vocabulary. Whatever else may be the case, says Mauss, "It is . . . important never more—except in a case of absolute necessity—to use terms from the 'savages' such as 'totem' or 'taboo'; they have caused sufficient harm to science" (Mauss 1906, 41–42). So, Mauss reverses himself and concludes that it is not such a good idea to "ask the natives." Instead, we must be active in constructing categories; we must deal directly with our conceptual problems by correcting the "faulty construction of nomenclature," by seeing to it that terms are "well constructed or named" (Mauss 1906, 41).

So thorough and deep is the confusion in Durkheimian thought that it sometimes occurs within the same work! In Hubert and Mauss's *Sacrifice: Its Nature and Functions*, the authors declare both empiricist and rationalist visions of science, even though few contemporaries seem to have noticed. While Durkheimian Robert Hertz, for instance, celebrated Hubert and Mauss's splendid "inductive method," they believe that they have written a work which shows up the shallowness of empiricism—in this case that of Robertson Smith (Hertz 1909, 219). He was, say Hubert and Mauss, "concerned above all with collecting and classifying documents . . . to build up an encyclopedic survey" (Hubert & Mauss 1964, 6). They, instead, were concerned "to disentangle the simple and elementary forms of an institution" (Hubert & Mauss 1964, 7); they were consumed with questions of "sacrifice's logical derivation" and "simplicity" (Hubert & Mauss 1964, 6), its "logical" priority to other institutions, not the "historical" sequence in which it might be found in a chronicle of rites. Hubert and Mauss said that they cared instead about discovering (what can now be appreciated as

Dee. au. has no sense of th [handwritten]

I misses soul, of lan... [handwritten]

oxymoronic) "typical facts" characterizing the institution of sacrifice (Hubert & Mauss 1964, 6). In their rationalist moments, Hubert and Mauss believed that they were embarked on a rationalist project of getting clear what *ought* to be meant by "sacrifice," rather than with some inductive survey of usages of the term enshrined in classic religious texts or authoritative commentaries (Staal 1989, 255–57). For this reason, Hubert and Mauss labored over several pages arguing how they believe the term "sacrifice" *should* be used, to what sort of phenomena it *should* be applied (Hubert & Mauss 1964, 9), about what the term "*must* designate," for what the "name must be reserved" and so on—even if they also believed that their creative theoretical constructions just happen to correspond to the reality residing in the "facts" (Hubert & Mauss 1964, 12). Yet, for some reason, even a colleague as close to Hubert and Mauss as Hertz imagined that above all he should congratulate them for their empiricist "inductivism" (sic).

Part of the cost of Durkheimian epistemological disarray has been to produce confusion about just how to execute a Durkheimian study of religion—a divide as wide today as it was then. Witness alone the epistemological gap between two sets of deeply conflicted Durkheimians, for example, conceptual innovators and theorists such as Mary Douglas over against the empiricists dominating mainline quantitative sociology. They show as little indication of reconciling what may be impossible differences as the Durkheimians themselves. Today, the embarrassment of assuming different epistemologies is at least mitigated by a division of labor: rationalists and empiricists keep out of each others' way. Perhaps the best way to excuse such conflicting epistemological foundations among the Durkheimians would, however, be to appeal to the overflowing richness and complexity of theoretical thinking which they initiated. David Pocock is probably right when he observes that on occasion Mauss's "researches had led him further than his original intent" (Pocock 1972, 2). The Durkheimians just got lost in their disparate thoughts.

4. An Historical Note: The Durkheimians, Tiele, and Anti-Empiricism

The Durkheimians interestingly enough seemed to have developed the constructivist side of their program in some, as yet unclear, relation with the religious phenomenology of Cornelis P. Tiele, and, to a lesser extent, Chantepie de la Saussaye—both of whom were well connected with the

the Fifth Section. Tiele's conception of phenomenology represented a departure from *histoire historisante* in at least three ways. It, first,
posited a putatively scientific, but actually theological, evolutionist model
of the development of religion. It showed "constant changes of form resulting from an ever-progressing evolution"—an evolution which was nothing
less than God's progressive revelation of himself to humanity (Tiele 1896,
27). Tiele thus affronted historicism by claiming access to what lay *below*
the empirical surface flow of data observed in connection with the many
"religions." Over against a relativizing historicist like Vernes, the extravagant diversity of the religions revealed a deep undercurrent of unity pointing in a definite progressive direction. Second, unlike Vernes again, Tiele
was anything but shy about inventing a scheme of classification and thus
identifying the elements making up religions. Furthermore, he then went
ahead and ranked the religions according to a definite scale of values
which he brought to his task from his pious Remonstrant Calvinist faith.
Third, having completed the work of the evolutionary sorting and ranking,
Tiele declared a sophisticated, if nonetheless transparent, theological
program. Beneath the rapid flow of the many religions, Tiele sought to find
the old steady stream of humanity's Natural Religion of the Deists, "*la
religion*," religion-as-such.

The Durkheimians too seemed to have been attracted to Tiele's anti-
historicist program at least until its theological character became clear to
them. Durkheim had sent Mauss on a mission to study with Tiele in Leyden
as part of a year's tour of leading foreign university efforts in studying
religion—a tour including studying under Tylor at Oxford and Frazer at
Cambridge. Linking Tiele and the Durkheimians (especially Mauss) was
their common desire for a history of religion which was "philosophical" in the
sense rejected by historicists like Vernes. Both Tiele and the Durkheimians
also sought to *explain* facts, and not simply to chronicle them; they both
sought to go beyond the "facts" by seeking the structures underlying them,
although the Durkheimians could not abide Tiele's theological ambitions
and theistic conclusions (Tiele 1896, 17–18).

Initially, Mauss lavished praise on Tiele's efforts at "morphology"—his
creative classification and grouping of religion into different forms (Mauss
1899, 540, 544). For Mauss, category formation, such as he and Hubert
undertook in their *Sacrifice: Its Nature and Functions*, was the part of Tiele's

work closest to the ambitions of the *Année*. Tiele's morphology, like the similar Durkheimian efforts, was, Mauss tells us, essential rudimentary scientific work, even if Tiele preferred in the end to make a theology of religion or a kind of "philosophy" in the sense condemned by Vernes, rather than the *science* of religion Mauss wanted (Mauss 1899, 544). As both Mauss and we know, Tiele did not stop with morphology. The "morphology" of the first volume of the *Elements* (evolution and morphology) prepared the way for the second volume and its "ontology" (theology) of religion-as-such. There Tiele sought to replace notions of religion in its historical variety by a menu of items transcending empirical observation—in Tiele's words, the "permanent elements within what is changing, the unalterable element in the transient and ever-altering forms" (Tiele 1896, 27).

Committed to a theological program from the very beginning, despite declarations as to the scientific character of his efforts, Tiele's "ontology" conformed to the major tenets of a theology of natural religion, distinctly flavored with Tiele's own brand of Remonstrant Protestantism. Tiele's view of sacrifice, for instance, articulated a model of sacrifice, which at the same time rehearsed the antiritualist theological polemic developed by the Reformation fathers. For Tiele, the only value in sacrificial ritual was the theological substratum which lay beneath the surface of "facts"—the inner attitude of heart, the "yearning of the believer for abiding communion with" God (Tiele 1898, 147). All observable features of sacrificial ritual, such as gift giving, the communal meal, feeding the gods, and immolations were superficial, and thus ultimately to be transcended by sacrifice as a "moral or inner sacrifice is the offering *par excellence*, of which all others are but lower forms, and, as it were, masks and foreshadowings; it is the only offering which is actually associated with worship, not as a mere symbol, but in spirit and in truth" (Tiele 1898, 147). Tiele's view of sacrifice demonstrates how his so-called scientific approach offered an alternative to historicism, but at the cost of becoming a species of Liberal Protestant theology.

Looking at the reactions of the Durkheimians to Tiele permits us finally to see how the Durkheimians positioned themselves over against antihistoricism of the theological sort: they recoiled from Tiele's program and waved high the flag of a "science" grounded in empirical observation. Yet, by contrast, when they did battle against thinkers even more empiricist than they, the Durkheimians promoted their rationalist or constructivist side. To me, this indicates that Durkheimian epistemological stances were at least sometimes conditioned by their polemic strategies rather than by some principled commitment to a vision of the nature of "scientific" concepts. Here, the Catholic biblical scholar and historian of religion Alfred Loisy presents a fine example of how the Durkheimians articulated their rationalist view of the origins of categories of inquiry in opposition to a paragon of historicism.

5. Loisy: Inventing Sacrifice or Finding It?

In reading modernist Alfred Loisy on Durkheim and the Durkheimians, it is sometimes hard to know which aspect of their program offended him most— its naturalist rejection of transcendental forces or its rationalist view of the invented origin of categories of inquiry.

Consider the Durkheimian methodological atheism first. The Durkheimians held that sacrifice and its functions are eminently observable: sacrifice "is a social function because sacrifice is concerned with social matters" (Hubert & Mauss 1964, 101). But Loisy would have none of this. For him, religious institutions like sacrifice mediate a non-empirical divine power. Sacrifice is a "transcendental action by invisible forces upon the world" (Loisy 1920, 8). Then, for the Durkheimians, sacrifice operated by natural causal means, and thus did not require the appeal to the transcendent required by Loisy. It is a "mechanism" or technology which Durkheim and the Durkheimians believed *caused* the experience of sacredness (Hubert & Mauss 1964, 2, 18). In reply to this position, Loisy reproached the Durkheimians, saying that "a power is supposed in the matter of sacrifice— a power which the rite has as its object to liberate, to intensify, to direct, to apply to its special ends and not precisely to produce . . . it is not at all created" (Loisy 1920, 8). In Loisy's words, sacrifice is "a mystical action, of unverifiable efficacy" (Loisy 1920, 9).

More to the point of the main argument of this paper, however, is Loisy's attack on the Durkheimian rationalist account of the origin of the categories of inquiry. While Loisy characterized his approach according to classic empiricist guidelines—"direct observation of facts, without preconceived theory"—he claims that the Durkheimians play fast and loose with the "facts" of the history of religions (Houtin & Sartiaux 1960, 195). For Loisy, doing history of religions is empiricist simplicity itself: the theological meaning of the texts is, as it were, written on them. In his review of the *Elementary Forms of the Religious Life*, Loisy thus accused Durkheim of imposing theory on data, of, in his words, "having been too pressed to construct a system where he keeps captive the truth that he has discovered" (Loisy 1913, 45). Durkheim, says Loisy, likewise misses the complexities of the evolution of a phenomenon by locking it in "a narrow framework of an abstract idea" (Loisy 1913, 71). Durkheim simply "puts himself in full contradiction with the facts" (Loisy 1913, 71). Thus, ironically what irritated the theologian Loisy was the hypocrisy of Durkheim's quasi-theological "dogmatism," his will to place theory before facts (Loisy 1913, 71). When these same methodological criticisms are applied to Hubert and Mauss's theory of sacrifice, Loisy feels that it too was out of touch with the facts. Loisy came to this conclusion because he felt that Hubert and Mauss had violently changed the meaning of "sacrifice"—which is of course what conceptual innovators like the Durkheimians sought to do! "The definition of the sociologists has well put into relief a power of sacrifice, but in exclusively interpreting this power as a social idea—as an expression of social force—it has changed its meaning. For the power of sacrifice does not seem at all to pertain to such and such an order of things purely social—if such an order even exists! This magical and religious power pertains to the physical and moral powers that religious thought postulates in the universe . . . transcendental action by invisible forces upon the world" (Loisy 1920, 8). Echoing *histoire historisante's* aversion to "philosophy," one of Loisy's collaborators, Paul Legay, characterized Hubert and Mauss's theory of sacrifice as "a kind of *philosophy* of sacrificial ritual—considered in itself, insofar as it is *abstracted from historic rituals*" (Loisy 1902, 281). Facts belonged ahead of theory, not the other way round as Hubert and Mauss's book on sacrifice seemed to indicate to them (Dumont 1986, 184). Thus, at one level, what really bothered Loisy about the Durkheimians was that they wrote as if our conceptions and theories *construct* facts, or sift out the facts that matter for a certain purpose. For Loisy, facts led immediately to theory.

6.   Why?

For better or for ill, it is not our fashion to believe that the data speak for themselves. Our contemporary attitude to reading data involves being critical of the reader as well as of what is read—an awareness that what the data are depends as much on *what* they are as *how* they are read. So it is not just an accident that Loisy's data speak to him theologically, while the same data speak sociologically to the Durkheimians. We rightly suspect Hubert and Mauss did not innocently focus on the functions for the human *sacrifier* either, even if they might plead innocence. Why should we believe Loisy read sacrifice any less naively? Loisy's data are doubtless constructed just as much as are those of the Durkheimians. How can he assure us that the God-man relation is always paramount? Are there no "ritual actions" in which the condition of the *sacrifier* matters most—especially in the mind of the *sacrifier*? Since we have no access to the minds of ancient *sacrifiers*, we must reserve judgment. We cannot therefore conclude with Loisy that the "data" simply speak in his voice. The "data" are open to several interpretations. Loisy has simply chosen to structure the data in a way more favorable to theism—as is his perfect right. I thus conclude that the debate about the definition of sacrifice becomes one resting ultimately upon competing polemics, competing strategies about doing history of religions—and strategies that may range all the way from academic to public or political ones.

We are thus left with the question of why proud empiricists should lapse into the constructivist invention of facts and why committed constructivists then should in their turn lean on the crutch of natural facts. Moreover, our question becomes even more tantalizing because these crossings back and forth apparently occur quite unconsciously—and to the very best of people! In the Durkheimian-Loisy contest, while in positivist mode, Loisy appeals to indubitable "facts" in trying to preserve some shred of theism or at least supernaturalism in speaking of religious matters. The upstart Durkheimians sought to change the prevailing common sense about religion, and thus construct a social alternative to put in its place. In order to establish his supernaturalist claims about the meaning and nature of religion, Loisy could have had no better grounds than a simple appeal to the literal meaning of the religious texts—to the common sense of religious scriptural accounts of sacrifice. In a way which totally contradicted his critical anti-literal approach to the Jewish and Christian Bibles when speaking to a pious Roman Catholic audience, it well suited Loisy, as a Collège de France historian of religion in anti-clerical France, to take religious texts as evidence, for example, of the transcendent in the reality of sacrifice. The same strategic aim to assert the existence of the transcendent did not suit Durkheim and the Durkheimians at all, since they sought to replace theism with sociologism—which was also in effect a step in replacing Roman Catholicism with a Durkheimian religion of humanity. Although it seemed that sacrifice was about the gods and their ways, it really was about something else not plainly visible to the naked eye. Yet, without much of a show of shame, the Durkheimians can turn around and speak as if the facts of sacrifice speak for them as well as for the theists. As we noted earlier, Henri Hubert said that the classification of "religious systems" is "demanded by the nature of things" (Hubert 1904, 219). And well it might be, but if so, why does not nature speak to everyone in the same voice? Why did not Loisy hear nature's call as did Hubert and Mauss? There is no answer to this problem—other than to see in the well-meaning and perhaps uncalculating attempts of great thinkers their ways of drawing lines between what we all surely know and that which we do not know, between what we think we simply discover, and what we must struggle to imagine and invent. These lines are drawn inevitably because the quest for knowledge is yoked to the larger life strategies of human beings.

PART THREE

The Vagaries of Religious Belonging

4

Durkheim, Judaism, and the Afterlife

 "To forget a period of one's life is to lose contact with those who then surrounded us."

–Maurice Halbwachs

"The past is not dead. It's not even past."

–William Faulkner

In considering future forms of community, we will not get very far unless we can conceive how individuals and members of communities living in the present have to do with both those in the past and the future. To put it otherwise, we will not be able to make satisfactory sense of the form of community we have with the past and future—short of recourse to beliefs in bodily resurrection or personal immortality—until we can conceive how the persons and events of our own day are related to the persons and events in the past. The Durkheimians thought about such matters and did so, in some measure, but not exclusively, like some of their Jewish compatriots and fellow-travelers. They also thought about such things like their positivist colleagues. I would like to lay out what the Durkheimian view was and how it echoed Jewish and other notions of those days. Then, I would like to ask what this may say about both the nature of the Judaism of Durkheim's day as well as about the possible Jewish character of Durkheimian thought.

The problem of conceiving how the living are related to the dead and to the yet unborn remains one of the primary puzzles of being human. For present purposes, I want to put to one side our relation to the yet unborn and limit myself to questions about relations with the dead and the past,

Reprinted from *Reappraising Durkheim for the Study and Teaching of Religion Today* (eds.) Thomas A. Idinopulos and Brian C. Wilson (Leiden: Brill, 2002), with permission of Brill Academic Publishers.

and in particular Durkheim's conception of these, and how they may be related to his supposed Jewishness. Having said this, we need to recognize that this question is really two questions. First, are questions about the relation of historical periods and events to each other—questions about the nature of the "past." Second, are questions bearing on the relation of individual persons across the life/death boundary, questions about the afterlife, personal immortality, the relation of matter and mind, body and soul, and so on. Let me deal first with how the Durkheimians treated the question of the relation of the present to the past, and then to immortality and the afterlife. But by way of doing so, let me begin with some remarks on the Jewishness of Durkheim.

I.   Was Durkheim a Jewish Thinker?

The main problem in seeing Durkheim as a "Jewish" thinker has always been that he deliberately fashioned his identity around the universalist ideals of the French Revolution and its secular humanism, rather than in terms of the particularist features of Jewish self-understanding. In this, Durkheim was like many of his "Jewish" contemporaries in the academic world of the Third Republic for whom French nationalism crowded out traditional religious or other identities. But having said this, it is also true that Durkheim himself believed that in principle, "Jewish" traits existed and could form character even in unconscious ways, thus passing on from generation to generation—at least relative to certain environments. Durkheim notes that Montaigne, for example, "stands out oddly amongst his contemporaries because of a practical cast of his mind (which derives perhaps from his Jewish origins." Durkheim is quick to add, however, that Montaigne's Jewish nurture does not insure his inheritance of a collective or social sense—a trait often associated with Jewishness by those who would make such claims (Durkheim 1977, 289).

In a glowing tribute to the liberal spirit of European Jewry, exemplified by the early twentieth century philosopher, Léon Brunschvicg, Emmanuel Lévinas raises this question of the Jewishness of the thought of those of Jewish birth, like Durkheim, who have transferred their loyalties outside the Jewish circle. Lévinas begins by calling attention to the ironies of the assimilated Franco-Jewish consciousness. As a typical rationalist atheist of the French variety, Brunschvicg dismissed Jewish or any other belief in an afterlife. Indeed, Lévinas reports that Brunschvicg was always tranquil and a bit amused in contemplating the subject of death, even his own. In a retort to Gabriel Marcel's existential agitation over the afterlife, Brunschvicg observed coyly: " 'I think that the death of Léon Brunschvicg preoccupies Léon Brunschvicg less than the death of Gabriel Marcel preoccupies Gabriel Marcel" (Lévinas 1977, 44). Put positively, however, Brunschvicg's Franco-Jewish consciousness stood for humanity. Lévinas notes that even in his domestic confinement during the Nazi occupation of Paris in 1942, Brunschvicg continued to "identify with human conscience," noting remarkably that "we do not find, in his *Diary*'s entries for the whole of 1942, the slightest trace of a specifically Jewish reaction. Brunschvicg is wounded only in his human-conscience." At the same time, Lévinas affirms that Brunschvicg's universalism was and is something to celebrate, partly because it did not necessarily require him to disown or hate being Jewish. Lévinas tells us that Brunschvicg

> was a member of the Central Committee of the Israeli Alliance from well before the war and never tried to forget his origins. But it is perhaps through this that he represents, even for those who feel they are men only through their Judaism, a profoundly respectable form of successful assimilation (which is so decried, and justly). Assimilation for Brunschvicg proceeded not from betrayal, but from adherence to a universal ideal to which he could lay claim outside of any particularism. (Lévinas 1977, 43)

This, I have argued in *Durkheim and the Jews of France*, was the way it was with Émile Durkheim as well. More than anything else, Durkheim loved the "republic," and identified himself totally with it. In dedicating himself to French secular republican values and identity, Durkheim might be said to have "forgotten" (or attempted to forget) his Jewishness. He lost contact with the self-identified Jews of his youth and did not seek or really reassemble another such self-identified community in their place. He surrounded himself instead with a community devoted to science known as the Durkheimian *équipe* or team, a group of young men equally well identified with the republic. "Only a few" of them, like Durkheim, were also Jewish by birth, and most of those no longer identified significantly with Judaism or

Jewishness (Pickering 2000, 80). The main exceptions to this rule of forget- *Mm*
ting their own Jewishness were Durkheimians Emmanuel Lévi, Isidore Lévy,
and, later, Robert Hertz. In terms of Judaism, the Durkheimians constituted
a community of forgetfulness. In this creation of a group of scientific collaborators with whom he had the most intense contact throughout his mature
life, Durkheim lives up to the promise of my opening epigram from Maurice
Halbwachs's *Collective Memory*, namely that "To forget a period of one's life is
to lose contact with those who then surrounded us" (Halbwachs 1980, 30).
Durkheim did not hate Judaism or his Jewishness; he simply wished in a way
to forget the circumstances of his own Jewish birth. He "forgot" his
Jewishness, then, by neither observing nor celebrating its essential rites of ⟩
memory. He, like Brunschvicg, neither denied nor publicly criticized Jews
and Judaism—and certainly not viciously, as several notable self-identified
quintessentially Jewish thinkers of the time—Bernard Lazare and Salomon
Reinach, for example—often did. He simply wanted other memories and
loyalties to fill his mind and heart and in that way he simply did not want
to remember that he was born Jewish.

Lévinas, however, has more to say. He puts the question to us whether
this is then the end of the "Jewish" story of so-called assimilated French
thinkers like Brunschvicg or Durkheim? His answer is a resounding "no!"
₄ Having duly registered the truth about Brunschvicg's distance from Judaism,
Lévinas goes on to claim that the thought of his old friend was profoundly
? Jewish, in spite of itself. For example, Brunschvicg's independence of
thought showed how truly Jewish he was, *malgré lui*. Adds Lévinas, "does he
not discover [Judaism's] . . . essential strains by affirming that at the heart of
the Infinite, where the intellect dwells, there is an independent man, master of his fate, who communicates with the Eternal, in the clear light of
intellectual and moral action?" Further, says Lévinas, other elements of
Brunschvicg's thoughts strongly echo those of great Jewish thinkers, and
therefore make mere coincidence seem unlikely. Lévinas notes that in
Brunschvicg's *Diary* entry of 7 October 1892, he claims that " 'one can only
work effectively for the future if one wishes to realize it immediately.' " Here
surely, says Lévinas, is "the thought of a Jew, a thought echoed in the famous
verse by [the late nineteenth- and early twentieth-century (1873–1934)
Hebrew revival poet, Hayam Nahman] Bialik: 'And if justice exists, it must
appear immediately.' " Thus, paradoxically, Lévinas claims that even in

Brunschvicg's ignorance of Judaism ("Brunschvicg ignores Judaism, since he does not know it," says Lévinas [1977, 44]), and in his "atheism," developed elsewhere in his thinking, he "is much closer to the One God than the mystical experiences and horrors of the Sacred to be found in the supposed religious revival of our contemporaries" (Lévinas 1977, 44–45). So, if Léon Brunschvicg and Bialik express the same ideas in practically the same idiom, do we not have the right to conclude that Brunschvicg is actually echoing his classic Jewish predecessor—whether consciously or not? Here, we may view Lévinas as articulating a theological position, instead of making a claim about a matter of fact. Namely, he believes that Judaism persists even in those who deny it. As interesting as this position may be, it may in the long run be costly to assert it. If the truth about us is to be found at the level of the unconscious, can we trust our conscious claims about our own nature and identity? What value can we assign them over against those supposedly unconscious aspects of ourselves? What value in particular could we then assign to those who claim openly to be Jews or Jewish thinkers? If the truth of things lies in the unconscious, they might conceivably be mistaken about their own identities! Placing such store in the unconscious or unwitting Jewishness may, moreover, cheapen open and explicit affirmations of Jewishness by Jews themselves. *A fortiori*, if Lévinas is right about the Jewishness of Brunschvicg's thought, might not something of the same be true about Durkheim and the Jewishness of his thought—especially since, unlike Brunschvicg, Durkheim did know a very great deal about Judaism? We will then be on the lookout for parallel passages between Durkheim and self-identified Jewish authors.

One is even more tempted to pursue this line of questioning when certain subjects are at issue. One such area of life (sic) is that of death, the question of human mortality or immortality, the nature of the afterlife, and the general relation of the present to the past. If some area of life should be susceptible to religious promptings and borrowings from classic traditional sources, it would surely be this area. It is in such considerations of the afterlife and the nature of the past that I believe we find discussions by Durkheim which seem to replicate the kinds of things his observant Jewish contemporaries were saying about the same issues in dedicated Jewish contexts—much as Lévinas hears unwitting Jewish echoes in the otherwise intentionally or consciously non-Jewish thought of Léon Brunschvicg.

Let me then turn directly to these parallels, and in doing so make bold to test Lévinas's estimate of the unwittingly Jewish nature of the thought of so-called "assimilated" French Jews like Brunschvicg and Durkheim.

.

2. Jewish Parallels? Sylvain Lévi and Jewish Historiography

In his presidential "allocution" before the general assembly of the Société des Études Juives in 1904, the great Jewish Indologist, Sylvain Lévi made what seems a remarkable claim about the nature of the past—it does not die, but rather is the reality of the present: "The present is no longer a spontaneous creation—autonomous and independent of the past. It prolongs the past; it continues it and condenses it. It is only the past itself on the way to being transformed" (Lévi 1913, ii). For Lévi, this belief gave rise to perhaps simply poetic, possibly mystical, but arguably also earnest and literal, views about the persistence of the generations in Jewish life. Nowhere is Sylvain Lévi's idea of the dead living on in our hearts and minds more beautifully put than in this same allocution to a general assembly of the Société des Études Juives. What is more, Sylvain Lévi says there that this life in our hearts and minds is an objective fact, and not just a thing of our subjective memory. Thus, Lévi tells his audience of Jewish scholars that in less enlightened times, Jews would escape the spiritual turmoil and mental stress of persecution by retreating into their libraries and scholarly work. There, they discovered a "dream" world of "eternal calm." These scholars of former ages are "the men who made us," Lévi reminds his fellows. But those selfsame dead do not leave us alone, cut off in time and space with little but reverent thoughts to connect us to them. Lévi claims that the old scholars go on actually—and apparently objectively—living within us, indeed initiate intrusions into our lives and, as it were, invade the minds of the living without waiting to be recalled into memory by us: "If we lend an ear to those secret voices in our minds [*consciences*], if we pay heed to those things we do without explicitly wanting to, if we get to the bottom of some of the subtle sources of the inchoate thoughts which play in our brains—we would hear *them*. We would take them by surprise. While we may believe that by means of history, we live in them, it is actually they who live in us. They continue their history through ours" (Lévi 1913, ii).

While such things may not be remarkable to hear from the mouth of an observant and at times conservative Jew like Sylvain Lévi, we hardly expect the same from Durkheim, as indeed we would not from the aforementioned Brunschwicg. Yet in Durkheim we do read much the same. In his study of the history of education in France—doubtless Durkheim's best historical work—he asks why the study of history is so important. Durkheim's answer, hardly different from that of his respected colleague and associate, Sylvain Lévi, is that the past is more real than the present, thus more important to study for understanding society. Says Durkheim, "the truth is that the present . . . is by itself nothing; it is no more than an extrapolation of the past, from which it cannot be severed without losing the greater part of its significance" (Durkheim 1977, 15). Durkheim thus felt that past events "continued" into the present in such a way that there was something of "chain of being" between all events in history stretching back to the distant past. He and Sylvain Lévi, in effect, anticipated the words of William Faulkner that "the past is not dead. It's not even past." Further, speaking in the same idiom as Sylvain Lévi, Durkheim says that the people of the past in fact "live" in us. Although lacking the poetry of Sylvain Lévi's mention of the old Jewish scholars haunting the mind of their successors, Durkheim nonetheless also sees the people of the past *objectively* alive in us. Early in the same work, Durkheim asks rhetorically:

> Indeed what do we even mean when we talk of contemporary man, the man of our times? It is simply the agglomeration of those characteristic traits whereby today's Frenchman can be identified and distinguished from the Frenchman of former times. But this cannot really give us a picture of the whole of modern man; for in each one of us, in differing degrees, is contained the person we were yesterday, and indeed in the nature of things it is even true that our past *personae* predominate, since the present is necessarily insignificant when compared with the long period of the past because of which we have emerged in the form we have today. It is just that we don't directly feel the influence of these past selves precisely because they are so deeply rooted within us. (Durkheim 1977, 11)

As if to emphasize the importance of this perspective, Durkheim concludes his history of educational thought in France by repeating and in some ways amplifying his view with talk about the unconscious nature of this indwelling of others in us:

> How can we fail to realise that we contain within us hidden depths where unknown powers slumber but which from time to time may be aroused according to the demands of circumstances? This extended and expanded view of humanity makes us realise more clearly how impoverished, flimsy and deceptive is the one yielded by direct observation of ourselves; for we must candidly admit that there exists in us something of all these styles of humanity which have historically succeeded one another, even if we are not currently sensible of the fact. These men of former ages were men like ourselves and it is consequently impossible that their nature should be foreign to us. Similarly, there live in us, as it were, other men than those with whom we are familiar. This proposition is confirmed by the findings of modern psychology, which reveal the existence of an unconscious psychic life beyond that of consciousness: a life which science alone is gradually managing to uncover, thanks to its special methods of investigation. (Durkheim 1977, 330)

Now, given these remarkable parallel statements about objective immortality, what are we to say about their possible Jewishness? To return to Lévinas's view of Brunschwicg's echoing of Bialik, is it not possible that Durkheim likewise reflects Sylvain Lévi, or at least a Jewish, possibly French Jewish, sensibility which both men shared? Is not Durkheim himself in fact admitting the very possibility of his own Jewish nurture and past acting upon him, given his talk of unconscious parts of ourselves, of "unknown powers" which "slumber but which from time to time may be aroused according to the demands of circumstances?" Does Durkheim subscribe to a Jewish agenda articulated by Sylvain Lévi? Can we perhaps speak of a common Jewish "influence" upon either or both men? If there is, I have not found one.

3. On Jewish Influences in Durkheim's Thought

Let us consider "influence" first. When we speak of "influence," several considerations need to be borne in mind. First, to credit someone as an "influence," real similarities need to exist between what the partners in such a relation say. This seems confirmed for the most part in the citations from Durkheim and Sylvain Lévi. But, however, a second requirement for justifying a claim to "influence" fails. To wit: there must be awareness of this supposed "influence," and real dependence on the thought of the "influence." Does either Durkheim or Sylvain Lévi need the precedent of Jewish thought to justify their saying what they did? In Sylvain Lévi's case, given his Jewish audience, he would probably need to assume that his hearers could recognize his claims about the continuous life of the old teachers as acceptable Jewish ideas—or at least acceptable French ideas. In the case of Durkheim, we would be left with the question of explaining why Jewish claims would have struck a sympathetic chord with him and his reading audience. How did Jewish claims get to be influential when there is so little evidence for this in Durkheim's writings generally? How did they graduate to the level of being so-called "influences"? "Influences" are not then just brute transmissions of information. They contain information which has attained a certain status, a status sufficient to be accepted as something which will guide or thus "influence" thought. Acceptance demands its reason for acceptance. And these go beyond the mere fact of transmission to the world of meaning in which these authors were situated.

To understand how and why certain claims about the eternity of the past, made by Jews like Sylvain Lévi, would have attained the status of the "influential," we need then to understand the motives, intentions, and projects of Durkheim which made it desirable for them to appropriate Jewish, or even specifically Sylvain Lévi's, notions about the nature of the past. In Durkheim's case, however, although Jews reading him might well be drawn to Durkheim's claims about the eternity of the past by their own Jewish values, it is unlikely that Durkheim was speaking in particular to French Jews. I say this because, as we will see, the Gentile intellectual and ideological circles in which Durkheim moved, even though many of their members were positivists and/or atheists, believed as well in the eternity of the past.

One such Gentile scholar well placed to move Durkheim toward a view of the reality and eternity of the past was none other than Fustel de Coulanges. While the coincidences of the statements of Durkheim and Sylvain Lévi are indeed striking, they do not stand alone. We in fact find the same attitudes expressed in the work of one of Durkheim's most influential teachers at the

École Normale Supérieure, the historian, Numa-Denis Fustel de Coulanges (1830–1889) (Jones 1999, 160–67). In the concluding paragraphs of the introduction to his classic *La Cité Antique*, Fustel de Coulanges sounds very much like the Durkheim of *The Evolution of Educational Thought* paying his debts to the living past. "Fortunately, the past never completely dies for man. Man may forget it, but he always preserves it within him. For, take him at any epoch, and he is the product, the epitome, of all the earlier epochs. Let him look into his own soul and distinguish these different epochs by what each of them has left within him" (Coulanges 1980, 6).

Although Fustel de Coulanges is often regarded as someone who stressed discontinuity between past and present, this applies to what one can call imagined, mythological, or ideological continuity (Jones 1999, 162). The polemic thrust of his classic treatment of ancient Roman and Greek religion and society, *La Cité Antique*, opposed such claims of historical continuity based on ideology. But when it came to real religious traditions, as opposed to ideological ones, Fustel de Coulanges could affirm continuity. For example, in the religious practice of ancient Romans, "they carry within them the authentic marks and the unmistakable vestiges of the most remote ages" (Coulanges 1980, 6). In 1864, Fustel de Coulanges thus challenged the received opinion of the followers of the revolutionary tradition that one could establish real continuity between the classic past of Rome and Greece and the (present) realities of French republican politics. This is largely ideology or myth. "In our system of education, we live from infancy in the midst of the Greeks and Romans, and become accustomed continually to compare them with ourselves, to judge of their history by our own, and to explain our revolutions by theirs. What we have received from them leads us to believe that we resemble them" (Coulanges 1980, 3). But this is to believe the mythological rhetoric of a revolution seeking to sever its ties with its Roman Catholic past as if it were fact. In truth, the past of ancient Rome and Greece is "another country," despite what the generation of 1789 and its offspring would like to believe. The Catholic (albeit non-believing) Fustel de Coulanges is, in effect, exposing the French Revolution's pretensions to real continuity with the ancient pre-Christian world as fraudulent. In particular, Fustel de Coulanges denied that the French Revolution's notion of personal liberty had any sort of ancient classic precedent: "They have deceived themselves about the liberty of the ancients, and on this very account liberty among the moderns has been put in peril. The last eighty years have shown that one of the great difficulties which impede the march of modern society is the habit which it has of always keeping Greek and Roman antiquity before its eyes" (Coulanges 1980, 3). Thus, adds Fustel de Coulanges, we have "some difficulty in considering" ancient Rome and Greece "as foreign nations; it is almost always ourselves that we see in them. Hence spring many errors. We rarely fail to deceive ourselves regarding these ancient nations when we see them through the opinions and facts of our own time." Adding a sense of urgency to his reproach are the contemporary political consequences of believing the revolutionary myth: "Now, errors of this kind are not without danger. The ideas which the moderns have had of Greece and Rome have often been in their way. Having imperfectly observed the institutions of the ancient city, men have dreamed of reviving them among us" (Coulanges 1980, 3). Now none of this should blind us to the overarching claim behind Fustel de Coulanges's demythologizing effort that, like that of Durkheim, believed, "the past never completely dies for man."

Of course, it might well be that Durkheim's thought about the reality of the past stems from Jewish influences all the same. And, as he said of Montaigne, Durkheim might think about things because he was raised in a Jewish home and community. It is just that in the present state of knowledge, we cannot determine whether this is true or not. Yet, a case might be made on circumstantial grounds if we take into account the possible opposition— political or otherwise—of the Durkheimians and French Jews to those who held an opposing view about the status of the past.

The first sector of French society to which Durkheim's affirmation of historical continuity might plausibly have been addressed was the Jacobin or revolutionary tradition as it existed in the politics of his day. Here we can return to the link between Fustel de Coulanges's skepticism about the revolutionary tradition's denial of its own debt to the long history of French Catholicism in favor of a mythical Roman past and his belief in the continuity of real religious traditions. In a spirit congenial to Fustel de Coulanges's claims, Durkheim's *The Evolution of Educational Thought* shows the same spirit of affirmation toward real historical traditions. Surprisingly, Durkheim has many good things to say there about the ongoing contribution of the French Catholic past to the formation of modern-day France (Jones 1999, ch 2). Durkheim approved of the unities of faith and reason, sacred and profane, religion and philosophy achieved by the Catholic middle ages, and indeed sought to "reproduce" them for his own time (Jones 1999, 52). Real history cannot be denied—indeed it is unscientific so to do. While a liberal and republican, it is not generally appreciated that Durkheim disapproved of revolutionary social change (Lukes 1972, 322–23). Insofar as revolutionary change spells radical breaks with the past, Durkheim's political attitudes here conform to his attitudes to historical continuity. Completing the parallel with Fustel de Coulanges, while in truth, a liberal much like Durkheim, Fustel de Coulanges could sometimes look to be as conservative as anti-Durkheimians such as Robert Nisbet have tried to make Durkheim out to be (Milbank 1990, 54–55; Nisbet 1966). Fustel de Coulanges's dissent from much of the Jacobin partyline of the revolutionary tradition made him easily exploitable by right-wingers in France like Charles Maurras (Boer 1998, 246).

A second segment of French political and religious society likewise to which Durkheim's views about historical continuity might have been addressed were the French liberal Protestants. While for the most part allied politically, on certain matters of social policy and public morals, the French liberal Protestants Jews, and the Durkheimians were far apart. I note the liberal Protestant tendency to theologize public policy about morals and moral education in a Christian direction as well as their resistance to the societist or collectivist methodological and public policy perspectives pioneered by the Durkheimians. Thus, there existed within the leadership of the Third Republic a liberal Protestant elite who held views of the past greatly at odds with those expressed by Sylvain Lévi and Durkheim. A prime example of such a figure was a Liberal Protestant intellectual, close to the Third Republic's leading politicians and public intellectuals, Albert Réville. He typified a certain mentality which sought to free France of her past—particularly, of course, her Catholic collectivist past and anticipated future. This led Albert Réville to hold what might be called a non-transitive or discontinuous view of historical change. As one stage of historical evolution succeeds another, such as the republic, it leaves the previous, Catholic France, the Empire and such, behind. "What has been, is not; what is, will not be," begins Albert Réville; "this is all that we can affirm," he concludes (Réville 1875, 235).

The present does not "participate" in the past for the likes of republicans like Albert Réville, because he seeks to liberate the present and future from the past. In the context of religious change, Jean Réville, the son of Albert, affirms his father's belief in historical discontinuity: "Doubtless each new degree of spiritual development negates that preceding it. . . . Monotheism only acquires its value and consciousness of itself in disengaging from its polytheistic context. . . . In this sense, to abolish is to fulfill" (Reville 1860, 388).

In terms of promoting a French Jewish agenda, Sylvain Lévi might have had several reasons for affirming the reality of the past. For one, it supports belief in the reality and continuity of the Jewish community itself—of course a prime value in itself for observant Jews. And, in political and cultural terms, this view of history as gathering the past into the present also functioned to guarantee the contribution of French Jews to French history. It legitimized their place in a time when attempts had been made to separate off the Jews of France from the history of the "real" (*sic*) French nation. At a certain point, the Durkheimians reacted to anti-Semitic attempts to alienate French Jews from the course of French life and history. The main problem with this scenario for linking Sylvain Lévi with Durkheim lies in Durkheim's apparent disinterest in the integrity and continuity of the Jewish community in France, cherished by an observant Jew like Sylvain Lévi. On the contrary, part of Durkheim's reaction to the anti-Semitism of the end of the nineteenth century was to predict that French Jews were on the way to disappearing as a distinct social entity in France. So, Durkheim seems to have had other than Jewish reasons for affirming the survival of the past which made him sound deceptively like a really Jewish intellectual such as Sylvain Lévi. These reasons seem tied to Durkheim's so-called "sociological realism" and not, of course, to any affinities he might have had with Christianity or some other traditional religion. On this view, "society" was seen by Durkheim to be real. But when Durkheim's thought about the reality of society is characterized as "real," we typically only imagine the society in question as real in the present. I am stressing, however, that Durkheim also wished to speak of society as existing over time and thus continuously through history. For him, speaking of the reality of the past was also a way to speak of the reality of society on a diachronic axis.

4. What Have "We" to Do with "Them"?

While Durkheim's general view of historical continuity and the reality of the past may thus *remind* us of Jewish thinking, they do not, at least on the historicist grounds from which I operate (*pace* Lévinas) necessarily confirm him as a Jewish thinker. So, let us try another tack. Perhaps his view of personal immortality—a much more sensitive issue and one at least open to considerations about supernatural being—can provide this link to Judaism?

People have disagreed quite sharply about how to conceptualize the fate of the dead. Some have imagined that the dead or their "souls" are not really dead in every sense of the word, but persist at another level of existence. Whether this place beyond death is one of a series, as in the Indian and Pythagorean beliefs about rebirth and reincarnation, or whether it is terminal, as in the Jewish, Christian, or Muslim idea of heaven, the status of the dead is assured. While they may be dead in body, they live "in spirit." In effect, they are not really dead. I call this the "spiritualist" position of "objective immortality" (Kselman 1993, 142). At the other extreme, in much of recorded and unrecorded history, others have imagined that the dead are utterly effaced. They are dead and gone, so to speak, vanished without a trace. They are "history," as we tellingly say in these days of casual killing and disdain for the past, conveying thereby our belief in the obliteration and irrelevance of the dead. This, I call the "annihilationist" position.

Between these extremes, still others have imagined that while the dead are not literally alive in some other space—the "spiritualist" position of "'objective immortality'"—they are nonetheless not utterly annihilated either, but continue their existence in some form. I distinguish two forms of such immortality—a "'subjective'" and non-subjective sense. I hesitate to call the non-subjective case "objective" yet, since I have just used that term for the spiritualist position. In the case of "subjective immortality," individuals are said to be immortal in a figurative or metaphorical way—only in the subjective, individual minds of people. In the non-subjective sense, the dead are claimed really to exist in some not just metaphorical or figurative way in their offspring, in personal dream and memory, in legend and literature, indeed in all representations of them, or further in the consequences of their actions, such as in shaping social institutions, in affecting the lives and personalities of those with whom they had significant contact, and even in the way the physical and material spaces of their environment were shaped distinctively by them, and so on. Let me call this alternative, "social realism" or "realism" for short. I identify this position with Durkheim and his school against the more typical characterizations of their view as "positivist" (Kselman 1993, 139–40). We will see that while Durkheim's position owes much to positivism, as in other aspects of Durkheim's thinking, he represents so radical a revision of positivism that the term arguably no longer applies.

In laying out the realist alternative, I would emphasize that I am not speaking of a so-called "figurative" life after death, or a so-called "metaphorical" immortality. Using terms like "figurative" or "metaphorical" to speak of these matters is really just another way of dismissing the reality of individuals' surviving annihilation upon death. It is to say at best that it is "*as if*" annihilation were not true. But in social realism, it is not "*as if*" an institution or practice, environment, and such had been shaped by the deceased, nor that the legends, stories, and memories of the deceased were of *someone else*, nor that one only *pretends* that the individuals had been socialized by the deceased. In every case, the deceased had in their ordinary lifetimes *really* caused certain states of affairs to be, even by the standards of the annihilationist. This claim falls far short as well of the claim spiritualists would have us make, since social realism asserts only that the dead live on in the *real* effects they have wrought in the *real* world of social relations and human affairs. Thus, the reality of the dead in the social realist view is not just subjective. What the deceased made during their lives remains what they really and objectively made.

Of course, the living center from which these effects emanated—the human person—is empty, and no longer generates effects. But the effects generated remain as long as they continue to exist. In that sense, the person in question lives on. Now, while these achievements may not in all cases be *recognized* for what they are, and thus not recognized as alive by the living, they have the objective ability so to be recognized. In this way, the continued existence of the dead is "recognized" in the way, say, Ruthenian nationality could be said to be recognized (Ash 1999, 54). A real social substratum beneath the name exists in the way the real social effects of the dead exist. Contrast, for example, the act of "recognizing" or trying to recognize an imaginary nation—a Ruritania—a nation in name only. "Recognition" here means nothing, since no one exists, nothing exists which could be the basis for the consequences of such recognition. In failing to recognize what the dead have done, we can therefore make them just "history"—in effect annihilate their memory. But on realist grounds, lack of *recognition* is our failure, not theirs. This is just another reason why rituals were so important for the Durkheimians: they maintained the collective memory of the acts of real people. Now, we must inquire whether Durkheim's social realism is Jewish.

5. Jewish Ideas of Immortality

Jewish conceptions of the afterlife at once showcase the glorious diversity of Jewish theology as well as serve as a source of bafflement to Christians. This diversity applies of course to matters outside the "halakhah" or to those matters not governed by the direct teaching of the rabbi of a particular Jewish community, such as for the contemporary Chabad under Rabbi Menachim Mendel Schneersohn. But outside such limits, however valued the opinions of the rabbis may be, they are not binding and a general lack of doctrinal or theological consensus typifies the tradition of the rabbis. Even the towering figure of Maimonides could not succeed against this Jewish essence of refusing to have a theological essence. He tried heroically to lay down what he took to be the fundamentals of Jewish orthodox belief in his famous thirteen principles, for example, the existence, incorporeality, omniscience, eternity, unity and sole worshipfulness of God, reward and punishment after death, the role of the prophets, with Moses as the greatest, the divinity and unalterability of the Torah, the Messiah, and the resurrection of the dead. But, even Maimonides could not command consensus on these arguably fundamental articles of Jewish faith. In Jewish theology, contest, conflict, and pluralism reign (Cohen-Sherbok 1987, 31).

As to *beliefs* proper about the afterlife, relatively little importance attaches to them and they vary a great deal. Before the period of the Second Temple, some belief in the spirits of the dead is found. But, Jews generally resisted cults of the dead. Jews further resisted elaborating or even developing ideas of the survival of the dead primarily because of the fear that the dead, as in many other cultures, would become deified and thus potential rivals to the one God. From the period of the Second Temple, belief in the resurrection of the body appeared among some segments of the Jewish theological population, but this is not accompanied by the belief in the existence of a soul or spiritual essence surviving death. Later, the Pharisees would champion the belief both in a human soul surviving death and in bodily resurrection of the dead—but only for the blessed and not for the damned. However, in keeping with Jewish traditions of dissent and disagreement, even though the pharisaic tradition would become relatively normative well into the middle ages, their opposite party, the Sadducees, would reject survival of death, resurrection, and final judgment.

However, if we make Jewish ritual practice and the witness of Jewish material culture our main criteria for measuring beliefs about the afterlife then we arrive at somewhat different conclusion. The evidence from archeology points clearly to the fact that Jewish funerary practice conformed closely to those of the host cultures in which Jews found themselves and no doubt was in some tension at times with rabbinic thought. Peter Brown does note the existence of cults of the dead among Jewish communities of late antiquity, and of the importance of tombs to the Jewish community (Goodenough 1965, 146). Yet, Brown also emphasizes Christian departures from Jewish practice. Christians "leaned on" the graves of their saints. In Christianity "tomb and altar" were joined as holy graves became sites of public worship; in Judaism, "holy graves and the rabbinate drifted apart" (Goodenough 1965, 145).

In the modern period, two opposed trends have emerged. First, belief in an immortal soul has tended to replace belief in bodily resurrection for both Orthodox and non-orthodox. Belief in resurrection faded as belief in the Messianic restoration waned. Indeed, in the Reform, belief in an immortal soul was seen as a refutation of belief in resurrection. Typical of the Reform's universalist humanist basis for this belief in individual human immortality was their view that humanity shared the divine nature—" 'in the Divine nature of the human spirit, which forever finds bliss in righteousness and misery in wickedness' " (Brown 1981, 10). Second, and opposed to what we might call a spiritualist view of human nature, a gradual increase in this-worldliness among certain segments of Jewish theological opinion has come to prevail. In the Reform, this takes the form of the ideal of the dead surviving, as it were perhaps only subjectively, in the living. Souls exist neither in isolation as individuals, nor even as resurrected re-embodied souls. Rather, it is in one's progeny and legacy to the world that one is said to survive death. Likewise, the foundation of the state of Israel has itself become the object of the hopes of many contemporary devoted Jews.

Thus, while there are affinities between the Reform's subjectively realistic conception of immortality being thoroughly human or even with materialist or nationalist trends of Jewish theology, we seem a reasonable distance from Durkheim's social realism, because for the Reform, it is chiefly only *as if* the dead survive in their offspring. Survival is a metaphor, not a statement about social ontology. Durkheim, however, argued for the reality of society. As such Durkheimian social realism might provide a theoretical basis for a Reformed Jewish view of objective survival—had the Reform wanted to avail itself of it. In this light it is instructive to compare how the later Jewish Reconstructionist American Jewish thinker Mordecai Kaplan seems to exploit Durkheimian social realism to make sense of the afterlife in realistic ways. Kaplan thus affirms something rather closer to the Durkheimian social realist position on the afterlife: "To limit our perspective on human life to the span of our earthly existence would destroy all values. Insofar as the good we do while we live bears fruit after we are gone, we have a share in the world to come. To be sure, we will not be there to enjoy the good achieved, but to ask that we be, is to refuse to accept the limitations which God places on individual life" (Brown 1981, 10). Further, in terms of connections with Jewish positions on the afterlife of his own time, it is striking that the two divergent trends in Judaism which characterize the Jewish problematic over the afterlife—one spiritualist, the other materialist—replicate the same opposition in Durkheim. As we will see, Durkheim's discussions of persons typically concerns itself with the soul or the spiritual essence of persons, on the one hand, and on the other hand, the belief in the real continuity of the past in the present. How "Jewish" then is Durkheim being in thinking across the entire spectrum represented by modern Jewish thought about the afterlife?

6. The Durkheimians, Spiritualism, and the Supernatural

Just *what* were the dead for the Durkheimians? For at least some of the most prominent Durkheimians, I shall argue that they were more than metaphorically, figuratively, symbolically or even just subjectively immortal, as the positivists proposed. The dead lived on in a more robust way as

extra-subjective persistent features of their lives, thus makir
for us to subsume the Durkheimians as easily to the positivist mou.
scholars such as Kselman, for example, have asserted (Plautt 1965, 33).

There are several indications that Durkheimian thought is to be read
this way. Staying with the matter of personal immortality for the moment, in
contrast to the positivists, Marcel Mauss, for one, seems to have trod dan-
gerously close to the belief in the kind of objective immortality which was
embraced in their later years by the positivists Renan and Comte, contrary
to all the explicit claims of the main lines of their thought up to that time.
Marcel Mauss seems to have trod close to Spiritualism, or even to the more
extreme Spiritism of an Arthur Conan Doyle, and thus to supernaturalist
conceptions of the reality of souls and spirits. In a recently discovered mem-
oir composed in 1930, Mauss reviews his life and career up to that point.
After paying tribute to the many losses of members of the *équipe* fallen in the
First World War, Mauss says despite the enormous losses of colleagues sustained in the war that "This team lives and has ever been reborn." What gave
Mauss, a severe rationalist and longtime atheist, the confidence to make
such claims—even if only meant figuratively? Mauss was after all part of the
generation surviving the First World War. Many of their number filled the
halls of popular lectures by members of the Spiritist movement. Sir Arthur
Conan Doyle was , for instance, a leading speaker for Spiritism. One wonders
then whether Mauss, and this is the point, even ventured beyond
Spiritualism and into the musty realm of Spiritism along with others who
grieved so deeply for those lost in the war?

One would be tempted to dismiss the literal sense of Mauss's apparent
assertion of a belief in immortality and resurrection, or even rebirth as ele-
giac poetic license, were it not for similar claims made elsewhere in his oeuvre. Speaking of Mauss's classic *The Gift*, Lévi-Strauss, for example, complains
that Mauss seemed to imbue the phenomenon of gift with (what Mauss at
least took to be) Maori supernatural beliefs in a spirit called the "*hau*"
(Kaplan 1956, 181; Kaplan 1981, 333). Mauss claims that the Maori believe that
the inherence of the "*hau*" in the gift given is the reason the gift is repaid
(Kselman 1993). But at the same time Mauss, in effect, affirms (what at least
he represents as) Maori Spiritism by himself asserting that essential to the
gift relation is the sense that in giving we give something of our own selves,
a portion of our "spiritual essence." The "thing given," says Mauss, "is not

inactive. Invested with life, often possessing individuality, it seeks to return to ... its 'place of origin'" (Mauss 1967, 12–13). Twitting Mauss for his credulity in the face of native beliefs, Lévi-Strauss reproaches his would-be master: "'Are we not faced here with one of those instances ... in which the ethnologist allows himself to be mystified by the native?'" (Sahlins 1972, 153–54).

But having dangled this tempting morsel before you, I must confess not being able to progress much further in establishing that Marcel Mauss on occasion seemed to give evidence of a belief in the immortality of the soul and the existence of spirits independent from the body. Had he believed in spirits, however, he would not have been the first critical intellectual so to do, and especially in the wake of the massive deaths of close friends and colleagues in the First World War. After the war, the belief in the reality of spirits and souls became something of a cultural vogue in Europe (Mauss 1990, 12–13). Whatever may be true about Mauss's supernaturalism, Mauss clearly felt that the dead lived in a way more real than talk of metaphors would permit. It is here in Mauss's perhaps budding supernaturalism, I believe, that we can triangulate on Durkheimian belief about the nature of the dead. For, one can make a case that Mauss was actually closer to being what I have called a "realist" about the life of the dead than to his more spectacular spiritist-sounding published statements. But to get at this view, we need to look to the source of many of Mauss's ideas—his uncle, Émile Durkheim.

7. Durkheim between Spiritualism and Positivism

Durkheim did not believe in the separate and autonomous existence of spirits or souls—Spiritism—although he enthusiastically identified himself with a revised form of Spiritualism, and was widely recognized by the commentators of his day for doing so (Gross, 2004 #3020, 85, 280).[1] In perhaps his deepest moment of personal grief after receiving definite news of the death of his son, André, in the First World War, Durkheim declared his disaffiliations from religion as unambiguously as perhaps could be.

> It is truly incredible that the therapeutic of moral grief should still
> be as Epicurus described it. I am not aware that anything new has
> since been said on this subject. It is inconceivable that this should
> be the great human malady and that almost nothing should have

been done to treat it. Of course I know that the religions are there, and that their practices are rich in experience that is unconscious and full of accumulated wisdom. But their wisdom is crude and empirical; nothing resembling ritual practices has been of use to me or seems effective to me. (Durkheim 1972, 556)

Despite the implications of such a stark acceptance of the annihilating death of his son, Durkheim was, however, no classic annihilationist or materialist about these matters. In another place, Durkheim defends himself vigorously against charges of materialism:

Nothing is wider of the mark than the mistaken accusation of materialism which has been leveled against us. Quite the contrary: from the point of view of our position, if one is to call the distinctive property of the individual representational life spirituality, then one should say that social life is defined by its hyperspirituality. By this we mean that all the constituent attributes of mental life are found in it, but elevated to a very much higher power and in such a manner as to constitute something entirely new. (Durkheim 1974, 34)

For him, then, the soul cannot be reduced to matter; it is especially not an epiphenomenon of the "extended matter" of Cartesian philosophy (Gross 2004 #3020, 280–83). The reason for this is that Durkheim felt that the so called "soul" was simply the presence of society in us. That is to say that it was a way of speaking of the presence of our values, our socially formed consciences, our basic concepts and assumptions about what is to be done and what we should do. And given his belief in the autonomy of society and social forces, this social soul was equally well autonomous of matter.

In addition, Durkheim felt on philosophical grounds that matter itself was equally as problematic a notion as spirit. This led him to reconceive both "soul" and "body," such that the one involved the other in paradoxical ways. In a typically ambiguous and tantalizing statement of this view, Durkheim said that unlike most spiritualists of the time going by that name, "our spiritualism admits that the soul is not a reality of a separate nature, arising suddenly in the scale of beings." Rather, "the mind finds itself in all degrees, only more or less rudimentary: everything lives, everything is animated, everything thinks" (Gross 2004 #3020, 280).

What could such a claim mean? We know that the soul is for Durkheim not ontologically different from the stuff of material things. In this sense, the soul is still material. Yet, the "soul" is "spiritual" in the sense that it is an autonomous perspective on the human person. It is an internal or social perspective on the human person. Spirit and matter are then two alternative ways of seeing the same entity. Thus, "what we call matter is no more than a collection of appearances, and the substance that serves as the substratum of these appearances can't be grasped by the senses" (Gross 2004 #3020, 283). Referring to the soul, Durkheim says that "there really is part of us that is not directly subordinate to the organic factor" (Durkheim 1995, 274). How is such a claim to be defended without recourse to the Spiritism of an Arthur Conan Doyle? Durkheim's answer is to see society as a mediating entity between brute matter and ethereal spirits.

8. Immortality Is Neither Subjective Nor Metaphoric

Answering our question of what it means to say that the soul is not "directly subordinate to the organic factor"—the body—Durkheim adds that there exists an intermediate realm between spirit and matter made up of "everything that represents society in us." This is also to speak of the entire domain of human culture and communication as an autonomous realm located between brute matter and ethereal spirit—in effect, what the phenomenologists have called the human realm. Says Durkheim, "all higher forms of psychic activity that society stimulates and develops in us—are not, like our sensations and bodily states, towed along with the body" (Durkheim 1995, 274). Human culture, although materially rooted in our organism, is not a simple evolute of the organism. Human cultures take form in ways which, at least until now, seem to operate by rules of formation and regulation unrelated to the rhythms and rules governing the body or matter in general. Sociobiology is still very much an unrealized and unfinished project, while patterns of political, economic, religious, artistic, and other behavior are quite well, if not precisely, understood. While one may admit, for example, that the behavior of the U.S. Congress in the impeachment of President Clinton can be understood in terms of their organic desire to survive, this tells us nothing about the intricate culturally-constituted tactics and strategies of political maneuvering that characterized this episode of the nation's history.

As a literally "eclectic" thinker, Durkheim thus seeks a balance between extremes of his own diverse position (Brooks 1998). His non-dualist perspective militates against conceiving immortality as involving belief in an eternal spirit, since the soul cannot exist independently of the body. But in denying rank materialism, he concedes some part of the views proposed by spiritualists. As far as Durkheim was willing to go in speaking of immortality, he felt that after death, *something* of us survives. Durkheim, for example, mentions that what survives of us may be described as something transformed or something of a non-personal nature (Gross, 2004 #3020, 281–83). Given the organic connection of individual personhood with particular body and mind, upon dissolution of the body, that something (not to mention the "somehow") seems best expressed in terms of what I have described as the real effects of our deeds in the world. We get closer to Durkheim's vision of the afterlife, I would suggest, by appealing to the idea that what survives of us are the effects our life has made in the world, the ways we have organized the space and time of our own use and that of others, the ways we have altered the nature of human institutions, human knowledge and understanding, and so on. One of Durkheim's most original followers, Maurice Halbwachs, articulated such view in his study of collective memory: "In addition to engravings and books, the past has left many other traces, occasionally visible, in present-day society. We see it in people's appearance, the look of a place, and even in the unconscious ways of thinking and feeling preserved by certain persons and milieus. Ordinarily we don't notice such things. But we need to alter our attention only slightly to see the outcroppings of the older strata underlying modern customs" (Halbwachs 1980, 66). Like Halbwachs, I am saying that Durkheim was what I have called a social realist about human survival of death.

Translating his social realist metaphysics into religious belief and practice, Durkheim would seem committed to a more robust view of the afterlife than that the dead live merely "metaphorically," as we say, in memory, in the minds, habits, and actions of living human beings. For him, that kind of living in memory was itself real, to the extent that it entailed informing the lives and actions of individuals and institutions. In this way, Durkheim's talk of the soul or spirits conforms to the pattern established in his talk of the *reality* of society—something whose reality is also often considered merely *metaphorical*, but which it is well known the Durkheimians considered robust, if not identical to the way individual human persons were real. How Jewish then are Durkheim's beliefs about the dead?

9. Spiritualism in the Third Republic

When we turn to other than Jewish contexts proximate to Durkheim and his world, we find a remarkable flourishing of beliefs about the afterlife in France. At least since the eighteenth century, in France, the religious traditions were hardly alone in offering solutions to life's perennial problem, and indeed as we will see, they were often deeply implicated in political agendas in which the Durkheimians were eager participants. Regarding influences upon Durkheim then, we will, first, find affinities between his beliefs about the afterlife and those of the non-Jewish alternatives I shall now discuss. We will also, second, find that he was aware of such non-Jewish ideas, and third, that he had good reasons for depending upon these non-Jewish sources and thus strong reasons for adopting them. Thomas A. Kselman, author of a recent fascinating study of these "alternative afterlives," notes that they flourished in opposition to the official Roman Catholic doctrines of objective immortality and their political concomitants, reaching a kind of peak during in the Third Republic, even if they mark their beginnings much earlier. The fathers of the French Revolution went to considerable lengths, for example, to affirm the immortality of the great men of the revolution and the human ideal. Falconet's article on immortality in the *Encyclopédie* celebrates the memorial use of sculpture for the way its solidity symbolized the " 'promise of immortality'" (Ozouf 1998, 333). Similarly, in 1791 Quatremère's intentions for converting the church of Sainte Geneviève into the Pantheon were informed by the notion that for the great men interred there "death was only a prelude to continued life . . ." (Ozouf 1998, 335). With an eye for where Durkheim might fit among such options, let me explore them at this point. These ranged all the way from the idea of subjective immortality celebrated by the positivists to the occultist spiritism of the *fin-de-siècle*. Within the intellectual circles in which Durkheim moved, the most salient of these doctrines were those one might call positivism and a cluster of beliefs not to be confused with the "spiritism" of Ouija boards, known as "spiritualism."

Intricately connected with these alternative doctrines of the afterlife were political concerns about the bases of public morality, stimulated by the dechristianizing policies of the French Revolution. How, the revolutionaries asked, could the state maintain moral order and a sense of ultimate account-ability for our actions in the face of the rejection of the then Roman Catholic notions of the afterlife? Kselman cites none other than Robespierre's remark-able plea for a doctrine of an immortal soul, made during the Terror of July 1794. In a raucous political debate against two of its antagonists, the atheists Anaxagoras Chaumette and Joseph Fouché, Robespierre shouted out:

> The good and the bad, tyrants and the friends of liberty, all disappear from the earth, but they do not suffer the same fate. Frenchmen, do not allow your enemies to debase your souls and to weaken your virtue by this deadly doctrine! No, Chaumette, no, Fouché, death is not an eternal sleep! Citizens, erase from your tombs this impious saying, which throws a funeral pall over nature and is an insult to death; carve there instead this saying: Death is the beginning of immortality. (Aulard 1897)

Kselman also reminds us that Robespierre's sentiments were by no means eccentric among the leadership of the revolution, nor were they offered as purely religious and apolitical doctrines (Kselman 1993, 126–43). As theists, the French Deists remained faithful to beliefs in the existence of God and the immortality of the soul; more surprisingly, the Directory supported the tenets of the neo-religion, Theophilanthropy, which affirmed beliefs in God and immortality as well (Mathiez 1973).[2] Both Deists and members of the Directory saw in such beliefs necessary bases for a well-ordered citizenry.

In the period between 1800 and 1850, the issue of the nature of the afterlife continued to remain politicized. Victor Cousin (1792–1867), an eclectic philosophical system-builder and political liberal, held a professor-ship at the Sorbonne during the Bourbon Restoration. Identified as the prin-cipal source of the very influential philosophy of Spiritualism, Cousin taught the same core lesson of the necessary link between theism and personal immortality, on the one side, and the stability of the social order, on the other. In the beginning, Cousin's motive was to provide a metaphysical grounding for morality to replace that supplied by the Catholic church, then enjoying renewed patronage under the restored Bourbons. Later, after 1848, Cousin redirected his rhetorical fire against the socialists, whose atheism made him anxious about the fate of public morals in the event of a socialist succession to power. So great was Cousin's influence that even Durkheim's great philosophical master and the unofficial philosopher of the Third Republic, the Neo-Kantian Charles Renouvier (1815–1903) formed a position on the afterlife similar to Cousin's. Justice required a God who would administer appropriate sanctions for human behavior and an immortal human soul which would survive death to reap the rewards or punishments for human deeds. Indeed, Kselman calls Renouvier one of the two most important representatives of the spiritualist movement in the last half of the nineteenth century—not an inconsiderable factor therefore in Durkheim's formulation of his own position on the afterlife (Kselman 1993, 131). Unlike Cousin, who taught and wrote under the threat of royalist oppression, Renouvier was free to reconcile spiritualism with republicanism. Given the affiliation of the Church with monarchist regimes, Renouvier concluded that the church must be dethroned from its dominance over the formation of the moral conscience of France. Renouvier attempted to articulate what he hoped would be a durable *laïc* civic morality. He argued for a "philosophical justification for a moral code that no longer relied on revealed religion and the authority of the Catholic clergy" (Kselman 1993, 132). Significantly, Renouvier was in great favor among liberal Jews and Protestants, who in the late nineteenth century shared beliefs close to the abstract religion of the Deism of the eighteenth century.[3] The liberal Protestants were disproportionately represented in certain key ministries, such as education, and in being so placed were able to introduce Renouvier's spiritualist theories of morality into the schools. Under the leadership of liberal Protestants like Félix Pécaut[4] and Ferdinand Buisson, the Third Republic gained the reputation as "the revenge of the Reformation" (Zeldin 1979, 263). Returning for a moment to the issue then of Jewish contributions to Durkheim's thought about immortality, their weight would seem small compared to the many references to Spiritualism and Spiritualist found in the Durkheimian corpus. By contrast, references to modern or classic Jewish authors or texts in Durkheim's *oeuvre* are relatively slight. This would seem to indicate that while Durkheim believed that the past lived on in the present, and thus in him, the past of which he saw himself part was the past of these great French scientists and philosophers. For Durkheim, his Jewish past was in this sense crowded out by the French public heroes of letters and science. It may have lived on in him, as he himself in effect admitted in his remarks cited earlier about the "men of former ages" who "live in us." But to Durkheim their voices would seem faint compared to those of the great heroes of the Third French Republic and its letters and science.

10. "Immortality for Positivists, Too"[5]

In the politicized religious context of the Third Republic, it was not only the Catholics and Spiritualists who found that conceptualizations of the afterlife were consequential items of public discourse. So did the so-called positivist or "laïc" thinkers of the early to middle nineteenth century. Major figures here are Claude Henri Saint-Simon (1760–1825) and Auguste Comte (1798–1857). Over against both the Catholics and the Spiritualists, they—at least the early Comte before the foundation of his "Religion of Humanity"—rejected beliefs in a God who shall judge the living and the dead as well as a belief in objective immortality (Kselman 1993, 134). Neither was necessary to maintain civic morality. Instead the positivists reoriented "salvation from a vertical to a horizontal plane." They planned to create "social rather than individual happiness . . . [and] felicity would be achieved in historical time as a result of human effort" (Kselman 1993, 133). In this vein, prominent figures of the Third Republic, such as Jules Ferry, the great reformer of the national French educational system, explicitly embraced Comte's positivism and argued that the values of human solidarity, progress, science, and family should be sufficient to fill the human heart and justify morality in a modern nation-state (Kselman 1993, 136). Neither Catholic nor Spiritualist metaphysical beliefs were required for the sound socialization of the youth of France into the duties of citizenship. Indeed, rightly or wrongly, Ferry felt that Catholicism's teaching of gloomy resignation and selfish otherworldliness stood in the way of the altruistic generosity of spirit and fellowship required of a motivated citizenry in a republic.[6] Ferry's policies finally succeeded with the hotly contested adoption of the education law of 1882. In it, Ferry established a plan for "'moral and civic instruction'" in the schools which officially severed the link between morality and religion[7] (Kselman 1993, 137–38). By 1910, after the official Separation of Church and State, Ferry's work was completed under the direction of Ferdinand Buisson, who installed a scheme of moral education in the French schools which in his words established "'morality apart from religion and meta-physics'" (Kselman 1993, 139).

It would be a mistake, however, to see the positivists as being merely interested in eliminating references to God and the immortal soul from public discourse. They were profoundly, indeed perhaps religiously, devoted to the nation and were thus vigorous advocates of the belief in the *subjective* immortality of, at least, assemblies of "great men," contributing to the French state (Ozouf 1998, 327). Because the positivists considered immortality as subjective, it required frequent and well constructed occasions to stimulate memory. In this, Comte and his Religion of Humanity provided some of the impetus for the intense cultic memorializing of the dead encouraged by the Third Republic from the middle of the nineteenth century. In truth, this intensification of public memorializing of national notables by the very individuals who were most contemptuous of religious cults of the dead had deep cultural causes. Comte's thought doubtless tapped into this sentiment in its own right (Kselman 1993, 134–35). The Third Republic's elaborate attention to secular cults of the dead expressed the need for a certain grounding of the present in the past, a certain solidarity between generations which the positivists had eliminated by severing links with religion and its theological notions of divine chosenness and French Catholic exceptionalism. That such attempts to legislate memory and immortality often failed—the Pantheon, that dour "Ecole Normale des Morts," being the prime example here—does not minimize the seriousness of the intentions of the hierarchy of France's secular religions, it only questions their wisdom and talents in affairs of the spirit (Ozouf 1998, 325–48).

Kselman ends his discussion of the positivists by noting the irony of the fact that some of those prominent in positivist circles, such as Comte and Ernest Renan, actually grasped at beliefs in objective immortality. Despite their rejection of traditional Catholic or Spiritualist beliefs, late in life both Comte and Renan, for example, took up praying to their respective beloved dead (Kselman 1993, 140–43). Whatever else these positivist lapses into supernaturalism may indicate, they underline Kselman's contention that while positivists delighted in the decline of Catholic belief, they also concurred with Catholics and Spiritualists that "death should be surrounded by a sacred atmosphere and an anxiety that was threatened by the profanity of the modern world" (Kselman 1993, 302).

11. Durkheim and the Secular Religions of France

Thus when we think of non-observant Durkheimians and their ideas of the afterlife, I would suggest that we need more to think of them as equally well participating in the thought-world of these alternative afterlives than in that of traditional or even modernist Judaism. In many ways, the Durkheimians remind us most of the positivists in their attitude to the dead. They were clearly neither traditional theists nor Spiritualists in the full and unqualified sense of the word. Nor is there evidence that the Durkheimians in general believed in the immortality of the soul, understood in the traditional sense. Yet, like the positivists, the Durkheimians were committed to the ideal of real solidarity across the generations. With the positivists, they felt that this shared sense of community reinforced claims for responsibility needed to sustain civic morality across time. With the positivists as well, they saw rituals as essential to stirring up the memory of the dead among citizens. With the Durkheimians, too, we see how personally they took such sentiments. Marcel Mauss, for example, was conspicuous for the degree to which he honored the dead among the Durkheimian group—and at great cost to his own career. Durkheim's famous nephew and perhaps the most significant member of Durkheim's *équipe*, he carried out the great work of memorializing the Durkheimians who had died in the First World War. For many years after the First World War, he dedicated himself almost exclusively to publishing the works of members of the *équipe* who had died during the war, Durkheim among them. For the Durkheimians as for many of the positivists, the *équipe*'s dead were neither "history," on the one (materialist) hand, nor potential ghosts, on the other (spiritist) side.

12. Conclusion

What is the moral of our story?

For historians and students of identity, part of the message must surely be how tricky it is, in the absence of direct evidence, to establish, with high degrees of certainty and on historicist grounds, the identities of persons in a world where multiple and plural loyalties are available. The main reasons the question of Durkheim's Jewishness presents such difficulties are thus two. First, in the presumed or enforced in more homogeneous social settings, he owed nothing professionally to his Jewish brethren, since he had made his career within the "laïc" circles of the Third Republic. If Durkheim's career was dependent upon any religious cosmopolitan world of late nineteenth and early twentieth century France, he enjoyed freedom from the social control set by traditional loyalties community, it would have been upon the favor of liberal Protestants, who filled many of the important posts in the Third Republic. In this sense, it is perhaps truer to say that instead of *our* having identities, *they*, in a way, have us. We have identities to the extent those bases of identity—Judaism, positivism and such—encompass our thinking, channel our action, mold us in their image. Second, in a time of especially heightened nationalism and in a time of rallying to the Third Republic by persons of Durkheim's political persuasion, he was presented with compelling alternative identities to those provided by his own particularist Jewish nurture in provincial Lorraine. Granted, as a Jew, Durkheim had additional interests in preserving the republic and resisting the rise of clerical political forces. But, the same was also true of every French religious minority, in particular the Protestants, and thus no particular Jewish interests were here at stake.

For Judaism, the moral of our story seems to be to support the wisdom of reaction to the extremes of Franco-Jewish assimilation. One way of putting this is to say that if Judaism (or Jewishness) is everything, then it is nothing. It is likewise to say, *pace* Lévinas, if self-consciously disaffiliated Jewish thinkers can be judged *unconsciously* Jewish, then so too could self-consciously, self-identified Jewish thinkers be judged in various cases *unconsciously* not Jewish! If, as prominent Franco-Jewish apologists claimed, the essence of Jewish tradition is fulfilled in republican France, then what is left of Judaism? In terms of the themes of this paper, if Judaism just teaches the same solidarity with the past as any number of secular religions, then what is Jewish about it? This, of course, does not mean that the values of historically different social and religious systems are never commensurable, only that they are unlikely to be identical. How, despite similarities, for example, can one identify the flavor and nature of the Jewish hunger for justice which emerges from adherence to the will of an essentially transcendent—and therefore capricious—deity with one emanating from the revolution's certainty of an unalterable moral law inscribed in nature herself? It was in part the dissatisfactions some Jewish thinkers of the late nineteenth and early twentieth centuries found with the colorlessness of Franco-Jewish theology which marked the beginnings of Jewish revival from their own ranks. Further work on such organizations as "Les Amis du Judaïsme" of the early twentieth century, and cultural conceptions of Jewish identity explored by Sylvain Lévi and his coreligionists might be especially pertinent for the study of the emergence of particularism in the midst of the purported universalism of metropolitan cultures such as France. The example set by Durkheim then should not encourage further quests for the hidden Judaism or Jewishness of disaffiliated Jews. It should rather stimulate Jewish theology to create compelling and durable conceptions of Jewish identity for the centuries to come.

5

Zionism, Brahminism, and the Embodied Sacred

What the Durkheimians Owe to Sylvain Lévi

I. "The Spirit Is Willing . . ."

How is that we so readily think of the essence of religion—the sacred—in tangible, spatial, temporal, socially and ritually "embodied" terms when, for example, the nineteenth-century pioneers of religious studies did not? The founder of the Fifth Section of Paris's École Pratique des Hautes Études Albert Réville, for example, indicted ritual devotion (here, to the sacred heart) as nothing more than an example of the "need to make use of religious forms, as if they were indispensable receptacles of the divine reality" (Réville 1874, 152). Cornelis P. Tiele, the early Dutch phenomenologist of religion, felt that the superiority of the spiritual to the bodily was manifest because it rested on for him what was the indubitable experience of a spiritualized personal identity: "while I hold that the content of doctrine and the forms of worship are by no means matters of indifference in religion, I can no more admit that they pertain to the essence of religion than I can regard my body as pertaining to the essence of my human nature, or suppose the loss of one of my limbs or organs would really impair my personality or true humanity." A really religious person will inform his or her sensibility with a religious "spiritualism," which results from a "more elevated moral and religious sense" (Réville 1874, 154).

Reprinted from *The Sacred and Its Scholars* (eds.) T. Idinopulos and E. Yonan (Leiden: Brill, 1996), with permission of Brill Academic Publishers.

Why, unlike them, are we *not* compelled to hold that "real" religion is always internal, a matter of "spirit and truth," something private and experiential, and that tangible social and cultural dimensions of religion are mere "externals," and thus of no particular importance? (Réville 1884). Why do we feel uncomfortable with their wholesale discounting of the idea that an embodied sacred is a perfectly fine sacred? Why do we think, for example, that religions based on sacred geographies, sacred territories, and such (everything from the Maoris to modern Israel and increasingly modern Palestinian Islam) are not *ipso facto* deficient because they locate sacredness in, and indeed identify it with, some concrete place?

Some of the answers to this problem of the historical origins of our thought about the sacred come from Mary Douglas in ground-breaking works such as *Natural Symbols* and *Purity and Danger*. There, she shows how the religious bases of methodological anti-ritualism in religion (her main concern) may be linked with the theological anti-ritualism of nineteenth-century liberal Christianity. But while Douglas has located the source of the problem, she has not, I think, targeted the source of the answers which emerge so richly and interestingly articulated in her thought. It is hardly controversial that Douglas's roots are set in the soil tilled by the Durkheimian *équipe*. But who precisely made the breakthrough from the liberal Protestant (but also liberal Catholic and Jewish) thought of the *fin-de-siècle*, which then smoothed the road for Douglas and our own generation?

Many have cited the influence of William Robertson Smith's ritualist conception of "primitive" religion as critical in the formation of Durkheimian interests in such "embodied" religious practice. Durkheim himself even dates this from 1895. But whether or not Smith was as dominant an influence as generally thought, the other two key members of Durkheim's group, Henri Hubert and Marcel Mauss, were already working along the lines of considering religion as an embodied thing close to 1895—and as we will see—from independent sources as well. Henri Hubert wrote his little known, and still less read essay, "Étude sommaire de la représentation du temps dans la religion et de la magie," in 1905. Stefan Czarnowski, Hubert's Polish student and author of *Saint Patrick* (1919), continued these working assumptions about the sacred by investigating "heroes whose feast days are marked off in *time* and reserved for special different *places*." As Hubert's inseparable co-worker,

Mauss cannot be excluded from anything done or thought by Hubert (Hubert 1919).

But can we push this trend to embody the sacred any further beyond the Durkheimians? I think we can. The great French Indologist, Sylvain Lévi, helped form the Durkheimian view that the sacred was itself an impersonal force, also spatial and indeed in this way concrete or material. He did so by virtue of the conclusions he reached on the nature of religion in India, articulated in part, as we will see, in terms of his meditations on his own Jewish identity. The Durkheimians tell us how much Sylvain Lévi's masterpiece of Indology, *La Doctrine du sacrifice dans les Brâhmanas*, mattered to them: "we have greatly drawn upon it," they say tersely (Mauss 1968, 293–95).[1] Their estimate will be borne out, I argue, in the late Durkheimian conception of a positive, impersonal, and material sacred—a sacred at once radiant with the highest ideals of the society from which it was born, thus bound to actual ritual performance, and marking out a domain in space and time.

2. Who Was Sylvain Lévi?

Next to Durkheim, Marcel Mauss considered Sylvain Lévi the most important intellectual influence of his life. Lévi was an observant and alert Jew. At different times, he served as president of the Alliance Israëlite Universelle and the Société des Études Juives. He wrote occasionally on Jewish subjects for the *Revue des études juives*; he was a critical figure in trying to conceptualize the relation of French Jews to a future Zionist state.[2]

Lévi's natural allies in the scholarly world were always those other great Jewish figures who mediated the world of orientalist scholarship with the other world of their own Jewish piety, community affiliation, and scholarship. Likewise, from the first, Lévi rejected the path leading to an exclusive concentration in Judaica. He never felt that he needed to depart from his home discipline of Indology to do his work in the comparative history of Judaism (Lévi 1926d, 49–54). Unlike others who would separate so-called "Aryans" and "Semites," Lévi always insisted that these two areas of study were better done in comparison with each other (Poliakov 1974, ch. 9; Simon-Nahum 1990, 26). To wit, against the divisive agendas of the German Aryanists, Lévi showed how Jewish thought contributed to other civilizations. Judaism stood alongside other great "world" religious traditions like Islam and Christianity as an equal in its cosmopolitan history, and thus as an object worthy of scientific study (Strenski 1993, ch. 10).

Despite this engagement in Jewish studies and life, Sylvain Lévi was most of all a master of Indology. Indeed, it was through his Indological work that Lévi exerted his direct influence on the Durkheimian idea of the sacred. By any standard, Sylvain Lévi (1863–1935) was one of the most distinguished Indologists of his day. Born in Paris of Alsatian parents, Lévi was educated in the rather conservative Jewish learning of the time. Although Lévi was poised to continue Jewish studies in Paris, he instead chose oriental studies. Deciding upon an area specialty, however, proved to be more difficult. Sylvain Lévi sought the advice of Ernest Renan, himself a former *élève* of the Indologist Eugene Burnouf. Renan had a special affinity for Indian studies, in no small part because he tended to follow German fashions of thought, one of which was the so-called "Aryanist" movement. The Aryanists were not only great promoters of the glories of Indian civilization, but more insidiously, scholarly anti-Semites, as was the young Renan in his own way. In his *L'Avenir religieux des sociétés modernes* (1860), Renan said, " 'The Semites have nothing further to do that is essential . . .' " (Poliakov 1974, 207). Nevertheless, Renan confided to Lévi that the resident Sanskritist, Abel Bergaigne, had no students at the time, and that he would therefore eagerly welcome an opportunity to take Lévi as his *élève*. By way of such a series of accidents, at age nineteen, Lévi began what would prove to be an illustrious scholarly career.

After finishing with Bergaigne, Lévi was unable to find a suitable academic post in his field. But the leadership of the same rather conservative rabbinic school in Paris where he had done his own seminary training was eager to have Lévi on their faculty. So when they offered him a position teaching traditional seminary subjects, partly out of a sense of obligation to his Jewish faith, he accepted. After several years teaching seminary students, Lévi eventually succeeded Bergaigne in the chair of Sanskrit at the École Pratique des Hautes Études, Fifth Section. By 1894, he was elevated to the Collège de France in Sanskrit Language and Literature, where he carried on until 1935.

2.1. *Sylvain Lévi: "Another Life As Well"*

Beyond scholarship, Sylvain Lévi lived an active life of Jewish philanthropy and religious practice.[3] Although a member of the Central Committee of the fervently anti-Zionist Alliance Israëlite Universelle, late in life Sylvain Lévi was not able to do more than adopt a still recognizably assimilationist, yet nuanced, position on Palestine as the Jewish National Homeland. Linked perhaps with a renewed sense of Jewish particularism, Sylvain Lévi was devoted to certain specifically Jewish religious causes. Here one may number his many articles advocating renewal of ritual life among the French Jewish community. In 1900, in *Archives israëlites* alone, Lévi wrote "Rituel du Judaïsme" and "La Régéneration Religieuse" (Lévi 1900a, 181; Lévi 1900b, 62). These were practical guides to religious practice, under the recurrent headline, "Études de culte." Unlike most Jews of his milieu and professional status, the conviction of Dreyfus began for him a period of active political life in behalf of causes near and dear to the Jewish community. In addition to his concern for the welfare of French Jews, he directed even greater efforts toward aiding foreign Jews, especially those fleeing the Russian persecutions toward the end of the nineteenth century. After the pogrom of Kichineff in 1905, for example, many young Russian Jewish scholars fled to France. Legend has it that Lévi solicited funds door to door for the relief of these young refugees, even though he met with personal rebuffs and indignities along the way (Level 1935, 97). Lévi tried to be blend reformist and conservative elements into his Jewish life. As Mauss put it, his "second uncle" Sylvain Lévi was

> a patriot, *un Français, un petit Parisien du Marais*, a descendant of Alsatian Jews—who showed in practice how much he felt himself to be a man both of his milieu and his work. He never wanted to break with his race, with his traditional milieu, from which he never wanted to be completely emancipated. And indeed during these times of trouble, he wanted to surpass the limits of duty. But he was also a citizen of the world, someone chosen by the universal spirit. . . . His will for peace, his intimate knowledge of people, the power of his thought, shaped all his activities. Alongside the life of a *savant*, friend, husband and father, Sylvain Lévi had another life as well. (Mauss 1969, 541)

Therefore, unlike everything we know of the non-observant Durkheim, Mauss tells us that Sylvain Lévi died a "saint" and "witness to his faith"—factors we may imagine, for the moment, made a difference to his intellectual life as well (Mauss 1969, 543).

3. Judaism and the Symbolic India

During Sylvain Lévi's lifetime, India was no mere domain of disinterested intellectual inquiry. Despite the geographical and historical distance between the religions of India and Israel, Hinduism and Judaism had been linked to each other symbolically, from at least the middle nineteenth century. This way of regarding Indian civilization was primarily the work of German "Aryanist" scholarship. The use German scholars made of such symbols was well understood in the 1930s. In an editorial commentary on the situation in Germany in the mid-1930s in the organ of the Alliance Israelite Universelle, the author cites the German Interior Minister, Dr. Frick, as saying that German cultural sciences generally wanted sharply to demarcate Germans from other peoples (anon 1935, 103). Thus, it was no surprise that the Nazis would seek to make of India a vast realm of symbols, rife with ideological significance for their campaign against Jewishness. They in effect staked out an "argumentative context" designed to decenter Judaism and the Jews of Europe. Aryanist anti-Semitism spoke the language of the history of the religions of India to discredit the worth of the religion of the Jews. India was thought to be the homeland of the Aryans, and thus in the minds of some, the homeland of European culture. Its religious traditions were thought as well to be the most ancient of any in history, and thus for some, the embodiment of religious traditions even more venerable than those of Israel. India was then felt by the Aryanist thinkers to represent a complete alternative and superior mirror image of the Jewish traditions of the West. Thus when the Aryanists seemed to be speaking about the religions of India, they were often speaking really (or also) about Judaism, here by deflecting it off India.

Sylvain Lévi's Indological studies in part counteracted the anti-Semitism encoded in the work of the Aryanists by standing anti-Semitic discourse on its head. Just like the Aryanists, Lévi spoke *of* one thing (Judaism), while speaking *with* another (India). But unlike the Aryanists, Lévi turned the arguments of the Aryanists against anti-Semitism; instead of using Aryanist symbolic discourse to disadvantage Judaism, he traded on it to enhance the reputation of Judaism (Lévi 1926c; Lévi 1926d).

Consider Sylvain Lévi's view of Buddhism. Even while affirming the Indian identity of Buddhism, Sylvain Lévi tried to deny it the "pure" Aryan roots it was claimed to have by the Aryanists. Buddhism was indeed,

Sylvain Lévi argued, substantially non-Aryan since it seemed to reflect a religious character for which there was no Vedic source! Where in the Vedas do we find the world renunciation, inwardness, and concern for psychological problems typical of the Buddhists? The "conventional wisdom" of scholars of the time automatically to assume that Buddhism was Aryan only revealed a prejudice symptomatic of the dominance of the Aryanist view of India. Thus Sylvain Lévi's answer to anti-Semitic isolation of the Jews from European history was to trade once more on the Indological code.

4. Hindu Survival and Buddhist Demise: The Benefits of Embodiment

We have seen how Sylvain Lévi's ventures into Indology facilitated his larger agendas. We can now probe further into the matter of his view that religion is a socially embodied reality, a "concrete" reality, and not merely an idea or abstraction. I believe that Lévi had developed such a notion at the same time as other forward-looking Jewish thinkers of his milieu, such as Maurice Liber and Hyppolite Prague. They worked out this socially embodied conception of religion directly in terms of Judaism itself, Lévi did so indirectly. A good example of this comes in how Sylvain Lévi explains the comparative Hindu success in surviving Muslim invasion to Buddhism's failure.

For Sylvain Lévi, brahminical Hinduism survived Muslim invasion because of its successful "embodiment" of its religious nature. Yet, this very fact of the embodiment of Hinduism presented Lévi with something of a dilemma. On the one hand, Sylvain Lévi believed India was the source of a rich universal humanism, an alternative to what he felt was our somewhat abstract disembodied humanism. We try, says Lévi, to "do away with local and national creeds"; this is in reality only another expression of "Roman power" (Lévi 1926c, 158–59). Indian humanism, by contrast, is incarnated in actual social and cultural realities: it sanctifies the local, and makes a human center of the "family house," understood as a nexus of "kinship" relations realized in the "joint family" (Lévi 1926c, 168, 170). And rehearsing his proposals for a Jewish national homeland in the code provided by Indian civilization, Lévi points out how Hindus have celebrated a notion of humanity which stresses "the continuity of men submitted to laws established and enforced by themselves . on the same piece of ground where their forefathers were living who originated them" (Lévi 1926c, 169). Even when it came to the Buddhism he dearly loved, Sylvain Lévi regarded it as a "secondary episode" from the viewpoint of Indian civilization taken as a whole, and that Buddhism too should be seen as having sprung from brâhminical interpretations of sacrifice (Lévi 1926b, 90).

Yet, on the other hand, something of this "embodied" Hinduism rubbed against Lévi's most cherished liberal religious preferences. Lévi was a lover of the egalitarian ideals of the prophets, French revolution, and Buddhism. Brahminical Hinduism was, however, the Hinduism of caste inequality and brutal ritual sacrifice. Yet Brahmanism saved Indian civilization—not, though, by being an abstract system of ideas or a neo-religion—but because it was embodied in the caste system and in sacrificial ritualism. However unlikable these might be to a religious liberal, they provided Hindus with the materials of cultural distinctiveness, a "means of defence against menacing absorption" by invading Muslim forces (Lévi 1926b, 88). So although Lévi had reservations about brahminical India, he found reasons to excuse it, at least in part, because of those very aspects of its social embodiment.

On the other side, "although brâhminism represents the national genius of Indian civilization," it is Buddhism which "expresses what was universal in it" (Lévi 1926b, 91). But Lévi stops short unambiguously of applauding these universal qualities in Buddhism. Lévi had definite reservations, for example, about the viability of an abstract Buddhism, a religion which had lost touch with its native "soil"—the Buddhism which decisively severed its ties with traditional Indian brahminical social structures and indeed anything which marked it with an incarnate Indian particularity (Lévi 1926a, 123). In Lévi's opinion, this led, in the case of Buddhism, to a religion which "more and more lost its national character . . . in order to take on a more and more human aspect" (Lévi 1926a, 118). In its Mahayana developments, for example, Buddhism even cheerfully dissolved its ties with India as an historical and geographic entity. The "new Buddhas" were in effect socially disembodied, says Lévi; they inhered in nothing, since they "had no sacred geography" (Lévi 1926a, 119).

Although this loss of geographical location and social embodiment might seem liberating (similar to that experienced by early Christianity),

Lévi felt that, in the end, it proved disastrous for Buddhism. Buddhism flourished most when it was embodied—when it acted to broker Indian civilization with the larger, outside world. But with its ties to India cut, it could no longer do this, and thus no longer enjoyed the benefits of dealing in cultural "trade" (Lévi 1926a, 125). One thinks of the benefits accruing to Christianity, for example, in some missionary situations, where its prestige was enhanced in being a conduit for Western medicine and education. Moreover, in universalizing, Buddhism lost much more that mere cultural identification: it "lost the inspiration which had animated it from its beginnings: it ceased being a church and became a school . . . a philosophical school" (Lévi 1926a, 123). Buddhism, in short, became a religion in the sense our nineteenth century anti-materialist students of religion valued—a "spiritual" thing without the cultural, social, and material forms or "particularities" which come with having a legal code, ritual life, or national character, without "any concern with social formation" (Lévi 1926a, 119). For Lévi's eyes, such a "religion" was a poor thing indeed. At least, embodied religions survive. Disembodied, however, like Indian Buddhism, Lévi felt that even his own Judaism would only weaken and then gradually disappear from Europe, much as Buddhism had from India.

Related to this tendency, Sylvain Lévi saw opposing features of religious life as "aspects" of a perennial ebb and flow in a long history (Lévi 1918, 22). In a particular time, one or the other aspect would be deemed desirable for a healthy religion, like Judaism, to embrace. Lévi thus also rejected a simple unilinear evolutionist model of religious progress. Neither Judaism nor Hinduism seemed to follow an irreversible historical trajectory. Instead of evolutionist talk of "stages," one ought again rather refer to *aspects* in the fluctuating life of a religion. The course of Hindu and Jewish religious histories moved to different, equally harmonious, rhythms. In the case of Judaism, while Lévi endorsed the liberal notion of "prophetic" Judaism, he did not condemn more conservative sorts of Jewish religion. Lévi celebrated the originality and its enlightened, universalist virtues of liberal Judaism, which often was identified as a descendant of the so-called "prophetic" Judaism. In an address of 1918 before the Ligue des Amis du Sionisme, Sylvain Lévi says that this prophetic, universal Judaism "holds out a fraternal hand to humanity to march in concert, anticipating the triumph of justice." But

Lévi does not stop with a standard celebration of religious liberalism: he goes on to applaud the particularist "aspect" of Jewish life and history in the same address. Lévi says mighty words in behalf of that sort of Judaism which draws inward and resists the universal Judaism of the prophets. Without rejecting prophetic ideals, he speaks unapologetically, as some- one gradually more and more confirmed in his own Jewish particularity of a so-called "Mosaic" Judaism. For Lévi, Mosaism is that *aspect* of the fluctu- ating movement of the perennial rhythms of Judaism where Judaism "tends to regroup the chosen people into its ethnic isolation, to multiply the barriers which separate it from the nations" (Lévi 1918, 22). While it is everything which "prophetic" Judaism is not, it flourishes in its own time and place, and is not to be denied.

4.1.   *Buddhism, Zionism, and a Jewish "Foyer National"*

Lévi's feelings for the importance of religion as socially embodied reality is interestingly confirmed at another level, from his nuanced and shifting engagement in the Zionism question. During the years just before and after the First World War, Lévi was the "official spokesman on the Zionist question to French Judaism" (Abitbol 1989, 69). Consistent with the high-minded idealist philosophical culture of his milieu and his adherence to the Francocentric ideals of the Alliance Israëlite Universelle, Lévi approached Zionism with "great discretion" (Abitbol 1989, 71). Since he also found poli- tics distasteful, he saw the fate of the world's Jews by and large as a problem of the "moral sphere" (Abitbol 1989, 69). Yet, by 1918, Lévi favored a Jewish national homeland in Palestine, although he opposed a political "state" of Israel (Lévi 1918, 14).[5] Lévi's remarkable report about a trip to Palestine in 1917–1918 is full of admiration for what he has seen that Jews can do for themselves. He applauded plans to settle Palestine with Jewish "colonies." He thrilled at the renewal of Hebrew, because "verbal effervescence responds to a boiling up of ideas and doctrines on their way to being real- ized." He marveled at Jewish enterprise in all areas of commerce and agri- culture, and especially how intellectuals worked the land as a way of recovering their Jewish identity. The orthodox may have denounced efforts of the Alliance to rescue Jews as "impious," but Lévi is all praise for the way Zionism has surpassed the Alliance in sheer "boldness." France should support its Jews in Palestine in the same way it rushed to the aid of Christians in Lebanon. Thus Sylvain Lévi's feelings about the desirability of an embodied Buddhism conform to his new-found enthusiasm for a Jewish homeland (Lévi 1918, 18).

Lévi's desire for a socially embodied Judaism in Palestine did not really constitute for him a break with the liberal universalist, idealist Judaism of his preference. He never became a Zionist in the normal (political) sense. While Jews should be free to migrate to Palestine, to reconstruct Jewish life there, even to cultivate Jewish culture there, it was neither necessary nor desirable to found a separate Jewish state in order to further the renewal of Jewish life in Palestine. To him, Zionism was a "work of sectarians." Lévi felt that Zionism would create intractable problems with Palestinian Arabs, that it would encourage the immigration of Russian Jews and their tendencies toward radical revolutionary politics, that it would make Jews the world over suspects of divided national loyalties (Abitbol 1989, 78–79).

Political Zionism, furthermore, betrayed the universal and humanist ideals of the Alliance and the kind of Judaism he embraced as a liberal French Jew. Consonant with the vision of the *Amis du Judaïsme*, Lévi's vision of a Jewish *foyer national* in Palestine was to be a cultural, not political, entity. Judaism was instead a cultural reality, a "religion," not a matter of statecraft, politics, or ethnicity. He thus distinguished the ideal of a Jewish "*foyer national*" from a Zionist state. Together with the leadership of the Alliance, he carried his fight against Zionism right to the highest councils of French and Jewish leadership, in the end only to be swept aside by the force of events (Level 1935, 97).

The ideal of a socially embodied religion, in touch with its own "soil," informed his scholarly judgment about the status of Buddhism set adrift from its home, as much as it informed his attitude to Judaism. Despite French national policies, decreeing that Judaism was just a "religion" alongside other "religions," historical events seemed to turn Lévi toward the view that this could not in practice ever be so. Although drawing well short of Zionism, Lévi asserted that Jews were a "people" and should assert their collective identity. The "law" of his thought was thus that as much as his universal aspirations favored Buddhism, the Enlightenment, and modernist, prophetic Judaism, the reality of a life of social embodiment put him more on the side of particularity—traditional India and Judaism.

5. Educating Mauss: "Things" and Rituals

I maintain that Sylvain Lévi made the Durkheimians—especially Marcel Mauss—a practicing heir to this "embodied" approach to religion, and thus to an embodied notion of the sacred. We should recognize that Mauss, like some of the other thinkers of his day, was also moving independently toward a collective and concrete conception of the sacred. But Sylvain Lévi contributed to Mauss's intellectual evolution, and provided much of the rationale for what Mauss would do with religion.

Nothing better describes the deep personal and professional relationship between the great Indologist and Durkheim's nephew than the words of Mauss himself. Sylvain Lévi was "my second uncle," he tells us. He "did more for us and all of you who have followed us [than one might imagine]" (Mauss 1969, 537). Sylvain Lévi was thus a great patron of the entire *équipe*, especially in the all important École Pratique des Hautes Études, Fifth Section. Thus, Sylvain Lévi's relation to the nucleus of the Durkheimian *équipe* could hardly have been greater. Mauss illustrates by recounting how Lévi oversaw the careers of each of his students. "He never separated a concern for our careers from the administration of our progress, work and our science. One of his great 'merits' was that he thought about each one of us in material, fatherly, and fraternal ways . . ." (Mauss 1969, 539).

In 1896, after having worked with Durkheim in Bordeaux, Mauss moved to Paris to do his doctorate with Sylvain Lévi at the École Pratique des Hautes Études, Fifth Section. His account of Sylvain Lévi as "guru" paints an admirable and intriguing picture of the great Indologist, telling us what Sylvain Lévi meant to Mauss as a scholar. It gave a completely "new direction to my career," says Mauss (Mauss 1969, 535, 537). Mauss came to Sylvain Lévi puffed up with the pretensions of the cosmopolitan idealist philosophy he had imbibed from his *maître* at Bordeaux, Octave Hamelin. Mauss tells us in effect that the time he had committed to plugging away at Indian culture with Sylvain Lévi would be short and uncomplicated. He would exploit Sylvain Lévi for a few "typical" facts, and force them onto the Procrustean bed of theory which he brought with him from Bordeaux (Mauss 1969, 537). Mauss's plans were, however, rudely upset. Early in his career as a student of Sylvain Lévi, Mauss presented the plan he and Hubert had conceived for *Sacrifice*. Lévi's immediate reaction was to reproach his inconstant pupil for having produced a mere piece of abstraction (Mauss 1969, 537–38). Lévi's colleague and coreligionist, Hartwig Derenbourg, put their common viewpoint directly: "As we conceive it the science of religion is not a branch of philosophical studies" (Derenbourg 1886, 302). Even though Hubert had given the prototype his firm historical touch, much remained for it to meet the standards of the kind of history Sylvain Lévi practiced. Thus far from indulging his rationalist philosophizing tendencies, Mauss tells us that Sylvain Lévi "made me plunge into a sea of facts." And, after two years of submission to Sylvain Lévi's historical method, no end was in sight. Mauss confessed in exasperation, "I kept on collecting and sifting facts" (Mauss 1969, 538).

If Mauss's words can be trusted, the abstract universalizing tendencies of his philosophical inclinations gave way to an historical and cultural particularism. The galloping speculation of philosophy was harnessed to respect for particulars (Dumont 1986, 184). By this route, Sylvain Lévi's more conservative Judaism, partly as mediated through his historiographical practice, seems to have formed Mauss's devotion to the collective, concrete, and embodied approach to religion, typical of the Durkheimians. Sylvain Lévi's emphasis on the collective and concrete thus shaped the Durkheimian agenda for the study of religion in at least two other ways—Durkheimian ritualism and their new idea of the sacred.

When Mauss arrived to study in the Fifth Section in 1896, Durkheim's équipe was a year or so from being formed, and plans for L'Année sociologique were just being made from Durkheim's provincial post in Bordeaux. In 1896, as well, Sylvain Lévi was doubtless in the midst of researching and perhaps writing his classic of two years hence, La Doctrine du sacrifice dans les Brâhmanas [1898]. It was a seminal time indeed.

From what we can tell, Lévi started Mauss straight off learning the lessons of historicist scholarship on religion with the subject of ritual sacrifice. Commitment to the study of ritual sacrifice contributed in no small degree to the articulation of the Durkheimian notion of the sacred as the positive force known as the essence of religion.

Taking ritualism first, Sylvain Lévi taught his élèves that Hindu texts should be read as indicators of rituals, rather than philosophical arguments (Mauss 1969, 539). Lévi's methodological ritualism seems to have taken its lead from Sylvain Lévi's own teacher, the Indologist Abel Bergaigne. Along with Bergaigne, Sylvain Lévi showed strong orientations to the arts, especially theater. Under Bergaigne, he wrote his groundbreaking doctorate on the history of Indian theater (1890). Indologist Louis Renou located this work within the context of a longer French tradition of interest in ancient Indian dramatic texts, but credits Sylvain Lévi with surpassing his teacher and becoming the first to master the entire range of Indian dramatic texts *and* performances from popular to classic forms. Sylvain Lévi went so far as to suggest general priority of various theatrical performances to the poetry attending them. This priority of performance over text became for Sylvain Lévi part of the polemics he and Abel Bergaigne waged against the German Aryan nationalists and even Max Müller (Renou 1937, xiv). Another part of this polemic was to have followed Bergaigne's reading of Andrew Lang's ritualist criticism of Müller. On this view, the hymns of the Veda should be read against the backdrop of the performative context of their settings; Max Müller, on the other hand, felt that the Vedic hymns had only "incidental dramatic value" (Renou 1937, xv).

The Buddhologist Paul Mus notes as well that Abel Bergaigne, as a great Vedicist, started a "heresy in traditional Indianism" by "showing that one ought above all to interpret the Vedas as explaining a ritual" (Mus 1937, 119). In a testimony of intellectual conversion remarkable in the history of science, Bergaigne tells us of being "suddenly stopped on the road leading to Damascus" shortly after an article of his on Vedic mythology, done in the solarist style of Max Müller, went to press. "What was it," Bergaigne asks, "if not the evidence of the texts, or in any case, something which appeared to me to be such, that could have been the reason for the change?" Bergaigne no longer believed: "I ultimately came to recognize that exclusively solar interpretations, just like exclusively meteorological interpretations . . . when they applied to the analysis of the Rigvedic myths, almost always leave behind a liturgical residue, and that this residue . . . is exactly the most important portion from the point of view of the exegesis of the hymns" (Bergaigne 1978, 283). Thus, the classics of Indological scholarship of Bergaigne, mediated by Sylvain Lévi, at least reinforced the Durkheimian determination to take ritual seriously as a key to the study of religion, and as we will now see, the sacred as essentially a (socially) embodied matter.

6. The "Sacred," Ritual, and Religion without God

Lévi's investigations of sacrificial ritual contributed as well to the related positive and non-theistic idea of the sacred, subsequently made famous by the Durkheimians (Mauss 1968, 353). In particular, Sylvain Lévi showed how Vedic and Brahmanic sacrifice assumed that ritual itself actually produced the gods. This meant, first of all, that the *definition* of religion could be separated from a belief in the existence or even the idea of God. Lévi says this because he was persuaded that the *nature* of the religion revealed in the *Brâhmanas* was constituted by sacrificial ritual. There, sacrifice "is God and God *par excellence*." Further, sacrifice "is the master, the indeterminate god, the infinite, the spirit from which everything comes, dying and being born without cease" (Lévi 1898, ch. 2). So potent, in fact, is the sacrifice, that even if gods are relevant, those very gods are "born" from sacrifice, are "products" of it (Lévi 1898, 54). Behind the figure of Prajapati, a major Hindu creation deity, is the sacrifice: "Prajapati, the sacrifice is the father of the gods . . . and its son" (Lévi 1898, 27).[6] Further, instead of the idea of the gods defining religion, the notion of an *impersonal* sacred power behind the gods and empowering them took over. For Sylvain Lévi, this power—the *brahman* of Indian thought—was a property of sacrificial ritual itself. It is an "impalpable and irresistible power which is released . . . like electricity." Like Hubert and Mauss's new dangerous sacred, Sylvain Lévi reports that "the force of sacrifice, once released, acts blindly; he who does not know how to tame it is broken by it" (Lévi 1898, 77). It requires little imagination, of course, to see here the *sacré* of the Durkheimians, which for Mauss was "fundamental"—"the ultimate aim of our researches [is] the sacred," was also the "highest reward of our work on sacrifice" (Mauss 1968, 353).

6.1. *The Sacred Is a Body*

Even beyond this general positive notion of the sacred as an impersonal power, Sylvain Lévi also taught the Durkheimians that the sacred was, in the words of François Isambert, "a 'milieu' one enters and leaves" (Isambert 1983, 189). Thus, Henri Hubert and Marcel Mauss observe in the second chapter of *Sacrifice*, "The Entry" into and "The Exit" from the domain in which the sacred is focussed—is the sacrifice. Mauss elaborates further about this in comments about Sylvain Lévi's course on the *Brâhmanas*. It "was personally destined for me. His *Idea of Sacrifice in the Brâhmanas*—his chief work—had been made for me. From its first words, it delighted me with a decisive discovery: 'the entry into the world of the gods'; there, right under our noses, was the starting point of the labors which Hubert and I realized in *Sacrifice*. We were only bearing witness" (Mauss 1969, 538). The sacred was, thus, far from being what it was for the religious liberals of the day—an idea or private mental state. It was instead something one might even call palpable, material, and bodily—like the "electricity" of which Sylvain Lévi spoke earlier. Citing Sylvain Lévi with approval, Mauss agreed that sacrifice and the forces it liberated were socially embodied. Sacrifice, thus, "'was a mechanical action, which acts by means of its own deep-seated energy.' It has its abode in the act, and finishes with the act" (Mauss 1968, 353).

That the Durkheimians came to their ideas about the sacred in this way is a matter of history. That we have not, up until this point, recognized Sylvain Lévi as one of the makers of that history is a matter of our ignorance. I hope that what I have written sheds light on how we have come to think about the sacred as we do.

6

The Rise of Ritual and the Hegemony of Myth

Sylvain Lévi, the Durkheimians, and Max Müller

I. Items

During the 1930s, Georges Bataille, a former student of Marcel Mauss, the pornographer, philosopher, and eventual head curator of the Bibliothèque Nationale, sought to establish Paris's traffic-choked Place de la Concorde as the venue for the revival of ritual human sacrifice.

Two other offspring of the original Durkheimian *équipe*, the Africanists Marcel Griaule and Michel Leiris, look out at us from a photograph. They are outfitted in standard-issue pith helmets, khaki shorts, and knee socks, typical of ethnographers in the 1930s. Sons of good family, they stand at attention before a mud-walled shrine and "prepare to sacrifice a chicken before the Kono altar at Kemeni, September 6, 1931, as a condition of their entry into the sanctuary" (Clifford 1983, 145).

2. Myth, Religion, and Ritualism

While many of us might draw up short of the ritual and sacrificial practice of these wildmen of religious studies, we need little intellectual persuasion that ritual constitutes a genuine part of religion. Along with myth, belief, social organization, ethics, experience, and art, rituals are "good to think," perennial foci of the study of religion and society at large (Smart 1968).

Reprinted from *Myth and Method* (eds.) W. Doniger and L. Patton (Charlottesville: University of Virginia Press, 1996), with permission of the University of Virginia Press.

Such attitudes are however relatively recent in the study of religion, and even to this day, often a cause of discomfort. Mary Douglas and Victor Turner, to name just two of our more influential contemporaries, devoted much of the effort of their mature work to establishing the claims of ritualism in one form or another (Douglas 1973; Leach 1968; Turner 1969). Thanks to them, some investigators have gone even further, arguing that religious life is shaped or caused by rituals; others indeed have closed the gap with Bataille, Griaule, and company, and seek to promote a revival of ritual life. For them, it is not enough that rituals are "good to think"; rituals must be "good to do as well."

Ritual has, however, not always been received so kindly; intellectual and cultural obstacles to its study, appreciation, and practice have been numerous (Douglas 1973). In this discussion, I want to examine an historical case of how ritualism in the study of religion overcame impediments erected against it by the hegemony of the idea of the special relation of myth to religion. This hegemony has persisted even to the present day, where it has ridden the backs of the modern leaders of religious studies, Joseph Campbell and Eliade, and Lévi-Strauss (Lévi-Strauss 1963; Lévi-Strauss 1971). But in a sense these contemporaries have only prolonged the priorities of the nineteenth century founders of religious studies, like Friedrich Max Müller, who slighted ritual and preferred to mark myth, however "diseased" a thing it might be, for the honor of being closer to the essence of religion.

The prestige of Max Müller notwithstanding, the early part of this century saw the first challenges to the hegemony of myth. On its other side, the challenge to myth was made in the name of ritual. In this discussion I want to understand how these first breaks in mythophilic and anti-ritualist sensibility were made. The main protagonists of this *coupure épistemologique* were those teachers of the Batailles, Griaules, and Leirises, the members of the original Durkheimian *équipe*, in particular Henri Hubert and Marcel Mauss. Now, although Hubert and Mauss (Durkheim as well) paved the way for what the *avant garde* achieved, they would not have lined up, chickens in hand, behind Bataille and his other partners in transgression. The Durkheimians always remained distant from ritual even while being patrons of its modern-day study. In this discussion, I want to lay out some of the cultural and intellectual conditions which made it possible for the original members of the Durkheimian *équipe* to become even the diffident ritualists that they were.

..e explore these conditions of Durkheimian ritualism, I want to keep in mind the way it arose, partly at any rate, at the expense of myth. Although Durkheim made much of the importance of myth in his analysis of religion, it is hard to know precisely how to read this enthusiasm in light of countervailing tendencies of Durkheim's thought (Durkheim 1915, 100). The Durkheimians continued the thrust of an anti-Aryanist cultural polemic aimed at the influence of the work of Friedrich Max Müller (Strenski 1993, 180–201). This polemic was in part a protest against the assertion, however nuanced, of the importance of myth by Friedrich Max Müller. In this the Durkheimians were not original. As Robert Alun Jones has powerfully argued, we must point to the widely accepted influence of William Robertson Smith (Jones 1981). I think however that this story needs to be filled out by showing how Durkheimian ritualism was occasioned by the anti-mythological— and anti-Aryanist—approach of the French ritualist critics of Friedrich Max Müller. This line of criticism began with the Sanskritist Abel Bergaigne, and was continued by the great Indologist, Sylvain Lévi. He, in turn, taught its lessons to his own student, and Durkheim's successor as head of the Durkheimian group, Marcel Mauss.

3. Four Kinds of Ritualism

In speaking about scholarly attitudes to ritual, what I have also referred to as "ritualism," we run the risk of conflating at least four distinct things. It would thus be good at this point to separate them one from another. These are ritualism in the sense of the causal or constitutive, methodological, practical and perennial uses.

First, when we accept, like the early Durkheimians, that ritual is central to the *nature* of religion, we are saying that the very existence of religion depends on the existence of rituals. For convenience sake, let me term this simply "causal" or "constitutive" ritualism. In its most perfect form, such ritualists will go so far, for example, as to say not only that rituals make or *cause* religions, but that religion essentially and simply *is constituted* by a set of rituals.

Second, given at least some form of causal or constitutive ritualism, we therefore assume that the *study* of religion ought to include the serious *study* of ritual. Let me call this "methodological ritualism." This sort of ritualism takes the form of recommending the study of ritual as an avenue into understanding the nature of religion. We recommend the study of ritual because ritual either *is* religion or is a key *causal or constitutive* factor accounting for its existence. Once again the early Durkheimians stand out as exemplifying this position.

Third, there are also those, like Bataille or some of our contemporaries such as Karen McCarthy Brown and Tom F. Driver, but unlike the Durkheimians, who draw certain conclusions from these positions for the sake of their personal lives (Brown 1991; Driver 1991). They are the "practical ritualists." They hold that participating or engaging in, even creating, rituals is a good thing.

Four, practical ritualists, in turn, also often hold that we *ought* to participate in ritual because it is essential to human nature and/or *perennial* in human culture. But one should immediately add that perennial ritualism does not require being a practical ritualist. For example, some non-practical causal or constitutive ritualists may also be perennialists simply because they feel that rituals have a place in any sort of society irrespective of its so-called stage of development or degree of religiosity. Rituals are a perennial facet of life, even if I personally may not care to practice them. This last position, I shall refer to as "ritualist *perennialism*."

4. Ritualist Clusters, the Probable and Improbable

Now, although the story of the rise of any of these senses of ritualism would be interesting, in this discussion I want to account for the historical rise of *causal*, *constitutive*, and *methodological* ritualisms. I do so because they prepared the way for the full-blown practical and perennial ritualisms of our own day. But for the purposes of this volume, these are the senses of ritualism which arose in historical conflict with the prestige of myth. How was it historically that we came to think about religion as constituted or caused by ritual instead of myth, and why we do believe it worthwhile to study religion by studying ritual, in conjunction with or even in preference to studying myth?

Now, having registered my intention to focus this discussion along the lines of methodological and theoretical lines, I will be the first to admit that it is not always possible *in fact* to separate matters of method and theory from other domains. Often enough, attitudes about one sort of ritualism "cluster" with others. Sometimes conclusions about one sort of ritualism may be drawn from holding or rejecting another. Indeed, they typically are. Here we can cite, for example, the relatively obvious conclusion that if one believes ritual *constitutes* religion, then one would doubtless adopt *methodological* ritualism in studying it. Thus oftentimes causal, constitutive, and methodological ritualism "cluster" in the thought of a single individual or school of thought. Less obvious, but more interesting from the viewpoint of historical and social analysis, are the possible historical clustering of ideology or religious commitment with causal, constitutive, and methodological ritualist positions. What conclusions, for instance, might be anticipated about the methodological views of an investigator or about their theory of the ritual (or non-ritual) nature of religion from the fact of their religious practice?

4.1. *Religion and Myth: When Anti-ritualism Was in Flower*

One such example of clustered ritualisms would be among the liberal Protestant founders of religious studies in France. There, the occurrence of rituals was considered *ipso facto* evidence of a "religion" having fallen into "superstition." To translate, if a "religion" were found to be constituted by rituals, it was deemed evidence that the religion had degenerated into something else, such as superstition. Rituals were sure signs of corruption, signs that where magic now was, religion used to be. Real religion had to do with purity of heart, philosophical ideas, or profound inner experience, but not with ritual. As a result, the methods used to study religion excluded the study of ritual: metholodological anti-ritualism thus "clustered" with constitutive anti-ritualism.

In Durkheim's France, a good example of the anti-ritualism typical among (especially the liberal) religious thinkers of the day was Albert Réville, the doyen of the École Pratique des Hautes Études, Fifth Section. Réville felt that ritual could not be the heart of religion, because all cultural or embodied forms of religion were examples of what Albert Réville (and others) called "religious materialism." Rituals were nothing more than examples of the "need to make use of religious forms, as if they were indispensable receptacles of the divine reality" (Réville 1874, 152). Interestingly enough, Réville is equally hard on the Anglican liturgical reformers of the mid-nineteenth century; saying that the "new ritualistic development in the Church of England" can lead to the "religious brutalizing and degrading of the people." Albert Réville lashes out with ever greater fury against the Evangelicals of his own day, saying that they "mistake nervous attacks for grace, and howlings for revelations of the Spirit" (Réville 1874, 155). Taken together, from the gentler Anglican expression of ritualism to the furious emotional ritualism of the Evangelicals, Albert Réville charges that rituals were "always more or less superstitious" (Réville 1874, 151). A really religious person will inform his or her sensibility with a religious "spiritualism," which originates in a "more elevated moral and religious sense" (Réville 1874, 154).

Réville had his own theological reasons for anti-ritualism, but he was joined in this attitude by many liberal Protestants of his day, most notably by his friend, the great student of myth, Friedrich Max Müller (1823–1900). Although on the surface, Durkheim himself was more concerned with refuting the naturism of which both Réville and Max Müller shared an equal part, what Durkheim went on to do in the *The Elementary Forms* was to place ritual at the center of understanding religion (Durkheim 1995, ch. 3). In this respect, I am suggesting that we can read Durkheim's position on ritual as a point at least partly made against such opponents of ritualism as Réville and Max Müller. Let me now turn to the man whom Richard Dorson believes "reoriented all previous thinking about the origin of myths," with the publication in 1856 of "Comparative Mythology," Friedrich Max Müller (Dorson 1968, 161; Müller 1881b, 299–451).

5. Max Mülller, Myth, and Religion-as-Such

In this heyday of the celebration of German folklore, language, and literature, myth was naturally enough a favored category of cultural expression (Strenski 2003, chs. 3–5). This was true for Friedrich Max Müller, even if myth, in turn, was for him both a derived feature of language ("only a dialect, an ancient form of language"), and, moreover, something which was symptomatic of a "linguistic breakdown" (Müller 1881b, 451)—the well-known theory of myth as a "disease of language." Thus, Müller says, "mythology is inevitable, it is an inherent necessity of language, if we recognize in language the outward form and manifestation of thought; it is in fact the dark shadow which language throws on thought, and which can never disappear till language becomes altogether commensurate with thought, and which it never will" (Müller 1881c, 590). Müller's belief in the importance of myth is thus secondary to his even deeper conviction of the overriding importance of language to culture. If a people's language should change, said Müller, soon too would its social arrangements follow suit (Müller 1881a, 24).

Typical of the idealism and romanticism of his generation of young German intellectuals, Müller's own religion tended toward pantheism, and he, like others of his class, much admired Vedanta philosophy (Strenski 2006, ch. 4). His religious sensibilities were accordingly cast in terms of a romantic nature mysticism. After describing the nature worship of the Vedas, Müller rhetorically asks: "And are so different from them?" In contemplating nature, "do we not feel the overwhelming pressure of the Infinite . . . from which no one can escape who has eyes to see and ears to hear?" (Müller 1889, 138). This meant that he had considerable appreciation and sympathy for religions that even he considered "low" on the evolutionary scale. Müller ranked the original nature religion of the ancients, what he called "Physical Religion," lower than the "Philosophical Religion" of his own day, but he nonetheless seemed to indulge some nostalgia for it. "Physical Religion," like the Vedas, may display certain "childish" features, but at the same time, it represented an approximation of the absolute (Müller 1882, 112). The Vedas were, for instance, "revelation" in their own way. Despite their "childish," sacrificial, ritual, and priestly character, was not their polytheism more precisely a "henotheism," and thus a waystation on the road to monotheism or monism (Müller 1882, 136–37)? A "Physical Religion" like the Vedas thus exemplified a vital progressive stage in the history of religions. And for Müller, the "real history of man is the history of religions: the wonderful ways by which the different families of the human race advanced toward a truer knowledge and a deeper love of God" (Müller 1882, 129). Müller's willingness to see what for him were the "precious stones . . . hidden" in the "rubbish" of the highly ritualistic "Physical Religion" put distance between him and some of the other liberal Protestant students of religion of his day.

As for the relation of myth to religion, Müller was considerably more ambiguous. This ambiguity of Müller's was also something Durkheim exploited to raise himself up as the new champion of the essential religiousness of myth—even though Durkheim was himself confused about the place of myth in religion (Durkheim 1915, 100). This ambiguity arises partly from Müller's own intellectual confusions, because of his attachment to a theory of natural religion, and finally because of his historicist tendency to stress the distinctiveness of different cultural configurations. We can pass over Müller's confusions and head directly to the matter of Müller's attachment to natural religion (Byrne 1989, 185–90).

For Müller, "religion" meant the many different historical religions studied by anthropologists, historians, philologists, and others; but "religion" also meant in a normative sense—*real* religion, religion in its true essence. This real religion we can call "religion-as-such," although it has also gone by the name "natural religion." For Müller, the real and essential religion cannot change, even if the history of religion is a history of change. Real, natural religion is the "deepest" root of the many religions which come and go over the course of the ages (Müller 1889, 104). Accordingly, the many religions were at best "sects if not corruptions" of the original religious natural impulse of humanity (Müller 1889, 54).

Müller often jumps back and forth between historical and normative uses of the term "religion," making it difficult to know the reference of his language about religion at any given time. Müller can say, for instance, that it is from religion-as-such that myths are said to arise, and thus that at the same time "religion" (referring in the collective to the many religions) cannot be equated with myth (Müller 1891, 292–93, 302). To explain this paradox, we need to see that for him, the religions were those melanges of cult, myth, and practice; but religion-as-such was the perfectly spiritual activity of the "perception of the Infinite," later modified to include the moral element (Müller 1891, 294–95). This notion of religion-as-such refers to something which existed "before" sacrifice, ritual, and myth, and thus was something which could not be equated with myth (Müller 1891, 302).

It is the dissociation of myth from this *normative* sense of religion in Müller's writing which drew Durkheim's attack. In his critique of Müller, Durkheim tells us that he will have none of the "abstract and philosophic" thinking about religious notions such as God, which results from the dismissal of myth from the religious domain (Durkheim 1915, 101). Durkheim is of course only partly correct, since he has in effect attacked Müller for not giving myth its due as part of religion-as-such. But insofar as the *religions* are concerned, Müller is quite pleased to declare, as we have seen, that religion and myth are integral to one another.

Thus, when it came to the Greeks, Müller could say, on the one hand, that he did not believe that the Iliad was their "Bible" (Müller 1881c, 585). But this did not stop him from turning around and declaring in the same lecture, "although mythology was not religion in our sense of the word . . . yet I would not deny altogether that in a certain sense the mythology of the Greeks belonged to their religion" (Müller 1881c, 585). Indeed, as he says in the same lecture, myth was "the religion of the ancient world" (Müller 1881c, 589). Going even further to assert the link between religion and Aryan myth, Müller said that in the case of ancient India, the Veda is "the real theogony of the Aryan races" (Müller 1881b, 381). Further affirming the perennial religious value of that great trove of myth and the love of his scholarly life, the Vedas, Müller said that in the Vedas, "we get one step nearer to that distant source of religious thought and language which has fed the different national steams of Persia, Greece, Rome and Germany, and we begin to see clearly that there is no religion without God, or as St. Augustine expressed it, that 'there is no false religion which does not contain some elements of truth'" (Müller 1882, 135).

Thus, for Müller, despite the failings of myth in capturing the high-flown abstract truth of philosophical religion-as-such which he preferred, the many ancient religions were often constituted by myth, and that proper piety presupposed a special reverence for myth, and at least in consequence, a playing down of the value of ritual.

5.1.   *Friedrich Max Müller and Aryanism*

Müller's spirituality was driven in part by a romantic German nationalist cultural politics which emphasized the overriding importance of the folkish and homegrown (Chauduri 1974, 84). These traditions, broadly inhospitable to ritual and institutional religious life as they were, thus shaped Müller's spirituality along the mystical lines of individualistic communion with the God who dwelled in all things (Byrne 1989, 186; Müller 1901, 294–95). In turn, they shaped Müller's sensibility to such a point that for him it was simply taken for granted that, despite its flaws, myth was a primary and essential element in the make-up of genuine archaic religion.

As a young man, Max Müller went to Berlin to study languages and philosophy. As an educated German of his generation as well as the son of Schubert's chief librettist, the romantic poet Wilhelm Müller, Max Müller had already come prepared by the popular romantic culture of Indianism and Aryanism (Chauduri 1974, 84). In Berlin, he was able to develop these tendencies academically and in tandem through oriental studies and comparative historical linguistics. As an admirer of Schlegel, for instance, he came under the influence of such pieces of early theoretical glorification of India as *Über die Sprache und Weisheit der Indier* (1808). As a student of Bopp, Müller trained as an Indo-Europeanist.

Müller was thus already a kind of religious idealist in that he saw what one might call intellectual and literary things as primary religious data. In this vein, beyond the spiritual ambience he assumed as a "child" of the German romantic movement, Müller gained an even more sophisticated appreciation of myth from his formal association in Berlin with F.W.J. Schelling, the first real philosopher of myth (Chauduri 1974, 84). Müller was especially taken with Schelling's attempts to rehabilitate myth in the manner of Herder and the German romantics in general. Over against the universalizing and iconoclastic tendencies of the enlightenment, the German romantics felt that myths captured the spirit of the peoples who originated them. This sense that the folk elements of a culture represented something noble about the "soul" of the nation spoke directly to Müller's rising sense of German cultural nationalism. Myths embodied a kind of folk wisdom, indeed, an ancient philosophy, which despite its simple folk origins expressed the essence of the self-conception of national groupings—like the Germans (Müller 1901, 152).

Although Müller felt that Schelling's knowledge of the religions of India was inadequate and misguided, he nonetheless became a devotee of the great philosopher of myth, crediting him with having "opened" up his mind to the possibilities of a systematic study of religion, myth, and philosophy (Müller 1889, 17). Indeed, Müller fancied himself Schelling's successor, but now arguing that a more thorough study of the Vedas than Schelling was capable of undertaking would fulfill the promise of the philosopher's program. Indeed, to Müller's mind, the study of the Vedas was fundamental to accomplishing Schelling's project. Müller's study of the Vedas was "only a means to an end, namely a philosophy of mythology and religion based on more trustworthy materials than those on which Schelling had been able to build his earlier philosophy of religion and mythology" (Müller 1889, 20). As a result of the influence of Schelling, whatever predisposition Müller may have had against ritual was surely given philosophical depth.

Both philosophic and orientalist lines of inquiry fed Müller's lifelong fascination with the so-called Aryans, and in particular the quest for the religion of the ancient Aryans. Like many others, such as Sir James Frazer, Müller was struck with a sense of the possible significance of the discovery of the relationships among the Indo-European languages (Ackerman 1987, 81). Müller in fact was the person who applied the term, "Aryan" to designate that group of peoples who spoke original Indo-European, feeling it was more appropriate than the cumbersome, then current, alternative, Indo-Germanic (Voigt 1967, 5). In Müller's view, ancient Aryan myths, such as the Vedas, were a repository of the ancient wisdom of the Aryans. In some real sense then the deepest content of the Vedas lay at the root of Western culture, and thus German national identity. "We are by nature Aryan, not Semitic," Müller said in 1865 (Müller 1882, 112). Max Müller's belief in the special place of myth in Vedic religion was thus in effect part of a deeper theological and sociological idealism, linked with Aryanist cultural ideology. Thus, when he encountered the Vedas, Max Müller felt as if he had fulfilled his own German romantic longings and the promise of his deistic liberal Protestant religious rearing at the same time. In the Vedic myths, he felt as if he had made contact with a pure, primordial contemplative nature religion, which, as the "bible of the Aryans," was at the same time the primordial religious lore of his beloved Germany. Müller's wife said of her husband that his " 'highest object was to discover reason in all the unreason of mythology, and thus to vindicate the character of our ancestors, however distant' " (Chauduri 1974, 364).

Because of their mythic qualities and because they seemed to be truly archaic, and thus closer to the natural religion of the dawn of humanity, the Vedas held pride of place for Müller. As such, they should be recognized as coequal in cultural stature with the biblical traditions and literature of the ancient Hebrews—but now most importantly as the source of properly European, read Aryan, cultural heritage. In the Vedas, Müller saw a record of the religion of a pre-European golden age. They provided a direct route into a profound philosophy, the primordial wisdom of the human race, and in particular, into what he believed to be the mother race of the West—the Aryans. It does not seem, however, as if this affection for the ideals of the Aryans, as revealed in the Vedas, moved Müller to embrace Schopenhauer's radicalism. The philosopher felt that Christianity should be revived by finding in the Vedas a new Aryan "old testament to replace its relatively inferior Semitic heritage (Poliakov 1974, 247). Citing Schopenhauer with apparent approval, Max Müller records the philosopher's delight in reading the Upanishads: "' . . . oh how thoroughly is the mind washed clean of all early engrafted Jewish superstitions, and of all philosophy that cringes before those superstitions!' "(Müller 1891, 36). Müller's thought thus pushes in the radical direction laid out by Schopenhauer, even if he does not go as far as the philosopher. Müller's way consisted in denying any religion a privileged place before the truth: "we share in the same truth, and we are exposed to the same errors, whether we are Aryan or Semitic or Egyptian in language and thought" (Müller 1891, 274). This meant then that Müller was free to rank the Vedas and other scriptures as "revelation" alongside the Bible (Müller 1882, 126; Müller 1889, 51). Thus, in this way, Müller at least relativized the religious value of the Bible, and put it on a par with other scriptures as an avenue to divine truth.

The implications of anti-Semitism suggested by Müller's links with Schopenhauer and the Aryanists dogged him during his life. But in truth Müller's responsibility for fostering anti-Semitism and racism in this manner is somewhat problematic. As early as 1865, even while asserting the Aryan nature of European peoples, he lavishly praised the Jews for having a history which was the "one oasis in that vast desert of ancient Asiatic history" (Müller 1882, 113). After 1871, Müller seemed repelled by the nationalist implications of Aryanism, confessing as much to none other than Ernest Renan. Léon Poliakov, certainly no friend of anti-Semitism, seems persuaded of Müller's sincerity in refusing to identify race and language—even if he calls Müller's retraction of earlier Aryanism, "timid" (Poliakov 1974, 214). Müller argued against German nationalist Aryanists that Indo-European philology had anything to do with race. There are, for instance, no Aryan skulls! Thus Müller himself became much less the representative of the sort of Aryanist supremacy contained in his views on these Aryans.

But with the genie out of the bottle, not even Max Müller could control "Maxmüllerism," which took on a life of its own. Those earlier Aryanist ideas influenced the racism of such disciples of Müller's as the American, John Fiske (Hofstadter 1955; Poliakov, 1974 #1483, 214).

6. Getting Serious about Ritual: Robertson Smith and Durkheim

The most substantial break with the approach identified with Max Müller came with the work of the Durkheimians (Jones 1981).[1] They, it is claimed, inaugurated our modern methodological, causal, and constitutive ritualism (Beidelman 1974, 64–68; Leach 1968, 520–26). Yet the fact remains that the place of Robertson Smith and the Durkheimians in aiding and abetting ritualism remains puzzling and improbable. In both cases, the Durkheimians and Smith were men of liberal modernist, and thus anti-perennialist and *practical* anti-ritualist, temperament. Their religious orientations—both Smith's Calvinism and the liberal Judaism of the Durkheimians—gave them every reason *not* to press ritualist trends in the study of religion. Indeed we have already seen how Durkheim attacks Müller for not giving a significant role to myth in identifying the nature of religion. Yet, the upshot of the work of Durkheim (and Robertson Smith through him) was to achieve just this turn toward the study of ritual. How is it, then, that they began a trend toward causal, constitutive, and methodological ritualism, when they neither practiced rituals, nor thought that they had unqualified perennial value? Let us look at Robertson Smith first.

7. Robertson Smith, Anti-ritualist

It is imprecise to credit Robertson Smith with advocating the unqualified primacy of ritual in religion. Indeed, he opposed such an affirmation of ritual in religious life. To be precise, we should say that only in his views of *primitive and non-*Christian religions was Smith a ritualist, and then only in causal, constitutive, and methodological senses. Seen from on high down the ladder of human cultural evolution, Smith saw ritualist religions as lower on the evolutionary scale than the religions of morality which he thought his own brand of Calvinist Christianity represented (Smith 1923, 53). Smith felt that (unhappily for truth's sake, as it happens) these primitive and non-Christian religions were thus caused and constituted by ritual, and that thus to understand primitive religion, we needed to be methodological ritualists.

But, when it came to what was for him "real" religion (to Christianity) or to practical and perennial ritualism, Smith turned his back on religious ritual: "a ritual system must always remain materialistic, even if its materialism is disguised under the cloak of mysticism" (Smith 1923, 440). Leaving no role for ritual in the "real" religiosity of his own faith, Smith proclaims that the "real living power ... in Christianity is *moral*; ... personal Christianity is not a play of subjectivities, but moral converse with God practically dominating the life" (Smith 1912, 317, 324). We should also not forget that Smith followed his teacher Paul Lagarde's anti-Judaism and anti-Catholicism. Lagarde disapproved of the rabbinic Jewish and Roman Catholic ritualism of his own day because he felt that both exemplified the "dessication" (*sic*) of a religious life dominated by rituals.

Even in 1875, when Smith seems to move toward a position granting substantive importance of liturgy, Smith steps back from the brink. For while it is true that he thinks liturgy matters, it matters only if dependent upon the state of individual personal piety and moral rectitude. On the ritualist side, Smith says that "the church is not a fellowship of Christian love which requires no unity of organization—but a fellowship of worship," and that "church fellowship has a moulding and upbuilding power on those who take part in it" (Smith 1912, 324, 330). But then putting ritual into dependent status, he undercuts what he means by this. In Smith's view, this "common worship of many individuals" is only an "expression in intelligible form of their common relation of faith towards God" (Smith 1912, 324). That is to say that ritual again comes second to the inner condition of the Christian soul. This likewise fits with his Reformation view earlier expressed in the same essay that "the effectual factor in the sacraments is not the outward sign, but the word of promise signified. [Thus] all participation in the benefits purchased by Christ is to be gained in converse with God, in hearkening continually to His Word" (Smith 1912, 319).

Such revelations about Smith may come as a surprise to those associating Smith with the celebration of the communion enjoyed during the "jolly feast," which was for him ancient Hebrew sacrificial religion. But a closer look will shed light on the truth of Smith's rejection of the view that religion in its essence is constituted by rituals. While it is true that Smith was initially fond of the communion aspects of sacrifice among aboriginal Hebrews, this attraction gave way to outright and thinly veiled disapproval. In Smith's eyes, after the primitive Hebrew period, sacrifice became dominated by the ideas of bribery or gift. Like the rest of ritual life, sacrificial rituals are "materialistic," indicators of the barbaric and uncivilized cultures producing them (Smith 1923, 440). Thus, Smith's ritualism (causal, constitutive, and methodological) is confined to the narrow area of human life where the religious spirit has not yet realized its own nature.

8. The Durkheimians as Diffident Ritualists: A Confused Causal and Methodological Ritualism

At first glance, the original Durkheimian group did not seem greatly to differ from the standard set by Robertson Smith for the study of religion by way of its rituals. Their ritualism was no more practical in terms of their own (lack of) religious behavior than was Smith's. Unlike Smith's Lutheran teacher, Albrecht Ritschl, for instance, they did not intentionally promote programs of liturgical reform (Lukes 1972, 338 n. 71).[2] Yet the Durkheimian position on the perennial value and role of ritual is more positive and nuanced than Smith's, even if this may mean it is only more confused.

The Durkheimians tended to believe that human life, and religion included in it, is everywhere and always, hence perennially, ritualist, even if they kept aloof from religious ritual themselves. Thus, the Durkheimians talk about the positive value of the *practice* of certain everyday rituals. In contemporary society, these would be such events as the celebration of Bastille Day, various civic rites, or indeed whatever is required to stir the community into a state of creative "effervescence" (Hubert 1968, 17; Pickering 1984). Granted, some of these modern rites may be best interpreted as "vestigial" rituals, impoverished forms of religious ritual life typically found in full flower in traditional society (Pickering 1984, 350). But another reading of the Durkheimians indicates that they felt that all societies needed their moments of effervescence in order to rise above emotional and moral mediocrity, as Durkheim lamented in his own day (Durkheim 1975, 71–72).

An early such figure we might add to the mention of Bataille, Griaule, and Leiris was a Protestant student of Hubert's, Philippe de Félice

(1880–1964). He wrote a rather popular book in 1936 called *Poisons sacrés; Ivresses divines* (Félice 1936). There, Félice repeatedly lavishes credit on what Hubert taught him about religion (Félice 1936, 372). Without prejudice, Félice merely records the many ways the religions of the world cultivated ritually-induced religious raptures, accompanied often by inebriants like beer and other more exotic drugs. It is a "general human phenomenon" fundamental to religion (Félice 1936, 363). Moreover, these ancient practices of quaffing "nectars" and "ambrosias" can be found also in the writings of the Church Fathers; they are even continued, Félice suggests, in the fervent expressive language of the mystics. A basic "need" exists, says he, "to transcend the self, which imposes itself upon human beings." We "desire to enter into the source of the immense river, where people, since their existence, have sought to refresh their souls" (Félice 1936, 317, n6). Rituals were instrumental in achieving these states of transcendence. Thus, rituals were not just appropriate to unevolved societies, but even to those organized along rational lines. In this sense, the Durkheimians might be said, unlike Smith, to be at least partial perennial ritualists.

In taking this line, Durkheim was committed to the view that evolution was continuous and in a way cumulative. The past was not in all respects effaced in the passage of time; it continued to live in its transformations. Durkheim here reminds one of Freud, who argued that the child lives on in the adult and is never lost in the course of human maturation. Working at the social level, Durkheim argued that ritual practices were concrete primitive practices which would later develop into abstract moral judgments (Wallwork 1972, 80). Ritual sacrifice continues into our day as civic sacrifice or altruism. Ritual sacrifice continues into our day as the "elementary form" of moral practice. The two realms are linked by a kind of organic historical linkage.

The Durkheimians were also more positive about myth—even as they shared Smith's causal, constitutive, and methodological ritualism. On the matter of the relation of ritual and myth or belief, for instance, the Durkheimians held that they were causally interdependent, albeit often a somewhat asymmetrical interdependence (Durkheim 1915, 121). Ritual, taken as society made visible, had a certain causal priority to myth or beliefs. In his 1887 review of Guyau, Durkheim announced what amounts to an appreciation of the causal priority of ritual. There he says that "Cult is religion become visible and tangible; like religion, it is based on a socio-logical relationship, formed as an exchange of services."[3] Making clear the causal priority of ritual to myth some years later, Henri Hubert colorfully says: "Myths are social products; it is in the rituals that society is visible, present or necessarily involved. The mythological imagination dances on the threshing floor trodden by rituals, and it is there that one might grasp it (Hubert 1919, xxxix). This reflects the Durkheimian view that rituals were somehow closer to the bedrock of social reality. They were the "*sine qua non*" of the maintenance of society" (Pickering 1984, 347). In another place, Hubert says, "First of all, as for a ritual, it implies by definition, the collab-oration of the entire society in which it takes place. The rite carries in itself the idea of its efficacy and reason for its observance. Secondly, every reli-gious act puts the *sacred things* into action" (Hubert 1902, 247–48).

Briefly, this is what is at stake. Against the antiritualist position of Jewish and Protestant liberals, Hubert and Mauss adopt a *causal or consti-tutive* ritualism. Religion *is* its rituals, not just its beliefs or even morality. Ritual is the locus of the positive power of the sacred that injects efferves-cence, energy and power into people, and because of which people are reli-gious at all. Thus, sacrifice is for them what *makes* (things) *sacred*, as the root meaning of "sacri-ficium" testifies. It even creates the gods. Sacrifice performs a positive function of creating the religious life of people. They say all this, of course, because as we noted in relation to the Durkheimian critique of the anti-ritualism of Albert Réville ritual is religion in social form, and thus "religion made visible and tangible" (Pickering 1984, 347).

But in a way, Hubert's brilliant metaphor also served as a recipe for a relation of interdependence with myth which the Durkheimians were apparently unable unambiguously to describe or explain. In "Individual and Collective Representations" (1898), Durkheim qualifies the rule of rit-ual causal priority (Durkheim 1974, 31–32). He says that once myths get launched, so to speak, they become causally independent of any rituals previously related to them. Thus, in certain contexts the Durkheimians saw myths affecting the shape of rituals, thereby making them worthy of study, virtually, in and of themselves—or at least as causally prior to rituals. They indeed take this line in *Sacrifice* in beginning their discussion of the sacri-fice of the god. There, they explain at the very heart of the book that their "main efforts will be especially directed toward determining the considerable part that *mythology* has played in this development"[4] (Hubert & Mauss 1964, 77).

Yet, while the Durkheimians wanted to admit that myths could acquire autonomy, they always seemed to want to keep their feet on the ground by asserting that flesh-and-blood social realities (like ritual) were the primary realities (Hubert 1919, xxxix). When we think about the range of things they studied, we see how the balance tips in favor of ritual: sacrifice draws their attention both in Hubert and Mauss's *mémoire* and in Durkhiem's great classic, prayer as an "oral rite" becomes the focus of Mauss's doctoral dissertation. The guiding methodological principle here is that ritual is a way society manifests itself, thus making it available to empirical study (Pickering 1984, 326). In the end, then, although the Durkheimians wanted to have it both ways in the balance between ritual and myth, ritual proves more equal than myth.

9. The Cultural Strategies of Ritualism

How was it then that the Durkheimians got to the point of embracing ritualism as much as they did? Why did not they turn out more like other cultural and religious liberals, such as their contemporaries, Albert Réville, William Robertson Smith, or Salomon Reinach? How was it that they parted the seams of the nearly seamless anti-ritualism of their times as extensively as they did? Part of the answer is, as I shall now show, bound up in the cultural strategies of the Durkheimian group.

We already know how Max Müller's preference for myth was embedded in a whole network of cultural strategies. The same is true about the evolution of the Durkheimians' ritualist positions. Where Müller was Aryanist and early on had acquired the reputation of being anti-Semitic, the Durkheimians were cosmopolitan and non-exclusive; where Müller was romantic individualism and mystic rapture, the Durkheimians looked to the Enlightenment fellowship and cooperation; where Müller saw society as formed by its language, myths, philosophy, and poetry, the Durkheimians saw society forming its modes of ideal expression; where Müller saw myth and philosophy, the Durkheimians saw ritual and concrete human relations.

But the Durkheimians were not original in reaching out for ritual; they owed their ritualism to the direct influence of Mauss's mentor in Indic studies, the Jewish scholar Sylvain Lévi (Reinach 1911, 437).[5] Sylvain Lévi's ritualism was in turn hammered out in opposition to Max Müller's mythophilic interpretation of the Vedas—and the cultural strategies it furthered. Lévi's ritualism was thus just as thickly nuanced by involvement in a program of cultural strategies as anything Max Müller and the Aryanists had attempted. Both ritualist opponents of Max Müllerism and the anti-ritualist mythophiles played the same game of religio-cultural politics but from opposite sides of the field. Let us now look at how this happened.

10. Ritual Makes the Gods

The first break in the idealist German Romantic reading of the Vedas came from the assertion of French scholars that the Vedas were not purely and simply "a profound philosophy,'" and one from which Indian religion degenerated into mindless ritualism (Lévi 1937, 7–9; Mus 1937, 119).[6] The ritual sacrifice of the succeeding texts such as the *Brâhmanas* could not thus be seen as symptomatic of a "long and profound degeneration of religious feeling," as the partisans of the Vedas as Aryan Bible claimed (Lévi 1898, 9). Sylvain Lévi thus struck at the heart of the theory of religious evolution typical of Robertson Smith, taken over from Wellhausen and the volkish Paul de Lagarde (Stern 1961, ch. 1).

Such a devolution from philosophy to ritual made little sense because it was not possible to separate the supposedly philosophic wisdom of the Vedas from practical ritualism. The supposed philosophical activity of the Vedic sages was thus not incompatible with their practical ritualism. Lévi indicated that the even the elaborate ritualism of the *Brâhmanas*, for instance, reached its peak among an elite class of brâhmins—who were at the same time philosophers. Ritual and philosophy are not mutually exclusive; they coexist under the same conditions. Even in the brutal brâhmanical sacrificial system ritual contains a speculative theological core which gives immediate rise to the lofty philosophical speculations of the Upanishads (Lévi 1898, 10).

But the French even went further toward recognizing the role of ritual in the earliest stages of Indian religion. Beginning with Abel Bergaigne and continuing with Sylvain Lévi, the leaders of French Indology taught that

Hindu texts would be better read as indicators of rituals, rather than philosophical arguments at all (Mauss 1968, 539). Once the mists of philosophy cleared, other readings of the Vedas could emerge. Bergaigne, for instance, believed that the hymns of the Veda needed to be set into the performative context of their settings. Significantly, Max Müller, on the other hand, felt that the Vedic hymns had only "incidental dramatic value" (Renou 1937, xv). If they were not philosophy as Max Müller in effect said, then they were myth. But with the growing attention to the performative settings of the Vedic hymns, Bergaigne for one began to suspect their mythological character as well. In a testimony of intellectual conversion remarkable in the history of science, Bergaigne tells us of being "suddenly stopped on the road leading to Damascus" shortly after an article of his on Vedic mythology, done in the solarist style of Max Müller, went to press. "What was it," Bergaigne asks, "if not the evidence of the texts, or in any case, something which appeared to me to be such, that could have been the reason for the change?" Bergaigne no longer believed: "I ultimately came to recognize that exclusively solar interpretations, just like exclusively meteorological interpretations . . . when they applied to the analysis of the Rigvedic myths, almost always leave behind a liturgical residue, and that this residue . . . is exactly the most important portion from the point of view of the exegesis of the hymns" (Bergaigne 1978, 283). In the words of the eminent Paul Mus, Bergaigne had started a "heresy in traditional Indianism" by "showing that one ought above all to interpret the Vedas as explaining a ritual" (Hubert & Mauss 1964, 64, n370; Mus 1937, 119). Thus, Bergaigne's rejection of Max Müller's mythophilic reading of the ancient Indian texts led him directly to ritualism.

Bergaigne's lead in Vedic studies was eagerly taken up by Sylvain Lévi. But to Lévi, as to Bergaigne, it was clear that the Vedas were heavily committed to ritual—a trend which continued into the *Brâhmanas*.[7] Sylvain Lévi's *La Doctrine du sacrifice dans les Brâhmanas* (1898) substantially argued the position that ritual, not the idea of gods, was the key to the origins of religion, as Louis Renou suggests in saying that for Lévi "ritual dominates mythology" (Renou 1937, xxiii). This differs from the point made by William Robertson Smith that to *understand* primitive religion, we should begin by trying to understand ritual life. Here the issue is the nature and origins of religion itself, not how to go about studying it. Confirming this, Sylvain

Lévi says that the *nature* of the religion revealed in the *Brâhmanas* is constituted by sacrificial ritual. Thus, in his review of Sylvain Lévi's book, Marcel Mauss cites passages from the second chapter where Lévi says that sacrifice "is God and God *par excellence*," or further, where he claims that sacrificial ritual "is the master, the indeterminate god, the infinite, the spirit from which everything comes, dying and being born without cease" (Lévi 1898, ch. 2; Mauss 1968, 293–95, 353). So potent is the sacrificial ritual, that even if gods are relevant, those very gods are "born" from sacrificial ritual, are "products" of it. Behind the figure of Prajapati, a major Hindu creation deity, is the sacrificial ritual: "Prajapati, the sacrifice is the father of the gods . . . and its son" (Lévi 1898, 27).[8] Sylvain Lévi in effect argues what Renou calls the "omnipotence" of ritual, what I have earlier termed causal ritualism (Renou 1966, viii).

10.1. *Mauss*

Marcel Mauss came to Sylvain Lévi at precisely the moment Bergaigne's ritualism had ripened to its full in the thought of the great Jewish Indologist. Early in his career as Sylvain Lévi's student, Mauss was submitted to an initiation test. He was told to assess the theoretical thrust of a text of which he, at the time, knew nothing. This book turned out to be the *locus classicus* of Bergaigne's ritualism, *La religion védique*. After three days of intense reading, Mauss returned to Lévi, reporting that he felt that Bergaigne had made his case. And, were Bergaigne correct, Mauss concluded, the major assumptions of Vedic studies would be overturned. Since he had made such a stark and uncompromising judgment on the book, Mauss awaited Lévi's reaction with some apprehension. But naturally Sylvain Lévi was pleased, and Mauss gained the confidence of his future teacher for life (Mauss 1969, 527). It is well to recall, however, that things might well have gone otherwise. Mauss was at that time very much an idealist philosopher and, thus in theory, more likely to be sympathetic to German idealist readings of the Vedas than to the emergent contextual and liturgical interpretations begun by Bergaigne and followed through by Sylvain Lévi. As it happened, the meeting of Mauss and Lévi was to be momentous for the future of Mauss's intellectual development as a partisan of ritualism— something which Mauss recognized in his review of *La Doctrine du sacrifice dans les Brahmanas*. There Mauss recites the lessons of Sylvain Lévi's view of the causal power of rituals, even to create the gods themselves (Mauss 1968, 293–95).

II. Sylvain Lévi and the Cultural Meaning of Ritualism

For Lévi, the cause of ritualism had been for some time important to him beyond the academic matters of interpreting religious texts. As an observant and politically attentive Jew, he knew that the mythophilic Aryanist program of Max Müller and his fellows posed special cultural threats to the status of Jews in Europe. Max Müller's interpretation of the Vedas as a body of Aryan, archaic European philosophical wisdom and mythological lore was at its worst a piece of Aryanist (and thus anti-Semitic) ideology. Lévi reacted against the Aryanists by leveling a devastating attack on the supposed superiority of the Vedic religion. The language of the Rig Veda was notoriously "barbaric";[9] the very existence of something called a "Vedic society" remained unproven; claims about its archaic character had been refuted by the discovery of the pre-Aryan Indus Valley civilization of Mohenjo-Daro (Renou 1937, xxii). In sum, the Vedas were far from anything marking a golden age with respect to which later Hindu religion—such as the *Brâhmanas*—could be seen to have fallen.

Sylvain Lévi's criticisms also took on existential pertinence because the German Aryanists symbolically identified later, post-Vedic, "degenerate" (*sic*) Hinduism with his own contemporary Talmudic Judaism. This follows the pattern assumed by biblical scholars in Germany, like Lagarde, Wellhausen, and, through them, William Robertson Smith; they had paired their admiration for long-gone ancient Israel with an equal distaste for "Judaism" proper—Talmudic Judaism. On the French Catholic side, the Assumptionist religious order published the influential newspaper, *La Croix*. There, contempt for Talmudic Judaism was widely deployed in the form of accusations that it was a form of anti-Christianity created in opposition to the new teachings of Jesus (Sorlin 1967, 138). Thus, in terms of symbolic relations, Talmudic Judaism was, for the German Aryanists, like Hinduism in decline *after* the glory of the Vedic period, and before the philosophical renaissance of the Upanishadic "reform."

To Sylvain Lévi, the course of Hindu and Jewish religious histories looked different from the picture painted by the Aryanists. While he agreed with them and with Jewish modernists that Jewish religious history ought to be divided along various lines, there were no *stages* of an irreversible historical evolution. What the evolutionists might call "stages," ought rather to be called *aspects* of Jewish religion, and "aspects" in a perennial rhythm of change. He addressed these issues oddly enough in a tract written for the "Ligue des Amis du Sionisme" (Lévi 1918). First, from his perspective as a republican French thinker, he recognized "prophetic" Judaism, doubtless echoing James Darmesteter, as enlightened, universalist or reformed Judaism (Darmesteter 1892; Lévi 1918). This Judaism "holds out a fraternal hand to humanity to march in concert, anticipating the triumph of justice." Sealing the pact with the French Enlightenment, he immediately adds that "French genius with its passion for universal humanity which expresses itself in its classics as well as in the Revolution is the closest relative of this messianic spirit. It is its natural safeguard against sectarians who have never renounced its suppression" (Lévi 1918, 22). But, in this tract, Sylvain Lévi also speaks as someone confirmed in his own Jewish particularity by the Dreyfus Affair. Without minimizing its difficulties from the viewpoint of "prophetic Judaism," he nonetheless applauds Zionism. He likewise recognizes the value of the "Mosaic" Judaism—that aspect of Judaism contrasting with the "prophetic." It is that moment where Judaism "tends to regroup the chosen people into its ethnic isolation, to multiply the barriers which separate it from the nations" (Lévi 1918, 22). Sylvain Lévi felt both aspects were perennial and, in their own times, desirable for Judaism to encompass (Lévi 1918, 22).

The Aryanists (although apparently not Max Müller) also sought to replace the very scriptural heart of Western culture, the Jewish Bible, with an "Aryan bible," the Vedas (Lévi 1898, 9). Alternative Aryan foundations for the religious traditions of the West would then replace those linked with Jewish traditions and religion. Although apparently not radical Manichean Aryanist like the work of his old professor of philosophy, Schopenhauer, Max Müller's work tended to decenter Judaism from its privileged relation with Christianity (Poliakov 1974, 247; Voigt 1967, 3). Thus, the radical cultural anti-Semitism of the Aryanist interpreters of the Vedas motivated Sylvain Lévi to undo their entire project. Part and parcel of the Aryanist program was a ritual-hating mythophilia to which Sylvain Lévi reacted by asserting the power of ritual.

12. The Significance of Durkheimian Ritualism

Bergaigne's methodological ritualism, mediated in this way by his student, Sylvain Lévi, passed on to Lévi's student, Marcel Mauss. Thus, through the classics of Indological scholarship of Bergaigne, mediated by Sylvain Lévi, Durkheimians like Mauss began taking ritual seriously as a key to the study of religion. Thus the real historical line followed by the movement to rehabilitate ritual in this century stems from France, and in particular, as I have urged, from the Durkheimian group. The French movement also included partisans of the *science du "Judaisme"* such as James Darmesteter, who as early as 1886 went to India in order to study Oriental languages in their concrete contexts (Monod 1897, 162–3). Darmesteter also emphasized the need for religion to be embodied in rituals in his *Prophets of Israel* (Darmesteter 1895, 59). This polemic line matters materially to the formation of our own sense of the value of ritual because Lévi's critique of Müller's preference for mythological interpretation of the Vedas aided the formation of the sociological approach to religion of the Durkheim school. In its Durkheimian incarnation, Lévi's opposition to Max Müller and myth amounted to an assertion that religion is primarily constituted by ritual, and thus that social life is founded on concrete human relations rather than merely upon ideas alone.

7

Durkheim, Hubert, and the Clerical Modernist Discourse on Symbolism

I. "Underneath the Symbol to the Reality . . ."

In his second publication, the 1887 review essay on Guyau's *The Irreligion of the Future*, Durkheim said, "Christ and the miracles now merely represent the deity. Why should God not himself be a symbol?" (Durkheim 1975b, 27–28). Every student of Durkheim's knows that this perspective became a basis for the claim that religion can be explained in terms of society. Society is what "god" really symbolizes. Further, this vision of reality lurking beneath symbol even informed two other central interests of Durkheim in morality and education. In *Moral Education*, Durkheim charts the way forward toward "a complete recasting" of the educational technique required to undertake effective moral education. There he says,

> We must discover those moral forces that men, down to the present time, have conceived of only under the form of religious allegories. We must disengage them from their symbols, present them in their rational nakedness, . . . and find a way to make the child feel their reality without recourse to any mythological intermediary. . . .
>
> We must discover, in the old system, moral forces hidden in it, hidden under the forms that concealed their intrinsic nature. We must make their true reality appear. (Durkheim 1961, 11)

Translated from "Émile Durkheim, Henri Hubert et le discours des modernistes religieux sure le symbolisme," *L'Ethnographie française* 91 (1) (1995):33–52.

In his classic, *The Elementary Forms of the Religious Life*, Durkheim again characteristically tells us that in the study of religion we "must know how to go underneath the symbol to the reality which it represents and which gives it its meaning" (Durkheim 1915, 14). Explaining religion, like understanding the grounds of morality, assumes a double-decker world of "symbol" concealing profound realities. Why does Durkheim talk this way? What rhetorical advantages would speaking in this way have among persons he would like to influence or combat? What is the "argumentative context" of his use of symbolic language? (Kibbee 1993, 167).[1] I shall argue that a symbolist approach to religion, however, was all the rage in Durkheim's day. Liberal Christians, "modernists" (a term I shall explain later), created the prevailing "symbolic" style of interpreting religion popular in the *fin-de-siècle*, and Henri Hubert was one of its main agents.

I believe the Durkheimians took for granted these religious "modernist" interpretive agendas as routine parts of their own thought-world. Instead, however, of joining religious modernists in an internal reform of the traditional religions, the Durkheimians usurped them. Ironically, in their similarly ambivalent and competitive approach to the clerical modernists, the Durkheimians repeat their similarly nuanced attitude to the Marxists. See in particular the disappointed reaction of Sorel to Durkheim. Once seen by Sorel as Marxism's great hope in France, Durkheim again and again showed that he would be Marxism's competition (Jennings 1985, 56). Thus, far from falling into totally distinct intellectual communities, the Durkheimians and the religious modernists or liberals are really differences within a common genus.

2. Symbolism: Neither Theology Nor Sociology Imitate Art

Until now, however, when attempting to locate the "argumentative context" of the Durkheimian symbolic approach to religion, historians have almost universally ignored religion, and consequently the "modernist" religious context. Only Samuel Preus considers a possible religious context of symbolist approaches to social and religious reality. For Preus, Durkheim's talk of symbols recalls "the classic formula of biblical hermeneutics, that the letter kills . . ." (Preus 1987, 163).

More typically, strategies to uncover the historical genesis of Durkheim's symbolism have focused on the more fashionable realm of the cultural *avant garde*. Sociologist Edward Tiryakian wants to link Durkheimian symbolism to the revolutions in the arts of the *fin-de-siècle*. The new cultural trends which swept through the Parisian scene after the death of Victor Hugo in 1885 apparently caught the Durkheimians in their surge (Shattuck 1967). In September 1886, Jean Moréas published his symbolist manifesto in *Le Figaro*; Baudelaire, Verlaine, Mallarmé, Rimbaud, and Maeterlinck flourished; impressionism, post-impressionism and expressionism, Van Gogh and Gauguin, followed later by Picasso, Braque, and Gris, all flourished exactly when Durkheimian thought was taking shape (Tiryakian 1979, 106). Tiryakian would have us believe that the Durkheimians participated in the radical Symbolism of the Parisian *avant garde*.

Durkheim's "going beyond the letter" thus reflected the Symbolist view that reality was no longer quite as "solid" as it once seemed. Behind it, hidden forces determined the shape of the seemingly stable surface of things (Tiryakian 1979, 108). These radical artistic departures correspond exactly to the new "paradigm" for looking at reality introduced by the Durkheimians; they too sought to plunge beneath the surface of mundane social appearances (Tiryakian 1979, 106).

But stimulating though Tiryakian's vision may be, it fails to fit the facts. Tiryakian fixes the Durkheimians into the wrong cultural coordinates. The mysticism and occultism of Symbolism puts it well beyond the Durkheimian pale. The Durkheimians never saw themselves as part of an *avant garde*, artistic or irrationalist or otherwise. Moreover, none of the major contemporary observers of the age saw the Durkheimians as Tiryakian has chosen to see them. That prominent barometer of the mood of these times, Agathon's *L'Ésprit de la Nouvelle Sorbonne*, attacked the rationalist trends of French positivistic thought[2] (Lukes 1972, 373). From its Bergsonian perspective, Agathon's list of targets was topped by the sociology of the Durkheimians—hardly then an advertisement for the supposedly radical *avant garde* pedigree of the Durkheimians (Antliff 1993, 149; Grogin 1988). If Tiryakian's thesis fits anywhere, it fits more naturally with someone like Bergson and his followers who, as Mark Antliff has shown, were close, or at least presumed close, to the *avant garde* and Symbolist movements (Antliff 1993, passim). Furthermore, as early as 1897, Durkheim makes abundantly clear his distaste for these and other radical cultural trends. "The anarchist, the aesthete, the mystic, the socialist revolutionary, even if they do not despair of the future, have in common with the pessimist a single sentiment of hatred and disgust for the existing order, a single craving to destroy or to escape from reality" (Durkheim 1951, 370). As champions of the rationalist spirit of the Sorbonne over against the then reigning Bergsonianism of the Collège de France, the Durkheimians saw themselves as scientists above all, even though their *moraliste* ambitions threw them into the same orbit as the religious modernists, as we will see. They sought to *explain* religion rather than give expression to it. After all, Durkheim does tell us that his symbolic approach, his going beneath the surface appearances, was simply what scientific explanation required (Durkheim 1915, 14). In terms of symbolic notions of explanation, Durkheim was especially disturbed by the view that people believed that science only saw the "surface of things," while religion got to the depths. On the contrary, Durkheim promised that sociology would usurp the role of religion by treating reality in a "symbolic" way: "We must closely examine these hidden sides of things, those supposedly mysterious realms that religion reserves for itself" (Turner 1997, 145). Accordingly, Durkheim attacked the very Symbolists Tiryakian wants to link with him. Durkheim accuses them of mistakenly attributing the epistemological power of science to religion: "Neo-mystics and litterateurs have strongly contributed to making this apparent contradiction fashionable" (Turner 1997, 145).[3]

Furthermore, Durkheim's scientism and his concomitant indifference to the arts characterized the entire *équipe.* Except for Henri Hubert (and here the exception proves the rule), the Durkheimians never considered the graphic arts socially significant. Art belonged to the "leisure life" of lazy sketching or Sunday afternoon dabbling in watercolors. In vain, further, do we seek evidence of a sensitivity to art which might be called "modern"— one which treats art for art's sake, as an autonomous mode of representation. Recently I had the privilege of seeing all the existing sketches and watercolors produced by Henri Hubert dating from his days of prankish adolescent caricature sketching at the École Normale Superieure right up to the end of his life where we see holiday scenes rendered in the easy style of a weekend artist at leisure: throw up the easel, and while away a pleasant Sunday afternoon painting. Nothing of high symbolist style is here, nor for that matter even the amateur's renditions of those cheerful baths of light and warm shapes made commonplace since the 1870s by the Impressionists.

As the only practicing artist and professional art historian among the Durkheimians, we might expect that Henri Hubert would have shown some orientation and understanding of the new modes of graphic representation. But on the contrary, he was apparently completely unmoved by the artistic fashions of his day—and this when he lived in the very same suburb of Paris, St. Germain-en-Laye, where Symbolists like Puvis de Chavanne lived, gathered, and showed their work. Even as late as 1913, when Hubert reviews a work on aboriginal African art, his attitude is not to celebrate the aesthetic of pure form or liberated abstract design; Hubert rather observes that a rich mythological tradition—and thus a world of collective representations—must lurk behind such painting and make it possible. Unlike the Symbolists and their ilk, Hubert believed that art was not important as something in and for itself. Thus, again and again, he subjected art to sociological and therefore *scientific* understanding.[4] The Durkheimians, then, seem to have been practically untouched by the greatest revolution in the graphic and plastic arts since the Renaissance— even though they literally lived right in its midst. But while he did not traffic among the *avant garde*, Hubert was well acquainted with some of the principal figures in the movement I call clerical modernism. By dint of his serious *moraliste* temperament, Hubert also fit more comfortably into their context of reform of the religious traditions of the nation. In what did this context consist, and who populated it?

3. Henri Hubert and Catholic Liberalism

At the very center of Durkheim's circle and at the same time in personal contact with prominent Catholic modernists and liberals like Alfred Loisy, was the Catholic-born Henri Hubert. Like other cosmopolitan liberals of his day, Hubert moved easily across religious boundaries. Yet, Hubert maintained relations throughout his life with certain liberal Catholic clergy, partly as a result of his education at the lycée Louis Le Grand. He is then quite likely to have been a principal conduit for what the Durkheimians knew about the theological symbolism of the day, since, as we will see, theological *symbolism* distinguished the standard mode of discourse of the French clerical liberals (or modernists) of Hubert's time and place.

In his personal behavior and interests, Hubert embodied some of the most attractive qualities of liberal French Catholic culture, even while not being one of its observant members. Hubert Bourgin, a one-time socialist who turned to the right after the Dreyfus pardon, included Hubert among those repelled by the zealous excesses of the anticlerical forces in the wake of the vindication of the innocence of Dreyfus. While Bourgin's words need to be weighed carefully against his manifest desire to justify his own rightward political course, Hubert's respectable bourgeois background and comfortable social situation surely would have made it difficult for him to stay too long in any extreme political location (Bourgin 1938, 381–83). Married to a German Protestant woman, who bore him two sons, he was a living example of the kind of bourgeois French religious and political tolerance typical of liberal Catholicism. As a student of religion, Hubert not only mastered the historian and modernist precursor Abbé Louis Duchesne's areas of expertise in the Greco-Roman world of primitive and Byzantine Christianity, but also in the Near East as well. His thesis on the Syrian goddess, completed before the turn of the century, is unfortunately lost (Hubert 1979, 156).

Hubert and Mauss met first in a Hebrew class at the École Pratique des Hautes Études, Fifth Section, elected by Hubert as part of his educational program (Drouin 1929, 48; Reinach 1927, 176). For Hubert, Christianity was essentially a Mediterranean religion of semitic origins, which could only be understood from the vantagepoint of its Levantine genesis, in the homelands of the Jewish people (Duchesne 1903, 1–10; Reinach 1923b, 400n2). Sometimes, Mauss and Hubert seemed to delight in confounding expectations about their special areas of expertise based solely upon their religious origins. Thus the "Jewish" Mauss reviewed Monseigeur Duchesne for the *Année Sociologique* while "Catholic" Hubert wrote on the great Talmudic and rabbinic scholar, Israel Lévi! Once again, Hubert reveals himself as a man of the middle, a man of reform and reconciliation, not a man of revolution and radical change.

His moral conscience was thus formed in the left-of-center liberalism typical of members of the Durkheimian *équipe*, and typical as well of the liberal Catholics of his day. The mood of conciliation with social change informing Leo XIII's support of Catholic participation in the Third Republic and his encyclical on justice for the working classes would seem hospitable to someone of Hubert's makeup. Whether as a stockholder in Catholic socialist Charles Péguy's Bellais press, *La Societé Nouvelle de Librairie et l'Édition*, or in joining the agitation in behalf of Dreyfus, organized by Catholic-born Lucien Herr, Hubert seemed the very picture of the liberal— if, however, "lightly" affiliated—Catholic (Besnard 1983, 24). Hubert was, moreover, personally associated with pious Catholic liberals like Albert Houtin, who in turn was close to Herr. Houtin would later in life also be Catholic modernist Alfred Loisy's biographer. But in 1916, he and Hubert worked together on common projects at the Museé Pédagogique (Houtin & Sartiaux 1960, 363–64). Reminiscent to some degree of Renan, Hubert thus showed the same combination of a sharp critical sense and qualified respect for religion as one of the makers of the culture which eventuated in modern France (Charlton 1963, 106). As he concludes one of his longer articles, Hubert waxes poetic about the path he believes he has helped clear to the center of religious life:

> In the midst of social life, religion has sprung up. It has burst into blossoms of prayer, sacrifice, mythology, morality, metaphysics, and even extravagant growths of magic. This tree has but a single trunk and its main branches are mighty. But so weighty are they that they bend to the ground. There, having taken root like the banyan, new branches spring up and hide the central trunk. As seasons pass and perspectives shift, the original shape of this tree changes so that one is hardly able to recognize it. Philosophers and historians mistake the tree for a forest—their error repeats the mistake of the early naturalists who defined beings in terms of external traits. But now we must clear away the branches and penetrate their sultry shade in order to catch a glimpse of the trunk. (Hubert 1904, xlviii)

But with what particular Catholic liberals of his milieu, and especially with individuals, did Hubert have actual intellectual and personal relations? Among historians, three "Catholic" figures stand out: Ernest Renan, Monseigneur Louis Duchesne, and Alfred Loisy. Hubert and Loisy knew each other, but were set against each other as competitors for the same academic posts. Loisy and Hubert were the prime candidates for the post

Hubert eventually won in 1901 at the École Pratique des Hautes Études, Fifth Section (Anon 1901, 257). For the purposes of this chapter, let me focus, however, on Monseigneur Louis Duchesne (1843–1922), confidant and teacher of both Loisy and Hubert, and leading historian of the Catholic mass of his day (Drouin 1929, 48).

4. Duchesne and Hubert: "Historiens Historisants"

A man of immense influence and distinction in his own time, Monseigneur Louis Duchesne is known to us today for his classic studies of the early history of the Christian church and the development of Catholic liturgy (Duchesne 1906, 1907, 1910; Duchesne 1920). Duchesne became personally and intellectually related to both Hubert and Loisy in his role as master historian. He, moreover, had definite opinions about studying the history of religion, since Duchesne in effect continued what Renan had begun. He was for Hubert one of the main conduits of the *histoire historisant* in the study of religion (Drouin 1929, 46).

Although trained at first in the traditional seminary system of Catholic France, Duchensne went on to study at the École Pratique des Hautes Études in 1868. There he was trained in history under the hellenist Édouard Tournier (Marrou 1973, II, 13), and then under Protestant historian Gabriel Monod, the leading "scientific" historian of his day. In his devotion to history, Monod gave institutional form to his own reform piety by carrying on the critical traditions of historical scholarship originating among Protestant biblical scholars in Germany (Carbonell 1979, 59–75). As the founder of that flagship of scientific history and bulwark of republican values, the *Revue historique*, Monod became for Duchesne a lifelong influence in his career as historian. Duchesne tells us he admired Monod's *ésprit positif* especially (Mayeur 1973, 319). As a teacher, Duchesne thus directly shaped the historical consciousness of a wide range of scholars in the spirit of Monod's example. These included the Catholic clergy especially, whom Duchesne wished to be as imbued with the spirit "methods of scientific work" as he was (Mayeur 1973, 326). Salomon Reinach similarly celebrated the way Duchesne "inculcated a severe scientific method among his pupils" (Reinach 1930, 431).

By this, Reinach apparently meant that Duchesne's example cut two ways. First, along with demythologizing historians like Renan, Duchesne taught a critical, skeptical history. He in effect taught historians to look beyond the accretions which had clouded the surface of legendary or mythological narratives and to seek what "really" lay beneath the appearances. Duchesne, for example, gained academic fame as a demythologizing critical historian of the popular and pious lives of the saints which had received circulation by Second Empire publishing houses (Savart 1985). Likewise, he published important books on the history of Catholic liturgical and ecclesiastical traditions, preparing the way for some of the liturgical reforms not seen until after the Second Vatican Council (Reinach 1930, 431; Vidler 1970, 24–25). Second, following the main trends of a French historiography selfconsciously seeking to model, but apparently exaggerating, German scientific history, Duchesne taught a kind of history obsessed with facts (Keylor 1975, 8).

Both aspects of this late nineteenth-century way of doing history were defining features of the informed liberal Catholicism Duchesne so well represented. Appointed Maître de Conferences at the École Pratique des Hautes Études, Fourth Section—*sciences philologiques et historiques*, Duchesne moved easily through the highest levels of secular learning and culture. Elevated to the Academie Française in 1913, he was honored thrice by the Third Republic's Legion d'Honneur in 1895, 1900, and 1905 (Mayeur 1973, 329–30). At the same time, he was also for many years professor at Paris's Institut Catholique (1876–1896), and then at the French École de Rome until his death in 1922. As editor of the wide-ranging Catholic review periodical, *Bulletin critique de littérature, d'histoire et de théologie*, Duchesne kept pace with the exciting intellectual developments of the times. Successive volumes of the then new *Année sociologique* were listed and reviewed by Duchesne's journal.[5]

In terms of internal Catholic theological controversies of the day, Duchesne was widely regarded a modernist himself, if not definitely a *precurseur* of modernism (Poulat 1979, 19). Yet, he kept a loyal and low profile throughout the period of most intense controversy. He never declared publicly for modernism, even though he and Loisy were close. Many believed that he privately harbored serious doubts about orthodoxy, all the while maintaining conformity in public for the sake of church discipline and unity. He was rumored to have been sent on periodic retreats in pious Brittany by ecclesiastical authorities to boost his wavering faith (Vidler 1970, 71). Mauss pokes at these tender spots in Duchesne's character by noting how Duchesne tried to reconcile the results of "historical critique with ecclesiastical necessities" (Mauss 1913, 310), and how he completely avoids the historical foundation of the doctrine of Petrine primacy (Mauss 1913, 311). Loisy was less kind to Duchesne's memory and expressed an embittered sense of betrayal. Loisy felt that Duchesne shared what he and the other modernists believed. But because of Duchesne's "eternal fidelity to the church," he remained silent. Loisy also charged Duchesne with a failure of courage to make common cause against the Vatican. Duchesne, like a good "sailor," says Loisy, always trimmed his "sails when the tempest arose" (Loisy 1930a, 478). Hubert, too, although for very different reasons, always maintained a strict discretion in matters concerning the internal politics of the Church. Thus, readers will look in vain for signs of public criticism of the Roman Church, or even public praise for the modernists. Hubert and Duchesne together seemed to practice a special kind of discretion when it came to matters sensitive to Catholics in the public domain (Hubert 1905, 290–91).[6]

On the personal side, Duchesne was also a great favorite of Jewish liberals like Salomon Reinach, and not only for his good-natured demythologizing flair. Duchense was a fearless philo-semite, who showed his mettle during the height of the largely reactionary Catholic anti-semitic campaigns of the nationalist revival. In this, he and Hubert show another dimension of the common values binding liberal Catholics in a time of trial for France's Jewish community. Hubert's philosemitic credentials should be evident from what we already know of his association with Mauss and Durkheim, as well as for his professional concern for the serious study of Judaism. Duchesne, for his part, exploited his position as an eminent historian of religion to defend a Jew against the charges of ritual murder which circulated widely in the Catholic press of the day. He wrote letters to prominent Roman Catholic journals bringing his considerable prestige to bear against a broad range of anti-semitic libels of those days (Reinach 1923a, chs xxx, xxxiv).[7]

4.1. Duchesne and the Politics of Hubert's "Étude sur la formation des états de l'Église"

Duchesne seems to have taught Hubert much of the art of doing the critical history of religions that is reflected directly in Hubert's early historical work. "Urged on by Abbé Duchesne," Hubert's first major publication in the history of religion, "Étude sur la formation des états de l'Église," appeared in Monod's prestigious *Revue historique*, the flagship of "scientific history" (Hubert 1899). The two-article series totaled over seventy pages of densely fact-ridden documentation. Among other things, these articles added to the literature demythologizing the "false donation of Constantine" by relating it to theological disputes between Pope and Emperor. The bearing of such scholarship upon the status of the Gallican church, the Church-State struggles during the Separation Crisis, and the efforts of Catholic liberals to soften the hard authoritarianism of Popes Pius IX and Pius X, as well as the edicts of the First Vatican Council, seem obvious. Not so obvious, however, was the ambiguous role played by Napoleon III in at once assisting the Italians of the Piedmont against the Austrians, but at the same time protecting the Papal States against the new republic.

By appeal to this fictitious grant, the papacy had justified its autonomous rights to political supremacy in the Western Empire, and thus in the future papal states. Rather than such a pact with Constantine, Hubert argued that theological controversies and political machinations lay *behind* the myth. Subsequent to Emperor Leo III's declaration of the prohibition of image worship, "the popes profited" from the ensuing "profound breakdown" between the Church and empire to carve out an independent domain of authority for the papacy (Hubert 1899, 2). The historical basis of absolute Petrine authority was also dealt a blow by Hubert's analysis of the Pact of Quierzy. Any claim to papal absolutism was apparently compromised by arrangements the papacy had made with the Franks. Concluding his articles on an ominous rhetorical note, Hubert said: "In 750 . . . Rome entered into a client relation with the Franks, and did not seek to get out of it. Will Rome be autonomous? Did the . . . Franks share in the power of the pope? Such is the suit which remained to be argued between the successors of [Pope] Stephen and the heirs of Pepin" (Hubert 1899, 272).

As an historian, then, with this work, Hubert reflected Duchesne's legacy as a critical demythologizer, as someone who looked *behind* sacred legend to what really could be documented to be there. It was not, as we will see, the full-blown symbolist approach of the newer generation of scholars trained by Duchesne. But we can see how the work of unmasking theological artifice made it natural to go on to think about many features of religion as dubious on their face. For those who, however, wished to retain religious affiliation, a positive answer was needed to the doubts created about the literal level of religious life and language. The modernists gave this answer. They had thus been initiated into the disenchanting methods of positive, scientific history. Now having absorbed the shock, they sought ways to construct a new religious epistemology. The symbolism of the clerical modernists was their answer. It was also in its own way the answer of the Durkheimians as well.

5. Religious Modernism and Durkheimian Symbolism

To orient ourselves to clerical modernism, it might be best to focus on the most conspicuous occasions of Durkheim's use of the language of symbolic interpretation of religion. Just where does Durkheim talk of a symbolic interpretation of religion?

First of all, in his second publication, his 1887 review of Guyau's *L'Irreligion de l'avenir*, Durkheim's religious "symbolist" sympathies are evident:

> To be sure, it has been said that dogma is untenable if taken literally, but why should we be confined to its literal expression? Words have no meaning in themselves; the mind has to seek the idea, and even the most sacred texts need interpretation. Unfortunately, once Luther had given the believer the authority to be an interpreter, he was instantly persuaded to put his own ideas in place of divine thought; and soon there were everywhere nothing but symbols, even in the most essential dogmas, including that of revelation. (Durkheim 1975b, 27–28)

What is more, this religious symbolist viewpoint persisted undiminished right through Durkheim's career. As late as 18 January 1914, Durkheim reaffirmed the same approach in delivering an expanded form of what he had said years ago in his review of Guyau. This speech was given before an association of humanist and religious (Gentile and Jewish) liberals, the Union of Free Thinkers and Free Believers. In his address, Durkheim is rather explicit about his affirmation of the symbolic reading of religious doctrines. Like the religious modernists, he held that they were revisable and thus (only) symbolic. With fundamentalists, no such fruitful conversation is possible:

> if he [the believer] values a denominational formula in an exclusive and uncompromising way, if he believes that he holds the truth of religion in its definitive form, then agreement is impossible and my presence here has no meaning.

Yet, for religious liberals, there is hope.

> If, however, he considers that formulae are only provisional expressions which last and can only last a certain time, if he thinks that they are all imperfect, that the essential thing is not the letter of these formulae but rather the reality they hide and which they all express inexactly to a greater or lesser degree, if he thinks that it is necessary as a consequence to look beneath the surface to grasp the underlying principle of things, I believe that up to a certain point there is an enterprise we can embark upon by common consent. (Durkheim 1975a, 184–85)

Durkheim thus identified himself, on this reading, as part of the larger "enterprise" of the symbolic reading of religion, which we know to be characteristic of the liberal or modernist theologians whom he addressed. A humanist philosopher and sometimes fellow-traveller of the *équipe*, Dominique Parodi, observed that the concern to explore the "symbolic value" of the old religious questions was indeed one of the characteristics of the times (Houtin & Sartiaux 1960, 286).

But who are these free-thinking theologians of the time, these practitioners of symbolic interpretation of religion? Who, like Guyau, is concerned about the future of religion, or its lack of a future? These are thinkers I shall call religious "modernists," and whom readers of Durkheim have already met making up the audience of "libres penseurs" and "libres croyants" to whom Durkheim addressed his "Contribution to Discussion 'Religious Sentiment at the Present Time.'" Durkheim's use of the idiom of the symbolic interpretation of religion participated in (and played to) the modernist religious concerns of his age.

Such powerful Durkheimian statements about symbolic interpretation of *religion* force us then to return to essentials, such as religion itself, and thus away from dallying in the world of the *avant garde*. At a minimum, if we take the contemporary theological context of his work seriously, Durkheim's talk of symbols would seem to be part of a context of attempts to *interpret* or *explain religious* discourse, under the conditions of *reform* and revision, rather than, say, radical anticlerical abolition of religion. Given these features of Durkheim's discourse on symbols and given the nature of the context of Durkheim's time, I believe that we should see the Durkheimians involved in "argumentative contexts" composed of the same interests and styles of discourse. These, I believe, are the discourses of religious "modernism." I use the terms liberalism and modernism synonymously primarily to short circuit current polemics in literary circles surrounding the terms "modernism," "postmodernism," and such. However conventional the term has become, the religious use of the term "Modernism" was first applied by the Vatican authorities to categorize and thus more easily deal with the burgeoning liberal movements in the Roman church (Kurtz 1986). By this logic, we should pay special attention to Durkheim and his *équipe* as men of these "modernist" religious *times*.

6. Religious Symbolism and Its Discontents

Modernists or liberals, whether religious or secular, Gentile, Jewish, or Durkheimian, generally stood for five fundamentals:

1. *Anti-propositionalism*: religious doctrines are not to be interpreted literally. Doctrines have no precise meaning. Rather they are to be read vaguely as tending to indicate certain states of affairs, whether internal or external to human consciousness.
2. *Symbolism*: Since the propositional meaning of doctrines is rejected, they are then interpreted as "symbolic constructions" (Besse 1913, 54, 63–64, 121; Nielsen 1986; Sorel 1909, 414, 441).
3. *Science*: scientific claims are, on the other hand, to be taken literally, whether these be in the human or natural sciences; religious doctrines are interpreted in concord with the claims of science—to be "inoffensive" to them (Sorel 1902, 547; Sorel 1909, 422, 429).

4. *Evolution*: the world of human affairs—religion included—is a world constantly changing, typically in adaptive or progressive ways. Even supposedly timeless religious dogmas undergo development.

5. *Beyond Divinity*: personal divinity is only a symbol of the ultimate reality, which may be described variously, but typically in more or less pantheist, impersonal, or undetermined ways (Sorel 1908, 200).[8]

We likewise know that the Durkheimians read and reviewed all the major theological works of their time. This was after all the heyday of the theological Symbolism of Fifth Section's Auguste Sabatier, as well as when the so-called Modernist Crisis among Roman Catholics split the nation (Nielsen 1987). When it comes to naming specific religious modernist thinkers with whom the Durkheimians had intellectual contact and conversation, Pickering correctly notes the prominence of the Catholic biblical scholar Alfred Loisy. Loisy wrote a long and thoughtful review of *The Elementary Forms*, and generously cited Durkheim as an important influence in forming the sociological dimension of his own thought (Loisy 1913; Pickering 1984, 143–44). Similarly, the Durkheimians reviewed many of Loisy's most important works in fields as initially distant from sociology as his *The Gospel and the Church* [1903]. Modernists such as Abbé Marcel Hébert even became models for literary characters, notably the *pretre symboliste* of Roger Martin du Gard's novel of the period, *Jean Barois*, for his character, Abbé Schertz. This dynamic cleric was the central figure in that chapter of the novel called "The Symbolist Compromise" (Martin du Gard 1949, 22–43). There, Schertz tries to win the heart of Barois for the symbolist cause: The doctrine of the "real Presence" of Christ in the Eucharist, declares Schertz, is no thing of magic, but "a symbol, a symbol of the divine grace acting on my soul." When Barois objects that Schertz has left out what ordinary Catholics take to be real, Schertz replies that he has instead found what is "essential"—"Our intellect rebels against certain points of dogma; that's a fact we must accept. But the symbol we extract from it is clear, self-evident; it satisfies our reason and furthers our spiritual well-being. So how can we hesitate?" (Martin du Gard 1949, 39). Schertz then draws his arguments for a symbolic reading of religion to a close in one last effort to console his troubled young friend.

> Truth and reality, they're different. Many people, I know, share your difficulty. But when you say "truth" you're thinking of "authenticity,"

which isn't the same thing. We should concentrate on the truth, not of the literal facts, but of their moral significance. We can admit the eternal verities that underlie the mysteries of the Incarnation and the Resurrection without admitting that they were concrete events, authentic in the historical sense, like the defeat at Sedan or the founding of the French Republic. (Martin du Gard 1949, 38)

Beyond their prominence in the national culture of the day, and besides the attention given to them by *L'Année sociologique*, we should take seriously the relation of the religious modernists to the Durkheimians because Loisy and Hébert took the Durkheimians seriously—as their peers. They felt that the Durkheimians were really theologians, despite their scientific intentions and pretensions. Of Hubert and Mauss's *Sacrifice: Its Nature and Functions*, for example, Hébert said that the Durkheimians pretend to absolute, quasi-religious knowledge by offering what they lay down as "*the* theory of sacrifice" (Hébert 1909, 71). Another Catholic modernist intellectual, Paul Legay, characterized Hubert and Mauss's work similarly, as "a kind of philosophy of sacrificial ritual—considered in itself . . ." (Legay 1902, 281). Similarly, in his long review of *The Elementary Forms of the Religious Life*, the leading religious modernist of his day, the Roman Catholic biblical scholar Alfred Loisy, relishes the irony of catching the anti-theological Durkheim doing with the scriptures pretty much what Loisy himself would: "The procedure of [Durkheim's] consisting in imputing this moral and social meaning to the origins of rituals is no more legitimate than that of the Christian exegetes who retrieve from the animal sacrifices described in Leviticus the prophetic symbol of the saving death of Christ" (Loisy 1913, 69). Thus, unlike Preus's biblical interpreters and Tiryakian's artists, these modernist theologians well knew Durkheim and his *équipe*. Even their discomfort with each other attests to this. Linking Durkheim to the religious modernists has, as well, the additional advantage of recapturing and integrating Durkheim's deeply ingrained and quasi-religious scientific vision. In a study of Durkheim's attitudes to science and religion, Robert Alun Jones argued that Durkheim believed that scientific study was more than an abstract and technical enterprise: it was also "morally edifying" (Kibbee 1993, 165).

7. Religious Modernism and the Culture of Liberalism

In temperament, the religious modernists represented a spirit of *reform*—the internal reform of religious traditions, approximating as well much of the Durkheimian program for a humanist morality based on Christianity. Like the Durkheimians, the religious modernists felt that revision of the old faiths was essential for national revival. The humanists wanted a religion based on universal human values, a religion or "morality" common to all (Besse 1913, 22). Such a *morale* was in their minds essential to revive the nation's spirits, and would become for France the "soul of its democracy" (Besse 1913, 198), or, even as the humanist Paul Doumer said, a "*religion de la patrie*" (Weber 1959, 36). As such, they were part of an even larger movement of religious humanism in whose spirit we can now see the Durkheimians share.

Modernists also felt that the traditional religions must square with the sciences, and that they therefore could not hold to their "letter." In 1924, Alfred Loisy noted that when doctrines conflicted with "reality . . . a new and broader interpretation of these formulas . . . was indispensable" (Loisy 1968, 245). Biblical literalism or absolute ecclesiastical authority were out; symbolic interpretation of religion was accordingly the stuff of their religious liberalism since it inoculated it from contradiction with the sciences. If the religious modernists stood for anything, it was application of the methods of scientific historiography (as then understood) to the study of religious traditions. They were great demythologizers of religious traditions, seeking the historical substratum *beneath* traditional or mythological religious representations (Turner 1997, 145). Guided by the example of the Germanically-informed biblical criticism of Renan, they were by and large products of German "scientific" history or "historicism." Durkheim, too, shared their scientific presumptions about dealing with religious materials. This is what Robert Alun Jones has called, in the context of Durkheim's affirmation of Wundtian experimentalism, Durkheim's German "scientific realism." Symptomatic of this approach was, for example, Durkheim's devotion to concreteness and the notorious notion of "things" in *The Rules* (Kibbee 1993, 164). As Georges Sorel argued, religious modernists were also basically like political revisionists (in some cases identical to them), rather than revolutionaries (Sorel 1908). For the most famous

French religious modernist of the period, Roman Catholic biblical scholar
Alfred Loisy, modernism was an effort to seek accommodation and reform
within the Church, not violent revolution. Modernism, Loisy tells us, "was
a more or less diffuse effort, intent upon softening the rigor of Roman
absolutism and theological dogmatism." Loisy wanted to "relax" the
Church's "intransigent attitude, to allow discussion of problems being
posed in the present day, [and] in doing so, to seek a good faith solution"
(Houtin & Sartiaux 1960, 286). In their religious thought the modernists
were content to retain appearances, so long as their inner meaning
changed. In their religious reformism the modernists were then like
Durkheim in politics. He was never a socialist, and certainly neither a
Syndicalist nor a Marxist. Thus, instead of the revolutionary aesthetic
ambitions of which Tiryakian speaks, the religious modernists and liberal
Durkheimians posit the symbolic nature of religion in order to press a plan
for revising and adapting traditional religious beliefs in light of "modern"
life, rather than overthrowing them. They and the Durkheimians marched
alongside each other for some way as fellow liberals.

Yet religious modernists did seek change at the level of religious culture
by means of the technique of symbolic interpretation. Religious liberalism
embraced the language of symbols because it meant that religion was always
open for interpretation: religion could be "modernized" by freeing it from
the "letter" of traditional religious belief and practice. Surface evidence
could always in theory be discounted as merely "symptomatic" of deeper
things. Thus rituals, for example, need not be taken seriously because they
are only symptomatic of deeper, essential human qualities, such as purity of
heart (Douglas 1973). It is within this context of such a religious liberal
agenda of interpreting religious beliefs in the modern world that we can in
part understand the program of Durkheim's sociology of religion. This type
of explanation would make sense to religious liberals because Durkheim
started on the same—"symbolic"—footing with the religious liberals. In the
case of the Durkheimians, they sought to explain religion as well.

8. Affinity Breeds Contempt

In the end, however, the Durkheimians preferred most often to hide their
affinities for the religious modernists. The Catholic Henri Hubert, who

would naturally have been well placed to approach Catholic issues, nevertheless chose his words about the Church very carefully (Hubert 1905, 290–92). Referring dismissively to one of Loisy's confederates, the philosopher Edouard Le Roy, Durkheim dryly observed that as a religious "modernist" he was part of a "neoreligious movement" (Durkheim 1960, 396). In terms of their position within French national politics, the Durkheimians did not wish to be stereotyped as unthinking opponents of the Church. Thus in public debates during the Modernist Crisis they took no position on the merits of Loisy's case (Hubert 1905, 290–92). Loisy himself voiced suspicions in his *mémoires* that the Durkheimians sought to thwart his ambitions for academic advancement (Loisy 1930b, 29–34).

More to the point, however, the Durkheimians were jealous of sharing the stage of social or religious reform with plausible competitors, such as the religious modernists. On the contrary, the Durkheimians apparently enjoyed polemics with their close religious brethren. In a letter of 1898, Hubert revealed how he relished the disruption his and Mauss's work on sacrifice would cause among the religious powers of the day. Writing to Mauss, Hubert said that "we are condemned, my dear fellow, to make religious polemics. We shouldn't miss a chance to make trouble for these good, but badly informed, souls. Let's stress the direction of our work, let's attend to our conclusions—so that they be pointed, sharp like a razor, and so that they be treacherous. Let's go! I do love a battle! That's what excites us!" (Fournier & Langle 1991, 2–9).[9]

With attitudes like these, plus their own ambivalences as "scientists" about being ideologues for a new *morale*, it is small wonder the Durkheimians tried to keep religious modernists at arm's length. The main framework erected around Durkheimian symbolic interpretation was not reform of any traditional religion. It was the building up of an, arguably quasi-religious, civic *morale* by way of symbolic reinterpretation and thus scientific explanation of traditional religions. Thus, although the Durkheimians may have sympathized from afar with this passion to revive traditional faith, they were not themselves given to the task of concentrating their efforts on the internal reform of any *particular* traditional religion. Suffice it to say that the Durkheimians were ready to profit intellectually and professionally from whatever happened to the traditional religions of France.

Simply because Durkheimian symbolic approaches to religion were *like* modernist ones, it bred competition for attention, even if it was competition for attention "within the same league," so to speak. In a way, the "affinity" of the religious liberals and the Durkheimians seems responsible for "breeding" a kind of "contempt." To the extent that Durkheimian civic *morale* was also something of an "ideology," their motives were of course similar to the "theological" ones of the clerical modernists. A major difference was that the Durkheimians could not admit it. They were compelled to deny their ideological ambitions by draping themselves in the laboratory coats of science.

PART FOUR

Institutions and Other Afflictions

8

Durkheim, Disciplinarity, and the "Sciences Religieuses"

I. What Is French "Discipline"?

"Disciplines" are one of the ways we regulate intellectual interests in the realm of knowledge. In France such regulation occurs largely through the power of the state to legitimate and recognize those species of knowledge we call the "disciplines." Thus, when the French noun "discipline" refers to something other than military order or punishment, it refers to a regime of rules governing an interest and craft, typically of scholarship and teaching within institutions of learning usually reliant on state legitimation.

But like other interests, these disciplined interests and crafts have a social and cultural character as well as an intellectual one. Here, I acknowledge debts to what Pierre Bourdieu, and lately Fritz Ringer, have written about "intellectual fields" (Ringer 1992). In Ringer's view, a "discipline" resides in what he calls an "academic culture"—"an intellectual field or subfield, a network of interrelated and explicit beliefs about the academic practices of teaching, learning, and research, and about the social significance of these practices" (Ringer 1992, 13). In this chapter, I want to show how the intricate relations among the intellectual, cultural, and political aspects of what was known in France from the mid-nineteenth century as the *science religieuse* played their parts in the life of a discipline. This is mainly to tell the story of the liberal Protestant intellectual and ideological bases of the Fifth Section of the École Pratique des Hautes Études and the

Reprinted from *Disciplinarity at the Fin de Siècle* (eds.) Amanda Anderson and Joseph Valente (Princeton: Princeton University Press, 2002), with permission of Princeton University Press.

way this Protestant study of religion was contested in *fin-de-siècle* France by no less notable a figure than Émile Durkheim and his team of collaborators in the Durkheimian group.

A brief survey of the involvement of political structures in the legitimation of knowledge illustrates a pattern repeated into the present day in France. The recognition of history as a particular species of intellectual interest and craft goes back to 1554, where we find mention of a royal *historiographe* charged with chronicling the doings of the monarch (Boer 1998, 54). In the time of Louis XIV, the crown in effect recognized certain disciplines by sponsoring various archives, libraries, and specialized research academies where activities recognizable by today's successors in the "disciplines" were carried on. The *ancien régime* continued this trend and founded institutions designed to promote certain practical disciplines, such as the applied arts of engineering and mining by founding the École des Ponts et Chaussées (1775) and the École des Mines (1778). Following this lead, the Revolution created the famed École Polytechnique (1794). In 1795, the École Normale Supérieure was founded to train a cadre of *instituteurs* charged with carrying the ideals of the Enlightenment into the classroom (Smith 1982). Closely linked with the disciplines of philosophy and the sciences, the École Normale Supérieure stood for a kind of *culture générale* which was felt to embody France's unique intellectual genius as informed by the revolution's vision of a transformed humanity. The nineteenth century saw the creation, as well, of a series of specialist craft-exclusive schools for training specialists of various sorts, for instance, the École Supérieure de Télégraphie (telecommunications), the École de Chartres (archivists), and the Écoles Françaises of Rome and Athens (archeologists). It was thus within these institutions and their attendant cultures that certain disciplined intellectual interests and crafts were nurtured.

In the humanities and social sciences in France in the late nineteenth and early twentieth centuries, the professionalization of scholarship changed much of the academic landscape. The rate of such legitimation and recognition, and along with it, the rapidity with which "disciplines" appeared, quickened with the foundation of the École Pratique des Hautes Études and its division into "Sections" in 1868. Because of its massive power to subsidize activities within it, the nation-state in effect played a role as exclusive guarantor of the legitimacy of disciplines. Thus, if no

chair of "The History of the Study of Religions," *
Fifth Section of the École Pratique, then one woul(
speak of this as a "discipline"—even though it ma
The original four "sections" and thus four discip
École Pratique were Mathematics (I), Chemistry a..._
tory and Physiology (III), and History and Philology (IV). In 188u, ..
Section (Sciences religieuses) came into being. Disciplines thus formed
within and around a variety of institutions of higher learning, archives,
libraries, research academies, professional associations, and even, as we will
see, under different circumstances around publishing ventures such as
academic journals.

2. Disciplines as Cultural Work

But while state action can *recognize* an intellectual activity as a discipline, it
is also possible to say that the disciplines did not necessarily *originate* from
state action. In France, private institutions, such as the many *écoles libres*
and amateur *sociétés savantes* flourished in France from the nineteenth century.[1] Witness to the vitality of the life of the disciplines in France were the
many *écoles libres* which sprang up in the late nineteenth and early twentieth centuries. In the absence of official recognition of economic and political studies, the Écoles Libre des Sciences Politiques was founded. It, in turn,
gave birth to the Collège Libre des Sciences Sociales, in the absence of official sanction for a school of social sciences in the École Pratique des Hautes
Études. After a while, the Collège gained some governmental subsidy and
became a consortium of independent institutions, the École des Hautes
Études Sociales in 1901 (Weisz 1983, 310). It was precisely within this milieu
of independent intellectual activity that the Durkheimians got their new
sociology started, even though individually they had been well ensconced
within the official world of the state apparatus of public higher education,
long before sociology was recognized as a discipline. Indeed, as we will see,
the example of the Durkheimians shows how a new discipline and a vibrant
intellectual culture can be formed outside the patronage of the state—here
around a periodical, Durkheim's *L'Année sociologique*.
  The Durkheimian *équipe* manifested all the requirements for being the
social basis of a "discipline" in the sense I am borrowing from Ringer and

dieu. Thus, in terms of its cultural identity, the members of *L'Année sociologique*'s support staff referred to themselves self-consciously as a kind of social grouping dedicated to advancing Durkheim's attempts to sociologize certain dominant disciplines such as philosophy and history. The *équipe* even captured something of this spirit of joint membership in a distinctive academic culture in referring to themselves in the late 1890's as a Durkheimian "team." The etymology and the then current use of the term *équipe* suggest focused labor as on a ship's crew, where indeed our words "ship," "skiff," "skipper," and such reflect the original root meaning of *équipe*. In Durkheim's day, *équipe* also echoed with the ideas of a competitive sports team, such as the *Equipe Casino* or *Equipe GAN* in the Tour de France. Pushing this analogy a little further, Durkheim's "team" of editors, reviewers, and contributors did indeed function like a competitive sports team, sharing a culture of common beliefs about approaches to the study of society, which set them apart from others. In its time, the zeal and swagger of the *équipe* in mounting vigorous partisan attacks on other clusters of scholars won them a good deal of ill will. In their private correspondence, Durkheim's closest confederates, Henri Hubert and Marcel Mauss, were not above making scathing remarks about their opposites in the camps of competing academic cultures. In a tone of determined, if cloaked, opposition, apparently, to the pious Christians in the Fifth Section, Hubert wrote Mauss in 1898 that he relished the mischief their "polemics" would spread among their religious colleagues: "We shouldn't miss a chance to make trouble for these good, but badly informed, souls. Let's stress the direction of our work, let's be clear about our aims so that they are pointed, sharp like razors, and so that they are treacherous. Let's go! I love a fight! That's what excites us!" (Fournier & Langle 1991).[2]

3. Taking the Fifth: Positivism and Protestantism

Perhaps sensing this contempt for their old-fashioned ways, many elements of the French intellectual and academic scene suspected the Durkheimians of gross ambition—the notorious "Durkheimian imperialism." They were correct. Indeed, the Durkheimians had targeted the *science religieuse* of the Fifth Section of the École Pratique for attack and conquest—a campaign not only aimed at a discipline but also at a way of life, an academic culture and more. What were at stake, both intellectually and culturally, were the Durkheimian attempts to replace the dominant Liberal Protestant culture of the *science religieuse* which had prevailed in the Fifth from its foundation.

From the beginning, the leadership of the Section in the person of Albert Réville (1826–1906)—a figure renowned for his "documentary interests"—articulated the norms of this common culture (Alphandéry 1906, 419). This "discipline" of what Réville understood to be a "scientific" study of religion—the *science religieuse*—was charged in Réville's words "'to study the facts, the testimonies, the texts, in order to extract from them their meaning and value, and to apply to them the fruitful methods of modern critical study, and never to allow theological passion to invade the serene temple of erudition'" (Anon 1918, 189). In this way, the Fifth was thus identified with and effectively dominated by "old school" érudites—"historicist" historians and philologists devoted to the careful study of religious texts and traditions. They reproduced faithfully the spirit of the critical historicist culture epitomized by the leading historical periodical in France from the middle nineteenth century, the *Revue historique*, in their own academic journal, *Revue de l'histoire des religions*.

But, like cultures of the ethnic sort, the academic culture of the Fifth Section was defined by opposition to the culture of religious belief and practice of others—chiefly the dominant religious culture of French Roman Catholicism. In many ways, the promotion of history as a "scientific" discipline—and hence the *science religieuse*—was the work of free thinkers and their ideological allies, French Liberal Protestants. "Science" for them provided a source of independent authority over against the claims of Catholic tradition. Among the religious communities of France, it was the Protestants, then, who mattered most in the field of the academic study of religion.

Before the First World War, French Protestants numbered only about 600,000 inhabitants, or 1½ percent of the entire population of France (Davie 1986; Davie 1987). Of these, only a fragment could be called theological conservatives or evangelicals. The rest are what have come to be known as Liberal Protestants or "Extreme" Liberal Protestants. Evangelicals and liberals differed primarily in their attitudes to Enlightenment rationalism. Thus, the more evangelical wing of the Protestant community tried to resist a total slide into rationalism by launching periodic religious revivals or evangelical awakenings (*réveils*). The *réveils* sought to reignite practical religious experiential life, and to assert a degree of doctrinal conformity in a movement perennially championing freedom of conscience and thought (Encrevé 1990, 83). Against the vaguely pantheistic Deism of the liberals, the evangelicals, then, reaffirmed the christology of the Athanasian creed (Jesus is "true God from true God, begotten not made, of the same substance as the Father'") (Smart 1984, 364), the sinfulness of humankind, the "'vicarious atonement and salvation by faith in the sacrifice of Christ,'" the divine inspiration of the Bible, and eternal damnation in hell (Encrevé et al. 1977, 272).[3]

By contrast with the Catholics, the Liberal Protestants practically merged with Enlightenment Deism and religious humanism. In Liberal Protestant theology, "one finds Locke, Condillac, Montesquieu, Rousseau, Voltaire, more easily than Calvin" (Ligou & Joutard 1977, 235). Deistic rationalism in this context (apparently largely Rousseau's) consisted in a belief in a supreme, but nonintrusive, god, creator of the world according to the natural laws we discover in the sciences, and whom we could know by reason alone, unaided by revelation (Grimsley 1973, 71–85). Humanity was portrayed as having been given in equal proportions a pure and unsullied primordial monotheistic revelation. But thanks to the Fall and those ever-conniving priests, humanity's grip on this religion weakened and it fell into savagery of broad dimensions: magic, political injustice or sheer ignorance, polygamy, bloody (sometimes human) sacrifice; "superstition," ritualism, fetishism, animism, and so on. The mission of Christ was to destroy these degenerate forms of historical religion which had arisen since the Fall, then to restore the primordial natural religion with a new and unprecedented "revelation." In its turn, the Reformation saw itself returning to the essence of Christ's mission, by destroying those "pagan" elements which it felt had re-entered Christianity through Catholicism.

Because of its generous scope and application, this particular kind of Deistic rationalism entailed universal humanism. People had no need of special divine revelation or institutional structures because all humans were innately and in essence "naturally" religious by virtue of their common humanity. Every human being shared a common primordial religion, even evident today beneath the many differences of the religions of the world. Albert Réville, for example, tells us quite explicitly that "the principle of humanity guides religion along higher paths . . . [and that the] truer a religion is, the more absolute the homage it will render to the principle of humanity" (Réville 1905, 254). Thus, another legacy of the Enlightenment was its universality, its affection for the ideal of humanity.

Despite the evangelical *réveils* of the nineteenth century, the greater part of French Protestantism (later to become the core of the Liberal movement) held fast to the Enlightenment rationalist religious norms. Samuel Vincent (1787–1837), the great forbear of French Liberal Protestantism, for example, took Christ to be merely an excellent guide of human conduct, not a transcendental spiritual being. In this way, despite periodic surges in evangelical popularity, the liberal traditions of Deistic rationalism held firm in France right through to the end of the nineteenth century. On the occasion when the evangelicals tried to enforce discipline at the 1872 Synod, they produced a formal split between "liberal extremists" and conservatives, ensuing in a series of spectacular defections of several leading liberal clergymen (Schram 1954, 54). Prominent among the rebels were a group of personal comrades, Timothée Colani, Edmond Schérer, Félix Pécaut, and Albert Réville, the father of Jean.

Colani was a disciple of Vincent. He studied theology at Tübingen, like the elder Réville, Schérer, and Pécaut. Tübingen was then the center from which the theory and practice of historical and critical study of the Bible emanated. Colani adhered to this standard of scientific study of the biblical documents, and, like Vincent, was led to deny standard orthodox doctrines, such as Christ's miraculous virgin birth, divinity, and resurrection, as well as original sin (Encrevé 1979, 372). Although Colani had founded the leading periodical of the liberal movement, the *Revue de théologie et philosophie chrétienne* (later to become the *Revue de Strasbourg*), he quit publishing it (1869) before his open rejection of the 1872 orthodox Declaration of Faith. Shortly thereafter, he abandoned theology entirely and even ceased church attendance (Encrevé 1979, 290, 293).

Schérer began his professional life as a professor of biblical exegesis in Geneva. After exposure to German biblical criticism, he broke with orthodoxy over questions of the inerrancy of scriptures, the incarnation and divinity of Jesus, original sin, and Jesus' resurrection. Later he would become a leading light at the Paris newspaper *Le Temps* and in the politics of the foundation of the Third Republic (Vigier 1979, 183–97).

Pécaut resigned his pastorate only months after his first assignment. While in the service of the church, he had gained fame as an author of a book declaring Jesus an ordinary mortal, *Le Christ et la conscience* (1859) and approaching the time of his resignation took to writing on the "religion of the future" in his *De l'avenir du théisme chrétien considéré comme religion* (1864). Later he was appointed by the Protestant minister of public instruction, Jules Ferry, to be director of the École Normale Supérieure at Fontenay-aux-Roses. There he sought to define the bases of a "secular faith."

All these men shared beliefs reminiscent of the old Deistic rationalism inherited from the days of the Revolution: resistance to supernaturalism, such as the belief in miracles, and thus an openness to science. As dissenters they cherished the freedom of individual conscience, religious tolerance, and freedom of thought. From their ranks many anticlerical leaders were drawn, since they arose from a tradition which originated in organized resistance to Catholic ecclesiastical authority. Commentators of the day characterized extreme liberal Protestantism merely as "a form of free thought touched with Christianity" (Robert 1978, 93).

Significantly for our story of the character of academic disciplines in the study of religion, as a result of his rebellion against the evangelicals, Albert Réville sought institutional refuge in the École Pratique des Hautes Études, Fifth (religious sciences) Section. There, under the patronage of the French state, he felt he could continue the trajectory of his Liberal Protestant intellectual interests free of ecclesiastical interference. As an institution, the liberal Protestant–dominated Fifth Section contrasted with institutions like the seminary, and officially ruled out "theology" and other practical or pastoral disciplines from its curriculum. Such self-definition-by-contrast reached such heights that at one point it was argued that a formal requirement for election to the Section be atheism! No believers need apply! A key feature of the common culture of the Fifth Section was then the "positivism" (borrowing again from Ringer) typical of much of the humanities in France in the late nineteenth and early twentieth centuries (Ringer 1992, 216–17).

Now, even though we can first, then, speak of a large overarching discipline of the positivist "*Le Temps* science religieuse"—in the singular—the Fifth Section was officially named as such in the plural "*Le Temps* sciences religieuses." This indicated no more than the division of the subject matter

into a number of specialized positive sciences, subdisciplines or "enseignement." The diversity of subdisciplines within the Fifth Section reflected as
well the existence of several positive sciences and their subcultures within
them. Thus, members of the Section brought with them something of the
academic cultures from which they had been drawn, chiefly philosophy, history, theology, philology, and so on, but also the many more narrowly delin-
eated "*Le Temps* sciences religieuses" such as the study of Rabbinic and
Talmudic Judaism, the religions of Rome and Greece, esotericism in the west,
religions of India—which, officially at any rate, were taught according to
canons of "scientific" history. The study of the texts of the sacred languages,
such as Hebrew or Sanskrit, would constitute additional subdisciplines,
taught according to the regulations laid down by the philological disciplines. A Durkheimian member of the Fifth Section, Henri Hubert, had, for
example, been trained as an archeologist and historian in the officially recognized schools and institutes created for this purpose. These qualifications
won him membership in the Fifth Section. He was "en enseignement"—
literally, taught the *histories* of the religions of pre-Christian Europe aided by
his archeological efforts under the rubric, "The Primitive Religions of
Europe." Yet, as a member of the inner circle of Durkheim's sociological collaborators, Hubert would well be counted a sociologist as well.

    Despite their common positivist culture and avowed commitment to
disinterested inquiry, the members of the Fifth Section tended as well to
affiliate and identify with partisan political tendencies and groups. Liberal
Protestants Albert Réville, Jean Réville (1854–1908), Maurice Vernes, and
others were just as loyal to the program of Gambetta's Republican anti-
clericalism and their own traditions of unitarian latter-day Deism as to any
ideals of disinterested "scientific" scholarship. For them, no conflict
existed between their loyalty to science, on the one side, and to the anti-
clerical republicanism of the Radical Party, on the other. They were really
one struggle fought at two levels.

    For their part, the Durkheimians identified themselves with many of
these same causes as the Liberal Protestants, but without embracing the
theological commitments often tacitly made by the Liberal Protestants.
More than anything else, they identified with their master and made membership in the *équipe* a principal source of academic culture affiliation and
disciplinarity. For instance, in being "Maitre de Conférence," Hubert

taught numerous courses—*conférences*—on topics concerning the "history" of primitive religions of Europe, such as courses on the survival of Germanic religion in ancient Gaul. He also employed his archeological expertise in courses on the study of prehistoric burial structures, and brought to bear the Durkheimian interest in myth and ritual in the lectures he gave on religious seasonal festivals of the ancient Germans, and so on. Thus, Hubert's approach to religious materials was shaped both by Durkheim's new discipline and by what he had learned during his previous intellectual formation as a "scientific" historian and archeologist.

Now, while the Durkheimians shared much of the critical positivist ethos of the Fifth Section, they differed enough so that in time they were seen (correctly) by the Liberal Protestant majority as a threatening foreign culture. The Durkheimians, in effect, challenged both the positivism of liberal Protestant scientific historical practice and the theological agendas prevalent among the liberal Protestant membership of the Fifth Section. First, the Durkheimians felt that the positivist erudition of the Protestant historians and philologists was insufficient to produce explanations. These historians were satisfied to chronicle events, but not to offer explanations for them. Indeed, since the positivists took the basic categories of inquiry as given, they could not and would not raise fundamental questions about their categorial status (Hubert & Mauss 1964). Notions like "sacrifice," "magic," or even "religion" circulated in the liberal Protestant study of religion, but without being subjected to fundamental questioning. The Durkheimians made it a part of their program to take responsibility for the concepts invoked in the study of religion. Thus, in their early work they published efforts seeking to lay down *how* notions like "sacrifice," "magic," "taboo," "mana," and such *ought to be* used. What should the responsible student of religion *permit to be counted* as an instance of "sacrifice"? Is sacrifice a kind of gift? What is the relation of sacrifice to the sacred? Is expiation necessarily contained in the idea of sacrifice? Should sacrifice be restricted to theistic contexts, or can we speak of sacrifice as independent of or even prior to the existence of gods? These questions, for example, would form the intellectual backbone of Hubert and Mauss's little book, *Sacrifice: Its Nature and Functions*. Second, the Durkheimians also went to war against the crypto-theologizing of the liberal Protestant philosophers, theologians, and psychologists because "these good, but badly informed,

souls," in Hubert's (fighting) words, begged all the very same important
questions about the nature of religion which the Durkheimians had determined to shape to their own needs. Where others—notably the Jewish
members of the Section—had been content, at worst, to live and let live in
the face of what must have been an often unbearable sense of Christian
theological triumphalism, the Durkheimians often attacked the views of
their Protestant colleagues.[4] Marcel Mauss felt that work of his colleague
in the Fifth Section and perhaps the leading Protestant philosopher of the
day, Auguste Sabatier, was "a matter less of analyzing facts than of demonstrating the superiority of the Christian religion" (Mauss 1909, 375). The
"discipline" of Durkheimian sociology was articulated in part in relation to
the prevailing positions held by the Protestants of the Fifth Section. It is to
this opposition that I now turn.

4. Christian Apologetics Emerges inside the Fifth Section

While the Fifth Section can be taken as being unified around its positivism, and divided into various sorts of positive sciences of religion, at
least two subcultures and thus subdisciplines should be distinguished
within the Fifth Section. Both of these subcultures stood for ways of unifying the theoretical basis for the work of the Section, but were ultimately in
deep contradiction with the positivism of the Fifth, even if at the time they
were felt to be consistent with its positivist scientific ethos. This contradiction arises mainly from the understandably unthinking assumption of
the Liberal Protestants in the Fifth Section that their pale religious views
could give no offense—even to liberal Catholics, Jews, and Freethinkers. On
the other hand, intransigent Roman Catholics could be ignored because
they could never win election to the Fifth Section.

This first subculture consisted of liberal Protestants who increasingly
turned toward the pursuit of positive theological agendas, all the while
without abandoning the positivist historical writing which was typical of
the Section from the days of its founding. This permitted the likes of Albert
Réville to speak of a discipline that was scientific, but also with the unmis-
takably imperious air of theology. Thus, the Liberal Protestant founders
spoke of "*the* science of religion" in the exclusive singular. In this, Albert
Réville merely reflected the ultimate origins of this odd combination of

scientific and theological programs pioneered by Friedrich Max Müller and his Dutch fellow-traveler (very influential among the Liberal Protestants of the Fifth Section), Cornelis P. Tiele. Max Müller's "science of religion" was committed to an *apologetic theological* program—a faith-guaranteeing search for evidence of a universal natural human religion—and at the same time, a search undertaken by the strictly "scientific" procedures of historical and philological scholarship of the day. When speaking in an historical idiom to the historians of his day, he would talk of uncovering empirical evidence pointing to the existence of a stage in human history dominated by a universal, primal, or natural religion—virtually identical in content to the beliefs of the French Liberal Protestants. In putting his views to psychological or philosophically minded thinkers, Max Müller would couch his arguments in terms of evidence of an innate religious mental faculty, a neo-Kantian religious *a priori*, if you will. One of its standard-bearers, Jean Réville, spoke accordingly of the "permanent needs and aspirations of religion in the human soul," echoing his father's similar sentiments concerning the religious *a priori* (Réville 1892, 516).

Such theologizing apologetics stirred little controversy at the time of the foundation of the Section for a number of reasons. First, as a variant form of the natural religion of Enlightenment Deism, it conformed to a major stream of secular religious thinking still alive and well among the unchurched elites of the Third Republic. With roots reaching as deep as the sixteenth century thought of Jean Bodin and carried forward into the modern age by many of the *philosophes*, the idea of a natural religion seemed (except for notable exceptions such as David Hume) self-evident. Such a natural religion was felt to supply the basis for morality, and thus for social stability—both desirable even in revolutionary periods. It was finally harmless, since unlike, say, Catholicism, it had little institutional basis and no clergy to conspire against the polity. How could the bourgeois humanism of the Third Republic find anything sinister in the "Fatherhood of God and the brotherhood of man"—a belief which was said to sum up the content of this tepid common faith? Albert Réville also believed in a common human religious evolutionary movement into which humanity was swept into a union with the divine presence. "In setting forth the intellectual and moral unity of mankind, everywhere directed at the same successive evolutions and the same spiritual laws, it brings into light the great principle of *human brotherhood.*" This common "evolution," in turn, forms a "basis of reason" for the "august sentiment of *divine fatherhood.* Brothermen and Father-God!—what more does the thinker need to raise the dignity of our nature . . . ?" (Réville 1905, 40–41).

But by the end of the century, the beginnings of a second more particularist Christian subculture formed primarily around Jean Réville, son of the Section's founder, Albert Réville. Reminiscent of some of our own postmodernist thinkers in religious studies, Jean Réville sought openly to bring theology—and even an explicitly Christian theology—into the Fifth Section as part of a then current revolt against positivism, all the while still giving lip service to science. In his day, for example, Jean Réville could declare "the greatest fidelity to the rigorous method of scientific history" (Réville 1886, 352). Yet, in virtually the same breath he also swore to go even further out on the antipositivist and apologetic limb of history writing in a series of pronouncements he made about the future of the history of religions (Réville 1892; Réville 1899; Réville 1901; Réville 1907; Réville 1909). Says Jean Réville: "Religious universalism, and I should add . . . Christian universalism—this is what the science of religion teaches modern society" (Réville 1892, 518). His break with the old pale Deism as well as the historicism and positivism dominant in the Fifth Section was part of a general dissatisfaction with the religious liberalism and historicism which we know came to a head in the *fin-de-siècle.* While leaders of this movement against historical positivism like Henri Berr and his new journal, the *Revue de synthèse historique,* sought a more self-consciously comparative, theoretical, and interdisciplinary sort of history, theologically inclined members of the Fifth Section like Jean Réville saw the rolling back of positivism as an invitation to Christian theologizing in the university (Boer 1998, 339–40; Keylor 1975, 125–40).

The story of Jean Réville's association with Henri Berr has it that the ever-entrepreneurial Berr commissioned an article from Jean Réville for the inaugural number of *Revue de synthèse historique* on the occasion of the First International Congress of the History of Religions in Paris in 1900 (Réville 1900, 211–3). Berr was to be proved right in his assessment of Jean Réville, given the plans Réville had already laid out regarding his own commitment to a thoroughly psychologized history reminiscent of Dilthey. Accordingly, with the target of the prestigious French practice of an *histoire*

parently in mind, the younger Réville asserted that the "histo-
iished his task until, with the aid of the testimonies which he
. ᴜᴏᴄɪved, he reconstitutes their exact tenor" (Réville 1907, 202). To Jean
Réville, the task of reconstructing the frame of mind of religious folk lays a
special burden upon the historian, and called forth, quite literally, a kind of
"methodological Methodism." As if reclaiming part of the vital Methodist
heritage of French Protestantism which we noted earlier, Réville says that
although he does not denigrate the many studies of religion done "from outside," one must now seek "the human soul" so that one can "find the underlying and true explanation of religious phenomena in the imagination,
heart, reason, conscience, instincts and passions" (Réville 1907, 203). Jean
Réville, however, died too soon thereafter to implement this new "methodological Methodism" into his otherwise strictly erudite history writings.

It was against these moves by the newly emboldened theologians, as
well as against the old positivism, that we might also speak of the beginnings of yet a third subculture consisting of the Durkheimians and their
sympathizers. Durkheimian efforts in the study of religion, along with their
attacks on the *science religieuse,* were just another part of their wholesale
quarrels with established disciplines like philosophy, psychology, history,
anthroposociology, and ethnography in the interests of establishing his
brand of sociology in France (Durkheim 1982, 175–240). Against Charles
Seignebos, a historian of great influence in the Fifth Section, for example,
Durkheim argued for a new look at the powerful claims of the discipline of
history against his own upstart sociology. Durkheim argued that history
was in effect a branch of sociology and not another "discipline" over
against sociology. How can they be opposed so exclusively when, in
Durkheim's view, sociology must always be historical (Durkheim 1975,
229). For Durkheim, sociology only differed from the old style erudite history practiced by most members of the Fifth Section in being both comparative and explanatory. So, sociology did the work of history even better
than history did itself.

Against the Liberal Protestant apologetic programs then launched in
the Fifth Section, the Durkheimians wished to establish a firmly naturalist
and societist foundation for the study of religion. Religion was not the special *a priori* inner extra-social something beloved of the theologians and
historians of Liberal Protestant persuasion. Religion was rather an eminently

social and human thing, and one demanding study with all the tools of positive science and scholarship. While the essentially unitarian and even innocuous religion of Liberal Protestantism underlying the *science religieuse* might have served in earlier times to ground the values of the Third Republic, that was no longer the case. For a host of reasons, notably the crisis of French nationalism of the *fin-de-siècle*, the Durkheimians felt that the individualistic and new sectarian notion of religion embodied in the liberal Protestant culture of the school, as expressed in the conception of the *science religieuse* prevailing there, would not fit out the nation for the dangers to France that lay ahead. With its Christian theological presumptions becoming more and more explicit in the pronouncements of influential figures like Jean Réville, the liberal religion articulated by the Liberal Protestants was not general enough to provide a moral center for the diverse Third Republic. Durkheim spent much of his adult life trying to articulate just what such a common moral system suitable for the Third Republic might be, and in doing so developed his well-known social notion of the nature of religion and the discipline of sociology fit for studying it and society at large.

5. Politics, "Sciences Religieuses," and Functionalism

What may surprise those unfamiliar with the ins and outs of the religious history of France is that the French should have pioneered disciplines devoted to the study of religion at all. Yet, the list of practitioners and institutionalized forms already mentioned gives the lie to this assumption. To their number we can also add Ernest Renan, Albert Réville, Georges Sorel, James Darmesteter, Jean Réville, Salomon Reinach, Sylvain Lévi, and others. On the institutional side, the foundation of the École Pratique des Hautes Études, Fifth (Religious Sciences) Section itself, a chair at the Collège de France and a world class academic journal, the *Revue de l'histoire des religions*, witness to the continued official national sponsorship of the study of religion since the middle of the nineteenth century. Today, this venerable institution houses some 48 established chairs within its halls. It is odder yet to think of a nation renowned for its anti-clericalism—at least among the modernizing elite of the republican regimes well known for their anti-clerical and dechristianizing zeal—to have chosen the leadership of the Fifth Section from a small subdiscipline within it, which went by the name of *science religieuse*. Yet, that is what this elite did. I have already suggested that the reasons for this are political. Let me conclude by filling out this story. It is like all political stories, a tale of control, regulation, and disciplining.

The need to control religion has a long history in France. Louis XIV's fear of national disorder caused him to seek control over religion. He felt that religious unity would function to promote the political unity the nation needed (Ravitch 1990, 21). A century or so later, Voltaire felt that it was in the interests of the state to maintain religion—but only in the interests of maintaining good order in the realm (Ravitch 1990, 52–53). Napoléon too assumed the same view of religion's political utility—even if that national religion was to be a traditional religion like Catholicism. His reasoning was complex. First, he, like the fathers of the French Revolution, felt that religion functioned better than any conceivable substitute for maintaining social order, thus for smoothing the way for trouble-free implementation of his own political goals. Furthermore, given the Catholic nature of France, it was simply more politic to sponsor it as the de facto religion of the realm than to seek to found a new religion. At any rate, obedience to the Emperor was the real "essence of religious obligation of the French subject and citizen" (Ravitch 1990, 58). This conviction repeated in so many different ideological contexts may help us understand why religion's *function* in society was defended so readily by later even anti-clerical tending figures from Renan to Durkheim. French social thought simply generalized from French political experience.

Behind the interests of the state, then, in disciplining and sponsoring the *study* of religion was their perennial political concern for order. Control over our *knowledge* of religion would inform our ability to control religion in the interests of the state. With social functionality in mind, it is then a short step to begin understanding how then a nation with such strong anti-clerical traditions among its elites might be among the leaders in sponsoring the discipline of the study of religion. It was only prudent that since religion did function in manifestly important ways in French society that those charged with obligation to the nation should well understand it. This spirit still prevails in today's France. It is no accident that France, with its large Muslim population, its former colonies in the

Muslim world, and its economic entanglements there today, should lead the world, if not Europe, in Islamic studies—much as the former Soviet Union had done and today's Russia still, to a large extent, does. In 1906, Jean Réville spoke with remarkable frankness in launching a spirited— functionalist—defense of the *science religieuse* as a way of getting intellectual purchase on the then troublesome intransigent Catholic opponents of the Third Republic. The "*science religieuse*," says Jean Réville, would notably serve the cause of liberal "tolerance" by "describing the rise and fall of all the various credos and dogmas that had been declared absolute and immutable" (Weisz 1983, 22–25).

6. Religion and Power in France

Given its particular traditions of state involvement in matters of education, it is therefore natural to think that in France, in order to speak about the academic culture or regime of an officially sanctioned discipline like the *science religieuse*, we need also to talk about political cultures or regimes at the same time. This point is cardinal because the kind of religion, in effect, officially established in the Fifth Section was Liberal Protestantism. Behind the discipline of *science religieuse* lies the uneasy history of the relation of religion—Roman Catholicism—and politics in France. From the time of Charlemagne, the religious and political forces of France have danced their little dance around each other. Religious forces have both shaped and been shaped by political ones; every political regime in French history has had in some way to contend with religion.

It is useful, then, to distinguish three levels at which politics has had to contend with religion. First, every regime in French history has had to take into account in one way or another the reality that the mass of its population consists of Catholics of varying degrees of faithfulness. This population supplies the social base of the persistently Catholic culture of the nation. It constitutes that vast population steeped in Catholic tradition, customs, and values, learned in churches, schools, and at the mother's breast. Even in periods of supposedly fierce dechristianization, such as the Revolution, recent studies have shown how much of the values and motivation of the Revolution itself, the quest for social justice prominent among them, were norms inculcated by the traditions of Catholicism

(Schama 1989, 349–50). Every regime, and in particular those like the Third Republic, perceived as antagonistic to Catholicism needed to find ways of allaying fears of repression or at least disguising them well enough to avoid out and out resistance to the state. A study of the decades-long struggle of the Third Republic to wrest control of education from the Catholic religious orders would reveal how protracted an effort this was (Partin 1969).

Second, at least since the reign of Louis XIV, the relation of "religion"— the organized church—to the state has been highly ambiguous. Even in periods where the political regimes have been regarded as dominated by "religion," the relation between religion and regime has more often than not been a constant tug of war in which throne and altar have alternately sought to pull the other under its domain of influence (Ravitch 1990). This is so no matter whether we consider "religion" to refer to the official ecclesiastical hierarchy or to one of the many religious orders or movements (Jesuits, Oratorians, Assumptionists or Jansenists) or lay organizations (Compagnie du Saint Sacrement) influential throughout French history.

At the risk of great, if not gross, generalization, I believe one can declare the state the eventual winner in this protracted struggle. Thus, for example, no matter how pious and popular the Jansenists may have been, nor how much the Bourbons took upon themselves the role of defenders of Catholicism against the Reformation, that did not stop Louis XIV from allying Catholic France with the Protestant powers against the Catholic Hapsburgs (Ravitch 1990, 21). Nor did Jansenist religious popularity do much to save Port Royal from suppression. Neither can we say that the fate of the even more redoubtable Jesuit order differed. While, from their position close to the Bourbon throne the Jesuits seemed to have been responsible for the demise of the Jansenists, royal suspicion of them by Louis XV effected their expulsion from France (Van Kley 1975). Similarly, no matter how much of a show of reconciliation with the Vatican Napoléon made, nor no matter how much his regime subsidized the salaries of the French clergy, in the end, these were calculating if not cynical attempts to bind religious forces to state policy in the compromising embrace of co-optation. This regular and successful employment of state power, whether by outright suppression or compromise, thus established a pattern of subordination of religion to politics in France that prevailed at least into the time when the discipline of *science religieuse* was established in France in the middle nineteenth century.

This then brings me to the third sense in which politics and religion are related—the very institutional foundation of the discipline of *science religieuse* at the École Pratique des Hautes Études, Fifth Section in 1886. Despite the great mass of French Catholic faithful in the population and the power, however compromised, of the Church, in France, the academic culture, and thus the *disciplinary* character of the *science religieuse,* was profoundly Protestant. Not only was the Fifth Section led by Liberal Protestants—a small minority in an already small (1½%) percentage of the national population—it continued to be led and staffed chiefly by Liberal Protestants into the early decades of the twentieth century when the Durkheimians made their appearance. Worse yet for the Catholics, the establishment of the study of religion in France was made at the expense of the Catholic faculties of the Sorbonne. With the creation of the École Pratique des Hautes Études, Fifth Section (*Section Sciences religieuses*) the Catholic faculties of theology were reconstituted outside the Sorbonne as the Institut Catholique.

Ostensibly, the official—and I think partly disingenuous—reason for banishing the Catholic faculties, while the Protestant Faculty of Theology stayed in place, was that the Catholics were charged with no longer performing their contracted (Napoléonic) roles of training clergy for practical ministry in parishes throughout France (Havet 1918, 188). They had instead constituted themselves as an agency for the production of knowledge about religion, but from a particularly Catholic perspective. Why this should matter to the government can, I believe, only be explained by the government's interest in controlling the production of knowledge about religion in the face of intransigent Roman Catholic dominance over the French church. It was thus not in the broad political interests of the Third Republic to foster this intransigent type of "Catholic" knowledge about religion, so to speak. Instead, the Third Republic seems to have decided it needed to seize authority over the most prestigious knowledge about religion always done, for *raisons d'état.* In the wake of the First Vatica‍ assertion of papal authority and with it the reinvigoration of t‍ gent and ultramontane parties in France, all hopes of liberal C‍ inance of the French church were by 1886 dead. Finding intransigent Roman Catholics impossible—not to mention unwelcome from the intransigents who clung to the restoration of monarchy through-out the century—the Third Republic acted in a perfectly expedient political way. They deprived the Catholics of hegemony over knowledge about religion and transferred it to a tiny faction of an already tiny portion (1½% of the total population) of France's religious communities—the extreme Liberal Protestants. The Third Republic was already regarded popularly as the "revenge of the Reformation," so the foundation of the Fifth Section, along lines laid out by leading extreme Liberal Protestant in their *science religieuse*, ought not to have surprised anyone.

The Durkheimians, with equally good credentials in the eyes of the anti-clerical Third Republic, were however never able to wrest control of the Fifth Section from the Liberal Protestants despite the Christian theological dalliances of the Révilles. The Liberal Protestant theological agenda itself, however, fell victim to larger historical trends outside their control. Both Révilles, father and son, died within months of each other, Albert in 1906 and Jean in 1908, and in doing so, effectively deprived the section of a theological articulation of the section's future. But, again contrary to what most present-day students of the social study of religion might imagine, the failure of the theological program of the Révilles did not at the same time pave the way for the triumph of the Durkheimians in the Fifth Section of the École Pratique des Hautes Études. In the Fifth Section, oblivion also awaited the Durkheimian project for a sociological study of religion. The Durkheimians were able to see only two of their number elected to the faculty of the Fifth Section during Durkheim's lifetime—Henri Hubert and Marcel Mauss—and these in 1900 and 1901. Further progress infiltrating the Fifth Section was effectively curtailed by the decimation of the Durkheimian "équipe" during the First World War, and the persistence of the òld historicism in the Fifth Section. In official circles, Durkheimian thought seemed to have attained influential levels only in the area of civic and moral education in the primary and secondary schools (Strenski 2002, ch 6). As the theological efforts of the Révilles died with them, the section then remained dominated by the old historicism of the Liberal Protestants, increasingly shorn of its once potent Deistic religious justifications. "Scientific" history had simply become common historical practice, even Roman Catholic historians, and thus no longer an ideologically charged issue between French Catholics and Protestants. The Durkheimians, on the other hand, became "sociologists."

In order for the Durkheimians to exert the kind of influence we recognize today, they had in effect to abandon the Fifth Section after fighting so hard to place their people in it. Instead, they created new official structures, such as the Institut d'Ethnologie, founded by Marcel Mauss and Lucien Lévy-Bruhl. Failing in attempts to create other institutions of this sort, the work of the Durkheimians was taken over by new schools of historians, such as the Annales group. While not formally associated with the Durkheimian équipe, they eagerly adopted the Durkheimian sociologizing lead and pioneered the ethnographic history of religion—history of religions "from the ground up," so to speak (Strenski 1993). The works of Marc Bloch on the social determinants of royal sacred healing or Lucien Febvre on the sociology of unbelief each reflect Durkheimian insights never so loyally followed up by the historians of the Fifth Section (Bloch 1989; Febvre 1982). Significantly, in order to do this new history of religions, the Annalistes eventually had to secure an institutional home outside the historicist Fifth Section in the relatively new Sixth Section. Here, the Annalistes established themselves and dominated research in a way in which the Durkheimians never did or could in the Fifth Section. It was then left to individuals such as Marcel Mauss (Hubert died prematurely in 1927), rather than institutions and disciplines, to pass on the Durkheimian torch. Louis Dumont's contributions to the study of religion in India, as well his latest work on modern ideologies, for example, all reflect the direct personal tutelage he enjoyed under Mauss (Dumont 1986). Durkheimian studies of religion first achieved their now familiar fame in England among the likes of Radcliffe-Brown or Evans-Pritchard (and students of theirs, like Mary Douglas). Dumont himself was moved to work in Oxford with Evans-Pritchard partly to reinforce the pre–World War Two Durkheimian trajectory of his thought. It is worth recalling that today we pay heed to the Durkheimians largely, but ironically, because in the late 1960's, Lévi-Strauss celebrated Marcel Mauss—(mis)leadingly as it happens—as a Lévi-Straussian structuralist before his own time. In fact, as Dumont shows, Marcel Mauss was in part committed to the same positivist l work pioneered by the Protestants and which would be a target Strauss's polemics against history for years. Thus, it was not Marcel i scholarly successes in the discipline of *science religieuse* as practiced in the Fifth Section which Lévi-Strauss celebrated in his years in the Fifth Section (Lévi-Strauss 1967, 7–11; Strenski 1987, 138–44). Instead, it was a mythical Marcel Mauss, fashioned in the service of advancing structuralism's prestige, which Lévi-Strauss holds up for admiration. Accordingly, although appointed to the Fifth Section as remote successor to Mauss, by way of direct succession to Mauss's student, Maurice Leenhardt, Lévi-Strauss took his first opportunity to flee the inhospitable disciplinary surroundings of the *science religieuse* of the Fifth Section for the independence of a chair outside standard French academic disciplinary boundaries in that home of the intellectual virtuosi, the Collège de France.

9

Liberal Protestant Theology and/or "Science Religieuse"

I shall argue that although theorizing religion in the turn-of-the-century Fifth Section was rare, a cryptic form of theologizing in its place was not. A subtle form of liberal Protestant theology informed much of the efforts in the study of religion of key members of the Fifth Section, such as Albert and Jean Réville. Despite their vociferous declarations in behalf of a so-called *histoire historisant* or "scientific history," the liberal Protestant leadership of the Fifth Section was thoroughly compromised by their theological ambitions (Keylor 1975, 52; Leroux 1998, 10). Thus, we are left with a paradox. While Albert Réville, for example, was celebrated for his "documentary interests" (Alphandéry 1906, 419) and Jean likewise reaffirmed "the greatest fidelity to the rigorous method of scientific history" (Réville 1886a, 352), both Révilles at the same time asserted their own theological orientations in the study of religion. In Jean Réville's words, "religious universalism, and I should add .... Christian universalism—this is what the science of religion teaches modern society" (Réville 1892, 518). In this paper, I wish to expose this vexing and seemingly contradictory development in the early years of the Fifth Section of a theologized religious studies within the *foyer* of dedication to a "scientific history" of religions.

Reprinted from *Ésotérisme, gnoses et imaginaire symbolique: Mélanges offerts Antoine Faivre* (eds.) R. Caron, J. Godwin, W. Hanegraaff, and J.-L. Viellard-Baron (Leuven/Louvain: Peeters, 2001), with permission of Peeters Publishers.

I. Vernes and the Historicism Too Historicist

Typical of the "scientific" way of doing history was Maurice Vernes, founder
of the *Revue de l'histoire des religions*, a member of the Paris Protestant theological seminary (from 1877) and a charter member of the Fifth Section in
the chair of biblical exegesis and the religions and history of the people of
Israel. Like many of his liberal co-religionists, Vernes's scholarly and personal religious life turned around with his encounter with the scientific history of nineteenth century German Protestant biblical scholarship of the
likes of Baur, Lücke, Weise, Zeller, and Strauss (Carbonell 1979, 61). But, after
a series of visits to the low countries and England to observe the comparative study of religions, Vernes extended his interest in biblical criticism to
the more general scientific history of religions. Of particular interest to
Vernes was how the Dutch had proposed as early as 1795 to replace the
teaching of theology with the history of religions. As editor of the *Revue de
l'histoire des religions* at this time, Vernes either commissioned the report of
van Hamel that appeared in the *Revue de l'histoire des religions*, or in some way
surely encouraged its publication (Van Hamel 1880, 379–85). Among other
points, Van Hamel mentioned that in the Dutch secondary schools, history
of religions occupies "first place" of honor in the curriculum (Van Hamel
1880, 385). So, we can conclude that its results would carry some weight with
the Fifth Section. For example, on becoming increasingly interested in the
prospects for a scientific study of the subject as pursued in the Netherlands,
Vernes sponsored other publications in the new field, notably among them
a French translation of the Dutch "morphologist" of religion, Cornelis P.
Tiele's significant work in this area of "scientific" endeavor, *Elements of the
Science of Religion* (Tiele 1877; Tiele 1896; Tiele 1898).

But the orthodox Protestants were ever watchful, and finally succeeded
in driving Vernes from his seminary post (Encrevé 1990, 91). Early in his
tenure at the Protestant seminary, the biblical literalists who dominated the
academic agenda attacked Vernes's critical or "scientific" historical studies
of the Christian scriptures. But they were even more enraged when Vernes
put theologizing to one side and urged that history of religions should be
taught as an "independent science" required of all students in the schools of
France. After being censured for denying the validity of the belief in divine
Providence in a public lecture, Vernes resigned his post. In 1880, he failed to

win the chair of history of religions at the École Pratique des Hautes Études, which subsequently went to Albert Réville. In the end, however, Vernes, like other disaffected Liberals, eventually moved over completely into the Fifth Section, where at first he found the security of an intellectual home which the Protestant Faculty would not provide. He remained there until his death in 1923.

Despite his arrival in the nominally more open Fifth Section, Vernes's woes had only begun. Hard upon his stormy departure from the Protestant Faculty, his work was attacked by his fellow Protestant Liberals in the Fifth Section! Chief among Vernes's attackers were the leaders of the Fifth Section—both Albert and Jean Réville—as well as the then liberal doyen of the Protestant Faculty of Theology at the Sorbonne, Frédéric Lichtenberger.[1] These erstwhile champions of the so-called "historical method" or "scientific history" laid an odd charge at the feet of their long-time colleague. In their view, Vernes's "scientific history" was just too scientific. Vernes's historicism was judged to be too historicist! His histories of religion, in the eyes of the Révilles and others, ended up being "positivist" catalogues of facts, exercises in "rigorous sifting" and "scrupulous" verification of data, and nothing more (Goblet d'Alviella 1885, 170–78; Réville 1886a, 349–57). Vernes shied away from discoursing on the meaning of the materials he studied according to the canons of the scientific historical craft of his day. Ironically, then, contrary to what we know about Liberal Protestant dedication to an ideal of "scientific" history, Vernes's practice of that very historicism put him into conflict with it. The Liberals wanted more. This "more" that the French liberal Protestants wanted was, I am arguing, theology. In this way, the French liberal Protestant attack on Vernes's historicism in the mid to late 1880's exposed these allegedly theory-free "scientific" thinkers as being deeply implicated in a theological effort all along.

Vernes was perhaps not totally surprised by such attacks from colleagues otherwise so close in fundamental beliefs about the study of religion. He warned of what he detected as an incipient theologizing tendency within the Fifth Section as early as the time of his arrival in the Fifth Section, in 1880. The Liberals, said Vernes, wished to insert what turned out to be theological "mental constructs" or models into the data, which had not themselves "emerged" from the "facts" (Goblet d'Alviella 1885, 174). For example, in place of a solid grasp of the Jewish historical context

of Jesus's thought, Vernes reproached the Liberals for projecting a model of
the moral man of the late nineteenth century onto the hapless Jesus. As a
result, in place of the at-first strange, yet nonetheless rich historical textures
of Jesus's Jewish life, the well-meaning Liberals had substituted an image of
themselves. They had just "read" Jesus along lines which were defined by a
theological "psychologism and subjectivism" reminiscent of the great nineteenth century German Protestant theologian, Friedrich Schleiermacher.
This resistance to psychological theology also put Vernes into conflict with
the Révilles, as we will see. Indeed, Albert Réville cites the great German theologian of the religious experience of absolute dependence favorably on at
least one occasion in his *Prolegomena of the History of Religions* [1881] (Réville
1884, 72). Somewhat later, toward the end of the century, we will see how
what thinkers like Vernes and his contemporaries called "philosophy"
would for a while again play a part in the development of a new style of
history and history of religions, under the inspiration of Henri Berr and
the Durkheimians, and to some extent by Jean Réville. Here to speak of
"philosophy's" role is simply to speak of a departure from the canons of
positivist history writing, and the acceptance of the privileged place
of prior presuppositions or models in writing historical narrative. François
La Planche reports that Vernes, in disgust at these theological maneuvers,
complained in his introduction to the first number of *Revue de l'histoire des
religions* that the typical Protestant "scientific" historian of religion "rarely
studies the past without some concern to discover its pet ideas in it" (Vernes
1880/1881, 10). Not for him such sectarian gambits: "we are definitely
not going to model [our approach] on them. The historian who doubles
as a dogmatist only produces a history which is suspect" (La Planche
1991, 94n10).

2. Evolution as Cryptic Theology

One of the chief liberal theological projections against which Vernes leveled his criticism was the idea of religious "evolution." Even though Vernes
no doubt was aware that the Liberals may not have thought that they were
violating the standards of "scientific" history in their view of evolution, he
was sure that they nevertheless were guilty of doing so. Vernes's assault on
liberal evolutionism provoked an angry exchange which in effect broke

relations between Vernes and the Liberal establishment. Albert Réville, for instance, believed in all honesty that the idea of the evolution "of humanity is not arbitrary." It reflected a "law of continuity" which applies to "successive evolutions of the human mind as to the animal and vegetable worlds" (Réville 1905, 4). In the minds of the Liberals, religious evolution was not then some "construct," "model," or "hypothesis" *projected* onto the data of religion. It was objectively "there." For them, evolution was the "quasi-certitude" which Belgian historian of religion Goblet d'Alviella had announced it to be—interestingly enough, aiming his words at the attack Vernes had launched on this very issue (Goblet d'Alviella 1885, 173).

For Vernes, however, the liberal view of evolution is "not at all historical," but only "reflects the ideological preferences of the historian" for a number of reasons which will no doubt strike readers today as remarkably compatible with our own principles. Vernes argued that in any religion in a given time, one could find simultaneously the representatives of the various stages of religious evolution which supposedly were lodged in discrete stages of historical evolution. Do we not, for example, find a kind of polytheism in the cult of the saints and Blessed Virgin in undeniably monotheistic Roman Catholicism? Does not any polytheist, when focused on a particular deity, at that moment not enter the spiritual frame of mind of the monotheist (La Planche 1991, 93)? Vernes thus rejected Réville's entire vision of a grand evolutionary march to monotheism up from animism, naturism, etc., which was, as well, characteristic of so much work by the French Liberal Protestant savants of the Fifth Section in the last years of the nineteenth century (Goblet d'Alviella 1885, 173). Weighing in with others against Vernes, Jean Réville argued that if the objectivity of religious "progress" were shaken this would have the intolerable result of placing all religions into the same developmental class. It is hard indeed to imagine a more damning admission of Vernes's accusations of the theological ambitions of the Liberal Protestant leadership (Goblet d'Alviella 1885, 173).

Despite the manifest (for us) merits of Vernes's criticism of liberal Protestant cryptic theologizing in the study of religion, his attack seems to have made no impact on the study of religion in the Fifth Section in his lifetime. Instead, his feuds with the Liberal Protestant leadership of the Fifth Section left him relatively isolated thereafter. The role of intellectual leadership belonged, as it had done from the creation of the Section, to the Révilles. Father and son continued to represent the Fifth Section in national and international professional worlds. Albert Réville conceived the International Association for the History of Religions and convened its first global meeting in Paris, 1900. Albert Réville was also France's representative several years before at the World Parliament of Religions in Chicago. Thus, at least, the most prominent members of the Fifth Section basically ignored Vernes's critiques of their thinking, and went on writing about religion as if religious evolution was the "quasi-certitude" which Liberal Protestant Goblet d'Alviella had said it was. When liberal evolutionism eventually faded—as evolutionism did everywhere—it apparently did not do so as a result of Vernes's polemics.

What this dispute between the Révilles and Maurice Vernes reveals is that the Liberals had gone far down the theological road, even while promising loyalty to "scientific history." The main question I wish to ask at this point is how this could be? Imagining for a while that the Liberal Protestants might be aware of this confusing mixture of orientations, how did they manage to justify such cohabitation of "scientific history" and theology to themselves? To answer this question, we might instructively look into the life and works of one of the chief Liberal Protestant thinkers of the Fifth Section who did: Albert Réville.

3.   Albert Réville, Tiele, and Comparative Study of Religions

The humanism and deistic rationalism of Réville's extreme liberal Protestantism led him, like Vernes, to surrender his ministry after a long career of ecclesiastical service. But Réville's professional life did not end there. The seeds of his often heterodox and dissident thoughts flowered into a new career in the study of religion. Much like Vernes, Réville too put to one side (although never fully abandoning) his original career as a biblical and ecclesiastical historian, and became his generation's leading exponent of the comparative study of religions, or "science religieuse," as this academic pursuit was known in its day. Along with this intellectual reorientation, Réville shifted institutional allegiance from church to university (Réville 1903, 432). It was in this role as president of their "Section" of the École Pratique des Hautes Études and as "secular" universitaire that Hubert and Mauss would have had to take seriously what Albert Réville said about sacrifice. But to understand Albert Réville's conception of the study of sacrifice we will have to understand the religion and scholarly projects of the one scholar who formed Réville's professional thinking about the study of religion more than any other, the Dutch scholar of religion, Cornelis P. Tiele.

In one of the only studies of significant length devoted to the thought of the Révilles, Franck Storne argues that by 1850 or so, Albert Réville had deepened his unitarian and rationalist commitments so much so that he found it necessary to surrender his ministry at the Temple Neuf in Luneray (west of Dieppe) (Storne 1985, 43–52). Storne, however, persuasively argues that we lack evidence to determine why Réville then left France for Rotterdam. Doubtless some mixture of political and religious causes might be cited, among which were probably Réville's desire to affirm his religious and political liberalism by association with the historically liberal Rotterdam church and those within its ambit, such as J. H. Scholten and Tiele (Storne 1985, 52). Réville worked abroad for twenty-two years in Holland, ministering to the needs of the expatriate French Protestant community in Rotterdam. There, in 1858, Réville first met Renan, who immediately invited Réville to use the pages of his *Revue des deux mondes* to sound out his liberal views to the French reading public (Storne 1985, 52). At the same time, perhaps also upon Renan's urging, Réville expanded his studies beyond the ancient Near Eastern and Christian worlds of his seminary training and ministry into the new field of the scientific study of religion then established in Holland (Storne 1985, 56). Réville and Renan enjoyed a veritable "parenté d'esprit" in matters concerning religion and politics (Reville 1860). Renan set an example moreover of how Réville might coexist with the Catholic majority of France, even though Réville was later to regard the Fifth Section as an "excellent engine of war for combating clericalism" —viz. Roman Catholicism (Storne 1985, 68). Renan's achievement was to persuade Réville that he could be both scientific and interested in religion, but that he need not provoke the suspicions of the Roman Catholic faithful in doing his scientific work (Réville 1889, x). Réville began publishing in the comparative study of religion in the late 1850's or early 1860's, focusing on the so-called primitive religions (Réville 1858; Réville 1862). But Réville did not undertake the fuller program of comparative study of religions until he met one of the modern founders of the field, Cornelis P. Tiele (1830–1902) (Réville 1902).

These two liberal Calvinists met in Rotterdam, where Tiele was pastor of the Remonstrant church. Albert Réville tells us that Tiele had been trained for the ministry by J. H. Scholten, a Leiden professor of theology who led the liberal so-called "modern theology" movement in Holland.[2] It was through these "modern theologians" that the new German methods of the critical study of the Bible arrived in Holland. In dogma, J. H. Scholten asserted that religion was a "natural fact and spontaneous tendency of human nature." It was thus not something "superadded," in Scholten's words, as he believed the Catholics held, still less a theoretical "construct" in language closer to our own time (Réville 1864, 280–81). Reminiscent of Rousseau's influence on the French Liberal Protestant movement, he also taught that human beings contained within themselves "the germ of a spiritual development, the objective ideal of which is God Himself" independent of any supernaturally originated special revelation (Réville 1864, 283). Because Scholten considered the existence of God a "fact," however exalted this "fact" might be, people could come to see and know God as He expressed Himself in and through His creation merely by contemplating the natural world with a pure and open heart.

For Albert Réville, Scholten's words reflected beliefs about the religious value of science long held by him.[3] Indebted as he was to Ernest Renan and the growth of the "scientific" historical disciplines in France, Albert Réville believed as well that "scientific" history of religions led its practitioners unerringly to the divine throne. What began in "scientific" history, then, ended in theology, indeed, in contemplation of the divine. Albert Réville held that historical research into the religions "purges" Christianity of the inessentials and moves its adherents closer to "the Eternal." It does so by revealing how humanity strives "towards the Supreme reality, mysterious, nay incomprehensible, and yet in essential affinity with itself, with its ideal, with all that is purest and sublimest." Thus for Albert Réville, the historical study of religion was religion itself; it was not only "one of the branches of human knowledge," but religious itself as well. Indeed, the very practice of the *history* of religions itself promotes a religious affiliation with Réville's *la religion*:

> in the domain of Religion . . . we can never lose our confidence that,
> if historical research may sometimes compel us to sacrifice illusions,

or even beliefs that have been dear to us, it gives us in return the right to walk in the paths of the Eternal with firmer step, and reveals with growing clearness the marvelous aspiration of humanity towards a supreme reality, mysterious, nay incomprehensible, and yet in essential affinity with itself, with all that is purest and sublimest. The history of religion is not only one of the branches of human knowledge, but a prophecy as well. After having shown us whence we come and the path we have trodden, it shadows forth the way we have yet to go, or at the very least it effects the orientation by which we may know in which direction it lies. (Réville 1905, 4–5)

This belief that the scientific study of nature and history would lead ultimately to direct experience of the transcendent had great, if finally destructive, repercussions for the study of religion. For Tiele and those like Albert Réville, since scientific activity led to spiritual vision, science and religion were complementary, and not opposed. Thus, while this meant that religious folk need not fear science, it also meant that theological claims could fairly intrude into the domain of science. Albert Réville sums up these sentiments eloquently, even though he seems totally oblivious to the barriers such a position would throw up to those not sharing his theism.

In virtue of his religious consciousness, man directly feels God, and even if he were to be the subject of a perpetual evolution, would never be able to avoid feeling Him. If we are able to admit the validity of this double method of finding God in nature and in the soul, I think that we may watch with perfect serenity all the progress, all the discoveries, all the transformations of science. If we open our eyes to the universe, God is there; and if we close them to look into our own nature, God is with us still. (Réville 1875, 242)

Given Vernes's severe scientific ethic, then, we can well appreciate his alarm as more and more of Albert Réville's theological orientation became apparent to him. Given Albert Réville's tender piety in these matters, we can likewise appreciate why his disputes with Vernes over the theologizing of the study of religion provoked such sharp clashes. The same applies to Durkheim's cautions about Albert Réville in a telling letter to Mauss. Referring to Albert Réville in most unflattering terms, Durkheim tells Mauss: "Don't do anything which might surprise or upset the old man. And, don't even bother to try to win him over" (Besnard & Fournier 1998, 292–93). As we will see later and at length, the Durkheimians well knew of Réville's theologizing of the study of religion, and sought to disestablish it within the Fifth Section.

While the precise origins of Albert Réville's so-called "scientific" theology are not totally clear, they match the general beliefs of key figures in close relation with Albert Réville—leaders of the so-called "science of religion," Friedrich Max Müller and Cornelis P. Tiele (Strenski 1996; Strenski 2005, ch. 4). In the context of Réville's own actual intellectual nurture, his mentor Tiele calls for special attention. At the very least, Tiele reinforces Réville's view that scientific—here meaning "historical"—research can have positive religious value, and not merely the negative demythologizing value typical of the French critics. Thus, says Albert Réville, historical criticism "should guide [our societies] in resolving the grave difficulties presented by the problems of the hour" and gets "us closer to 'the Eternal'" (Réville 1905, 4, 5). Given this conviction of the factual nature of the real presence of God immanent in nature, Tiele (and Réville) felt justified in referring to the study of religion as a "science of religion"—understood along the antitheoretical lines of nineteenth century positivism. Needless to say, others would find this odd blend of "reason" and "faith" a good reason to reject the assumption of scientific status by the so-called *science religieuse*.

In 1873, Tiele went on to become professor at the Remonstrant seminary in Leiden, and in 1877, professor of the history of religions at Leiden. Until his death in 1902, he maintained formal academic relations with the Fifth Section and the *Revue de l'histoire des religions*. Tiele's books were cited routinely in the *Revue*, with Albert Réville even publishing a French résumé of Tiele's *Inleiding tot Godsdienstwetenschap* in installments over a period of four years—apparently in lieu of a critical review which never appeared in the pages of the *Revue de l'histoire des religions* (Réville 1897). With Tiele, Réville seems also to have begun to taken on the study of the so-called "primitive" religions—however ironic, as we have seen, his attitude to them was. These interests emerged later in a notable public debate with William Gladstone over the nature of "primitive religion." There Réville argued that the primal religious sensibilities of the "primitives" were "natural" and not the result of any extraordinary divine intervention or revelation.

And as such, they were open to scientific study. With Charles Renouvier and other partisans of what we might call "natural religion" or the kind of deistic rationalism described in the previous chapter, Réville believed that the "primitives" were inherently endowed with a "moral sense" of God's existence. The problem was, however, that the "primitives" often seemed grossly deficient in adhering to this natural morality, as evidenced by their gruesome sacrificial rites (Réville 1884, ch. 3). In the course of his long career as historian of religions Albert Réville wrote many articles as well as several general surveys of so-called primitive religion (Réville 1883), and some specialized books on the religions of the world, such as "the religion" of Mexico and China (Réville 1885; Réville 1886b).

4. Tiele and Theory: Morphology Becomes Theology

Now, unlike the French pioneers of the study of religion, Renan and Vernes, the "philosophical" Tiele was committed, institutionally or otherwise, neither to historicism nor even to the writing of historical narrative. Because of Tiele's strong influence on Albert Réville, he no doubt was responsible for steering Albert and Jean Réville in a conceptually more constructive direction.[4] In 1881, in the same address in which he spoke in favor of "scientific" history, Albert Réville in effect distinguished his approach from Vernes's positivism in asserting the creative role of the historian in theorizing and concept formation. The historian's task is "to choose in this mass of [data] the typical facts, the "standard facts" which reveal [their] spirit—the true originality of a definite religious state" (Réville 1883, iv). As Tiele sought the underlying forms of historically variant religions, Albert Réville argued in the same address for an investigation into the hidden laws governing religious phenomena. Specifically aiming his remarks against Tylor's view of traditional folk as "primitive philosophers," Réville urged those studying the religions in a direction very different from that of Vernes. In the "non-civilized," they should "study and admire in them, their involuntary and unconscious brainwork—the internal logic of the human spirit, though yet uncultivated, no doubt following its own guiding principles and workings, and revealing that unthinking logic in their religions and religious practices" (Réville 1883, 24).

Tiele thus was a generation in advance of the anti-positivist revolution in French historiography of the end of the century (Keylor 1975, chs. 8–10). As Tiele put it, the study of religion should be truly *scientia* and not merely *eruditio*. To him, this meant a departure from the historical positivism of a Renan or Vernes; such a study sought to take hold of religious phenomena and "penetrate to their foundations" (Tiele 1896, 15). Tiele then moved well beyond the realm of brute data, by actively encouraging the efforts which theory always makes to explain phenomena in terms of causes at another strategic level than what is given. Calling this approach also "literally the philosophy of religion," Tiele quite explicitly rejects the "onesided empirical method which culminates in positivism and only ascertains and classifies facts, but is powerless to explain them" (Tiele 1896, 18). Tiele even called for a "deductive method" of the study of religion, one which while not "speculative . . . starts with the results yielded by induction, by empirical, historical and comparative methods" (Tiele 1896, 18). Tiele thus began from a perspective at odds with the critical or positivist history practised by Renan, Maurice Vernes, or, for that matter, probably even Albert Réville at the time they met in the 1860s.

Sadly enough for those who seek to keep theology from a place within the "science religieuse," Tiele's new anti-positivist approach to religion tended in just the same theological direction as we have seen in the work of Albert and Jean Réville. I refer here to Tiele's work on religious "morphology" (Tiele 1896). Tiele's "morphology" flew in the face of positivist canons of historiography which dominated the study of religion in France in at least three ways. First, Tiele presumed an evolutionist model of religious development behind the data, in effect, at a theoretical level. His "morphology" of religions sought the "constant changes of form resulting from an ever-progressing evolution" (Tiele 1896, 27). Second, in doing his morphological classification and ranking of the religions, Tiele offended positivism by claiming access to the general species of religion which lay below the chronological surface flow of the data and facts of the many "religions."

However, the "morphology" of the first volume of his great work, *The Elements of the Science of Religion* (evolution and morphology), prepared the way for the second volume and its "ontology" (in truth, just a "theology") of religion-as-such. There, Tiele enjoyed access to the "permanent elements within what is changing, the unalterable element in the transient and ever-altering forms" (Tiele 1896, 27). Having completed the evolutionary ranking of "religions" over against the transcendent standard of *la religion*, Tiele emerged to advocate a sophisticated, if nonetheless transparent, theological program. The putative "scientist" of religion, Tiele, and with him in varying degrees, the Révilles, was more than just a naturalist critic of positivism, but in fact a man of faith seeking to found a new theology.

10

The Durkheimians and the Protestants in the École Pratique, Fifth Section

The Dark Side

In spite of the picture recent commentators, such as Laurent Mucchielli, have tried to paint of cordiality and cooperation between the Durkheimians and the French liberal Protestant leadership of the *Revue de l'histoire des religions* and the École Pratique, Fifth Section (Albert Réville, Jean Réville, Léon Marillier) (Mucchielli 1998), I believe the situation was virtually the opposite. Instead of unity, I argue that profound underlying tensions disturbed the otherwise placid surface of civility of relations between the French liberal Protestants and the Durkheimians in the late nineteenth and early twentieth centuries. These tensions were fed by the continuing attempts of the French liberal Protestants to persist in confessional theologizing and Durkheimian distaste for it. Yet, rarely, if ever, did this opposition emerge into public view, although they were very much there for the sleuthing eye to detect.

Expressions of antagonism were characteristically reserved for confidential communications, some of which are only now coming to light (Besnard & Fournier 1998; Fournier 1994). In a letter of 1901, Marcel Mauss referred to "the Protestants" as a political bloc against whom it would be wise to guard, since they acted in concert for their own sectarian interests to promote, in this case, their own candidates for positions in the Fifth Section (Fournier 1994, 192). As early as 1898, and thus while still students

Reprinted from *Durkheimian Studies/Etudes Durkheimiennes* 6 (2002):105–14, with permission of the General Secretary and Co-Director of the Durkheim Press.

in the Fifth Section, still several years before they won their posts there, Henri Hubert wrote a remarkable note to Marcel Mauss revealing the hidden antagonisms of the Durkheimians toward the liberal Protestants. In this letter, Hubert tells Mauss how thoroughly he relishes the mischief their "polemics" would spread among the religious powers of the day— meaning perhaps both the Liberal Protestants holding sway in the Fifth Section as well perhaps as the Roman Catholics so vocal in public affairs bearing on religion. Hubert tells Mauss how we "shouldn't miss a chance to make trouble for these good, but badly informed, souls," and concludes with a conspiratorial call to arms: "Let's go! I love a fight!" (Fournier 1994, 151). Far from being isolated instances, we also now know how Durkheim had long plotted to maneuver his "men" into positions of power in the Fifth Section. We also learn from another recently available letter that Durkheim had directed Marcel Mauss, then interviewing Albert Réville, the Section's president, for a chair in the Fifth Section, to conceal his sociological agenda in order to smooth his entry into the Section. Dated November 1901, Durkheim wrote Mauss:

My dear Marcel,

A few words in haste, since I am very busy today.

I'm so happy with the news you passed on. Regarding your visit tomorrow with (Albert) Réville: just watch out for yourself! Don't do anything which might surprise or upset the old man. And, forget about trying to win him over. The important thing is that you don't give him any reason to think ill of you. Let *him* run the conversation, and don't pressure him. You're there so he can get to know *you*, not so that you can preach to *him*. It will get you nowhere if he knows exactly what you do, and what methods you employ. In fact, if he asks you about these, just answer as simply and cleverly as you can. E. D. (Besnard & Fournier 1998, 292–93)

Thus, in and around the Fifth Section, relationships were calculated and political to a high degree instead of constituting anything one might call a "zone d'influence" (Fournier 1994, 187n2). Indeed, I would argue that the Durkheimians were routinely, deliberately, and systematically devious in their relations with the Liberal Protestants in charge of the *Revue de*

l'histoire des religions and Fifth Section. One can well come to another conclusion given that the then upstart Durkheimians never publically attacked the positions of the major liberal Protestant members of the Fifth Section. They only did so after Hubert and Mauss had safely won their chairs in the Fifth Section and thus attained a degree of security against counterattack. Until Hubert and Mauss gained their footholds in the Fifth Section, the Durkheimians diverted their critical fire onto the Dutch Protestant co-religionists associated with the Révilles, Cornelis P. Tiele, and Pierre Daniel Chantepie de la Saussaye. The Révilles and Tiele shared common religious affiliations with the Remonstrant wing of Calvinism (Réville 1864, 275–77).[1] Thus, an attack on Tiele or Chantepie de la Saussaye, for example, would serve the same polemical strategy as an attack on the Révilles—to expose the unfitness of theological discourse for the public realm in a secular state. It would do so, however, without risking the potential acrimony an attack on another French scholar would provoke. Focusing attacks on the Dutch instead of the French seems to have kept matters civil, thanks to a certain level of Durkheimian prudence.

As Durkheim's letter to Mauss shows, the Durkheimians were keen to avoid being targeted as enemies by the very men who controlled their academic careers in the Fifth Section. Such direct attacks would surely have sunk the candidacies of Hubert and Mauss for the chairs which they avidly sought in the Fifth Section. Indeed, the radical reputations of Hubert and Mauss had already begun to circulate when Hubert and Mauss were pursuing their candidacies, and appointment there would be anything but sure. We will shortly examine Jean Réville's testy review of an early work of Hubert's, showing how hostile the Liberal Protestants could be to the antitheological intentions of the Durkheimians.[2] But, as we will see, the Durkheimians succeeded in passing the tests for their admission into the Section. Once the Durkheimians were safely ensconced in the Section, though, they put political prudence aside and attacked the subtle theologizing carried on under the name of *science religieuse* by the Liberal Protestants.

This strategy becomes clear when we note the disparity between Mauss's rather soft criticism of the work of the great Liberal Protestant scholar Auguste Sabatier *before* he had won appointment to the Fifth Section and a sharply critical attack on Sabatier which followed shortly thereafter. In

1898, before election to the Fifth Section, Mauss complimented Sabatier's *Esquisse d'une philosophie de la religion* for having put the "social and external character of dogma into bold relief" (Karady 1968, 535). He likewise passes over the theologian's treatment of primitive religion. But in his never completed PhD thesis, *La Prière* (1909) he calls Sabatier's treatment of primitive religions "cavalier" (Mauss 1909, 535). Similarly in 1898, Mauss politely notes about Sabatier that the "preoccupations of the soul sincerely burning with his religious faith compromises the uses of method here" (Karady 1968, 531). Yet, from the security of his post in 1909, Mauss damns Sabatier's entire discussion of prayer as "predetermined by the faith of the author" (Mauss 1909, 375). In 1909 Mauss also notes that Sabatier's progressivist story of religious evolution is "broad and facile . . . (Mauss 1909, 536). It is a matter less of analyzing facts than of demonstrating the superiority of the Christian religion" (Mauss 1909, 375).

I.   Hubert and Mauss against the "Science of Religion"

The French liberal Protestants had certain clear ideas about what religion was. For them, it was essentially spiritual and internal, largely a matter of personal experience and individual moral conscience. As budding "sociologists," the Durkheimians, on the other hand, could hardly have thought differently about religion, and thus about sacrifice. Most of these points of difference emerged in the Durkheimian critical writing about the Dutch scholars of religion, Cornelis P. Tiele and Pierre Daniel Chantepie de la Saussaye (Van Hamel 1880).[3] Rejecting Tiele's psychologizing of religion, Mauss felt that since religion was at the very least a human thing, and since humans were social, the social dimension of religion was just as likely (if not more so in his case) to be "essential" to the nature of religion as any sort of mental state (Karady 1968, 547). Referring explicitly to Tiele, Mauss argued that when "one tries to reach . . . [key religious facts] at one go, by simple introspection, one just substitutes one's own prejudices, personal impressions and subjectivity for the things one wants to understand" (Karady 1968, 548).

This turning from realism to subjectivism by Tiele and the Révilles in Durkheim's time was in a way extreme, even by Protestant standards. As Jones has shown us, Durkheim had been full of praise for what he took to be the original Protestant contribution to the formation of just the sort of realism he had admired among German scholars—the practice of studying "things" (Jones 1999, 66–68). Durkheim's French liberal Protestant contemporaries had apparently lost their way from what could have been the salutary beginnings of a real "*science religieuse.*" Instead, it turns out to have been the Durkheimian role to reassert early Protestant "realism" by way of their study of society and their sense of that study as a study of "things." Only in this way could one help provide our introspections and subjective feelings with some sort of external check, and thus achieve something worth of the name "*science religieuse.*"

On top of its subjectivism, Tiele's psychological approach to religion was also bedeviled by its apologetic purpose and structure. Tiele made no secret of this. From "the inmost depths of our souls," he said, religion radiates a "power . . . which the assaults of the keenest of the adversaries of religion with the keenest shafts of their wit, with all their learning and eloquence, . . . are in the long run unavailing and impotent" (Tiele 1898, 24). Religion therefore dwelt in the secret recesses of "the heart"—an impregnable and autonomous fortress fashioned by the liberal Protestant piety of the day, thus rendering it ultimately resistant to inquiry (Tiele 1898, 14). Quite naturally, the Durkheimians concluded that Tiele's assertion of the privileged autonomy of religion simply exposed the confessional theological nature of his entire discourse of religion. Science had no way inside this kind of religion. When Tiele spoke of this "interior God," concluded Mauss, "he truly seems to be teaching a theology" (Karady 1968, 547). Such a conception of religion, said Mauss, "retiring more and more from social and material life in order to take refuge in the individual conscience" simply made the study of religion impossible (Karady 1968, 544).

2. Against Chantepie de la Saussaye

Having done with C. P. Tiele, the Durkheimians took on Tiele's countryman, Pierre Daniel Chantepie de la Saussaye. They did so, however, in a way which was deliciously devious. In 1897, Chantepie de la Saussaye published the second edition of his lengthy 1887–1889 "phenomenological" handbook of the world's religions under the title, *Lehrbuch der Religionsgeschichte* (Chantepie de la Saussaye 1897). Interested as they were not only in new data about religion, but also about novel ways of studying it, in 1904, Henri Hubert and Isidore Lévy gathered a team of translators to produce a French edition of this massive work, under the title *Manuel d'histoire des religions* (Chantepie de la Saussaye 1904).

Durkheimian sponsorship of de la Saussaye was not, however, as innocent as it seemed to be at first glance. The Durkheimian project was shot through with disingenuous political purpose. While nothing at all was controversial about the avowed public purpose and content of the translation of the text itself, the Durkheimian use of it was Hubert wrote a most peculiar introduction to the volume, taking much of its *forty-three* pages severely to attack many of Chantepie de la Saussaye's main theses! In fact, the book was so problematic, said Hubert, that it would be "useless to remake it" (Hubert 1904, v). Adding insult to injury, Hubert then turned de la Saussaye's *Manuel* into a vehicle for laying out the main lines of a Durkheimian "manifesto" for religious studies (Berr 1906, 18; Goblet d'Alviella 1913, 195). Noting, for example, that Chantepie de la Saussaye, like Tiele, had wedded the study of religion to a theologized introspective psychology, Hubert reasoned that Chantepie de la Saussaye's work rested squarely on things which could not be "known," but relied on acts of faith. The only path to redemption for this putative "science of religion," said Hubert, was "to extirpate the unknowable from its domain and to ban theology from it as well" (Hubert 1904, xix). Thus, deep in the heart of a putatively "scientific" project was a clear confessional agenda—and one which Hubert made it his business to expose and exploit for Durkheimian purposes. In so using Chantepie de la Saussaye's book to bolster Durkheimian ideas, Hubert had then simply "hijacked" the *Manuel* and "drove" it off to do Durkheimian work.

3. Jean Réville

Within the otherwise clubby confines of the Fifth Section, Hubert's translation and introduction in particular created a major flap, showing how serious were the conflicts between the Durkheimians and the Protestants. That Hubert should undertake this project was no surprise, since we already know how concerned the Durkheimians were about breaking with historicism by promoting a comparative study of religions informed by the critical study of categories and religious morphology.[4] Yet, as Hubert had promised in his letter to Mauss of 1898, he had something much more "mischievous" in mind in commissioning the French translation of Chantepie de la Saussaye's book (Fournier 1994, 152). Not surprisingly, Liberal Protestant reactions to Hubert's treatment of Chantepie de la Saussaye were unfriendly indeed for what was an age of rather gentlemanly academic discourse. The "bite" of the Durkheimians upon the "*science religieuse*" was apparently beginning to be felt. There was doubtless as well a sense of personal betrayal. Despite his Catholic family background, Hubert showed much the same profile of intellectual orientations as many of the French Liberal Protestants. Hubert had been *agrègée* in the "Protestant science" of history, a past contributor to Protestant Gabriel Monod's *La revue historique*, and a model of historicist erudition. The French Liberal Protestants of the Fifth Section may well then have felt betrayed by one they counted as their own. Hubert's attacks on the public and scientific pretensions of the Liberal Protestant "*science religieuse*" could not be avoided or totally ignored.

In 1905, a leading figure in Liberal Protestant circles, Jean Réville, took direct aim at Hubert's critique of Chantepie de la Saussaye's theological approach to the study of religion in a featured review in the *Revue de l'histoire des religions*, the official organ of the Fifth Section (Réville 1905, 75–82). There, Jean Réville barely seems to be able to control his rage, as Réville's biographer noticed. The biographer singled out Jean Réville's review of Hubert's "Introduction" as "one of the rare doctrinal statements" which Réville made during his career (Goblet d'Alviella 1913, 197). An intimate of the faculty of the Fifth Section, the Belgian historian of religion Goblet d'Alviella confirmed these bad feelings among the Protestant faculty created by Hubert's "Introduction." Reporting this without ascription, Goblet noted that certain unnamed *esprits chagrins* (apparently, Jean Réville) had "reproached" (Goblet d'Alviella 1913, 195) Hubert for having misrepresented Chantepie de la Saussaye's historical work, making of it in the process a "veritable manifesto . . . of neo-sociology" (Réville 1905, 78).

Goblet d'Alviella's aggrieved mood fit well the tenor of Réville's angry review. In a word, "doctrinaire" was how Jean Réville described Hubert's imposition of a sociological notion of religion onto Chantepie de la Saussaye's book—the furthest thing of course from the Dutch theologian's mind (Réville 1905, 81). Without arguing the particular merits of the

Durkheimian claim, Jean Réville simply vented his fury against the Durkheimians for making society central and essential to religion, over against his own Protestant belief that religious experience and "religious individuality" constituted the essence of religion (Langle 1991, 5). Thus, Hubert's assertion of the social nature of religion as well as his attack on the Protestant doctrine of the privileged interiority of religious life brought out into the open how Protestant "theorizing" about religion was really theology, how it remained a private discourse of an admittedly liberal religious confession rather than the makings of a language for speaking in the public arena about religion. And so the lines of battle were sharply drawn between Liberal Protestant theology and Durkheimian theory. Perhaps this was where Hubert was fulfilling his promise to Mauss that we "shouldn't miss a chance to make trouble for these good, but badly informed, souls . . ." (Fournier 1994, 151). Whatever else he had done, by making a public issue of Protestant theologizing of the *science religieuse*, Hubert had certainly made his share of "trouble" for the universalist pretensions of these "good, but badly informed souls" of the Fifth Section.

4. Durkheimian "Foxes" and Protestant "Lions" in the Fifth Section

One could go on and spell out other examples of the profound, yet concealed, antagonism between the Durkheimians and the French liberal Protestants of the École Pratique, Fifth Section and *Revue de l'histoire des religions*, such as the struggles of Hubert narrowly to win his chair in the Fifth Section over Protestant objections. But this would tax us with too much to explore and analyze in full for this short chapter, which at any rate I have mapped out in detail in my *Theology and the First Theory of Sacrifice* (Strenski 2003, 165–71). Suffice it to say, it was only after several rounds of voting that Hubert got the minimal "relative majority" (seven of thirteen voting) rather than the "absolute majority" of the total membership (eight of the fourteen-member Fifth Section) necessary for clear election (Anon 1901a; Anon 1901b; Strenski 2003, 165–71). Arrayed conspicuously against Hubert were Albert Réville, Jean Réville, Léon Marillier, Eugène De Faye, and Georges Raynaud. The intensity of this struggle among scholars of religions should then give the lie to Laurent Mucchielli's unduly eirenic characterization of the relationships between the French Liberal Protestants of the Fifth Section and the Durkheimians. It seems to me wrong for Mucchielli to speak of "la communauté des historiens des religion" and still more mistaken to speak of the manner in which this supposedly cordial relationship can be said to "souligne la relative facilité avec laquelle" the Durkheimians, Hubert and Mauss, "ont pu pénétrer d'autres reseaux institutionnels." The institutional "penetration" of the Durkheimians into the Fifth Section was, as I have argued, anything but "facile."

And whatever anyone else at that time or now may think, the Durkheimians were keenly aware of this, and of the gravity of their institutional triumphs. Thus, elated by Hubert's election against such odds and through such trials, Durkheim shared his delight with his young collaborator for what he saw as a political and institutional victory for "sociology." "In general, it is not without interest that sociology has now penetrated the École Pratique des Hautes Études. For, even if this time [the term "sociology"] . . . does not appear on the [official] posters [announcing courses and faculty], it is really there in this choice of [you] and in your personal presence there. Now, those are reasons to celebrate!" (Fournier 1994, 185–86). The main point to underline in reviewing how the Protestants and Durkheimians differed on the study of religion is how this academic debate spoke to the question of the nature of public discourse about religion in a religiously diverse society. Not only did the struggles between the Durkheimians and the Protestants involve careers and national and global prestige, but their outcome would also attempt to influence the shaping of national policies of moral and civic education, and the way religion would be conceived in the public domain. These were matters about which neither the Durkheimians nor the French liberal Protestants invited interference in the plans they were hatching for the nation. On the Protestant side, Jean Réville planned for a "scientific theology" to assume its place in the realm of public higher education (Réville 1899, 412). So apparently emboldened was he by the prospects for success for such a program in "Catholic" and secular France that Jean Réville asserted his theological ambitions in baldly Christian terms. In Jean's words, "religious universalism, and I should add . . . Christian universalism—this is what the science of religion teaches modern society" (Réville 1892, 518). Sad to say, we will never know exactly what the explicit theologizing of the history of religions would have entailed for public education in France. Nor will we enjoy the polemics of the actual public debate which its implementation would have excited: Jean Réville's new effort to theologize the study of religion was cut short by his premature death. On the Durkheimian side, however, the French educational establishment went some distance in implementing a Durkheimian scheme for teaching civic morals in the schools, which both its Catholic and rightist critics called equally well dogmatic and religious as anything a traditional religious community would have produced (Halls 1996, 124, 126). Such charges generally failed to carry against Durkheim's efforts at moral education until the Vichy regime came to power in 1940 (Halls 1996, 129–30). Recognizably, if not explicitly, Durkheimian manuals of civic morals were used by teachers of civic morals in the schools for decades prior to the time that the Vichy government took control of French education (Hesse & Gleyz 1922, 139). But the whole story of the fate of the Durkheimian effort is beyond the scope of the present chapter and must wait for another occasion to relate its fortunes (Halls 1996).

PART FIVE

Politics and Pedagogy Today

11

Durkheim Sings

Teaching the "New Durkheim" on Religion

I. The New Durkheim   -]√ *Zeitlin* ?

As a combined undergraduate philosophy and sociology major, with special interests in religion, at the University of Toronto, I had been dunned with the standard orthodox drill about Durkheim. He was a dull and uncomplicated combination of old-fashioned "scientist"—the number-crunching positivist of *Suicide* or *The Division of Labor in Society*—and head-in-the-clouds theorist—the hopelessly metaphysical Idealist of *The Elementary Forms of the Religious Life*. His over-generalized and reified concept of Society put him into a theoretical Never-Never Land and out of touch with the particularities of the diversity of societies and certainly their detailed histories. Yet, as a classic "Great Man," he single-handedly created sociology and pioneered the sociology of religion. In terms of religion, however, not much was there to be learned, since he crudely reduced "God" to "Society" and flew in the face of everything believers said about their own experience of religion. In terms of his underlying vision of human life, morality, and the like, he "misplaced" the "concreteness" of the individual and imagined that Society—writ large—itself was some kind of "thing." As a stiff and naive moralist, he had his mind fixed only on the problem of social order which, above all things, he sought to maintain in classic conservative, if not statist, ways.

Reprinted from *Teaching Religious Studies* (ed.) Terry Godlove (New York: Oxford University Press, 2004), with permission of Oxford University Press.

With the publication in 1974 of Steven Lukes's *Émile Durkheim: His Life and Work*, however, a new Durkheim came into focus. A new generation as well of historical reappraisal and study was initiated into the life and works of Durkheim, the benefits of which we are only now a quarter century later beginning to reap. Here, Durkheim is located within the context of his real life and times, and not tailored to fit the needs of theorizing in the social sciences, such as quantitative sociology, or the dogmas of mainstream ideologies, such as bourgeois individualism.

This historical re-evaluation of Durkheim has resulted in a new view of the great thinker, departing substantially from the received view dominant in the human sciences since the mid-1950s. It became clear from the work following in the wake of Lukes's great work that, far from working alone in the splendid isolation typical of history's "Great Men," Durkheim presents us with a paradigm of collaborative multifaceted scholarship. In the France of the late nineteenth and early twentieth centuries, Durkheim had assembled a "team" of research round the periodical he had founded in 1897, the famous *Année Sociologique*. At the center of this active "team" of collaborators in the cross-cultural and comparative study of societies, he directed research across a wide range of subjects unequaled in the history of the human sciences for the real collective work it embodied. He emerges as a thinker still alive to the problems of philosophy, respecting the status of the historical sciences, even as he sought to transform them. While seeing sacredness resident in the interaction of human beings in collective enterprises, Durkheim was alert to the sacrality and importance of the individual in society—as witness by his singular defense of Dreyfus in the face of the conservative political forces of his day. Far from being a simplistic sociological reductionist, Durkheim was always the eclectic: he was as active in thinking about the social nature and function of religion in society as he was in exploring the moral or religious nature of society. All the while, Durkheim was a passionate and thoughtful progressive thinker as skeptical of communism or socialism, patriotic jingoism or mob rule as he was of the myths of an abstract and selfish individualism embodied so thoroughly in classic utilitarian economic ideology and in many of the social arrangements connected with the market mentality.

How then could and should this "new" Durkheim be taught in religious studies?

2. "The Problem of Religion" and the Causes of Religious Experience

I speak from the experience of having taught Durkheim for the past six years in a one-quarter undergraduate course called "The Problem of Religion" (RLST 100) at the University of California, Riverside, and for some years previously at both University of California, Santa Barbara, and Los Angeles.[1] Parenthetically, I might add that this course has been taught for the past six years as an interactive videoconference course tying together the Davis and Los Angeles campuses of the University of California system. In terms of content and authors read, RLST 100 ranges from the theorists and advocates of what has been variously called "natural religion," Jean Bodin and Lord Herbert of Cherbury, through the classic "naturalist" thinkers of religious studies, such as David Hume, Friedrich Max Müller, E. B. Tylor, J. G. Frazer, Sigmund Freud, Max Weber, Robertson Smith, Gerardus van der Leeuw, Ninian Smart, Mircea Eliade, and Emile Durkheim. Of each figure introduced, I ask how they have "problematized" religion, how have they made a problem for religion?

Although this array of thinkers might signal the stock "methods and theories" course, "The Problem of Religion" is far from it. It is my view that these so-called "methods and theories" courses are in reality "wannabe" analytic philosophy of religion courses. One takes the theoretical views of the founders and considers them solely as collections of arguments and for the sake of their arguments. The propositions in these arguments are then analyzed critically to determine their viability. The two most likely results of the "wannabe" philosophical approach are the Tool Box and Prince Charming. As "Tool Box," one regards most or all of the contributions of the classic thinkers as having some utility, like the variously useful items collected in a good box of tools. These Tool Box "methods and theories" courses in principle never come to a single conclusion as to the best theory or method sufficient to guide students in their work. Pragmatic in its outlook, the Tool Box approach finds bits of each theory or method of potential use. So, when one needs theoretical help, one just dips into one's "Tool Box" of theories to pick out the one, or the parts of one, most useful to the particular task to hand. All the theories are right in their own ways and for their own purposes. On the other hand, with the Prince Charming alternative, we meet the "methods and theories" course as ideology. Here, the instructor is wedded to a certain single theoretical approach and seeks in this way and that to vindicate it. The

"Prince Charming" method and theory courses then become elaborate con-
trivances aimed at showing how a true theory thankfully arrives amidst all
the other benighted wrong ones littering the history of past theorizing. Thus,
when treated as philosophy, these "methods and theories" courses become
either forays into the Tool Box or quests to crown Prince Charming.

As its title, "The Problem of Religion," indicates, RLST 100 seeks to show
how religion has been "problematized" in the course of the study of religion.
If anything, RLST 100 is much more a history of the study of religion, built
around the notion of religion becoming a problem for Western thought than
an attempt critically—acontextually or abstractly—to decide or pronounce on
the truth or falsity of various approaches to the study of religion. What historical conditions have led thinkers to see religion as a "problem"? Thus, the
main question guiding RLST 100 is not whether a given conception of religion
or its study is true—although these questions can and should be enter-
tained—but why the thinkers in question *thought they were right* in speaking
and thinking of religion as they did. Why did this array of classic thinkers
bother to interrogate or theorize religion, instead, for example, of just being
religious? And why did they think their questions were the right ones to ask?
What sorts of happenings in the context of our culture have forced people to
think about the nature and function of religion as they have?

3. Durkheim's Problems of Religion

Taken together with the emergence of the "new" Durkheim, this orientation to religion as a source of problems suggests a certain way to teach
Durkheim in religious studies. While I shall only describe my own efforts in
"The Problem of Religion," I would submit that the new scholarship on
Durkheim makes him, his thought, and that of those he influenced available across a much wider spectrum of courses in religious studies than ever
imagined. The writings of Durkheim and his "team" might inform many a
course in our curricula—Durkheim himself on morality, ritual, and nationalism; Henri Hubert, Marcel Mauss, Georges Bataille on gift and sacrifice;
rice Halbwachs on memory; Michel Leiris on the sacred in everyday
Robert Hertz on pilgrimage, shrines, and saints, to mention a few
les. Let me discuss how I teach Durkheim in RLST 100, "The Problem
ion."

The classes on Durkheim come toward the end of the second part of the 10 week run of RLST 100 just before Eliade, just after Freud. In the second part of RLST 100, I argue that the focus of theoretical problems in the study of religion, at a certain point in the nineteenth century, doubtless the result of Schleiermacher's influence, became religious experience. This focus contrasts on the whole with the way problems of religion arose from issues having to do, for example, with predominantly historical quests for the identity of the first or most fundamental religion—the discourse of "natural religion"—typical of sixteenth-century thinkers such as Jean Bodin, seventeenth-century thinkers such as Lord Herbert of Cherbury, or the eighteenth-century Deists. Likewise, the relatively modern obsession shared by Durkheim with making sense of religion by making sense of religious experience contrasts as well with the nineteenth-century critical philological and historical focus on the way the study of sacred texts—the Bible as well as the Vedas and other religious documents—problematized religion in the West by putting into question the status of religious texts. Here, one thinks not only of a D. F. Strauss and the "higher criticism" of the Bible, but also of Friedrich Max Müller's historical and philological criticism of the scriptures of India, what Max Müller and his ilk thought was an alternative—"Aryan"—Bible.

These contrasts make the case that the work of Durkheim on religion is better seen as akin to other investigations of religion focused on the experiential dimension of human religious life. In his day, even while the quest for natural religion persisted, as for example, with Max Müller, it took a distinctly psychological turn, as in the work of Cornelis P. Tiele and the Liberal Protestants and neo-Deists who dominated the study of religion in France in Durkheim's time—Albert Réville and his son, Jean Réville. To wit, in the same league, although "playing" for different "teams" than Durkheim, would be Otto, Malinowski, Weber, Freud, Jung, and Eliade, among others. Thus, like Freud or Otto, for example, Durkheim sought to explain the psychological state or individual experience of dependence upon the sacred that seemed characteristic of religion. But, unlike Freud or Otto, for example, Durkheim argued that this feeling of dependence was not some residue of early childhood experiences or instead a "being experienced" by the "Wholly Other," respectively, but ultimately a function of participation in social groups—effervescent or otherwise.

4. Making Durkheim Plausible: The Case of "Strong" and "Weak" Durkheimianisms

The first challenge in pedagogy here is to make Durkheim's view plausible to students typically hostile to its societist character. Here, I do not primarily have in mind that part of the Durkheimian view that urges us to study religious institutions and social organizations—what one may call a "weak" Durkheimianism. This "weak" sociological apperception contributes to the study of religion as a "natural" part of present-day religious studies as the study of beliefs, doctrines, morality, and such have been. Historically speaking, positions in anthropology or sociology of religion in religious studies departments are far outnumbered by those in the historical, philosophical, or theological study of religion. This appropriation of Durkheim would indeed take religious studies beyond these more prevalent approaches to the study of religion in terms of religious beliefs, myths, morals, and the like and bring out the nature of religions as social institutions. Marcel Mauss, for example, seeded Durkheimian societist insights throughout the many reviews he wrote for *L'Année Sociologique*, and notably in his joint writings with Henri Hubert. In a review of one of Hubert's mentors, the great Roman Catholic ecclesiastical historian, Abbé Louis Duchesne, Mauss complains that he pays no heed at all to the social contexts of the rise of Christianity, when he well should have (Mauss 1913a, 312). He ignored, for instance, the role of the synagogue and changes in its rites upon the early church (Mauss 1913b, 345). The "weak" Durkheimian perspective thus brings social considerations to the fore, showing, for example, in connection with the synagogue, that not only was it as a social institution decisive for the formation of Judaism, but also an institution that gave birth to the great flourishing of religious sects of the day. Religious groupings, such as "sects"—Christianity for one—were formed as "epiphenomena" of the synagogue. Christianity was not the lone work of Jesus or Paul, or even the groups that formed around them (Mauss 1908, 588f). Judaism too was subject to sociological analysis in order to illuminate singular figures such as the prophets. Mauss argued that the prophets were far more tightly bound to the societies against which they seemed so often to be poised than orthodoxy would allow. "Social conditions ... modify the religious state of the people, necessitating the prophetic movement—the prophet as moral leader and preacher was only a natural instrument of the renovation" (Mauss 1902b, 312).

What I would call a "strong" Durkheimianism, however, generally meets much greater resistance in the study of religion. "Strong" Durkheimianism asserts that religious experience is caused by social forces, by the action of groups upon the psychology of their members. It is not then surprising that, given our native Western individualism, often coupled with an individualist religious piety, students instinctively object to Durkheim's social view of the origins and causes of religious experience. They protest that religious experience is essentially transcendent and/or personal. It cannot in principle have social causes, such as Durkheim describes, for example, in his discussion of the relation of totemic beliefs to the collective activities or rituals—essentially social features—of totemic religion itself. Since God dwells within and/or since the individual human person is thought to be an absolutely autonomous being, the occurrence of religious experience is therefore felt to be independent of extra-personal or worldly location. Put into another form, the objection raised is as follows: How does the Durkheimian account of the causes of religious experience explain the frequent occurrence of religious experience in solitude? Therefore, in order to get students to make Durkheim plausible, one needs to confront "strong" Durkheimianism and the issue of why Durkheim would have thought he was right in advancing his "strong" societist view of the causes of religious experience.

Since "strong" Durkheimianism goes well beyond the fairly acceptable propositions of "weak" Durkheimianism, namely that we should attend to religious institutions as well as religious beliefs, myths, morals, and the like, a little more argumentation is required. This takes us into some fairly sophisticated intellectual territory. To begin, we need to attend to epistemology and then to what I would call social ontology.

5. Epistemology, Public Knowledge, and "Strong" Durkheimianism

In terms of epistemology, early in "The Problem of Religion," I argue that the study of religion differs from being religious, and that this has certain consequences for the way we proceed in talking about religion in the public domain. In our discussion of the problems for religion thrown up by the critical study of the Bible and religious texts in general, I argue that one needs, for example, to distinguish between what Christians believe Jesus to be and what, as a matter of history, it is possible to say about Jesus' life and works. We can thus distinguish between the claims made about Jesus by a particular Christian community from those it is possible to affirm in the broader public domain. This is not to say that one is true and the other not—that, say, the Jesus of faith or of a particular Christian group is a "myth" and thus not true, while the Jesus of "history" or of the public domain necessarily tells the truth about Jesus. It is however to say that "history" and the demands of the public realm in diverse and pluralist societies differ in certain key respects from "myth" and the demands of a believing community. To wit, we can ask what it is possible to say about Jesus from the viewpoint of the epistemological standards of "history" as a public academic discipline and to compare that with what it is permissible to say about Jesus from the standpoint of a particular Christian community and faith. In the classroom of a public university such as the University of California, we are situated in the public domain, and in that sense we are governed by a different set of rules about what constitutes "knowledge" than in a particular Christian church. Interestingly enough, Durkheim was aware of this distinction and was moreover dedicated to addressing this broader public domain. Although, for example, there are elements of liberal Judaism in the thought of Durkheim and his collaborator, Marcel Mauss, as well as aspects of liberal modernist Roman Catholicism in Henri Hubert, another close co-worker in the Durkheimian group, none of these Durkheimians participated in articulating or in any way developing the respective confessional discourses of religious liberalism proper to either the Judaism or Roman Catholicism of their day. Their focus was public and extra-ecclesial, so to speak.

In studying Durkheim, we are therefore considering someone studying religion, someone seeking moreover expressly to advance knowledge about religion in the public domain. This aim, in turn, calls forth an epistemology governing Durkheim's claims about the nature of religion, the causes of religious experience and such. To wit, Durkheim must play by the same rules governing what counts as public "knowledge" as any other player in the arena of knowledge about the world. One of the requirements of such claims made about the world would be that they must in some sense be empirical and publicly falsifiable, such as in the case of the historical "sciences." With his efforts shaped by these rules, Durkheim could not—in principle—advance a claim about religion that made appeal to religious faith or transcendent causes—even had he wanted so to do. The reason of course lies in Durkheim's seeking to advance public knowledge. While one may not like his claim that association with a social group causes religious experience, such a claim is legitimate within the world as it is bounded by the epistemology of public knowledge about the world.

6. Social Ontology, Religious Reality, and "Strong" Durkheimianism

Once, however, students get over the issue that inquiry is public, and that public knowledge is sought, we can begin taking the measure of the more fruitful appreciations of Durkheim's "strong" approach to religion. This brings me to the issue of the social ontology of religion. This issue arises immediately concerning Durkheim's views about the underlying reality of religion—the ontology of religion—best summed up in his religion-society/society-religion identity, the identity of society and the object of religion (the sacred).

As an identity relation, "Religion, God, the Sacred ≡ Society" (I call this D1) is interestingly ambiguous. (One will note as well that Durkheim and his peers called his sociology of religion by the equally ambiguous title of "*sociologie religieuse*.") Our identity is ambiguous because it can just as fairly be read, "Society ≡ Religion, God, the Sacred" (I call this D2). That is to say that the identity expressed is to be read in both directions at the same time—either with "society" being the object of predication (D1) or with "religion" playing the same grammatical role (D2). Yet, when scholars speak of the religion-society/society-religion identity, they are often tempted to read this identity in the typical reductionist way characteristic of the old scholarship of Durkheim (D2). Thus, by this reading, "Religion, God, the Sacred ≡ Society" implies that Durkheim argues simply that the underlying reality of religious experience, and thus of the nature of God or the sacred and so on, is society. Religious experience is thus caused by those very social forces that can be detected and investigated in the pub-lic way we have just discussed.

But logically speaking, this reductionist reading is not logically privi-leged. Strictly speaking, no member of a pair in an identity is prior. No mem-ber of the pair identified is privileged with position in the expression of identity: the religion-society identity is just as much a society-religion iden-tity; neither D1 nor D2 is prior. This means we can read this identity (D2) as stating that "Society $\equiv$ Religion, God, the Sacred" with equal logical justifica-tion as D1. Read in this way as D2, from the point of view of what is predicated of society, it follows that Durkheim is asserting that society, social life, and so on have a religious nature. Society is for Durkheim no mere sociobiological massing of individual organisms, but a collectivity informed with what one might call spirituality, or in older parlance, values, ideals, and such. Durkheim is predicating religious traits necessary to the existence and main-tenance of society, not only the other way around. Durkheim "sings."

7. Society *and*—Not *or*—the Sacred

The main point in drawing these deductions is to shift the typical religious studies student's perspective on Durkheim, sufficient for giving Durk-heimian scholarship on religion a plausibility which it may not have hith-erto had. Beyond, then, the benefit of "weak" Durkheimianism, of taking a social approach to religion, there is thus more. Beyond the benefit of focus-ing on religious institutions and social forms—e.g. asceticism and monas-teries come into focus as social institutions and forms of social organization, rather than just the beliefs, morals, or myths of monks—there is the core of at least part of "strong" Durkheimianism that can be appreciated. To wit, the "strong" Durkheim, properly understood as affirming the religion-society/ society-religion identity, is asserting that all social reality can be said to par-ticipate in religious reality. This would be no more or no less than saying society participates equally well in political or esthetic dimensions of human life. Since there is no society without values, without what Durkheim himself called a non-materialist or natural "spiritual" dimension, there is no society without a religious dimension (Durkheim 1974).

How then does appreciating Durkheim's positing of religious traits onto society play itself out in a course in religious studies? Here, the choice of texts is crucial. Instead of the better known classics like *The Elementary Forms of the Religious Life*, I have used Durkheim's passionate and brilliant polemic essay of 1898, in behalf of the innocence of Dreyfus, "Individualism and the Intellectuals" (Durkheim 1898). This piece is most effective in showing how Durkheim links certain social arrangements and values to the sacred or religiousness in a way that hardly seems to make his societism an obstacle to thinking seriously about the propositions made about the nature of religion.

Durkheim here is arguing against the attacks made upon the defenders of Dreyfus led by the Roman Catholic writer and polemicist, Ferdinand Brunetière. At the time Durkheim wrote, it was becoming increasingly clear that Dreyfus was quite plausibly innocent and thus both unjustly condemned and punished. To stem the tide of a popular movement to exonerate Dreyfus, Brunetière argued, in effect, that the honor of the army and state required that protests should cease and Dreyfus's conviction not be challenged. In a time of national danger, said Brunetière, matters of mere individual innocence must be subordinated to "saving the face" of the national government. Better, like Jesus, that one man—even though innocent—suffer for the sake of the people of France, than that the nation's key institutions be humiliated and perhaps delegitimized by admitting their errors. The trouble in the France of his day, argued Brunetière, was those noisy protesting "intellectuals," who were the chief advocates of Dreyfus's innocence. In the name of transcendent values of justice and the integrity of the individual, they argued that Dreyfus should be rehabilitated, no matter what embarrassment this would cause to the nation as a whole.

Going by expectations normally associated with Durkheimian societism, the case Durkheim made for Dreyfus is remarkable and shows how crude the old view of Durkheim was. Against Brunetière, Durkheim argued nothing less than the case for the *sacredness* of the human individual. As sacred, an individual like Dreyfus was due justice absolutely. His rights as a sacred being were transcendent and could not be compromised to the national interest, as Brunetière wished. Indeed, for us, Durkheim says, the human individual is a sacred being.

This move, then, establishes at least one feature about the place of religion in Durkheim's thought—namely that he approved of at least certain kinds of religion—here a version of the "religion of humanity," that neo-religion affirming the transcendent sacredness of the human individual. If Durkheim were a reductionist and in this sense insincere about his claim that the individual is sacred, then we would no longer have a "new" Durkheim, but just the old one. But our recent scholarship—at least since Lukes, but also anticipated by Robert Bellah and his notion of "civil religion"—shows that we do indeed we have a "new" non-reductionist Durkheim. We have a Durkheim who saw religion as something valuable in itself and a pervasive element in modern societies—especially the ideal of the sacredness of the human person.

Readers may ask, however, what has become of Durkheim the reductionist sociologist? I answer that Durkheim is still present at the heart of this argument, although not in a way that I think ought to be called "reductionist." Durkheim here resists reductionism because he integrates his societism and his individualism, rather than making one an epiphenomenon of the other. By arguing first that the individual is a value for "us"—at least for France—and, second, that it is so because to be a value is to be valued by the community—whether the historical or present-day community does not matter—Durkheim links individual and society internally. Thus, in defending Dreyfus, Durkheim is defending the rights of the individual as an instance of the more general French national and social values inscribed in such foundational documents as, for example, the Declaration of the Rights of Man and Citizen. Although there is a social causality in that our values are necessarily the products of groups—like all human values—there is no reductionism, because the sacredness of the individual is real, and as real as anything emanating from the human realm could be.

8. Making Durkheim Plausible: The Bible beyond Cognition

Another source of antipathy to Durkheim among students of religion stems from the assumption that he does not belong to the lineages of religious studies. He is neither historian nor phenomenologist of religion. As either a pedagogue or sociologist, Durkheim's institutional affiliations are not those of anyone in the main institutions of the study of religion in France—the Science Religieuse (Fifth) Section of Paris's École Pratique des Hautes Études. Nor does he even seem much aware of his contemporaries, Albert Réville, doyen of École Pratique, Fifth Section, Jean Réville, his son and successor, or Maurice Vernes, founder of the august *Revue de l'histoire des religions*. Likewise, Durkheim does not seem to be in conversation with the founders of the classic origins of religious studies in the late nineteenth and early twentieth centuries like a Sir James Frazer, Friedrich Max Müller, Edward Burnett Tylor, Cornelis P. Tiele, or Pierre Daniel Chantepie de la Saussaye. From this perspective, Durkheim is not "one of us," but rather a foreign intruder into our field of religious studies, and worst of all, someone seeking to "reduce" it to sociology.

But, as I have already shown, the Durkheimians were in conversation with all the founders of the study of religion. One of the major areas in which their contribution to the study of religion sets out a new direction is in what students of religion have always considered their private reserve: religious texts. After all, the École Pratique des Hautes Études, Fifth Section, France's main institution dedicated to the study of religion, now well over 100 years old, was created expressly for the purpose of the critical study of sacred texts, essentially modeled on the work of the German pioneers of the Higher Criticism of the Bible. However odd to Anglophone ears the word "pratique" in the title of the School may sound, in French academic parlance, it indicates critical study of texts. Let me conclude, then, by discussing the Durkheimian contribution to the study of religious texts, since it shows both their uniqueness and therefore how they might contribute to the teaching of religion.

When it comes to the study of religious texts, one commonly practiced manner of studying them has been to treat them as a source of doctrines, meanings, and contents. By contrast, a Durkheimian approach would focus more attention on the religion of sacred texts themselves, and their dynamics, rather than on their esthetics or their literary qualities—understood in their various aspects, such as entities primarily to be illuminated in terms of their text-historical natures, the intricacies of their canonical or literary formation, and such. In a review of the history of religion and cultic practices, Henri Hubert put it well in congratulating the author for writing of "religious life" and "not just 'religion,'" which as Henri Hubert tells us was to treat "not just doctrines, but systems of actions and the feelings to which they adapt" (Hubert 1901, 226). What does this mean?

First, Durkheimian approaches would focus our attention on the ways religious texts illuminate the nature of religious phenomena, by raising what I have discussed as problems of religion. A Durkheimian approach would rededicate religious studies to the centripetal tasks of the study of religion over against centrifugal, and finally fissiparous, tendencies for us all to hive off in pursuit of the agendas of generally older and more venerable sub-specializations, including, but not exclusive to, the study of biblical literature. Mauss, for example, argued for a socialized approach to beliefs, one of those cross-cultural religious categories usually thought independent of social aspects of human life. Thus, Mauss urged that the belief in spirits, for instance, ought not be excused from interrogation about the conditions of its appearance. Why did the belief in spirits occur in one particular time and place, and not in others? Mauss's answer suggested this had to do with the particular social context and period in which such beliefs are found. Whatever else, for the Durkheimians, beliefs are not free-floating and autonomous entities, but are rather things that need to be connected with other features of life, such as their social location (Mauss 1913c, 591–2). The Durkheimians would thus call home students of religion from the dispersal of their energies into varied agendas represented by the Association of Asian Studies, Middle Eastern Studies Association, the Association of Jewish Studies, the American Historical or Philosophical Associations, the Modern Language Association, the Society of Biblical Literature, or the American Schools of Oriental Research. By rededicating scripture studies to the central problems of religion, the Durkheimians, ironically enough, would help religious studies go some way to finding and owning a common voice within the university.

Second, a Durkheimian approach puts emphasis on texts as actions or as related intimately to actions, rather than as ideas, as simply cognitive. This means seeing scripture and aspects of scripture, such as the myths and stories contained therein, as part of certain social undertakings, such as in their ritual contexts. Mauss, for example, argued that the study of myth leads invariably to the study of a rite, especially sacrifice, since sacrificial rites demanded extensive mythical and other justifications (Hubert & Mauss 1968, 4f). Or, in connection with the frequent mention of prayer in the Bible, Mauss argued that all prayer, which he tellingly terms "verbal rites," is derived from social—ritual—contexts. Prayer does not stand on its own as a lone, detached piece of religious oratory, or an inner meditative condition, but requires certain social conditions and is performed in them as well (Mauss 1983, 148). Many prayers occur, for example, as a normal and required part of sacrifices (Hubert & Mauss 1968, 4). Others are themselves straightforwardly performative, like the words of baptism. There, the prayers at baptism effect the results of which they speak. They become actions themselves. Here, the Durkheimians would find common ground with the work already being done by biblical scholars on how religious texts really work in religions.

American biblical scholar Vincent Wimbush has shown how African-Americans use scripture in other than strictly literary or linguistic ways, including non-cognitive uses of scripture—healing, direct worship, "magic"—in salient contexts such as Latin America and Africa (Wimbush & Rodman 2000). Texts may, therefore, inform religious action in their being physical sacred objects that in turn themselves are felt to be symbolic or even magical, like the words of baptism. Texts may themselves *perform* religious functions, rather than being mere vehicles for the words and meanings that they contain. Swearing on the Bible in courtrooms is such a case where the physical object of a sacred book becomes the source of legitimation rather than anything mentioned in the book itself. The conspicuous display and, often hostile, brandishing of Chairman Mao Tse-tung's *Little Red Book* or Ayatollah Khomeni's *Green Book* were taken to have powers of their own to bring about desired results for those who adhered to them. Similarly, sacred texts may be just as much direct objects of veneration and worship, of incarnations of God—the Word made flesh—as containers of meaning. Here, of course, the liturgical use of Gospel books in the Eastern Orthodox Christian tradition stands out. While I am sure something of the content of the ornate Gospel book before which my Rusyn grandmother bowed conditioned the effects sacred scripture had on her, I was never sure how much of her religious life actually consisted in entertaining those meanings over against how much it had to do with the sacramental, even talismanic, power of the bejewelled Gospel book that sanctified her world and her place in it. Aside from the meanings—even religious ones—conveyed by religious texts, the ways that scripture enters into the religious life need to be ascertained empirically, and not simply assumed a priori.[2] Such empirical studies will enrich our understanding of religion beyond that dictated by either liberal modernist tendencies to exalt the cognitive in religion or even biblical literalism's deification of the words on the page of a book.

The Durkheimians are not, of course, arguing that the study of religious texts has no place in religious studies. Nothing could be further from the truth, as their sometimes excruciatingly detailed study of sacrificial texts, for example, shows (Hubert & Mauss 1964). Nor am I arguing that the meanings derived from religious texts never hold interest for them in understanding a particular religion or religious situation—only that in recommending the insights of the Durkheimians, what I might call a cognitivist approach to scripture should not be assumed a priori. The very rise and fall of cognitive readings of scripture is, as well, one of those problems of religion that Durkheimian religious studies would try to understand and explain. Even in cases where religious people apply a cognitive approach to scripture, we need as well to devote ourselves to the problem of understanding how that happens. Is this because of what is said in the text—its cognitive value—as in counsel, or in a directive or commandment? Or, is it because of the way a text may create an atmosphere or put a group in a particular frame of mind—as in the case of dramatic and moving, but perhaps uninformative, passages from the Book of Revelation?

Lest one think I protest too much, I cite a particularly infuriating example of how scriptural cognitivism bedevils public discourse about religion. In studying the Bible, it is easy for those attracted to cognitivist (and certainly literalist) approaches to neglect to look further than the letter or cognitive meanings of scripture. At least as far as the mass media are concerned, it is now commonplace to assume that if one wishes to understand Islamist calls to jihad, say, we need—first and virtually exclusively—to turn to the Quran, as if that text settles all questions. Here, the Quran, removed from all historical contexts, from other Islamic sources of authority and such, is cast as an unambiguous road map of clear instructions about getting from point A to point B. Scholars of Islam, however, inform us that the Quran does not seem to indicate a consistent message about the duty to jihad, understood narrowly as taking up arms against another individual or group, for example. This is hardly surprising, since the Quran, like every religious text, speaks in different voices, and oftentimes not at all in the cognitive language of instruction or precise religious directive. Jews and Christians certainly know this as well. Do "the mountains [really] skip like rams," as the Psalmist says, "and the hills like lambs"? And, even when religious texts deal out instructions, the Quran, like the Hebrew Bible, for example, lays out all sorts of maps charting or implying all sorts of routes in differing degrees of clarity to different destinations. The Allah of the Quran is not only "the best of devisers" and thus may lead people into sin for his own inscrutable reasons, but he is also the "merciful"—to refer to just two of Allah's attributes. If anything is a constant in the relation of religious texts to religious life, it is the variety of practices and beliefs that can be legitimized by the selective citation of the well-chosen scriptural passages. While one is aware of Muslim or Christian "fundamentalists" basing their views on their fidelity to the words of scripture, there is nothing in principle preventing moderate Muslims or Christians from doing likewise. The *Los Angeles Times* reports precisely such movements among moderate Muslims in Malaysia combating radical Islamist movements by appealing with equal authority to the literal words of the Quran (Marshall 2002, A4). As Shakespeare reminds us, "Mark you this, Bassanio, the devil can cite scripture for his purpose" (*Merchant of Venice* I, iii, 99). And so, too, can the angels.

Durkheimian approaches would deviate from cognitivism, and also complicate our understanding of scriptural narratives. But I would wager that they would at least bring out greater depths in our appreciation of the religion underlying them—and in ways that are unexpectedly familiar to modern biblical scholarship. Thus, over against this tendency to use scripture unhistorically and acontextually, for example, Mauss argues that the biblical text is not virgin territory, but is rather only a surface phenomenon beneath which lie the remnants of many social activities, such as theological contests, mythical imaginings, and other things that had constructed the text itself in the Jewish community (Mauss 1913c, 302). Likewise in his review of Frazer's *Golden Bough*, Mauss follows the great mythologist's estimate of the vogue for the story of Christ's resurrection. Mauss pointedly asks how one can insulate the popularity of this myth, and the belief attached to it, from the social context of the day where numerous myths of the sacrificial death and resurrection of several Mediterranean gods circulated and made such beliefs commonplace (Mauss 1902a, 134). Does not the story of Jesus's resurrection have to be seen—at least at some point—against the backdrop of other such stories in the same cultural *Sitz im Leben*?

If the Durkheimians sound like good classical Higher Critics of the biblical texts, it is because they descend intellectually from some of the very founders of the so-called "Higher Criticism," such as Julius Wellhausen, and more immediately, from Wellhausen's student, William Robertson Smith (Smend 1995). For Robertson Smith, the Bible was not to be read primarily as literature—although he was a master linguist and philologist—but as containing information about an episode in the *history* of religion (Smith 1912, 229–33; Strenski 2006, ch 6). As it happened, for Robertson Smith, this history was theological to a high degree. It was indeed a triumphalist and supercessionist *Heilsgeschichte* (Reif 1995) of the "gathering up into one whole of all God's dealings with men from the fall to the Resurrection of Christ, the history of true religion, the adoption and education, from age to age, of the Church, in a continuous scheme of gradual advance" (Smith 1912, 232). But, despite the theological intentions that he brought to his work, Robertson Smith was notable for asking questions—posing problems that are peculiar, or peculiar enough, to religion—much as Mauss showed how, despite and perhaps because of his sociological perspectives, he was also able to pose fundamental problems about religion. Robertson Smith laid out immensely fruitful suggestions for understanding both the religion of the Bible, and indeed, religion itself (Bediako 1995). His classic *Lectures on the Religion of the Semites* is nothing less than a study of the religion of the Bible in pre-biblical times. It does so by means of exploring what are plausibly critical biblical notions, such as sacrifice, ritual, purity, the sacred, as well as religious institutions.[3]

Robertson Smith thus concentrated on the role of religious ritual in what for him was the religion of a good portion of the Hebrew Bible. In doing so, he challenged the degree to which the cognitive features of religion, such as its beliefs, played a role in the Bible's own religion. In Robertson Smith's view, the Semitic tribes he investigated legitimized their institutions, for example, by means of rituals, rather than beliefs, oral myths, or the texts of religious scriptures, if they indeed had anything that might be called "scriptures" at all. Robertson Smith therefore showed us how to problematize religion, how to devise and put questions that raise fundamental problems about the nature of religion that go well beyond the text as literature or as a mediating device of ideas.

More recently, Mary Douglas, in her *Purity and Danger* and other books, demonstrates how one can penetrate the sometimes opaque features of biblical religion—proscriptions against eating certain animals, for example—by problematizing aspects of biblical religion in terms made possible by comparative analysis (Douglas 1970). Her investigations into the intricacies of avoidance of various animals at bottom show how these apparently trivial proscriptions reveal something of the religious vision of the Hebrew Bible. One avoids contact with certain animals—they are impure—because they reflect a distortion in the plan God devised for humans. What God wants more than anything is conformity with the order of creation that he has set out. No pork, because while the pig has cloven hooves like a cow, it does not chew its cud. It is actually some mysterious deformation of creation—a monster. What God wants of humans is perfection according to his divine plan—and not monstrosity.

Of course, ever since the splash made by Douglas's book, this kind of questioning of the religion of biblical texts has proceeded as never before in so broad a way within biblical studies. But how far off am I in feeling that Douglas's raising of religious questions, her interrogating of the religious cosmology of the Hebrew Bible from a cross-cultural comparative point of view, indicates that scriptural scholars needed to be prodded from outside their profession's research agendas in order to raise what I call religious problems about scripture? Rightly or wrongly, Douglas herself felt that even further nudges from outside the guild were needed. She applied herself to this task, guided in part by Jacob Milgrom, and followed up her work on purity and danger with an extensive study of the *Book of Numbers*, published as volume 158 in the distinguished series of publications of biblical scholarship, the Supplement Series of the *Journal for the Study of the Old Testament* (Douglas 1993).[4] Knowing even more than Douglas about the Bible, as they do, the expertise and learning of biblical scholars positions them to make even more substantial contributions to the study of religion as a phenomenon than even she has managed.

I say all this, as well, in full recognition that many of today's adherents of, at least, Judaism, Christianity, and Islam, respectively, believe their scriptures to be just the sort of unambiguous road maps of clear instructions that scholars like modern biblical critics, as well as Robertson Smith and the Durkheimians, would decry.[5] Knowing just what to do in one's life is today a very big problem. Fundamentalist or, at least, cognitivist readings of scriptures, like horoscopes, are open enough for anyone's life to squeeze in, and straightforward enough to provide the confidence needed to move on.

I thus agree that religions, at certain moments in their lives, can resist broad, conflicting, allegoric, symbolic, loose, or non-cognitive readings of their scriptures. It is only to say that they need not, in principle, do so, and that it is an historical and empirical problem of religion whether they do or do not. It is precisely these different ways of reading scripture—its cognitivizing or its rejection—that students of religion should busy themselves in understanding and explaining.

12

Christians, Durkheimians, and Other Animals

Of critiques leveled at Durkheimian sociology of religion, one of the more notable is "neo-orthodox" theologian John Milbank's charge that it is "only a theology, and indeed a church in disguise, but a theology and a church dedicated to promoting a certain secular consensus" (Milbank 1990, 4). Milbank is only the most recent in a long line of critics accusing Durkheim of seeking to launch a neo-religion under the guise of a secular science of sociology, and thus of being a kind of "theology." But the secret source of Milbank's hostility to Durkheim is the exclusion of his own kind of "theology" from the curricula of public universities. If Christian theology cannot be done in the secular university," Milbank in effect reasons, "why should a 'crypto-theology' like Durkheim's sociology?"

The merits of Milbank's case are worth dedicated treatment, and one to which I have given attention in the tenth chapter of the present volume. There, I shall argue that Milbank is fundamentally taking issue with the notion that Durkheimian discourse about religion, the "sacred," and such is unfit as public discourse—or at least that it is as fit (or unfit) as his brand of Christian theology. Ironically, however, Milbank's hostility to Durkheim and Durkheimian thought blinds him to the significant utility Durkheimian theoretical notions about religion might have in furthering the development of his own Christian theological projects—undertaken, of course, in their proper institutional contexts in a school of divinity or theology. I shall argue here that while Milbank seeks to discredit Durkheimian sociology for being "theological" or religious, he misses an opportunity to exploit Durkheimian sociology to assist Christian theologies in addressing a perceived vulnerability in the "animal liberation" debates. Durkheimian thought can be quite useful, I am arguing, in providing Christians with a way of articulating a morally defensible and theologically orthodox position on the comity between humans and non-human animals (hereafter just "animals" for short) (Fern 2002; Linzey 1998). I shall do so, however, not simply to make polemic points against Milbank, but in a spirit of earnest exploration of certain values where Durkheimian thought and certain pre-Reformation Christian theologies find an unanticipated harmony.

Such a discussion should interest Christian theologians in part because of the persistent charge that Christianity has no coherent or consistent theological resources with which to overcome the gap between humanity and nature (Singer 1975). It should interest non-Christians as well, given the powerful influence of religion in our contemporary politics, as witnessed in our divisive "culture wars" over homosexuality, procreative rights, Darwinian evolution, "animal rights," and such. In our democracy, how do we negotiate the animal rights issue, for one, given that one position holds that once God gave Adam and Eve dominion over the earth and all its creatures, no room at all is left for such frivolities as "animal rights"? As a matter of public debate, since the mid-1970s debates about animal rights have become intense, as witnessed by movements such as PETA and films like *Babe*, provoked for the most part by perhaps the single most influential book written on the subject, Peter Singer's *Animal Liberation* (Singer 1975).

I wish to proceed by engaging a close and more informed reading of the history of Christianity on the issue of comity between humans and animals. This will reveal weaknesses of Singer's arguments against Christianity, and ironically—at least as far as Milbank is concerned—that Durkheimian insights may provide just the occasion to articulate the kind of animal-friendly theology many Christians want. What is more surprising—at least to those like Milbank who can only read Durkheim as reducing religion to society ("religion≡society")—is the existence of a major Christian theological tradition asserting the comity of animals and humans, but on Durkheimian principles. While I would not go so far as to assert the "hidden Christianity of Durkheimianism," we will see how at certain times in its history Christian theology was informed by notions that are eminently Durkheimian, and that these notions formed the bases for an assertion of comity between animals and humans. As foreign, therefore, as it is for the present author to play the role of a Christian theologian, I take somewhat perverse, but nonetheless amiable, delight in doing so for the sake of vindicating Durkheimian thought against the hostility of its theological critics. Let me begin by setting the situation of Western attitudes to the relation of animals to humans into a broader context, and once having done so, show how Christianity in its many forms has played a role in articulating the nature of that relationship—ironically on the basis of unrecognized Durkheimian principles!

I. Humanity, Utility, and Nature

In the first decade of the nineteenth century, William Blake penned these verses about two men who were arguably the fathers of modern science and technology, respectively Isaac Newton and Francis Bacon.

> I see the Four-fold Man. The Humanity in deadly sleep
> And its fallen Emanation. The Spectre & its cruel Shadow.
> I see the Past, Present & Future, existing all at once
> Before me; O Divine Spirit sustain me on thy wings!
> That I may awake Albion from His long & cold repose.
> For Bacon & Newton sheath'd in dismal steel, their terrors hang
> Like iron scourges over Albion, Reasonings like vast Serpents
> Infold around my limbs, bruising my minute articulations.
> (*Jerusalem*, ch. 1)

To Blake, Newton and Bacon epitomized all that was hateful about the scientific project of his day. They laid on the "iron scourges" of necessity, since their thought was "sheath'd in dismal steel" by their unfeeling mechanical insensitivity to all things "natural." Today with the new sensibility toward the environment and the plight of living things, many Christians share the same or at least a sympathetic version of the poet's repugnance for the predations of technology and arrogance of scientism, or for the prevalent and overwhelmingly dominant utilitarian view of humanity's relation to nature. Then, and in part now, nature was seen in strictly machine-like and utilitarian ways. That is to say, nature was seen principally as interesting only to the extent that it served concrete and practical human ambitions and projects.

That sensibilities differ today, and that at least a large portion of our population would find these common hyper-utilitarian and mechanistic worldviews of the eighteenth century repugnant, shows us how much our values have changed in favor of organic and dialogic values. I am arguing that the difference between our time and Blake's is that we have at least begun to establish (or re-establish) what is, in effect, a variant of a pre-Reformation Christian attitude to nature as something with which human beings can establish comity, kinship, or society. The question is, however, whether and how this view of the ideal of a society composed of humans and nature is and can be sustained over against the still powerful pragmatic and utilitarian attitude to nature so deeply embedded in our whole way of life. Or, the question may be put as to how our utilitarian attitudes, properly understood, might conceal a "kinder, gentler" attitude to nature than one might at first think. Do such "kinder, gentler" views of our relation to nature have authentic and substantial Christian roots and precedents? And, if so, what theological commitments would the ideal of a society encompassing humanity and nature entail—say, in the articulation of Christian attitudes toward abortion or euthanasia—or in Christian attitudes to ritual slaughter by rabbis for the sake of adhering to laws governing *koshrut*? Is the social ideal merely a "nice" way of thinking about nature on Monday, Wednesday, and Friday, while we busily go ahead and exploit nature for our own enrichment on Tuesday, Thursday, Saturday, and Sunday? And, if not, what are the conditions for bringing the entire "week" of human behavior and experience under the governing rule of comity, kinship, and sociability?

Since the term "nature" names a realm impossibly vast, I shall confine myself to the relation between humans and nonhuman animals. For convenience sake, but also at the risk of perpetuating an error, I shall sometimes employ the shorthand, "animals," when what I really mean are "non-human animals." Since humans are as fully animal as are horses, cows, pigs, and dogs, it is an odd, but telling, way of speaking about "nonhuman animals" to label them with the general name of "animals," while humans are given a pass by being contrasted to them. Still, as long as it is understood here and now that I am not using "animal" in a sense that excludes "humans," I, at least, will not perpetuate this error any more than I need so to do.

At the same time, in resisting the exclusive use of the term "human," I should declare that I am not simply going to rehearse the program of animal liberationists like Peter Singer, for one. In fact, what I shall argue in part seeks to reform some of the major views advanced by Singer in his classic, *Animal Liberation*, especially his characterization of the role Christianity has played in forming our attitudes about the relation of humans and animals (Singer 1975). For, contrary to what Singer argues about the broad speciesism of Christianity, I shall argue that while Christianity does not generally entail vegetarianism, its attitude to nature is far more complex than Singer would allow. And here I am not referring to Francis of Assisi—that standard fall-back paradigm of Christian affection for nature and especially animals—but to a larger Christian religious mentality of which Francis was but a single instance. This religious mentality, as we will see, is conditioned by a sense of relationship, kinship, social bonding, reciprocity, and the like—all eminently Durkheimian theoretical notions.

In introducing a notion such as a "larger Christian religious mentality," I do not underestimate the complexity and confusion of Christian attitudes to animals. Some of this diversity and thinking at cross purposes can, for example, be captured in the varying fortunes of sacrifice in Christianity. Like Judaism and Buddhism, Christianity is in a way a post-sacrificial reli-gion—at least in the literal sense of sacrifice as ritual killing. In this sense, René Girard and his colleagues have a point in claiming that Jesus puts an end to ritual sacrifice in an analogous way to what we might say about the rabbis and the rise of the synagogue marking the end of temple sacrifice or the Buddha and meditative practice marking an end (at least for Buddhists) of brahminical animal sacrifice (Williams 1997). This is not to say that sac-rificial imagery and metaphors vanish from Christianity, Judaism, or even Buddhism. But, they are radically transformed for the most part. Thus, while Roman Catholics perpetuate sacrificial thinking within the sacra-mental economy of the Eucharist and in a related ethic encouraging an anti-individualist self-effacement, and while Jews today will speak of the age-old ideal of sacrifice in images drawn from worship in the temple, par-ticularly insofar as the continuation of the existence of Israel is at stake, only a small minority of Jews today advocate the restoration of animal sacrifice in the temple at Jerusalem. And while the most popular literature of the instruction of the young in Theravāda Buddhist countries—birth stories or *jātakas*—very often cast the Buddha-to-be in literal acts of self-sacrifice unto death. Buddhism is classically nonviolent. Thus, the general religious practices of these three traditions, at any rate, no longer embrace actual ritual sacrifice, and it is very hard indeed to imagine that they ever would again.

The upshot of these considerations about sacrifice is that in judging Christianity and its relation to nature—or at least the prospects of a future articulation of a relation of Christianity to nature—I am saying that there is more to determining what a plausibly normative Christian attitude to nature might be than what the balance of the Christian past has held. I would argue, as well, that there is also much more to the matter of articulating a Christian theology of nature today than deciding the arguably minor point of whether or not we eat our fellow creatures. After all, even the Buddha—someone who plausibly could be said to have invented "nonviolence"—did not forbid meat eating to his followers, and is reputed to have died as a result of perhaps overindulging in a savory meal of bad pork! I submit, this "more" is whether or not, from a Christian perspective, today's Christians can plausibly and meaningfully see themselves and the animals as partners in that most Durkheimian of notions, an inclusive society.

2. Peter Singer's *Animal Liberation* and Christianity's Allegedly Essential Speciesism

Beyond the question of what one eats, there is, however, Singer's larger point that needs to be addressed in any consideration of Christianity's relations to animal rights. To wit, does Christianity merit most blame in perpetuating and legitimating speciesist cruelty to animals (Singer 1975, 217)? In effect, is Christianity incorrigibly speciesist, and does this account for the massive history of cruelty to animals commonplace in the West?

One needs to say straight out that Singer seems quite confused on this point, even though he continues to lay blame at the feet of Christianity. Let me explain. Singer doggedly clings to his view of Christianity's primary guilt for speciesism, even though *Animal Liberation*, like Blake, fingers the mechanistic philosophy of Newton and Descartes as guiltier parties in the modern foundation of speciesism. Singer quotes an eyewitness account of a live animal experiment in Descartes's day, such as then was becoming widespread in Europe—something I believe without exact parallel in the annals of Christianity—at least short of the practice of judicial torture in church-supported criminal procedures from 1250 to 1780 (Peters 1985):

> "They administered beatings to dogs with perfect indifference, and made fun of those who pitied the creatures as if they felt pain. They said the animals were clocks; that the cries they emitted when struck were only the noise of a little spring that had been touched, but that the whole body was without feeling. They nailed poor animals up on boards by their four paws to vivisect them and see the circulation of the blood which was a great subject of conversation." (Citing Fontaine's *Dictionnaire Philosophique*, "Bêtes" [Singer 1975, 200])

What is particularly Christian in any of this, one might ask? Aren't mechanism and scientism enough to explain such cruelty? Singer's answer to this apparent confusion is—incredibly—to blame Christianity for Descartes' mechanistic views! And, are either mechanism or scientism plausibly derived in any significant way from Christianity, or what Singer never seems to care about, the Christianity of its day? Is Singer's view that Cartesianism is the "most painful outcome of Christian doctrines to emerge in the first half of the seventeenth century" any more plausible (Singer 1975, 217)? While it is true that Descartes drew upon the spiritualism granted him by a substantial part of the Christian tradition, the origins of the new mechanistic worldview of the Newtonian scientific revolution that he married to his spiritualism seem not to have Christian origins. And, while one cannot and should not deny or minimize Christianity's great role in rendering "so low" the status of animals that little deterioration could be imagined, Descartes, in particular, does take us even further into the depths of "speciesism." With Descartes we no longer just have the assertion of superiority of humans over animals, or even the relegation of animals to the use of humans; we have torture for its own sake and aggravated sadism. After all, for a dualist like Descartes, the seat of sentience in the soul is radically separate from the body. Since animals had no souls, they could feel no pain. While Christians likewise did not attribute eternal souls to animals, Christian philosophers like Thomas Aquinas attributed temporal souls to them, and thus the ability both to feel pain and to enter into communion with other "souls." Thus, philosopher Lex Newman has shown that "Unlike Descartes," the Scholastics "hold that the automatic processes involved" in animal behavior "are under the direction of the soul, namely the powers of vegetative and sensitive souls. Heartbeat and digestion require the guidance of vegetative souls. And such behavior as involves the pursuit of, or flight from, the objects of sense—as when sheep flee wolves—requires the powers of sensitive souls" (cf. Aquinas, ST 1a.80.1, 1a.81.2–3). The theory entails that sensory awareness of the objects of pursuit or flight is as indispensable to the production of such behavior as are the "physiological contributions, themselves under the direction of the soul though they involve no cognition" (cf. ST 1a.78.1) (Newman 2001, 496). Thus, in depriving animals of their "souls," Descartes and his mechanist fellow-travelers arguably provide more of the ideological underpinning for an abrogation of an ideal of comity or of a society embracing humans and animals than does Christianity.

Beyond Descartes's scientific and theoretical mechanistic philosophy of animal life, and internally related to it, is, of course, the entire revolution of thinking about the world characterizing early modernity. It is no accident that a mechanistic philosophy of animal life coincides historically with the rise of the industrial application of mechanics as well as economic systems of production designed to exploit the logic of mechanism. Thus, while it is a long way from today's Japanese factory fishing fleets, "scientific" Marxism, or battery hen operations to Descartes's *cogito*, it is much closer than one would imagine. A mechanistic philosophy of nature rationally justifies our confidence in the regularity of mechanisms; it also permits us to measure their utilities, to calculate their inputs and outputs as accurately as we are able by the instruments to hand; and it finally makes reliable exploitation of nature possible. In effect, the utilitarian calculus applied to real mechanisms is the way nature is rationalized—in the Weberian sense of the term—and thus how, together with all those spiritual features of the history of the West, exposed—more or less—by Weber, they built (or retroactively justified) the edifice of the modern industrial economy. If mechanism and rationalization be here, can battery hen operations be far behind? Our historical experience tells us they are not.

Completing his unrelieved attack on Christianity, Singer notes that the coarseness induced by Cartesian attitudes to animals and nature would soften, but not thanks to Christianity! Enlightenment anti-clericalism and the proto-romantic rediscovery of nature spurred by Jean-Jacques Rousseau are Singer's heroes. In his prejudices, Singer typically passes right over the rich Christian theological traditions of the Enlightenment, typified by Bishop Joseph Butler, who argued for the existence of souls in animals, and thus for their ability to feel pain and, accordingly, to merit our compassion (Butler 1834, 13–30).[1] Even more emphatic about the nobility of animal dignity was the Reverend John George Wood (1827–1889), "an eloquent and prolific writer on the subject of animals." Wood believed that cruelty to animals prevailed because people of his time did not realize that animals not only had "animal" souls, as the Scholastics held, but also that they had "immortal souls and would enjoy eternal life"![2] While Peter Singer and others have taken ample opportunity to emphasize Christianity's responsibility for cruelty to animals, they have thus distorted the record which, while ambivalent to this day, contains a "single, coherent and remarkably constant" tradition of kindness to animals from at least the fifteenth to the nineteenth centuries (Thomas 1996, 153). Indeed, Keith Thomas adds that the familiar spirit of kindness to animals of our own times, dating from the end of the eighteenth century, was informed significantly by Christianity, so much so that Thomas adds that "all the essential ingredients of" our own modern feelings of relationship, kinship, and kindness to animals are to be found in the history of Christianity, as perhaps the earlier examples given of Bishop Butler and Reverend John George Wood suggest. The ideal of kindness to animals is so much a part of Christian tradition that Thomas notes that in the seventeenth century it became a fully articulated "religious obligation": " 'Love God, love his creatures.' " "Cruelty" toward animals was seen as an "insult to God," a veritable "blasphemy against his creation" (Thomas 1996, 156). Whatever defects or malicious behaviors animals might manifest were as well the responsibility of humans. After all, it was we who caused "The Fall," and thus we who corrupted all creation by our sin. Therefore, we should show due "mercy" and kindliness for the animals (Thomas 1996, 157). By the same token, since animals shared in the results of human sinfulness, so also they were taken to be candidates for redemption as well. They were assumed to be part of the "society" contracted between God and Israel, both in some Christian as well as Jewish theological traditions (Thomas 1996, 137). And although the matter of whether animals would be resurrected on the last day

was hotly debated as late as the seventeenth century, many theologians of
the same period taught that animals had "souls" and that they and the souls
of animals would enjoy both an afterlife and participation in the general resurrection (Thomas 1996, 138, 140). Why else, some of these divines conjec-
tured, was Christ born in a stable—unless he meant to be " 'the redeemer of
man and beast out of their bondage by the Fall' " (Thomas 1996, 140)? At the
very least, it was widely believed that in the kingdom to come, animals
would be restored to their innocent prelapsarian condition—along with the
whole of the natural world (Thomas 1996, 139). The biblical support frequently cited for this belief was Romans 8:18–22, where Paul says,

> I consider that what we suffer at the present time cannot be com-
> pared with the glory that is going to be revealed to us. All of creation
> waits with eager longing for God to reveal his children. For creation
> was condemned to lose its purpose, not of its own will, but because
> God willed it to be so. Yet there was the hope that creation itself
> would one day be set free from its slavery and would share the
> glorious freedom of the children of God. For we know that up to
> the present time all creation groans with pain, like the pain of
> childbirth.

Instead of giving Christianity its due, Singer ransacks sources of non-
Christian Enlightenment sensitivity to nature, and indeed the general sensibility of the Romantic movement, such as its debts to Hindu religious
thought, recently made possible by the pioneers of Western orientalism
(Singer 1975, 221). What Singer conveniently leaves out, as a result of his own
anti-Christian bigotry, are the gentler features of Christian Enlightenment
thinking that informed a policy of the defense of animals, culminating in
England in the nineteenth century, in laws punishing wanton ill-treatment
of animals and in the foundation of the Royal Society for the Prevention of
Cruelty to Animals.

Singer is similarly notably silent about the legacy of the persistence of
the Enlightenment's utilitarian anthropocentric attitudes, but also about
the aforementioned Christian sources of animal liberation in the eighteenth century. When Marie Antoinette uttered the call to her courtiers
and entourage—"Come, let us be shepherds!"—as she led her jolly throng of
pre-Romantics into the mock peasant hamlet she had had constructed in

the Petit Trianon of the park of the Palace of Versailles, she was not, we must presume, imagining herself and her lion king husband lying down in fraternity with the lambs gathered there for her delectation. She was after all in drag as a shepherdess, and she imagined herself doing what shepherds and shepherdesses do—at least employing sheep for her exclusive human use as domesticated farm animals, not to be to let free to roam untended like the packs of merry Aquarian dogs chasing about such neoromantic havens in this harsh world as Berkeley, California.

Now, it is true that in the nineteenth century, Darwin's thought—or at least the ground from out of which Darwin's thought sprang—contained significant anti-anthropocentric elements. These found expression in the new British laws of the early nineteenth century. Yet, interestingly enough, even Darwin's vision of the kinship between human and nonhuman animals did little to prevent the continued exploitation of animals as wholly subservient property placed at the service of human beings. Alongside and in competition with Darwin's naturalistic sensibility, utility—as well as a new industrial economic order, now flexing its soon-to-be awesome muscles—still reigned. Thus, even here in animal-loving England, where laws were set in place in the early nineteenth century to protect animals from human predation, kindness to animals did not follow automatically from the promulgation of these laws. Although theory and indeed certain new laws pointed to a kindlier attitude toward animals, actual everyday practice did not significantly change from what it had been before. Darwin's belief in the common descent of human and nonhuman animals did not, for example, convert him to vegetarianism. Singer thus calls this period nothing but an "era of excuses" (Singer 1975, 227). It remained anthropocentric at bottom. Indeed, Richard Martin, the MP who proposed the first legislation to prevent cruelty to animals, in the end only succeeded in his initiative by offering his bill as a protection of private property—which the animals were taken to be. No notion of a social bond emerged here, even in the most progressive arena of animal liberation (Singer 1975, 223).

It is important to note again that Singer's explanation for the failure of non-anthropocentric theory to bring about non-anthropocentric behavior seizes on Christianity as the perennial villain. Arguing from what one might call the thesis of eternal and omnipotent embeddedness, Singer believes—without fully explaining why—that the Christian "moral attitudes of the

past were too deeply embedded in our thought and our practices to be
upset by a mere change in our knowledge about ourselves and of other animals" (Singer 1975, 232). A principal moral, then, to be drawn from Singer's
story is (once again) that Christianity chiefly bears the blame for the justification of cruel behavior to animals, for our carnivorous lusts—even long
after its influence has waned.

What, among other things, one can accept from Singer's arguments,
and what seems to reflect deep Christian values, is the abhorrence of pain.
Because pain is the absolute evil in Singer's view—rather than death, for
example—Singer is not a strict vegetarian. His criterion of what animals can
be eaten by humans rests on whether our doing so entails pain for the animal concerned. For Singer, there is all the world of difference between the
anguishing foreknowledge about their imminent doom afflicting highly
intelligent animals like pigs or the physical agony suffered by them and
other stock in the process of their slaughter over against the insentience
and inertia of an oyster as it slides down my throat or as it catches a whiff
of the catsup and horseradish sauce on the plate beside it. Never eat something that has a face, that can look you in the eye, are maxims that capture
the spirit of Singer's view. I shall be arguing that these can also be embraced
as values with Christian bases and affinities, and that they are grounded in
the ideal of a social bond with living things.

But, why should pain be an absolute evil—from a Christian point of
view? The answer to this question recalls what Sarvapalli Radhakrishnan,
the great Indian philosopher and former president of the Republic of India,
offered to a challenge to Hindu traditional practices of mortification and
poverty. "The only kind of poverty worth having," said Radhakrishnan, "is
voluntary poverty." Let me then first qualify our question about pain by saying that I mean *inflicted* pain. The pain we ourselves choose—except in
extreme cases where someone is a classic "danger to themselves"—can be
excluded. "No pain, no gain" is a formula for higher-order pleasure, not a
tormentor's credo. But pain which is inflicted upon an unwilling subject
bears names we all understand, and labels phenomena I believe we all
abhor—namely torture, cruelty, torment, and the like. So why is torture
wrong—in particular, torturing animals, whom not even I, and much less
Singer, imagine to be full moral agents or beings who might qualify, at least
in most senses generally accepted today, as subjects of salvation?

4. Vagrant and Enduring Sources of Christian Comity between Humans and Animals

Now, in thinking about how Christians might conceive a relationship between human and nonhuman animals, Christians must, I believe, acknowledge much of the force of the critique of Christian speciesism in the work of Singer and others. But this does not mean, as I am arguing, that Christians lack sources for kindlier views about a relation to nature in the traditions making up the rich texture of the history of Christianity.

But to acknowledge that sources can be found is also to assert that Christians will need to admit at least two things about the way the Christian tradition and the Bible are read. First, to read Christian tradition and the Bible is to interpret them in a creative and open way. Quite frankly, one will have to read Christian tradition selectively partly because there is largely no other way so to do. As to the Bible, even so-called fundamentalists or biblical literalists read scripture selectively, even while not admitting it. The Bible does not itself tell us how it is to be read.³ In that case, how *are* Christians to read the Bible? Second, as to reading the Bible, let me call to mind to those given to a literal reading of the Bible that reading the Bible exclusively in a literal way is a relatively recent way of reading sacred scripture. For over a thousand years, the Bible had been read in numerous ways, and the most prominent among them, for example, until the Protestant reformation, was an allegorical reading of the Bible. Let me explore this older Christian way of reading the Bible. As we will see, its overthrow coincides with the desacralization of nature, which, in part, marks the beginning of speciesism in the Christian tradition. So, what was this reading of nature and the Bible as a single text like? (Harrison 1998).

For Christians of an earlier, pre-Reformation age, God had provided humanity with two "books," as it were—the Bible and the "book of nature." Seeing nature as revealing the creator meant that the entire natural world spoke to pious Christians in various and sundry ways. Everything, no matter how humble and useless to human purposes, was a symbol of some, often quite small, part of the divine plan. "Animals," historian Peter Harrison tells us for example, "had a 'story,' they were allocated meanings, they were emblems of important moral and theological truths, and like the hieroglyphics of ancient Egypt they were to be thought of as the characters of an intelligible language" (Harrison 1998, 2). The attacks of wild animals, for instance, were seen as instruments of divine punishment. In the seventeenth century, Abbé Pluche preached that worms, flies, and other destructive pests "'are employed by the Almighty to humble the Pride of Man'" (Harrison 1998, 162). Such animals as pigs, for example, while not proscribed to Christians, were nonetheless warnings to the faithful of the sins of mindless gluttony and the filth—both moral and physical—attendant upon devotion to this classic vice.

But even more important in appreciating how the Bible was read is the fact that the meanings invested in the book of nature in their turn informed the reading of the Bible itself. As Harrison puts it, the "interpretation of the two books, moreover, took place as part of an integrated hermeneutical practice, premised on the principle that the meaning of the words of scripture could not be fully known until the meanings of the objects to which the words referred were also known" (Harrison 1998, 3). Such readings of scripture are what Harrison calls "allegorical." But by allegory, he does not mean our way of reading "multiple meanings into the words of texts, but [it] was rather a process through which the reader was drawn away from naked words to the infinitely more eloquent things of nature to which those words referred" (Harrison 1998, 3). No accident, the Christians of that time thought, that Jesus should send a herd of pigs over a cliff to their ruin in casting out an evil spirit. The pigs of the Bible story were fulfilling their cosmic destiny, in a way, by living up to their innate divine symbolism.

For the most part, all this changed with the Protestant and Catholic reformations—perhaps especially with the Protestants. To begin with, the reformers severed the allegorical link between nature and the Bible. In this way, the reformers positioned the Bible at the center of Christian life by denying the "book of nature" its previous status as having intrinsic symbolic or religious meaning. Only the words of the Bible carried meanings bearing on salvation. Nature had religious value only insofar as it was an arena in which humanity put nature to use for humanity, and in doing so worked out God's purposes for humankind. Nature was no longer a "text," to use current jargon. Only texts were "texts." Nature no longer was a vast and densely populated "forest of symbols" celebrating divine majesty and goodness, but instead became a vast arena in which utilitarian human purposes were to be worked out. In place of sacramental significances, nature's hidden code was articulated in terms of abstract mathematical relations (Harrison 1998, 162). Instead, then, of what some would call the "passive" reading of nature for the symbolism inherent it, this new generation of reformed Christians were enjoined to undertake "an active investigation of things which uncovers their material utility" in the service of humanity (Harrison 1998, 167). It is no accident, too, that the Jesuits—in a sense Roman Catholicism's answer to the Protestant reformation—were led by the same slogan directing all mundane human activity to the divine "A. M. D. G."—"all for the greater honor and glory of God." In the words of William Derham, an early eighteenth century divine, "Scripture not only commends God's works," but also should be a spur to those " 'curious and ingenious Enquirers that Seek them out, or pry into them.' " As such, the severing of the allegorical link between nature and scripture provided a basis for the independent study of nature and scripture alike. In a way, this moment spelt the very beginnings of science and technology. The new science was, after all, to be put to use for the practical, utilitarian purposes of humanity.

In light of what both Catholic and Protestant reformations wrought, it would indeed be odd to speak about the Christian bases for a notion of comity or of a society comprehending animals and humans. The injunction to use nature, and thus animals, for human purposes alone as a means of realizing the new Christian ideal makes the idea of relationships, kinship, and, thus, a social bond with animals theologically awkward, if not absurd. If John Bossy is right in arguing that both Protestant and Catholic reformations share more in common with each other religiously than they did with the era immediately preceding, then Christians who wish to begin again to think, feel, and speak about animals in ways which are not exhausted by their utility to human purposes will have to recapture something of the spirit of Christianity before the reformations—or at certain remarkable points thereafter (Bossy 1985, ch. 6).

5. When Christianity Was Durkheimian and Irish Godparents Were Wolves

First, then, to the Christianity before the reformations. One place to begin thinking about a society encompassing human and nonhuman animals is oddly enough to reflect on the place of the idea of relationship, community, society, kinship, and such in various strains of pre-Reformation theology. This is to recognize those moments in Christian thought when its values and Durkheimian values most closely approximated each other. I have in mind those moments in the history of Christian thought when kinship, community, and such had highest value, such as John Bossy brings to light in his *Christianity in the West, 1400–1700* (Bossy 1985, 14–34). These were periods, closer to 1400 than to 1700, before the popularity of the personal tomb, individual family cemetery allotment, or even the private church pew, and, instead, a time when burial in common and prayer en masse were the norm. This was when holy "communion" meant sharing in the fellowship of the church, not in the private sacramental enjoyment of the savior, when "charity" meant the "simple affection with which one was in and out of regarding one's fellows," not an "act of benevolence towards the poor," when "penance" meant payment of a social obligation in order to achieve social peace, not handing over "money in return for goods and services," what Bossy describes as a shift from an "ethics of solidarity to one of civility" (Bossy 1985, 168–69). This was in effect a period when Christian spirituality, theology, and practice lived by norms that would later be characteristic of Durkheimian values and theory. Notions like comity, society, relationship, and kinship—all values celebrated by the Durkheimians—were also seen by these pre-Reformation Christians as essential to their understanding of Christianity.

In order to establish the Christian bona fides of an ideal of comity, society, kinship, and such between humans and animals, I shall start with the core of Christian theology: christology. In certain pre-Reformation strains of christology and soteriology, ideas such as kinship, relationship, society, and the like controlled fundamental conceptions of who and what Jesus was thought to be, and thus by extension, how creation was related to the savior-creator, in just the same general ways that I have described. A peculiarity about this fifteenth-century christology was its "obsession" with the humanity of Jesus, and eventually with Jesus as part of a family, kinship group, society, and so on (Bossy 1985, 7). A landmark theological document of the period was Anselm of Canterbury's (1033–1109) *Cur Deus Homo?* Despite the controversial nature of its soteriology, it faithfully reflected the popular religious sentiment of late medieval Christianity in emphasizing this very humanity of Jesus. For both Anselm and the mass of ordinary

Christians, Jesus not only redeemed humanity by sacrifice, as prevailing atonement soteriology presumes, but most importantly, by virtue of the sacrifice of his human nature, rather than his divinity. This view was moreover so long-lived and widespread that historian John Bossy claims that it reigned from Anselm's twelfth-century world until the time of Luther (Bossy 1985, 5). For Bossy, in "Anselm's reading, the redeemer is Christ the man, not Christ as God. That with which he satisfies the Father is his Godhead, but he who is satisfying must be man. Godhead is a sort of quantity with which Christ operates, a mysterious possession of the man. This was certainly how his double nature appeared to the average Christian of the late Middle Ages, for whom Christ was simply 'God.'" Thus, in seeking assurance of redemption, the principal concern of the pious Christian of the late middle ages "was to know that this God was an actual man, from whose redeeming sacrifice he was accordingly entitled to benefit" (Bossy 1985, 6).

But, how did these pre-Reformation Christians convince themselves of Jesus's humanity? For them, as for Durkheimians and perhaps for Christians today, Jesus's humanity is guaranteed by the sure knowledge of his having a network of blood relatives and kin—of his being a fully social being in the normal human sense of the term. As Bossy notes: "To show, in the fifteenth century, that Christ was a real man, it was not necessary to resort to biology, and not sufficient to see that he was a child of known parents: it was necessary to know that he was someone with human kin" (Bossy 1985, 8). Thus, for the Christians just prior to the reformations, Jesus was most assuredly human for the same reasons the Durkheimians thought that humans were different from non-humans—because Jesus could be located within a familial social web, a network of the blood relatives and kin.

An additional curiosity of this line of late medieval reasoning emphasized the special value of Jesus's having kin within Mary's family. Thus, we count blood kin of Mary's recorded in the "much-read" *Golden Legend* of Jacobus de Voragine: her parents, Anne and Joachim; her cousin, Elizabeth; a first stepsister, Mary Cleophas, the mother of Simon and Jude, described as Jesus's brothers in the gospels; and a second stepsister, Mary Salome, wife to Zebedee, and mother of the apostle James and John the Evangelist. Indeed, by the reckoning of *Golden Legend*, fully one half of Jesus's apostles were his blood-kin on Mary's side—and none, as far as one can tell, from Joseph's (Bossy 1985, 11). Bossy goes on to show how Jesus's location within a nexus of familial social relations made many of the mysteries of the Gospels clear for the Christians of the late middle ages. For instance, the social location of Jesus explained that the

> wedding feast at Cana had been given by Zebedee and . . . (Mary Salome), the virgin's (second) step-sister, for their son John the Evangelist. Mary the Virgin, as senior sister, was evidently in charge; it was natural that Jesus, for all his prudish reservations, would help with the supply of drink, though not surprising that he should carry the Evangelist off to virginity once the feast was over. Similarly, it was perfectly natural that Jesus should particularly love his step-cousin John, and should commend him to Mary on the cross, to take him as her son in lieu of himself. . . . (Bossy 1985, 9–10)

Thus, as late as the time of Leonardo Da Vinci (1452–1519), the holy family, so-called, of this period, was composed of the trinity of Mary, Jesus, and Anne, rather than with Joseph, the head of Jesus's nuclear family of modern conception (Bossy 1985, 9–10). Bossy shows that Joseph was held in a good deal of contempt until the end of the middle ages. He was just a "doddering ancient, an unwilling spouse and a jealous husband, whose conviction that his wife had committed adultery" characterized what Bossy calls this "dismal figure" (Bossy 1985, 10).

How, then, does this conception of Jesus's saving role as bound up with his human relationships bear on our relation to animals? Quite simply it thrusts Durkheimian notions of affiliation, comity, social relations, kinship, friendship, and thus society right to the fore across the board. For along with the kinship-articulated christology that I have described, we also find kinship-based notions informing the understanding of ideals of human perfection or sainthood at the very heart of the religion of the high middle ages. Before the Reformation, saints were of two kinds: those stern ascetics who gained their repute by enduring "penitential hardship and self-denial" and a "more benign" ideal of saints as "friends of God." Crucial here is the notion that such comity or friendship with God was not chiefly a matter of their self-involved virtue, whether the saint had furthered "friendship among" others—whether they furthered such (Durkheimian) notions as sociability. Saints as friends of God were then the classic peacemakers that Matthew's Gospel of course tells us are "children" of God—his kin (Matt. 5: 9). Thus, for these pre-Reformation Christians, classic Durkheimian social virtues such as comity, reconciliation, and friendship carried a remarkable theological weight: they were the very stuff of being part of God's family or social circle, of being one with God.

One cannot emphasize too much the defining power of this social notion of saintly perfection. Our current sensibilities permit us to understand how humans might be saints because they were "friends" of God, or because they were "friends" of our fellow human creatures. In the high middle ages, animals could also be "friends" and thus form social bonds with humans, and, so, with God. Bossy relates the story of a faithful dog in the legend of St. Roch who saved the life of the saint by fetching him food during the saint's illness. The dog was later canonized for the same reasons St. Roch himself had been: St. Roch died a friend of God and therefore in high middle ages Catholicism was a "saint." Since the dog was a friend of this friend of God, he too was a saint. Likewise the story of the thirteenth-century St. Guinefort, "dog and martyr" tells the story of a faithful dog who tended his master's baby, but who was mistaken for the baby's killer, and "martyred" by the irate father. The people of the region were sure that Guinefort was only being a "friend" of God, and thus deserved sainthood, in serving so selflessly—even unto death. Bossy concludes, in fact, that the spiritual sensibilities of the day indicated that "a dog might be a better friend to man than other men," and that their religiosity was eminently authentic since for the Durkheimians, "'religion' means the extension of social relations beyond the frontiers of merely human society" (Bossy 1985, 13). Accordingly, some of these pre-Reformation Christian forbears regarded animals—at least some animals, such as our domestic and farm animals—quite naturally as we do in these post-Romantic times—as friends and companions, as part of our community. Indeed, the French for "pet" dog in this case retains this sense in the term *chien familier*—literally "belonging to the family." Similarly, the German *"Heimtier"*—"animal of the home"—may capture the same sense of a nonhuman animal as part of the household, as kin. Significantly, while these animals, such as dogs, are companions in a quite full sense of the term, they are at the same time not really treated sentimentally as is our custom of referring to them as our "children." In the high middle ages, it was thought that the "Irish chose wolves as godparents since the friendship so created would oblige the wolf to do them no harm . . ." (Bossy 1985, 16). The reason for this is that while we can easily say they keep us company and even in the literal sense share our bread (com-panion), treating them as our "children" not only stretches the idea of offspring, but denies animals their otherness in essentially being assimilated to us as our children. This inclusion of animals into human society and its social institutions, such as in the legal courts, also accounts for the many criminal trials of animals—as "enemies" of humans—from at least 1266 through the high middle ages (Cohen 1986, 20).

So the relationship which the Christians of the late middle ages conceived of having with at least certain kinds of animals might remind us of ways in which we today affirm that our relation to animals has a correspondingly religious and moral dimension. While it is true that Christians differ from Jains or Buddhists, for example, in regards to their not having an explicit commandment against killing animals, our attitudes to the treatment of animals certainly has a moral dimension. If you think this reeks of sentimentality, reflect for a moment on our common feelings toward those who dump or abandon their pets, whether they be people on the move, unable any longer to accommodate their pets or those who find the attention to them required inconvenient, or the all-too-familiar phenomenon of students dumping their pets at the end of the school year. The violation here is precisely the abrogation of a relationship, the unilateral severance of a system of exchange of which one has had the benefit. It is immoral in the same sense—although arguably not to the same degree—as copping out of other relationships in which one has acquired obligations of reciprocity.

6. Conclusion

Now, where does all this leave us? In some ways, while I think I have provided a defense of the case that in Christianity there is a legitimate tradition of considering the reality of a society encompassing humans and animals, Christians remain perhaps as "hopelessly conflicted" today about the precise limits of such a society as they did in the late middle ages or in post-Reformation England (Thomas 1983, 301–3). Consider the conflicted emotions over the mass slaughter of potential carriers of hoof and mouth disease. One can, I think, speak of a public grief or sorrow for the fate of these diseased animals, yet they are the very same animals normally bound for stockyard and abattoir! Why the difference in emotional reaction? Is

there perhaps even more, as yet to be explored, feeling for our fellow creatures in our utilitarian attitudes to animals than we realize? And, what of the
contradictions listed by Keith Thomas that are signaled by such situations
as our children, who may take their teddy bears to bed with them at night,
yet who demand to visit Ronald McDonald whenever possible. Or, what of
the contradictions contained in our cherishing certain animals as pets or in
the wild, yet at the same time trying to rid the world of pests and vermin?
Thomas reports that Oliver Goldsmith observed that the animal lovers of
his day " 'pity and . . . eat the objects of their compassion' " (Thomas 1983,
301). Worse than that, I am not sure how and where to go with this particular way of articulating a social bond or kinship with animals, especially in
the harder cases of those animals not part of our households, with animals
that, by definition, avoid relationships with humans. I refer here to the so-
called "wild" animals of our forests, deserts, and seas. What of animals with
whom exchange seems otherwise highly problematic or impossible—I
think of that tasty oyster again? I am frankly just not sure how one would—
or could—articulate relations of kinship in cases of such remote relationship. Perhaps, like every good tool, Durkheimian thought reaches the limits
of its utility here? But at least it has taken us this far. What I, at least, hope I
have been able to do by accessing these eminently Christian traditions of
community with animals and Durkheimian insights into the relationship
of exchange and comity, is to provide to those who are moved to the love of
living things—whether Christians or not—at least a way of taking strength
for their efforts from the traditions of Christianity and the wisdom inherent
in Durkheimian thought.

13

Sacrifice, Gift, and the Social Logic of Muslim "Human Bombers"

The way we "talk the talk" sometimes conforms to the way we "walk the walk"; the way we think about things sometimes determines how we will act. The heavy artillery of political and religious rhetoric is routinely wheeled into place alongside the machinery of military combat. Thus, whether it is the world of the latest Intifada or that of post 9–11, the struggle to control the discourse about these conflicts is just as fiercely contested on the battlefield of language and concept as are the material struggles related to them. In the pages of *Terrorism and Political Violence*, Raphael Israeli has argued correctly, I would submit, that careful use of terminology is therefore "not a matter of mere semantics, but of great importance in order to discern notions and mind sets and their significance" (Israeli 1997, 96). I agree. In thinking about Al Qa'ida, for example, it is vital that we think about them in ways that illuminate what they do and are. Ought they be thought of as hijackers, murderers, suicides, and fanatics, or as martyrs, saints, sacrifices, and "gifts"? And what of the Palestinian bombers? Are they, as well, martyrs or suicides, sacrifices, homicides, "gifts" and/or what Raphael Israeli calls them in the quest for a neutral designation: "human bombers" (Israeli 1997, 96)?

In this chapter, I shall first attempt to sort through some of the conceptual issues thrown up by naming the particular phenomena that Israeli

Reprinted from *Terrorism and Political Violence* 15 (3) (2003):1–34, by permission of Taylor & Francis Group, LLC, http://www.taylorandfrancis.com.

has argued we should call "human bombs." I shall propose that we need to pay greater attention to the "sacrificial" designations of these "human bombings" as made by Muslims and as rooted in Islamic discourse. I do this not in the interests of celebrating the acts of "human bombers," but for the sake of understanding them better. When we succeed in understanding the sacrificial aspect of the Islamic "human bombings," I believe we will better understand the purposes and facilitating structures of these acts. Until we do so, we will miss something central to what they are—at least in the minds of those perpetrating these acts.

I. Jihad, Sacrifice, and the Many Voices of the "Human Bombers"

Before pressing ahead toward an analysis of "human bombings" in sacrificial terms, two points must be kept in mind, first, about the relation of the "human bombers" to mainstream Islam and, second, about the content of the "human bomber" ideology. First, the "human bombers" are a modern deviant form of Islam, a fringe "opposition" to mainstream Islam, although disproportionately influential in ways that we are only now discovering. And accordingly, as extreme forms of Islam finding embodiment in such movements as Al Qa'ida, Hamas, Hizballah, and others, they and the innovations they assert are widely rejected by mainstream Muslims (Israeli 1997; Israeli 2002). As such, the rise of the Muslim "human bombers" signals tensions within Islam itself. Second, the image of external, militant jihad must be kept firmly in focus as a leading conception of what "human bombers" see themselves to be doing.

Regarding sacrifice and suicide in particular, it is, indeed, arguable that "jihad" holds the key. I shall refer at length to Raphael Israeli's persuasive arguments that jihad certainly overshadows and indeed invalidates the view that "human bombers" should be called "suicides." Raphael Israeli notes, for example, that even for extremists, the Quranic prohibition against taking one's life creates cognitive dissonance. Even if a "human bomber" may claim purity of motive, Islamic theology always leaves the final judgments to Allah. So, self-inflicted death, even with conscious religious intent, can never guarantee one's place in Paradise (Israeli 2002, 35). I am also considerably less sure that jihad is a mightier concept in these examples of self-inflicted death than "sacrifice." In fact, I am arguing that "sacrifice" is set on a course of its own, although it is woven into the discourse of jihad as well. At the very least, I shall try to show how multivalent the discourse about "human bombers" is, with "sacrifice" being one of the most prominent "voices" making up the chorus.

Nonetheless, a place for "jihad" at the head of the conceptual table cannot easily be denied. In some cases, "sacrifice" might be subsumed to the notion of jihad. The recent "appendix to an issue of the Muslim fundamentalist organ *al-Islam wa-Filastin* (Islam and Palestine)," referred to by Raphael Israeli as a "manual of Islamic fundamentalist terrorism," makes this point. There, we hear the author tell us that self-sacrifice is merely what jihad requires (Israeli 2002, 34–35).

This is to say that whatever else the "human bombings" may be, they are about killing Jews, Israelis, and eliminating Israel itself. The declarations of Hamas and other organizations involved in them have made this abundantly clear. Little is mentioned of sacrifice in the Charter of Hamas, for example, but a great deal is said of jihad and eliminating Israel (Israeli 1997, 111). Hamas, for example, focuses on the suffering caused to the enemy by the "human bombers" rather than "extolling their own suffering and sacrifice." Hizballah likewise demands that the deaths of their "human bombers" be justified by the suffering of the number of casualties inflicted on the enemy (Israeli 2002, 30). These examples, informed as they are by the discourse of jihad, should also counsel caution about speaking too simply of sacrifice in connection with the "human bombers," since sacrifices are not typically directed against the interests of another.

Despite the clear jihadist conception behind "human bombings," they persist in being conceived as sacrifices by their perpetrators—even if this produces a "convoluted" or internally conflicted discourse (Kramer 1996). Despite their action in service of jihad, the "human bombings" are also seen as supreme gifts given in the interests of enhancing the conditions of others. Multivalence reigns. One way that this gap between the utility of military attack and the symbolism of the sacrificial deed is bridged will be by recourse to the alternative description of these "human bombings" as "martyrdoms." They are deaths suffered in active struggle in behalf of Islam or Palestine. Thus, sacrifice bombers can also, and at the same time, be martyrdom bombers in the view that I shall elaborate. But this only adds yet another "voice" to what I have already referred to as a kind of "chorus" of voices all singing in the unison provided by "human bombings."

Even if we grant jihad a prominent place at the conceptual high table of "human bombings," in order more fully to understand even some jihadist aspects of "human bombings," we may have to adopt something even closer to the viewpoint of a segment of Islam that repeats again and again that they are sacrifices. I am urging us to pay more attention, then, to the nuances, qualifications, and inner contradictions of the standard interpretation of "human bombings" as simple instances of jihad attacks (Kramer 1996). Jihad, I think, is only part of the story of the "human bombers." Thus, even as practical military acts of jihad, these operations are fraught with an ambiguity and multivalence that I shall try to exploit in bringing to the fore the idea of sacrifice in this discussion.

Even from a strictly military point of view, it seems strategically ineffi-cient to undertake operations that in effect guarantee the loss of one's fighters in every assault. David C. Rapoport has, for example, argued that the classic movement of Assassins did not assign highest priority to the efficiency of their operations—at least in the commonplace sense of "efficiency" often employed in military operations (Rapoport 1984, 675). Thus, strictly from the perspective of the ugly calculus of jihadist military efficiency, aimed at actual military victory, would it not make more sense if, instead of killing themselves in the process of making their attacks, the "human bombers" could have gone on killing many more Israelis in subsequent non-suicidal attacks, instead of just those they typically kill in killing themselves? Ambiguity and multivalence as well, thus, afflict the calculation of a rational ends/means calculus. Although perhaps militarily defensible if only for the terror incited and for the economic costs to Israel, the strictly military rationality of these operations does not seem necessarily or undividedly the only priority of these self-inflicted deaths.

"Human bombers," however, have a kind of efficiency of their own. Kramer has shown that for the Lebanese "human bombers" in the 1980's, self-martyrdom needed to be seen as "productive" in order to receive clerical sanction. Killing oneself in a futile and unproductive attack wins no merit (Kramer 1996). The "human bombers" can get close; they can choose their time and place of attack with great precision; they cannot be interrogated afterwards for information about their future plans. Still, strictly from the perspective of the ugly calculus of jihadist military efficiency, the loss of such devoted fighters at some point may be subject to the law of diminishing returns. But then again, the demographic imbalance between an Arab Muslim population in the many tens of millions against Israel's five million makes such calculations rather theoretical. Ambiguity and multivalence affect this calculation of a rational ends/means calculus.

With Raphael Israeli, then, I believe we need to adopt even more an "Islamic frame of reference for definition and perhaps a diagnosis . . . if we are to comprehend the underlying motives of this sort of unparalleled mode of self -sacrifice" (Israeli 1997, 107). A great part of that "Islamic frame of reference" for the "human bombings" is sacrifice. If in Israel/Palestine, one goal of these deaths is to attack others outright in jihad, then another, and simultaneous one, is to create a Palestinian political entity by making a sacrificial offering to Allah and the umma. While the "human bombers" aim to kill Jews, they also are embedded in their families and communities, and in a world encompassed by a supreme being that has a political teleology of its own beyond killing Jews. The meaning of the actions of the "human bombers" derives at least in part from the web of human and divine relationships in which they seem themselves to be living, now and as they imagine their extended families and people living in the future. There is more to "human bombers" than jihad, and certainly more than suicide. There is, as I shall now argue, sacrifice.

2. Sacrifice or Suicide?

Once attention is drawn to talk of violence, we see rather quickly that words like sacrifice, suicide, or homicide are not neutral designations, but "loaded" words—evaluations of certain actions. This is to say, language becomes an integral part of the physical struggles involved, and not something set aside and independent of them. For this reason, we will need to clear up some conceptual or terminological issues from the outset.

It seems uncontroversial that calling a death a suicide or homicide is rhetorically aimed at delegitimizing it, while calling it a sacrifice or an act of martyrdom is raising it to lofty transcendent heights—thereby, of course, to religious levels of discourse and behavior. In calling a death sacrifice, it is typically ennobled, raised to a level above the profane calculation of individual cost-benefit analysis—to the level of a so-called "higher" good, whether that be of a nation or some transnational or transcendent reference, like a religion. For this reason, the neutral term coined by Raphael Israeli, "human bombers," serves a useful purpose (Israeli 1997, 96). For this reason, we will need to clear up some conceptual or terminological issues from the outset.

I make no claim to originality in remarking on the rhetorical character of our talk about sacrifice and suicide. Indeed, Israeli has recently made the question of the distinction between the two a major feature of his important discussion. Israeli believes that at least Palestinian "human bombers" might be best termed "Islamikaze" (Israeli 1997, 96). Revealing, among other things, his psychological orientations to the phenomenon of the "human bomber," Israeli takes pains to show that at least Palestinian "human bombers" do not fit the "psychological or pathological" profile of a suicide (Israeli 1997, 96), but rather conform more to that of the Japanese "kamikaze"—in explicit contrast to "suicides" such as "hara kiri." Israeli likewise reports that Al Qa'ida even maintained formal "Kamikaze Barracks" in Afghanistan (Israeli 1997, 97)! In support of this rejection of the description of the "human bombers" as "suicides," Israeli notes how the motivational profile of suicides differs from that of those whom Israeli calls "Islamikazes" and "human bombers" (Israeli 1997, 97). Like "kamikazes," the "human bombers" are dedicated to "wreaking havoc on their enemies," not primarily to their own destruction, like "hara-kiri" (Israeli 1997, 99); they seek to minimize their own losses, while maximizing those of the enemy (Israeli 1997, 20). They, in short, embody the ethic of jihad that we discussed at the outset.

3. Suicide or Sacrifice?: A Sociological and Religious Solution

While accepting Israeli's analyses in terms of personal psychological motivations as useful and instructive, I would like to move things along by introducing sociological and theological factors. In my view, whether to commit suicide or to do sacrifice, people act not only because of personal, self-contained motivational structure, but also because of their relationships with others—whether these be relationships with other human beings or with divine superhuman persons, conditions, or states of affairs. I am in no way accusing Israeli of deliberately excluding social and religious causal factors in the behavior of the "human bombers," only that his treatments thus far of sociological and religious insights have been inadequate because only incipient. Thus, while I believe we can find in Israeli's articles the beginnings of sociological and religious analyses, these need to be robustly exploited.[1] Let me then turn to what a sociological or religious perspective on "human bombers" might yield.

Well over a hundred years ago, France was plagued by outbursts of terrorist violence, haunted by impending war, and troubled by an epidemic of suicides. The great French sociologist Émile Durkheim obsessed about these issues, about the way that they could best be minimized and explained, and about the possible hidden connections among these apparently disparate phenomena that escaped the untutored eye. How do we account for the disparities among different populations in terms of the occurrence of suicide in modern France? Why were French Protestants more likely to commit suicide than, say, French Catholics of roughly the same socio-economic and regional membership? Should we regard these suicides in the same or different light as we regard death in a hopeless cause on the battlefield?

While sociologists will recognize Durkheim for his first book on this subject, aptly titled *Suicide*, it is less well appreciated that his theory of sacrifice in *Elementary Forms of the Religious Life* (1912) and that of his co-workers, Henri Hubert and Marcel Mauss in *Sacrifice: Its Nature and Functions* (1899) are conceptually linked with the work on suicide (Durkheim 1951; Hubert & Mauss 1964). Again, were the suicides among rootless industrial workers, for example, related at all to the prospect of "suicidal" infantry assaults in the upcoming war? Or were these kinds of death only superficially similar in their hopelessness? Further in this vein, in *Suicide,* Durkheim was particularly puzzled about how to conceive the occurrence of what he called "altruistic suicide"—cases of individuals giving up their lives—sacrificially—for others, as, say, in a war where a soldier dies to save his comrades. Since he was viscerally averse to suicide in any form, Durkheim puzzled over the question of how it was possible that these altruistic suicides were seen by otherwise admirable societies as praiseworthy. If those who praised altruistic suicides were correct in their valuation, should we not call them something else—something signaling their lofty moral stature? Are they not a sort of "sacrifice" instead? And, if we chose so to do, what were we implying in our use of the term, "sacrifice"? Did it mean that the "sacrifice" incurred in dying for one's comrades was like sacrifices elsewhere, say, in the Catholic "sacrifice" of the Mass, or in sacrifices in the world religions, like that done on the Hajj by Muslims? And, if there was something linking these various uses of the word *sacrifice*, what could it be?

Durkheim made little or no progress on this dilemma, although in connection with the relation of suicide to sacrifice the conceptual thread that he left dangling was to be picked up a generation later by one of his most talented co-workers, Maurice Halbwachs. While hugely loyal to the Durkheimian legacy, Halbwachs was never satisfied with the way that Durkheim handled the conceptual relation of suicide to sacrifice. In a dedicated study of his own on suicide, *The Causes of Suicide* (1930), Halbwachs revisited the question of the relation of suicide to other kinds of deaths, in particular to ones highly regarded, such as altruistic or sacrificial deaths in warfare (Halbwachs 1930). Here, Halbwachs came up with a formula that seemed to him at any rate to ease the conceptual tangle over sacrifice and suicide left behind by Durkheim. Curiously, Halbwachs's solution to was to be more Durkheimian than Durkheim, in a way. He simply relativized the matter of usage by referring these terms to their social contexts. Whether something was a "sacrifice" rather than a "suicide" depended upon the viewpoint of their respective societies of reference. Halbwachs tells us straightforwardly that "society claims sacrifice as its own proper work," accomplished "within the bosom of the community, where all the spiritual forces converge . . ." (Halbwachs 1930, 477). Society thus "presides" over sacrifice, says Halbwachs; it "organizes" it and "takes responsibility for it." By contrast, society "repudiates" suicide (Halbwachs 1930, 475). Thus, to Durkheim's attempt to define suicide—"We call suicide all those cases of death resulting from an action taken by the victim themselves, and with the intention or the prospect of killing oneself"—Halbwachs first added the phrase "and which is not at the same time a sacrifice" (Halbwachs 1930, 475). This seemingly innocuous formula brought sacrifice and suicide into conceptual relationship to one another as limiting cases of each other. Halbwachs was, in effect, saying that the only feature making the suicidal and sacrificial deaths different was society's attitude to them. Suicide and sacrifice differ because of their relation to society. A death, such as that of a *satī* in traditional India, might be considered a sacrifice under those conditions typically prevailing there, but it most certainly "becomes a suicide if it loses its ritual form" (Halbwachs 1930, 477). Halbwachs's insight is one that I think we can capitalize upon in discussing the matters to hand of religious violence.

Confirming the value of the sociological apperception that Halbwachs's conceptual work brings to our subject, Avishai Margalit recently published an analysis of the so-called suicide bombings in Israel and the territories that is worthy of Durkheim and Halbwachs. While these deaths seem to be the calculated utilitarian acts of individuals, Margalit argues that they are motivated by a vengeance marked by a strong desire for "spectacular revenge." They are thus signs meant to be read and received by certain audiences and therefore profoundly social acts. Their success seems necessarily to rely upon the kind of communal recognition and subsequent ritual celebration of the operations by the community from which the bomber comes. Margalit observes, as well, how much social prestige accrues to the bombers. Everyone knows their names, Margalit tells us—even, and perhaps especially, "small children" (Margalit 2003, 38).

Raphael Israeli also brings home the point of the "jihadist" nature of the "human bomber" attacks, as we have already discussed. But he notes beyond this that such an individual death is a profoundly social act: it is done so that the "entire Islamic *umma* is rescued" (Israeli 2002, 37). Bin Laden likewise made clear that, in his mind, the 9–11 hijackers belong intimately to the community and are duly celebrated: "The 19 brothers who sacrificed their lives in the sake of Allah were rewarded by this victory that we rejoice in today."[2] Or, if we are to take radical Islamist Palestinians seriously in describing the self-immolating deaths in Israel and the territories as "martyrdoms," then we need to think about these acts of religious violence in ways that we have not perhaps yet done with sufficient thoroughness—as "sacrifices."[3] This, I take it, is precisely what Halbwachs had in mind in speaking of society "claiming sacrifice as its own proper work," of sacrifice accomplished "within the bosom of the community, where all the spiritual forces converge . . ." or of a society that "presides" over sacrifice, "organizes" it and "takes responsibility for it" (Halbwachs 1930, 477). Sacrifice is a profoundly social action, essentially involving a network of relationships, typically, as we will see, actualized in terms of systems of social exchange. Sacrifice is not something to be understood solely in terms of the dynamics of an individual's psyche (Kramer 1996, 5).

What is more, sacrifice is not just a social deed. It has potent religious resonances as well. Durkheim and another two of his co-workers, Henri Hubert and Marcel Mauss, argued that sacrifice is more than just a socially sanctioned kind of self-inflicted death. It is also a "making holy," as the Latin origins of the term indicate—*sacri-ficium* (Hubert & Mauss 1964, 9). Sacrifice for the Durkheimians is indeed a giving up or giving of that makes something holy. Thus, for Durkheimians, these "human bombings" would not tend to be conceived as simply utilitarian acts. As we have learned, the "human bombers" are regarded as "sacred" by their communities of reference. They have been "made holy" in the eyes of the community that "accepts" them and their deed. They are elevated to lofty moral, and indeed, religious, levels, as sacrificial victims themselves or as kinds of holy saints. Thus, bin Laden celebrated "Hani Hanjour from Al-Ta'if, the destroyer of the centre of the US defence," the Pentagon, in appropriate words to this newly perceived reality of the self-sacrificing human bomber "victim." He concludes that because of this act of self-immolation, Hani Hanjour should win acceptance by Allah, thus sealing his having been made holy in the process of his human bombing: "Clear purity and a splendid sacrifice. We beseech Allah to accept him as a martyr."[4] Finally, like all those one regards as holy, the bombers cast themselves as innocents. As young people, and now notably young women, indeed, in many respects, they are classic candidates for attributed innocence. Thus, especially when young "human bombers" die in the course of an operation itself deemed morally meritorious, they attempt to turn the moral tables on the enemy. It is as if they are saying in their self-destruction: "See what you have made us do!" (Margalit 2003, 38).

In employing the language of the perpetrators of "human bombings," I am, of course, neither justifying nor elevating their self-described "sacrifices." I am not urging anyone to lavish the praise or to attribute the prestige these operations seem to have from their radical societies of reference. For Americans or Israelis, no amount of argument will make us accept the "human bombers" as "sacrifices"—nor should it! Using Halbwachs's language for distinguishing between suicide and sacrifice, we did not "preside" over the acts of the 9–11 agents and thus for us, these acts are not "sacrifices." To adapt Halbwachs's words again, we did not "organize" these operations and "take responsibility for" them. Indeed, we "repudiate" these deaths as "suicides." But that should not stop us from seeing things from the point of view of Al Qa'ida. For them, these operations are entirely different in character from what they are to us: they are gifts, sacrifices, martyrdoms, and so on.

This is the point to be made here—the language of sacrifice and suicide is "loaded"—which is to say that their meanings are relational. Unless Americans see how Al Qa'ida can imagine things in this way, I do not believe that we will be able to access their deeper processes of thought. It should go without saying, then, that I am not urging understanding here to cover for sympathy. But I am urging us at least to take up Halbwachs's point and see what those promoting these deaths and self-immolations think that they were doing, and consequently why they think they are right in so doing. In this way, I think we can begin to explain their actions—and with that knowledge do what we will. We are still free to deplore, deter and punish what those promoting these deaths and self-immolations are doing even when we understand them better. But I can see no benefit in ignoring what they think that they are doing, especially for those who wish to prevent them from promoting these deaths and self-immolations. At the risk of wearing out a cliché: if you understand their "talk," you may just be able to predict their "walk."

Taking together both that social recognition and high religious or moral qualities of innocence color these bombing operations, I conclude that they are easily described as neither straightforward utilitarian attacks nor pitiful suicides. They are not mere attacks because they are systematically careless of preserving the life of the attacker and in doing so seem to take their meaning and rationale from the prestige accorded them by their social group of reference, and especially their transcendent religious location (Rapoport 1992, 120–21).

They are, nonetheless, not just suicides, in part because they remain offensive attacks, but also because they have high moral or religious purpose imputed to them. This is why I am arguing that we should at least see if we can gain further insight into these phenomena by taking seriously other sorts of descriptions that accommodate the social and religio-moral qualities of these acts. In this case, I suggest that we can acquire just these sorts of insights by referring to the insider point of view of these deaths and immolations. From within this view of the world, these bombings and immolations are routinely and regularly described as "martyrdoms" and "sacrifices." (Rapoport 1992, 120–21).[5]

4. Mighty Shi'a Martyrs

In broaching the question of "the" Muslim view of sacrifice and martyrdom, we must be careful not to offend the diversity of Muslim opinion, here made acute, as we will see, by the modern innovations introduced into the discourse of sacrifice, martyrdom, and jihad by the Islamists. As it turns out, that diversity of opinion runs along rather different lines than it has in the past. No longer, as we will now see, are Shi'a and Sunni quite as opposed to one another as those we may call moderates and extremists—no matter what their sectarian affiliation. In order to gauge this deviation from Muslim traditions, both of greater longevity and much broader present-day allegiance, let me begin this part of my discussion by seeing how the Muslim, here primarily Sunni, mainstream regard "martyrdom" or "sacrifice." Much that we will meet here will be familiar to Western readers since the notions of martyr and sacrifice derive from elements of a common Abrahamic tradition, mean roughly what they do in Judaism and Christianity.[6]

Of the two notions, however, "martyrdom" shows the most difference in meaning between Muslims and Christians (Cowdrey 1985, 46). Instead of the passive Christian sense of martyr as a literal "witness" in God's behalf, for Sunni Islam, the death suffered in martyrdom is one endured in active struggle in behalf of Islam. The overwhelming consensus of Muslim tradition, furthermore, holds that martyrdom is not a "status to be achieved by the individual warrior, and performed as though it were his own private act of worship" (Makiya & Mneimneh 2002, 21). It is instead a defined social role, as Halbwachs would well understand, heavily regulated by communal standards, debated extensively in that most social of languages—that of jurisprudence. It is, in any event, always "something bestowed by Allah as a favor on the warrior for his selflessness and devotion to the community's defense." It is never an individual act voluntarily undertaken on one's own authority.

By contrast, Christians seem less certain, although not always consistent from time to time and place to place, about the application of the title of "martyr" to all cases in which Christians might have died in some connection with the interests of Christianity.[7] Thus, for example, while in a context where one might have expected official ecclesiastical sanctioning of death in battle against the enemies of the Church, such as in the Crusades, "references to martyrdom are quite, but not very, common," and then primarily found in the writings of the medieval historians of the crusades, often from addresses given to crusading societies (Cowdrey 1985, 50–51). But by the twelfth century, martyrdom had become "an integral part of the crusading experience," with the likes of St Bernard of Clairvaux articulating its ideal (Cowdrey 1985, 53). It still, however, seems rare to find either those who participated in the Crusades, or even those who died in battle during a Crusade, officially canonized as "martyrs" because of that participation or, it seems, even death.[8] This appears so even under the broadest definition of a "crusade"—the eight generally recognized Crusades dating roughly from 1095 to 1699.[9] Perhaps the clearest example of a Crusader who subsequently becomes a "saint"—but still not martyr—was San Juan de Capistrano. In 1454, he assisted at the Diet at Frankfurt in its deliberations concerning a "crusade against the Turks for the relief of Hungary." Against the Turks at Belgrade, Juan actually led a "wing" of the army commanded by the fifteenth-century Catholic patriot and governor of Hungary, Janos Hunyady.[10] Another example of the sainted crusader—although again not canonized for his martyrdom—was Louis IX of France. He led both the Sixth and the Seventh Crusades, and died in 1270 at the outset of the Seventh. And while he suffered captivity and imprisonment by the Muslims from 1244 to 1249, he was not declared a "martyr" for this, or for any other reason, at his canonization by Pope Boniface VIII in 1297. Actually, Louis survived his many ordeals in the Levant only to die of dysentery. Similarly, the thirteenth-century Yorkshire Crusader, St. Leonard of Reresby, attained sainthood apparently in some obscure connection with his miraculous release from a Saracen prison, and not because of any death—martyrdom or otherwise—suffered for attempting to liberate the "Holy Land."[11]

On the other hand, while there seems to be no evidence of Crusaders officially canonized as "martyrs" for their having died in a Crusade, those who suffered persecution or death by the Muslims were described as martyrs, following the spirit of the classic pattern. The old passive pattern of dying for the faith by refusing to betray it is retained in the Crusades, although also supplemented. Thus, in an eleventh-century account of the First Crusade, *The Deeds of God Through the Franks*, a medieval historian of the Crusades, Guibert of Nogent, says that "We have heard of many who, captured by the pagans and ordered to deny the sacraments of faith, preferred to expose their heads to the sword than to betray the Christian faith in which they had been instructed."

These count as martyrs for Guibert (Nogent 1997). Yet the theme of an active martyrdom, as preached before Guibert's time, and thus before the First Crusade, may well have prepared the way for recruitment of its participants and for the legitimacy of their efforts as evidenced in Guibert's history (Cowdrey 1985, 46). Thus, Guibert's sensibilities in regard to Christian warriors as martyrs rests on the centuries-old prestige of martyrdom, properly reaffirmed to characterize the deaths in battle of Christian knights, at least since the time of Charlemagne (Cowdrey 1985, 47–48).

On the other side, the lack of such consistent and robust canonical recognition may, in large part, only be a feature of a peculiarity in its bureaucratic mechanisms of implementation. The Roman Church tended to discourage the pursuit of martyrdom after Constantine's Edict of Milan and the official recognition of Christianity as the religion of the Empire. The Roman Church certainly forbade Christians "seeking" martyrdom, and counseled a piety of prudence in its place.[12] But when we turn to levels of ecclesiastical recognition below the canonical level, and especially in the Crusades where Christians find themselves pitted against non-Christian forces, such as Islam, Communism, or Nazism, an altogether different attitude prevails. Edith Stein, a Jewish convert to Roman Catholicism and a Carmelite nun, recently canonized in 1998, is regarded in the Roman Catholic Church by both Catholic laity and hierarchy as a "martyr" for having cared for other inmates in Auschwitz and for having been murdered there by the Nazis. There, the classic passive pattern seems to have adapted to the aggressive tendencies of popular and non-canonical piety and preaching of the early Crusades. Medievalist Jean Flori, for example, has broken with the habit of looking on the Crusades as pilgrimage, even as "armed pilgrimage," and has argued that they were "holy wars," that is to say, the equivalent of jihads (Flori 2001)! Here, an active conception of the warrior martyr obliterates the differences between Christianity and Islam (Cowdrey 1985, 46; Flori 1991). Once again, Guibert of Nogent's *The Deeds of God through the Franks* provides the text:

No land on earth will ever see soldiers of such nobility fighting together. If you wish, I shall relate the story of every kingdom, speak of battles done everywhere; none of these will be able to equal either the nobility or the force of these men. They left their paternal lands, abandoned conjugal bonds, their children were unattractive to them, remaining at home was punishment for them; in every knight the desire for martyrdom burns. (Nogent 1997, 50–51)

As for today's Muslims, observers of the Islamic world judge that the theology of Muslim martyrdom has taken even greater turns from the common Abrahamic root in recent time. In the hands of Sunni extremists, it has been described as an "entirely modern innovation" since it would "justify calling someone who kills civilians and noncombatants a 'martyr'" (Makiya & Mneimneh 2002, 21). Martyrdom in this way is seen as "a human response to the call of Allah to sacrifice oneself for the sake of Islam, and to inflict loss on the enemies of Allah" (Israeli 2002, 35). Thus, it is utterly non-traditional for Sunni extremists to refer to a Palestinian "suicide" bomber as a "martyr"—(*sheheen*) or Usama bin Laden and the 9–11 suicide hijackers in the same way. "Violence," in Islamic tradition, instead "must be proportional and that, in repelling an aggressor, only the necessary amount of force should be used" (Israeli 2002, 30; Makiya & Mneimneh 2002, 21). Yet, the Islamist extremists claim that "martyrdom is a pure act of worship, pleasing to Allah, irrespective of Allah's specific command." This, their Muslim critics charge, is simply "a terrifying new kind of nihilism," influenced, as we will see, by radicalized Shi'a militants like Hizballah and the Ayatollah Khomeini (Makiya & Mneimneh 2002, 21).

A similar kind of extremist transformation of traditional concepts of martyrdom also conspicuously marks the Shi'a, long noted for the prominent place reserved in their spirituality and ritual life for the idea of martyr. The Shi'a notion of martyrdom is rooted in the commemoration of the death of Muhammed's grandson, Imam Husayn, in 680 in a straightforward military battle at the hands of the forces of the local Umayyad governor, Ubayadallah ibn Ziyad, at Karbala in present-day Iraq. No martyrdom, in the strict literal sense of the word, thus originally took place. Some scholars suggest that Husayn was simply poorly prepared for war, and in all respects, this was just a political struggle with the Umayyads. Shi'a piety nonetheless plays upon the failures of others to aid Husayn, upon his abandonment by those from whom he had expected assistance, whether wisely or not.

The pathos of the death of Husayn thus produced at least two religious consequences. First, the Shi'a religious imagination is driven by a sense of _____ bout responsibility for Husayn's death. His devotees affirm that, if y could be reversed, modern day Shi'a would rush to Husayn's aid (1997, 41). But since history cannot be undone, Shi'a devotees ritually reenact efforts to aid Husayn, or indeed to shed blood and even die for him. This ritual participation in the drama of Husayn's death is commemorated annually by pious members of the Shi'a community in Ashura, the tenth day of the Muslim month of Muharram (Halm 1997, 41–88). These ritual practices seek to demonstrate willingness on the part of the faithful to undergo privation and death in a mystical attempt to show that they would have risked all to save Husayn, had they been present at Karbala in 680. Thus, ritual self-flagellation (*mâtam*) expresses and realizes a resolve to share the fate of Husayn or mystically to come to his aid. By ritual extension, in our own day, this resolve to save Husayn is converted into the willingness to accept death in order to fight other Muslims threatening the Shi'a people, as was proved by the deaths of young Iranian soldiers in defense of the Islam of the Iranian revolution against Iraq (Halm 1997, 143, 150). Some Iranian prisoners of war, upon being released from Iraqi captivity, confessed "shame" at not having died in order to defend the new Islamic republic of Iran (Halm 1997, 150).

Second, rising to the level of symbol, Husayn then becomes increasingly regarded as having died a martyr's death on the Sunni pattern—as an active fighter against injustice. Those following Husayn thus resolve to prepare themselves to be martyrs as well. Martyrdom thereby takes on a more active aspect, for example, in reinterpretations of Husayn's death as a sacrificial struggle. Here it may be waged against Muslims or anti-Islamic practices by either Muslims or non-Muslims. Opposition to a supposedly non-Islamic institution, such as the monarchy of the (Muslim) Umayyads, is as said by some Shi'a to have caused Husayn's military campaign in the first place. Raphael Israeli has argued that the Sunni extremists reflect the influence of Shi'a militants, such as Hizballah in Lebanon, and advance this extreme version of martyrdom in contemporary days. Even more radical, since 1986, and spurred on by the theological innovations of the Ayatollah Khomeini, they have also projected back onto the victimization of Imam Husayn at Karbala in 680 CE a heretofore unknown desire for his own self-immolation in the course of jihad (Israeli 1997, 96)! So, what we find, in sum, is a cross-fertilization of extremist ideologies and theologies of both the Sunni and Shi'a, and an emergence of a radical ideology of martyrdom, self-immolating sacrifice, and jihad, culminating in one way or another in the phenomenon of the "human bombers."

5. Abraham or the Prophet, Routine or Extreme?

Despite the increased influence of Shi'a conceptions of sacrifice and martyrdom upon the entire Muslim world, attention must be given to the longstanding, widespread, and still prevailing views of sacrifice proper to the majority Sunni population. One of the common words for sacrifice here is "adha"—the same "adha" in the name of the great feast celebrating the end of Ramadan, the "Eid al adha." The roots of sacrifice in such ritual contexts reach down into the very traditions of ritual sacrifice in Islam. These are generally conditioned by Muslims' readiness to give of themselves for Allah and routinely for the Muslim community in its routines of *zakat*, the charitable giving counted as one of the pillars of Islam. But all is not so unproblematic. Theologically, a crisis lies in wait for Muslims, since in the face of an omnipotent deity it is hard to see how devotees could justify limiting the extent of their devotion and giving by routines and rituals, however piously engaged. In narrative form, this crisis comes to a head in the case of Abraham's problematic attempted sacrifice of Ishmael.[13] Understanding the exact complex nature of Abraham's obedience, his willingness to give to the utmost what Allah requires, yet Allah's relaxation of the demand for Ishmael's life, in turn informs the thinking about sacrifice for Muslims. This is so no matter whether these sacrifices are ritual, existential, or metaphoric. Abraham becomes a model for pious Muslims to emulate in their everyday lives, even if the meaning of the model is contested.[14] In general, the Abraham/Ishmael story has legitimized a moderate view of sacrifice. In our own time, however, in at least two ways, the moderate model has been challenged by the rise of the modern deviations from the traditional Abrahamic model. In both cases, the tone and extent of sacrifice are ratcheted up either by replacing Abraham with Muhammad as the model of sacrificial behavior, or by an extreme interpretation of Abraham's attempted sacrifice of Ishmael.

In the case where the Prophet replaces Abraham, he is cast as the chief exemplar of both self-sacrificial death and self-sacrifice (*tad'hia*) linked essentially with jihad. Abraham, though, as we will see in due course, seems to exemplify moderate, everyday, prudent sacrifice—a giving of a victim or a portion of one's treasure, by contrast with the total giving up signaled by modern extremist commentary on the example of Muhammad. Thus, the choice as to kind of sacrifice demanded of the Muslim would depend upon

whether or not Muslims felt that the umma's very existence were threatened—a highly subjective matter to be sure. In normal times, the prudent
"giving of" would suffice. But *in extremis*, the ultimate "giving up" would
become the norm (Israeli 2002, 33–4).[15] As Raphael Israeli notes, this interpretation of the Prophet's behavior in times of extreme danger is supported
by extremist scholars who point to "the famous Hadith, where the Prophet
undertook to die for Allah, to come back to life and then die once again.
This means that there was no bigger goal in the Prophet's own existence
than to die for Allah, and repeatedly so. Therefore, this tenet constitutes, in
the author's mind, a divine guideline that applies everywhere at all times."
Annihilating self-sacrifice thus becomes integral to situations where jihad
is enjoined. This sort of self-immolating jihad should then become "the
standard behavior of all Muslims who seek battle at the highest level of
risk"—although not, apparently, at levels of routine, everyday risks (Israeli
2002, 4).

Before considering both the tradition of Abraham's attempted sacrifice
of Ishmael/Isaac and the uses the extremists make of it, a theological note
is in order. It seems to me that, like other theological efforts, such as theod-
icy, the efforts undertaken by these extremist Muslim theologians to reconcile their advocacy of self-sacrifice with the explicit Quranic declaration of
the "sanctity of human life," are bound to look "convoluted" (Israeli 2002,
32). These interpretations look convoluted because they are! Like perennial
efforts to "justify the ways of God to men," the Islamists are not likely to reconcile all things, because the levels of divine and human discourse are so
essentially different. Furthermore, these extremist interpretations are also
likely to continue to both look and be convoluted because they seek—
impossibly, it could be argued—to force the many rushing streams of Islamic
theology into a channeled orthodoxy.

6. Abraham's Dilemma: Total Sacrifice or
Prudent Sacrifice?

Of all sacrifices performed by Sunnis, the most exemplary, traditional and
routine has been that done in imitation of Abraham and Ishmael during the
Hajj. It is being challenged today by the extremists in several ways, as I shall
discuss shortly after accounting for the traditional view. First, then, to tradition. At a key point in the Hajj, pious Muslims will ritually slaughter and

sacrifice a certain intermediary victim, traditionally prescribed as a bovine animal, such as a goat. In this way, the pious Hajji gives of themselves in the act of ritual sacrifice ("qurbani")—literally a "bringing near" (i.e. to Allah).[16] So much part of everyday Muslim spiritual formation is this sacrifice, that efforts are made for any and all Muslims to perform it. Thus, since it is expensive both to make the Hajj to Mecca and to purchase a suitable sacrificial animal for qurbani, elaborate means have been devised for universal participation in this sacrifice. Thus, although the price of £140 is quoted for a sheep in Palestine, for a relatively small sum of £45, pious Muslims wishing to perform their qurbani can send either corned or frozen portions of a properly butchered sheep to their less fortunate Palestinian brothers and sisters.[17] Deployed and embedded even more broadly in Islamic religious life, the term "qurbani" is often used more generally to name all aspects of Muslim charitable giving.[18] There is, for example, a website called "On-Line Qurbani" where one is invited to donate to feed families in several countries.[19] Far from anything to do with jihad, then, a critical strand in the Muslim understanding of sacrifice (qurbani) is as a gift, and as a limited, modest, or even partial one at that.

Emphasizing this sense of normal Muslim sacrifice as the prudent giving of over against the extreme giving up, typical in many ways of Abraham, one notes that despite the pervasiveness of the Muslim sacrificial tradition, in both ritual and moral senses, self-immolation, self-sacrifice, and certainly human sacrifice are never optional. Along with the ritual sacrifices of bovine animals, it is instead the limited practices of self-denial, such as mortification, fasting, charitable giving, and such that are regarded as paradigmatically sacrificial. Thus, sacramentally joining with Abraham in substituting an animal victim for the sacrifice of Ishmael, Sunni Muslims do what may be regarded as sacrifices of the spirit, or of bodily mortification or gifts of their material wealth, in further imitation of the submissive spirit to Allah's command. Highest on this list of rituals connected with sacrifice is the festival banquet bringing to an end the period of self-denial typical of Ramadan, the "feast of sacrifice"—the Eid al Adha. The extreme of giving up is held at arm's length from normal everyday Islam.

But Abraham's sacrifice, no matter how comprehended under normal circumstances and across the great length of Muslim history, is still embedded in a story of the relation of humans to an incomprehensible divinity.

Because of this essential connection with the divine will, the nuances of the story also become the bases of consequential interpretive disputes among Muslims hearing about how extreme the sacrifice demanded of people really might be. For example, given the Quranic reverence for human life, how was it that Allah could really command Abraham to sacrifice his son, Ishmael? Was this order, perhaps, a devious piece of deception set to test Abraham's loyalty to Quranic values? Therefore, did—either or both— Abraham or Ishmael accept this command, as earnest and true? Or, did they hear it as something laced with divine irony or only meant to be enacted symbolically—say by substituting a ram, as Muslims today do on the Hajj's ritual sacrifices? Other interpreters, less enamored of the Quranic valuation of human life and more impressed with the equally Quranic assertion of the mystery of divinity's ways, claim that both father and son did indeed embrace the command to sacrifice Ishmael literally and earnestly. Giving up gradually begins to push giving of off center stage, at least among these interpreters:

> People today may see themselves as individuals and that they are independent, that they have no responsibility to anybody, that the ahkam sharia does not apply to them, they don't care about that the Muslim Ummah is facing, they say that Islam only applies to indi- viduals in their houses and should have no affect in life.
>
> Did Ibrahim (as) carry this idea that he is independent, that he is an "individual" who does not have to take the orders of anybody? Was he selfish? Did Ismael take his own benefit rather than what Allah had commanded? Did Ibrahim (as) disobey the command of Allah to sacrifice his son? On the basis that he was an individual and that was against his benefit?[20]

The answer to this series of rhetorical questions is that he did not.

Other Muslims (I shall call them Muslim humanists), however, take the contrary view that Abraham always understood the command to be a kind of test to see if he could distinguish a diabolic deception from a divine order. Would he follow an unrighteous order—an order in conflict with Quranic values and Allah's true nature? In defense of this interpretive tactic, the Muslim humanists note that the patriarch did, after all, arrive at the idea of sacrificing Ishmael by the mitigating medium of a dream. The Quran tells us straightforwardly that Abraham says to Ishmael: "O my son, I have seen in a dream that I should sacrifice you."[21] The Muslim humanists deny that Allah would ever sanction the sacrifice of a human individual—even as a test. They project a rather different sort of sense of Allah and human obligations to Allah than those who do not. For them, Islam values the human individual. A modern-day Muslim humanist argues by analogy: "How is a wall built? How do the individual blocks 'join ranks' to turn into a solid and impregnable wall?" The answer comes swiftly and clearly in terms of an assertion of the value of the human individual: "As a wall is composed of many building blocks, so must our communities be built upon the strengths of individuals like yourself . . ."[22] Therefore, in the story of Abraham and Ishmael, there was never really any danger of either of them understanding the command to sacrifice Ishmael as earnest and straightforward, since this would contravene Allah's well known valuing of the integrity of the human individual.

There are as well other ways in which the interpretations of Abraham's attempted sacrifice of Ishmael reinforce the position of Muslim humanism. One may shift the particular aspect of the episode to be celebrated, for example. Some interpreters focus on other features of this complex incident than either Abraham and/or Ishmael's submission, or Abraham's restraint, however minimal it may have been. In these cases, it is the sparing of Ishmael from death that Muslims hold dear and emblematic of the incident. In the example following, taken significantly from a religio-political context, Abraham's sacrifice is read as about saving Ishmael from any sort of sacrifice at all. The duty of Muslims, the text tells us, is "to remove the real knife from the throat of oppressed Muslims from Bosnia to Kashmir, from Somalia to Palestine. Let us revolt against the heartless worshippers that we have become. Remember our Eid is not an Eid of victory. It is the Eid of sacrifice (adha)."[23] Still other Muslim humanist interpreters of this classic episode of the scriptures of the Abrahamic tradition dispute as well whether Abraham himself really meant to sacrifice his son at all. In reality, Abraham intended instead only to assent to Allah's command in a kind of perfunctory way, knowing full well that Allah would provide a substitute—as indeed Allah did.[24]

In any case, what I would like to underline is that both the potential ferocity of the divine will as well as the willingness of people to follow such commands are mitigated equally well in the objective Quranic text (a dream) and in the interpretations of this incident. Further, whatever previous positions may have been held, Muslims generally share the same conclusion to the Abrahamic sacrifice story—namely humans are not sacrificed in Islam.[25] Rendered as a formula of the mainstream, Muslim sacrifice as a "giving of" oneself, of one's alienable property—animals, portions of one's wealth, and so on—is very highly valued and enjoined; but sacrifice as a "giving up"—as a total negation of self or an inalienable subject (Ishmael)—is at most highly questionable—at least in the Quran and some of the commentarial literature that I have cited. There is, it must be emphasized, only so much that one can read out of scripture that actually shapes a religion at a particular time. But based on both Quranic and commentarial authority, Muslims seem very much like Jews and Christians when it comes to sacrifice. To wit, while it may well be that Allah could in principle require absolute self-immolation—since Allah is the supreme being and does after all require absolute submission—the extreme of annihilationist sacrifice is not the kind of sacrifice Allah decides, out of the mysteries of the divine will, to require. There, a goat will do, as it were. As the modern tract, "Sacrifice: The Making of a Muslim" declares, sacrifice is a central Muslim value, but it is sacrifice as "giving of," not as the extreme giving up:

> First, imagine where we would be today without the heroic efforts, sacrifices, and patience of Prophet Muhammad (peace be upon him) and his devoted Companions in building the vibrant Islamic society of Madinah? . . .
>
> Sacrifice means giving up things which are valued or desired. Those things may be (1) tangible, countable like our time, wealth or life, or (2) intangible, immeasurable, like our feelings, attitudes, opinions or aspirations. They are given up for the sake of something that is more worthy or more urgent to us (Quran 6:162). Without sacrifice our lives would be devoid of harmony and cooperation, full of conflict, and prey to self-centredness and immediate gratification of desires.

Making explicit that sacrifice as "giving up"—as annihilation of self or others—is not required, this tract goes on to assert how deeply Muslims value human life:

> How is a wall built? How do the individual blocks "join ranks" to turn into a solid and impregnable wall? As a wall is composed of

many building blocks, so must our communities be built upon the strengths of individuals like yourself . . .

When the wall is seen from a distance, the blocks may look indistinguishable due to their uniformity, but like human beings, each retains its inner individuality. *No one is required to sacrifice this.* (my emphasis)[26]

7. Sacrifices Are Also Special Kinds of Gifts

From this rich tradition of Muslim sacrificial discourse, we can begin to bring to bear some of the things we have learned from the comparative study of religions to illuminate Muslim sacrifice. I would single out three aspects for particular note. As I intimated earlier, at least in part, sacrifice can be seen as a very peculiar kind of gift by Muslims. But sacrifice is also peculiar as a kind of gift in that the gift (as victim) is destroyed in the process of giving it. Finally, in the course of this act of destruction and giving, the gift/victim is made holy or sacred—a *sacri-ficium* (Hubert & Mauss 1964, 9). In thus classifying sacrifice as a special kind of gift, it will show all the same characteristics of gifts in general, but with the added feature of at least portions of the sacrificial gift being alienated from the human realm in the process of something being made sacred. Let me begin to elaborate this in connection with the "human bombers" in considering first the obligatory quality of the gift.

The author of the single most influential book on gifts, Marcel Mauss, argued that gifts are never free, despite what people tend to think about their disinterestedness and spontaneity. Despite the show of pure generosity gift givers typically display, gifts are always given under obligation—the obligations to give, to receive the gift, and to reciprocate (Mauss 1990, 1–2, 11–12). A kind of systematic deception prevails between the appearance of freedom in giving and its actual restricted nature. In the initial instance, the giver first feels obliged to give—as anyone invited to a birthday party or wedding will keenly appreciate, or as anyone burdened by the onslaught of Christmas shopping and its endless obligations can attest. Taking matters a step further beyond the obligation to give, there is, second, the additional obligation to receive or accept the gift. As the burdens of Christmas shopping should recall the obligation to accept or receive the gift can be quite oppressive—adding as well to the weight of the cloud of obligation that settles on the gift in the first place. And, topping both these first two obligations is a third, perhaps even more strongly felt, namely, the obligation to reciprocate, to give in return. This recursive logic accounts for the way that gift exchange develops into "rings," cycles or systems of exchange, as Malinowski first demonstrated in his analysis of *kula* in his 1922 *Argonauts of the Western Pacific* (Malinowski 1961, 49–80).

Because I am going to suggest what may first seem absurd, namely, that a "human bombing" can be understood as a "gift," let alone a sacrifice, a few words of further explanation are in order. "Gift" is a very capacious notion and phenomenon, capable of very wide application. It is not limited to handsomely wrapped "presents" or the items for sale in a "Gift Shop"! Literally anything can become a gift, given the understanding Mauss provides of it. All that is required in a prestation or exchange is the tell-tale gap between the appearance of disinterestedness and spontaneity on the one side and the reality of the three-fold set of obligations on the other. Thus, gifts come in many forms—in actions, deeds, or objects of all sorts, in greetings, courtesies, kindnesses, or gestures, in legacies, time dedicated, or in deference paid to others, and of course in all the myriad "things" people give to one another. None of this means, then, that just because anything can be a gift, everything is a gift. As a subclass of exchange, gift is not, for example, a form of unidirectional access to goods or services, like taking, theft, or creation ex nihilo. Gift involves an offering, but one that likewise entails an exchange.

Gift also differs from other common sorts of exchange, such as economic exchanges like buying and selling, "truck and barter," or mere commercial transactions. Gifts are "in theory" voluntary, disinterested, and such. They carry something of an aura of "freedom" about themselves, although we usually tend to make too much of this in our sentimentalization of alternatives to an economic society. In straightforward economic transactions, everyone knows that the deal is "interested" by definition, no matter how much a pretense may be made in the course of the transaction that no one really seeks a profit!

As I have already averred in discussing the case of Abraham—and here we begin to broach the matter of sacrifice—gift also can range from a moderate "giving of" or a more extreme "giving up." Gifts can range from alienations of part of one's goods or services to near-total alienations thereof. These may range from an ordinary expenditure of time or resources such as in routine philanthropic grants or common holiday gift giving, through to special gifts, such as the giving of family treasure or heirlooms to members of the next generation, or in the most extreme cases, to the kinds of large scale, massive (relative or absolute) givings away that characterize something like the Potlatch of the Pacific Northwest Native Americans.

In these last extreme forms of giving, we seem to shade into, if not arrive at, sacrifices, because no ordinary reciprocation or exchange seems possible. What is given in potlatch is destroyed, as is the victim in a proper ritual sacrifice. Indeed, the point of potlatch giving is to make it virtually impossible for the initial gift to be reciprocated without courting ruin. Small wonder that Mauss called potlatch the "monster child of the gift system" (Mauss 1990, 41). Recalling my earlier discussion of sacrifice as a special mode of giving in which the victim given is typically destroyed, and in being so is made (or at least regarded as) holy or sacred, let me return us to the matter of the "human bombers." Perhaps monstrous in its own way, I believe that the same sense of gift exchanges articulated by Mauss will apply equally well to "human bombings" as sacrifices.

8.   "Human Bombers" as Sacrificial Gifts

Without minimizing the importance of the utilitarian jihadist conception of these bombings, as well as their multivalence, permit me to pick up some of the many strands of meaning that dangle from the claim that these so-called suicide or martyrdom bombings need also to be considered carefully as sacrificial gifts. The elements of sacrifice are there in such abundance and pervasiveness that it would be irresponsible to ignore them. Whether the sacrificial factors weigh more than practical ones will have to be determined, perhaps on a case by case basis. But they at least need to be factored into the equation of the motivation of so-called suicide operations committed by radical Muslims. Once they are factored into the equation, the careful researcher will need to measure and weigh the results of the mix between the sacrificial and practical aspects of these operations, assuming that this is analytically possible due to the multivalent and perhaps hopelessly confused nature of motivation here. In order that this factoring may begin, let me further expand my discussion of these bombings, deaths, and such as sacrificial gifts.

There is, first, no doubt that the Palestinian bombers give themselves in a spirit of obligation characteristic of the gift that I described. Their deaths are seen as a sacred duty to sacrifice, to give themselves up totally. That they seek the deaths of as many Israelis as they can take with them only witnesses to the multivalence of their acts. Significant here is the fact that even when attacks sometimes fail, the bombers will detonate their charges anyway. This implies that foremost in the minds of some bombers is the intention to give up one's life in the process—to sacrifice—even when no practical benefit in terms of an attack can be accrued.

I am further persuaded of the wisdom of describing bombings and related death as gifts, sacrifices, and such from other data originating from beyond the radicalized Muslim world. Consider, for example, the self-descriptions of the notorious Black Tiger units of the Tamil Tigers of Sri Lanka, or as they prefer to call it, of Tamil Eelam. While the Black Tiger bombings have had considerable utilitarian value in killing many Sri Lankan soldiers in deliberately offensive operations, the Black Tigers typically see these operations as "gifts," further distancing themselves from mere suicides in any form. A recent New York Times article reports a Tamil leader as saying that the Black Tigers explicitly decline to use the word "suicide bombing" for their operations. The Tamil name for these operations is thatkodai, meaning to "give" oneself, as opposed to the word "thatkolai," meaning simply to "kill oneself." A thatkodai " 'is a gift of the self—self-immolation, or self-gift,' " said a Tamil Tiger representative. "'When one enlists, there is no remuneration. The only promise is I am prepared to give everything I have, including my life. It is an oath to the nation,'" the same leader went on (Waldman 2003, A8).

This therefore returns us to the matter of the socially and religiously formed mind of the bomber, and most of all to the conception that they may have of their action. Here, what escapes the observer of narrow purview is the network of social relations in which an individual bomber is located. Fixing only on the individual bomber, or the individual bomber as an agent posed against someone, hides the sense in which bombers see themselves as embedded in a network of social relations to which they may be said to belong or want to belong. And here sacrificial gift makes a triumphant return. Once grasped as a relational reality, it becomes natural to ask to whom and for whom, then, are the lives of these Palestinians given up? Gifts are necessarily relational, not solitary actions. Recalling the logic of obligation inherent in gift, we may then ask who is obliged to accept them?

One answer arises as to the intended recipients of sacrifice. If we link these self-immolations closely with the ritual sacrifices of Ramadan and Hajj, they are intended for Allah. This was how bin Laden, for example, tells us that the WTC-Pentagon hijackers were meant to be seen. The theological problem that I see in this case is that the gifts given exceed what Allah expects of pious Muslims. Muslim sacrifice is normatively a giving of, rather than the extreme giving up typical of the hijackers and self-immolating bombers. Indeed, there are many references in the current literature issuing from Muslims saying that such deeds of self-immolation are illegitimate and at odds with Islam. This however may only underline the radical and original aspects of bin Laden's version of Islam.

If we then press the question about who—besides Allah—is obliged to accept these gifts, I think we can grasp how and why the political arena is the natural place for these deaths to occur, and why on top of this, they merit the description of being "sacrifices." In the case of the Israel/Palestine dispute, besides Allah, I suggest that it is Palestine or the imagined community of Palestine that—at least in the minds of the bombers—is obliged to accept the offering of the death of such a self-immolating bomber. It is literally and ritually to Palestine and Palestinians that these sacrifices are offered, who therefore are obliged to accept them, and then in some appropriate and equivalent way, to reciprocate.

In light of the relational nature of sacrificial gifts of themselves made by the "human bombers," certain policy consequences might flow. Thus, to the extent that these bombings are viewed by their actors and the communities to which they belong as "sacrifices" and "gifts," they might be encouraged or deterred in the way ordinary gifts are encouraged or discouraged. If to deter these operations were the aim, then the societies of reference in question here would have to make it clear that such gifts are not desired, or that they are inappropriate. Offers of such a gift will be rejected. Thus, the social logic of such a deed as a gift, as a sacrifice, would to some extent be encouraged or undermined in the same way, respectively, that a desired suitor or an unwanted one were urged on or dissuaded. Their gifts could be, respectively, increased or stopped by clear welcome or, alternatively, refusal to accept them. The success or failure of sacrifice bombings then is relational. It would seem, then, to depend on the willingness of the intended recipient to accept the gift. Perhaps instead of seeking to dissuade sacrifice bombings by concentrating on the bomber as an individual unit of analysis, we therefore need to concentrate on those for whom the bombers bomb. This points to the weakness of our cruder forms of economic explanation of such matters, further enfeebled by liberal guilt, that economic disadvantage breeds such bombings. The facts are quite the contrary, since it is now well attested that most of the sacrifice bombers are formally educated and hail from comfortably middle class families (Atran 2003, A27).

Finally, who is to reciprocate for the sacrificial gifts thus offered? And, how are they to reciprocate? By the logic I have sketched, it would be Palestine and Palestinians who are expected to reciprocate for these deaths. And, how? By continuing the struggle, of course, but by continuing a struggle in which what is at stake is Palestine itself—or at least a certain imagined community of Palestine. As long as we are thinking about Palestine, it would be well to recall that sacrificial death for Israel has as well always been held in high regard. In the famous Israeli nationalistic poem, Natan Altermann's "The Silver Platter," we meet a young couple—significantly pure and innocent as sacrificial victims are classically represented—confronting the nation with the sacrificial price which must be paid for the continued existence of Israeli nationhood itself. The poem concludes with their final words:

"We are the silver platter
On which the Jewish state has been given you." (Tamir 1997, 235,
    240–41)

Similarly, although some commentators on the Warsaw Ghetto Rising see it, like Masada, as a "suicidal" gesture, what also seems clear is that even in sacrificing their lives in a fight they knew could not succeed militarily, the Ghetto fighters knew that they were doing their part in making Israel. " 'All we had were grenades, some guns and bottles with flammable liquid. We were like ants attacking a regular army which had conquered all of Europe . . . We did it to honor all the Jews,' " recalled Masza Putermilch, 79, a Jewish ghetto fighter who spoke at the Warsaw commemoration of the sixtieth anniversary of the Rising in April of 2003 (Kasprzycka 2003, A15). The only response to

their sacrificial gift was to reciprocate by following through with the foundation of the real historical state of Israel.[27]

9. The Gift of Sacrificial Death Makes "Human Bombers" Holy

Now what of sacrificial gifts as those special kinds gifts that involve a "making holy"? Beyond being a rite that destroys something, sacrifice is one that
transforms something offered—the victim—into something else—something
sanctified. The sacrificed Passover lamb becomes, for Christians at least, and
by several steps admittedly, the Lamb of God. Thus, the part of the victim that
is destroyed is, as it were, and in theory, alienated unto the gods. That which
is sacrificed is what belongs to the gods, and is therefore sacred. The victim
becomes ipso facto sacred in being sacri-ficed. That is what sacrifice does. By
extension, as well, much that comes into contact with that which has been
made sacred by the sacrifice, itself becomes sacred by contagion. The sacrificial precinct, that place where the "making sacred" happens, becomes ipso
facto a sacred place, a place bounded by tabus and removed from ordinary
concourse. The officers of sacrifice, those who pay for the rite, those who
receive the sacrificial communion, all participate in the sacredness created
by the sacrificial act of this special kind of giving. Raphael Israeli notes
accordingly that the notorious videos produced before the bombing are
devised to provide education and the image of "role models" for further
"human bombers"; they are far from being like the typical self-pitying or
despairing suicide note (Israeli 1997, 105). Further, the forms in which the
community supports the "human bombers" draw on a variety of standard-
ized, local religious models. The meager belongings of the "human bombers"
are collected and revered as "relics." Songs are composed about them and
their acts, and sung openly in the streets. Their pictures "become the object
of worship-like adoration." The families of the "human bombers," by a kind
of contagion of the sacred, are viewed as "precious in the eyes of the public."
They are viewed with "awe and admiration" (Israeli 1997, 105–6).

The notion that these immolations are offered to or for Palestine permits us to dwell for a moment on the peculiar property of sacrificial gifts of
making things holy. As the name, "sacri-fice" indicates, while the immola-
tion consists in a gift, it is also at the same time, a "making holy." The

paschal lamb, like the goat in "qurbani," for instance, is not "ho.. sacrificed. So, also, in performing sacrifice for the sake of Palestine, on. ipso facto "makes" the bomber holy. At the same time, the sacrifice performed there makes the territory of Palestine "holy," since Palestine is a site of an event of making something holy, as well as an intended recipient of sacrifice. One affirms the precincts of its "holy of holies"—its national borders—as holy by making its territory an arena of sacrifice—much say as the WTC site is now generally considered a sacred site, if we are to judge by the persistent invocation of the heroism of the firefighters and police lost in the collapse of the buildings.[28] Notice that nothing of the same sacredness seems to have adhered to the Pentagon, where, as well, many lives were lost, but no conspicuous acts of sacrifice on the part of rescuers were much noted or perhaps even performed. Perhaps coincidentally, this intifada bears the name al-Aqsa Intifada, referring to the mosque located within the sixty-six-acre site known to Muslims as the Haram al Sharif ("the Noble Sanctuary") and to Jews as the Har ha-bayit or Temple Mount, both places regarded as holy, although contested, territories. Whether pretense or not, this intifada, in the eyes of some—or at least enough— Palestinians was provoked by Sharon's visit/intrusion into the sacred place of the Haram al Sharif.

Informants in Israel tell me that the Israelis immediately erase any evidence that the sites of Palestinian sacrifice/suicide bombings have ever been the sites of such acts. These sites become, as it were, negative memorials—places of deliberate forgetting—by their rapid return to normal profane uses. Contrast these unmarked—and perhaps unmarkable—sites of the loss of Jewish life to others, such as are embodied in the memorial to the Warsaw Ghetto Rising. There the event is embraced with considerable pride, as well as, of course, with deep sorrow.[29] And compare again the Ghetto Rising memorial to the difficulties afflicting modern representations of the death camps. After so many years, they are still waiting to be comprehended within an appropriate classification at this writing. Are these to be seen as museums, monuments (and to what?), cemeteries (Webber 1992)? If all this be so for Jews, in a future Palestinian state, one might well imagine that the very same sites of sacrifice/suicide bombings will become memorials to the bombers who did their sacrificial deeds on what is now for Palestinians sacred ground.

In the sense of sacrifice as an act of destruction, there is contained at least the opening for a rejection of a utilitarian or pragmatic calculus. While sacrifice may confer benefits, there is no immediate return, no one-for-one correspondence between what is given and what is gained. Indeed, in sacrifice, it may seem that nothing is returned at all to the person offering the sacrifice, and certainly not in the sense of something immediately reciprocated. The sacrificial gift in most respects is thus removed from normal circulation or exchange. Although an animal, for example, given in sacrifice is often shared to be eaten by those offering the sacrifice in a kind of communion meal, at least a portion of the sacrifice is given to the "gods" to be eaten—and in being so, is removed from the world of humans. It is no longer available for practical human purposes, such as further exchange, and is, by virtue of that, made sacred. The removal of the sacrificial victim from the human world, of course, has never stopped people from calculating how their particular gift to the gods might win them some handsome, if remote and unpredictable, reciprocation. This is not to say that just because part, at least, of the victim is removed from the human world, that something might not be removed from the divine world and returned to the human. People never seem to stop calculating their advantages, or working the angles. We probably all remain political and economic animals, even at times when we seem to shed concerns for power or gain. What in part makes sacrifice so intriguing, however, is how it seems capable of working both sides of the street of disinterestedness and gain.

10. Nation-Building and Meaning-Making by Sacrifice

Thus, despite the extremity of radical Islam's interpretation of sacrifice, I am urging us to understand those goals and the means by which those goals are imagined to be realized through the interpretive lens of sacrifice. We need to think about them as sacrifice bombings as much as we do so as martyrdoms or suicide/homicide bombings.

However distasteful it may be to extend understanding to those whom many would see only as killers, I urge that it helps to understand what other—sacrificial—goals the deaths and immolations are meant to bring about. And here I think appeal to "sacrifice" may help us focus. The kinds of extreme sacrifices of giving up are, as we have seen, not what Abraham performed and which are arguably the normative sacrifices as giving of for the Islamic world. Human sacrifice is precisely what Abraham finally did not do, and in which the Abrahamic religions eventually declined to engage at a certain point in their development.[30] Nevertheless, I am urging us to see that these suicides or homicides are sacrificial gifts of an extreme sort, offered to attain something in exchange—Palestine—to keep it alive, to realize it, in a way, to create it, in return for the sacrifice of young lives (Rapoport 1992, 128).[31]

The main reason nation-building in this way reeks so of religion is, then, because nationalism is exposed as religious. Whatever else they may be, nations are, like religions, meaning-making entities of grand and transcendent sorts, creating an aura of sacredness about all their central doings. Not only do national borders mark boundaries of a sacred precinct as "tabu" to the intruder as any temple's holy of holies, but the accessories of nationalism—its flags, monuments, anthems, and such—partake of the same transcendent religious glow of the nation as sacred being. In terms of national ritual, nationalism has taught us notably that "sacrifice" will routinely be required of individual citizens in one form or another. As such, in sacrifice the nation (and religions of certain kinds) shows itself as the highest form of collectivity demanding human loyalty, transcending palpable human individuality. Thus far at least, for all the efforts of universal cosmopolitan "humanity" to rally people to common human causes, it has yet to outdo the nation or religion in calling forth the loyalty of people and in getting them to lay down their lives for it. Whether the same can be said for the newer transnational ambitions of Al Qa'ida remains to be seen. (Part of the larger significance of attempts of trans-national religious movements, like Al Qa'ida, as briefly successful in Taliban Afghanistan, or recently as threatened in Indonesia, is precisely to challenge and overwhelm the nation-state. How the nation-state will react to such attempts to usurp its monopoly over the use of force within its own borders remains to be seen.) At any rate, Benedict Anderson has argued that the readiness of individuals to kill others and to sacrifice themselves can be understood only in terms of the religious nature of fellowship achieved by the nation-state—that place where religion and nation are not usefully distinguishable (Anderson 1991, 7).

People do not sacrifice themselves for "administrative units," such as the EEC, but lately for nations—whether actual or imagined—like Bosnia, Serbia, Ireland, Israel, and Palestine or, I would add, potentially for religions like Islam and Christianity, on the other.

Thus, we would be wise to pay attention to differences in language about violence in politics corresponding to differences in fundamental viewpoint. From an Israeli viewpoint, the independence struggle was fought for the imagined community of the "nation of Israel," and not for the "mandate of Palestine"—even though the two territories are virtually identical. In that struggle, the deaths of Jewish fighters counted as "sacrifices" and martyrdoms, and not—as the British who were arrayed against them, insisted that they were—as "terrorist atrocities." Similarly, from a contemporary Israeli view which seeks to contain or deny Palestinian "nationality," those who die in so-called suicide or homicide bombings are "murderers," "terrorists," or pathetic mad men. But, seen from the viewpoint of those who want to make the imagined community of Palestine into a nation-state, these suicide or homicide "bombers" are better seen as "sacrifice" bombers, martyring themselves for "Palestine," Islam, and such. For them, these deaths are meaningful, and in this way "religious" deaths, not the random acts of mad men or visceral responses of an overly stimulated organism.

As such, the West Bank, Gaza, and the rest are for the Palestinian religious nationalists not the "administrative units" which they are for Israel, any more than was the imagined community of the British Mandate of Palestine for the Jewish independence fighters. The reason that nationalism is so saturated in religious meaning is that "administrative units" do not create meaning while, in a sense, religions and nations do nothing but create meaning—however gruesome it may be (Anderson 1991, 53).

14

A Durkheimian Text in Turkey

Ziya Gökalp, Hüseyin Nail Kubali, and Muslim Civil Society

I. Hüseyin Nail Kubali and *Professional Ethics and Civic Morals*

In 1950, Professor Hüseyin Nail Kubali, then dean of the Faculty of Law of the University of Istanbul, directed the publication of a set of lectures by Durkheim under the title *Leçons de sociologie physique des moeurs et du droit* (Durkheim 1950). These later appeared in English translation as *Professional Ethics and Civic Morals* (Durkheim 1957b). The lectures in this book were first given by Durkheim in Bordeaux between 1890 and 1892 under the title "Physiologie des Moeurs et du Droit." Much of the content of these Bordeaux lectures was later incorporated into the first edition of *The Division of Labor* published in 1893. While still at Bordeaux, between 1898 and 1900, Durkheim "profoundly" transformed these lectures to emphasize the place of morals in them. From that point on, they remained essentially the same when Durkheim again offered them in Paris in 1904, 1912, and then shortly before his death in 1917 (Kubali 1957, ix; Mauss 1969a, 478). Witness to the importance of these lectures, no less a figure than W.S.F. Pickering, the dean of Durkheimian scholarship, claims that these lectures "contained in summary form nearly all [Durkheim's] major hypotheses on religion: the notion of the sacred, religion as a non-illusory reality, the divinity as a symbolic form of society, the modern cult of the individual and so on" (Pickering 1984, 71). Historian of religion Jonathan Z. Smith that these lectures are the "single most provocative treatment idea of the sacred, at least in the Durkheimian corpus (Smith 200.

303

For his part, Kubali was effusive in his loyalty to the Durkheimian tradition, saying, "There are many like myself in Turkey who bear the stamp of Durkheim's school of thought" (Durkheim 1957b, xi). The story of how a Turkish scholar became the facilitator of the publication of this important work is an interesting and consequential chapter in the study of modern, comparative religion and politics, the significance of which is the subject of this chapter.

In the early 1930's, Kubali was studying for his doctorate in law in Paris. The reputation of Durkheimian thought among republican reformers pressing their programs of social reconstruction in Turkey had been so extensive that Kubali seems to have felt that a thorough study of the alleged nineteenth-century "precursors" of Durkheimian sociology might be particularly germane to Turkey's situation in the 1930s.

> The French School of Sociology has for us a double value: first of all, thanks to its strictly scientific method, it has contributed in an original way to an explanation of judicial problems. And, in view of the long standing influence of French culture in Turkey, it also holds out a growing interest for us. This School has earned, here as in France, the keys to the city.
>
> Given that fact, it is quite understandable that we would not have been able to resist wanting to know what their precursors thought about the state. Such is the essential motive for this present study. (Kubali 1936, 5)

It seems to me significant that at a time when the fact and theory of "statism" was uppermost in the minds of Turkish political thinkers, Kubali should seek to see whether various "statist" thinkers might have left their marks on Durkheimian thought, or whether Durkheimianism seems to have resisted statist tendencies. How, in particular, did the concept of the state advanced by the likes of Frédéric Le Play, Gabriel Tarde, Gustav Le Bon, Joseph De Maistre, or Alfred Espinas square with that of Durkheim? Kubali believed that each of these thinkers left his mark on the rise of Durkheimian sociology. Did they with equal measure leave distinctive views of the nature of the state on Durkheim's thinking?

In time, Kubali's doctoral thesis became *L'Idée de l'état chez les précurseurs de l'école sociologique français* (Kubali 1936). Early in the process of writing—1932—Kubali tells us that he felt that to do justice to his topic, he needed to explore the most mature ideas of Durkheim on the "problem of the State" (Kubali 1957, ix). Kubali's first efforts at researching this topic, however, turned up little in Durkheim's published work. Kubali thus turned to Marcel Mauss to inquire about other items by Durkheim that might be useful to him. Mauss at the time was engaged in the long process of preparing Durkheim's unpublished works for the press. Among these materials, Mauss identified a set of Durkheim's lectures that eventually would become part of those that would later be assembled under the title *Leçons de sociologie physique des moeurs et du droit*, or *Professional Ethics and Civic Morals* in its English translation. These had been continually revised by Durkheim since their first delivery in Bordeaux in 1896, later in Paris in 1904 and 1912, and finally in the years just prior to his death in 1917. Mauss entrusted a number of these lectures to Kubali. Some years later, Mauss succeeded in publishing three of these (on professional ethics) in 1937 in the *Revue de métaphysique et de morale* as "Physique des moeurs et du droit"—"The Nature of Morals and of Rights" (Durkheim 1937; Kubali 1957, ix). The other lectures—six on civic morals—however remained unpublished, despite Mauss's best intentions. Years later, after Kubali had returned to Turkey to assume a post at the University of Istanbul in the Law School, he undertook a Turkish translation of the six lectures on civic morals given him by Mauss, and he published them in 1947 in the *Revue de la faculté de la droit d'Istanbul*—the first time they had seen official light of day. In 1950, and in Turkey as well, thanks to access granted Kubali by one of Durkheim's daughters, Madame Jacqueline Halphen, Kubali acquired a total of fifteen lectures on civic morals to add to the three that had been published earlier by Mauss on professional ethics in the *Revue de métaphysique et de morale*. Kubali edited and published the entire set of eighteen lectures under the title of what we know today as the *Leçons de sociologie physique des moeurs et du droit* (*Professional Ethics and Civic Morals* in its English translation) (Durkheim 1950; Durkheim 1957a).

I have labored the matter of the dates of access and publication of these materials because they bear on the larger purposes of my argument—one of which is to discuss the place of Durkheimian theoretical thinking about politics and religion in the new Turkish republic's policy about the place of religion in a modern nation-state. Accordingly, I am first of all asserting that despite the French origins of *Professional Ethics and Civic Morals* in lectures given by Durkheim, the fact of their anthologizing and

publication in Turkey establishes a *Turkish* provenance of the published
work. This, in turn, makes an understanding of modern Turkey particularly pertinent to an understanding of the text and vice versa. Indeed, I
would go further. Despite the fact that these lectures were conceived and
written by Durkheim, in their present physical form as an anthology of the
text of lectures, they cry out for interpretation within the historical context of the Turkey of the life and times of its facilitating editor, Hüseyin
Nail Kubali. In this chapter, I am seeking to make sense of the relationship
of the publication of Durkheim's *Professional Ethics and Civic Morals* in modern Turkey to the life and political thought of Hüseyin Nail Kubali.

Second, and related to this investigation of the context of publication
of *Professional Ethics and Civic Morals*, the chronology of Turkish access to
Durkheim's writings, especially in relation to the subject of corporatism and
occupational groups, holds an as yet untold significance for an evaluation of
Durkheimian thought in light of its practical political nature. No other
European thinker was appropriated more enthusiastically by key Turkish
intellectuals in their attempts to articulate a vision of a modern Turkish
nation-state than Durkheim. Given the reputation of Kemalism from at least
the middle 1920's as an authoritarian, even fascist "corporatist" political
regime, and given the great influence of Durkheimian corporatist thought
in Turkey since the beginning of the twentieth century, the question arises
of whether it is fair to see Durkheimian social theory as a kind of "*scholarly
forerunner*" of Kemalism, and thus of Turkish fascist corporatism? Further,
was Durkheimian corporatism practically *operationalized* as a blueprint for
actual fascist or fascist-tending corporatism, such as some scholars have
identified in sectors of and at periods in the history of Kemalist Turkey
(Parla & Davison 2004, 13, 265ff; Ranulf 1939)?

For Durkheim's part, he definitely meant his meditations on the subjects treated in *Professional Ethics* for practical application. No matter how
sketchy Durkheim's plans in *Professional Ethics* may have been, he intended
them to guide reconstruction of societies in the modern age in deliberate
opposition to Marxist class-based visions, liberal individualism, and fascist
corporatist schemes for the future shape of society (Mauss 1969b, 504). I
shall accept the recent arguments made by Andrew Davison and Taha Parla,
however, that Durkheim actually articulated there what has been called a
"solidarist corporatism," as opposed to "fascist" one (Parla & Davison 2004,

12). Later, in the hands of certain segments of the Kemalist party and regime, a fascist reading was given to a scheme of social organization that was essentially not fascist at all (Parla & Davison 2004, 244, 246, 255–66). As we will see in detail, Durkheim's sketch of the "corporate society," his vision for the reconstruction of modern society, called for a harmonious assembly of professional or occupational groupings (Hawkins 1994). There are, however, some readers who will need to be convinced that Durkheim's plans for a corporate society do not point toward a Durkheimian justification of fascist corporatism, in that they believe that anything short of liberal individualism entails fascist corporatism. Durkheimian societism does, indeed, require that the individual's location within a social group should become actual and significant, even if Durkheimians would not say that the individual is utterly absorbed in or subordinated to corporate interests.

Readers familiar with the issues arising about the political import of Durkheimian corporatism, especially in the 1920s and 1930s with rise of fascist corporatism, will hear the distinct echo of the theme of the fascist import of Durkheimian thought. I am thus deliberately referring to the controversy spurred in 1939 by the infamous charge of the Swedish sociologist Svend Ranulf that Durkheimian societism was guilty of being a "scholarly forerunner" of fascism for the Europe of the time (Lukes 1972, 338 n71; Ranulf 1939). Similar charges have made indirectly against Durkheimian social thought in connection with Turkey by the Turkish sociologists Uriel Heyd and Faruh Birtek, respectively (Birtek 1991; Davison 1998, 95–99; Heyd 1950, 55–57).

Such charges of facilitating Turkish fascism would, in theory, be much more consequential in Turkey, since the leading ideologist of Turkish nationalism, corporatism, and, allegedly, the fascist corporatism linked with Kemalism was the Durkheimian sociologist, Ziya Gökalp (1875–1924). It was Ziya Gökalp who, in effect, introduced Durkheimian thought into Turkey, and enthusiastically promoted it in Turkey in the first two decades of the twentieth century. Thus, insofar as Gökalp can be said to be the key theorist behind Kemalism, and to the extent that Kemalism can be said to be a form of "fascist corporatism," one would have to conclude that Durkheimian thinking—at least indirectly—participated intimately in theorizing and intellectually legitimizing a fascist political order (Parla & Davison 2004). The main question, of course, that needs to be faced here is the justice of the charges that Durkheimian thinking about professional and occupational groups—either as interpreted by Gökalp or as directly conveyed by Durkheim—was either in theory or practice a form of fascist corporatism. Central, then, to the questions at play in this discussion is whether the leading Turkish Durkheimian of his generation, Ziya Gökalp, taught a fascist corporatism based upon Durkheimian thought. Finally, alongside these questions, we will want to ask where the work and thought of Hüseyin Nail Kubali fit, with his publication of Durkheim's outline of his brand of corporatism, *Professional Ethics and Civic Morals*.

2. Durkheimian Solidarist Corporatism and Civil Society

Aside from any of these or other considerations, one reason for doubting the justice of the fascist corporatist characterization of, at least, Turkish Durkheimianism is the place occupied by Durkheim's corporatist thought as articulated in *The Division of Labor* and *Professional Ethics and Civic Morals* in theorizing the diametrically opposed political social formation known widely as "civil society." Taking Durkheimian thought along this opposite political axis, other commentators have seen *Professional Ethics and Civic Morals*, for example, as anti-totalitarian, in its articulation of the social conditions standing in the way of such staples of the fascist program as statism (Emirbayer 1996a; Emirbayer 1996b; 1994; Kumar 1993). The Durkheim of *Professional Ethics* writes to articulate nothing less than the "associational relations of civil life"—what lies between the state, capitalist economy, and the individual, "the intermediate domains of social life," as Mustafa Emirbayer tells us (Emirbayer 1996b, 112). In a work of the same genre, according to Emirbayer, Durkheim's *Evolution of Educational Thought*, Durkheim is enthusiastic about the way the pedagogical theories of the humanists along with the break-up of monolithic Christianity produced "'movement toward individualism and differentiation'"(Emirbayer 1996a, 273, citing Durkheim 1977, 171). Emirbayer celebrates precisely the anti-statist features of Durkheim's thought that he celebrated in the rise of free thought and the cult of the individual—those movements that "emboldened rising social groups to press their right to deviate from existing beliefs" (Emirbayer 1996a, 273). Long-time student of Durkheim and politics J. M. Hawkins, as well, brings out the way the Durkheim of *Professional*

Ethics emphasizes the nature of occupational and professional groups as a means not only to discipline an unruly egoism, but also to clear a political and moral space independent of the state in which individuals could be nurtured in default of the weakening of family ties in industrial society (Hawkins 1994, 474–76). Although he never demonizes the state, neither does Durkheim indulge a "mystique" of the state (Davy 1950, xxxix). Rather, Durkheim seeks to "devise intermediaries between it and the rest of society. 7. The state must have a relation to the nation without being absorbed in it. . . . (It must) intercalcate between the two some resistant bodies which will temper the action that has the greater force" (Durkheim 1957b, 101). Again, the question of the justice of these characterizations of Durkheimian thinking about professional and occupational groups as facilitating the creation and sustenance of civil society must be addressed.

In this discussion, however, I want to take at least one step beyond the prevailing theoretical or analytical character of their discourse. While these theoretical discussions of Durkheimian corporatism make for interesting analyses of Durkheimian *texts*, they are mute about whether or not the antifascist principles of civil society were ever *implemented* in the way the fascistic ones are claimed to have been, or even whether these more liberal readings of Durkheim attracted any practical *following* in Turkey. Is the liberal, or solidarist, reading of Durkheim's corporatism nothing more than a hopeful idea without any actual application to the real Turkish state? In the present discussion, I shall argue that besides the Durkheimian thought of Ziya Gökalp and those in Kemalist Turkey tending in the direction of fascist corporate society are those who read Durkheim (or at least certain texts of Durkheim) to support a notion of solidarist corporatism typical of proponents of civil society. The thought of Hüseyin Nail Kubali and his publication in Kemalist Turkey of *Leçons de sociologie physique des moeurs et du droit*, in particular, shows that, at least in highly placed quarters of the Turkish Durkheimian intelligentsia and political leadership, an anti-fascist re-appropriation of Durkheimian thought was well under way.

3. Durkheim in Turkey: Ziya Gökalp

In this vein, Kubali's publication of *Professional Ethics and Civic Morals* seems to represent an attempt to put Durkheimian corporatism in Turkey definitely on the side of the formation of just the sort of civil society of which Davy, Emirbayer, Hawkins, and others have written. By publishing a work like *Professional Ethics and Civic Morals* that features Durkheim's commitment to human rights, especially the sacredness of the individual, found there, Kubali would have been asserting again, several generations later, Durkheim's original intent. While, at this point, I can only hazard the hypothesis that Kubali is doing so in part to rehabilitate Gökalp by retrieving the democratic legacy of Durkheim from the right wing of the Kemalist movement who would use the prestige of both Durkheim and Gökalp for their own purposes, one might keep such a possibility in mind for future research.

Right-wing and, in particular, statist readings of both Gökalp and Durkheim have a history in Turkey, especially in connection with Gökalp's ardent Turkish nationalism. What is sure, however, is that most of the discussion of Durkheimian corporatism and right-wing political arrangements stems from the application and interpretation of Durkheimian thought in Turkey under the aegis of Ziya Gökalp. Historian Robert Devereaux and other scholars of modern Turkey have argued that one of the "most influential Turkish writers of the twentieth century" and one to whom "more than any other one man, belongs the credit for reviving Turkish national pride, which Atatürk later exploited" was none other than Turkey's leading Durkheimian sociologist, Ziya Gökalp (Devereux 1968, ix). The main figure of my attention in this chapter, Hüseyin Nail Kubali, writes similarly in his Preface to the 1950 edition of *Professional Ethics*. Kubali, for example, affirms these reports of the powerful and direct influence of Durkheim in Turkey, especially upon the fervent Kemalist ideologue Ziya Gökalp (1875–1924). Referring to his publication in Turkey of *Professional Ethics and Civic Morals*, Kubali notes:

> The publication in Turkey of this posthumous work of Durkheim is not in any way a matter of chance but rather, we might say, the result of a kind of cultural determinism. For in Turkey, Durkheim's is the only sociology, apart from that of Le Play, Gabriel Tarde, Espinas and others, to have become a standard work, especially since the books and teaching of Ziya Gökalp, the well-known Turkish sociologist. There are many like myself in Turkey who bear the stamp of Durkheim's school of thought. (Durkheim 1957b, xi)

For this reason, the question arises, however, whether one would thus say that, whatever Durkheim's political orientations or intentions, Ziya Gökalp meant to use Durkheimian corporatism in a "fascist" way? The answer, as the most recent scholarship on modern Turkey by Andrew Davison and Taha Parla, for example, argues is that the thought of Ziya Gökalp, and Durkheim by association, cannot be merged with statism. While a strong nationalist, Gökalp represented a solidarist corporatism, derived ultimately from the French solidarist, Alfred Fouillée (1838–1912), and from him to Durkheim, one cannot derive the worship of the state that can be associated with certain twentieth-century right-wing thinkers going back at least to Kaiser Wilhelm's state philosopher, Treitschke (Durkheim 1885). What, then, of Gökalp and the issue of statism?

Born in Diyarbakir, an historic cultural center on the banks of the upper Tigris in the Kurdish areas of southeastern Anatolia, Ziya Gökalp was the son of a notable provincial official (Findikoglu 1935, ch. 1). The rich and diverse ethos of Gökalp's home city doubtless enriched the intellectual scope of the young man, given the way it was placed at the intersection of vibrant religious piety and practice, on the one hand, and avant garde politics on the other. Diyarbakir was not only home to many sufis, poets, mullahs, and philosophers, but also nurtured an emergent democratic movement in the midst of later Ottoman times. While still at secondary school there, Gökalp began reading the great Muslim philosophers, Al-Kindi, Ibn Khaldun, Al-Ghazali, and other original thinkers from the Muslim middle ages. Gökalp's father, Tevfik Efendi, especially encouraged his son's wide reading in the adventurous thinker Ghazali, and also provided him with an example of principled political commitment to liberal and democrat causes, of which he was a conspicuous promoter, despite his prominent position in officialdom.

The intellectual environment of provincial Diyarbakir nonetheless had its limits. After Gökalp completed his first excursions into formal education, he moved on to higher education in the more cosmopolitan environs of Istanbul in the mid 1890s. Due to economic reasons, however, Gökalp was compelled to train in a practical field of study, and chose veterinary medicine. The young man's heart was never in such work: his mind, then, always wandered off into the loftier realms of social theory and philosophy. So, while pursuing an occupation in the capital, Gökalp satisfied

his inexhaustible appetite for philosophy and politics by an intense program of reading and an active life among his intellectual peers in Istanbul.
It was here that he first learned French, and was drawn to the writings of
influential thinkers of the Third Republic, such as Gustav Le Bon, Gabriel
Tarde, Alfred Fouillée, and Durkheim (Findikoglu 1935, 19). Nietzsche, as
well, was influential in Gökalp's thinking. But in Istanbul, too, Gökalp
immersed himself with equal zest in the national culture—Turkish arts,
popular literature, poetry, theater, and philosophy. In his course work,
Gökalp was attracted to opposite poles of interest—on the one hand to
mathematics and the natural sciences, but with as much fervor to Muslim
theology and spirituality. Gökalp even speaks with delight of how he
derived a kind of intellectual "charge" from entertaining such polar opposites of inquiry (Findikoglu 1935, 6).

Inevitably, Gökalp was drawn into the swirl of Turkey's political revolutions of the beginning of the twentieth century. He joined one of the secret
political societies of the day organized by the radicalized medical students of
Istanbul, and was imprisoned for his participation in their activities. He was
thereafter exiled to his home city of Diyarbakir, but continued his political
activities there, although subject to police surveillance (Findikoglu 1935, 12).
In 1908, Gökalp played a major role in the Young Turk Revolution, largely as
its main ideologist, offering a coherent vision of what Turkey's future might
be. He also gave financial support to the rebels. Led for the most part by
physicians from the Military Medical College, they later became the core of
the Committee of Union and Progress (CUP) that, in effect, pushed aside the
newly established constitutional monarchy. By forcing the sultan to recall
parliament, the "Young Turks," in effect, restored representative government. In spirit, they were a heady mix of romantic Nietzschean moral revolution and scientistic French positivism—both qualities that gave their
leadership a distinctively fresh, but elitist character. In prescribing their
political remedies, these doctors of a "sick" nation felt that "they knew best,"
so to speak. (Smith 1995, 46–47) The central committee of the CUP invited
Gökalp to represent Diyarbakir at the general national party congress in
1908. From this point forward, Gökalp was launched into a national political
career. From that time, as well, he put to full use his command of the
vast learning he had acquired over the intervening years, especially of
Durkheimian sociology (Findikoglu 1935, 15).

It was from about 1909 that Gökalp intensified his focus upon Durkheimian thought. He believed that Durkheimian social theory could afford him the best theoretical basis for conceiving the broad future shape of Turkish national life. In 1910, Gökalp instigated the mission of a Turkish student, M. Nermi, to Paris both to study Durkheimian sociology and also to collect texts and notes from Durkheim's lectures. Together with this effort, Gökalp set about gaining official support for an *école normale* devoted to instruction in Durkheimian social science and philosophy. Here is where he began teaching Durkheimian sociology in earnest.

The purpose of both Gökalp's teaching and the establishment of French sociology in Turkey was done with an eye to the direct application of Durkheimian social theory to Turkish social life. Like the reform-minded Durkheim in his *Professional Ethics and Civic Morals*, it was practical social reconstruction, as well, that Gökalp had foremost in mind when he decided to bring Durkheimian sociology to Turkey (Findikoglu 1935, 21). From time to time, during the years 1913–1915, Gökalp also taught Durkheimian sociology in one of Istanbul's Muslim seminaries (*medrese*). Finally, in 1915, Gökalp moved on to a new chair of sociology at the University of Istanbul that he had himself worked to create. He remained at the university until 1919, enjoying an extraordinarily fruitful period of work. He not only saw to the normal official duties of a university professor, but also founded academic journals, one of which was modeled expressly on *L'Année Sociologique*. He likewise worked to see that Durkheimian texts were translated into Turkish (Findikoglu 1935, 22).

3.1 Gökalp's "Turkism"

As Turkey moved toward involvement in World War I, and as it suffered a humiliating occupation by Western forces after the defeat of the Ottomans in the war, Gökalp, like many of his countrymen, was moved by the call to patriotism. During the war, Gökalp especially worked on ideas having to do with the nature of Turkish national identity. Taken together, these ideas formed the basis of what Gökalp called "Turkism." For Gökalp, Turkism "means to exalt the Turkish nation" (Gökalp 1968b, 12). Despite the political ring of the term, it was "not a political party but a scientific, philosophic and aesthetic school of thought. Or, to phrase it differently, it is a course of cultural effort and renovation" (Gökalp 1968b, 125). As such,

Turkism encompassed radical renovation in the arts, language, morality, law, religion, philosophy, and the economy, as well as in politics. It was a statement of the content of a new Turkish national identity.

But declaring a doctrine is a far cry from actually implementing it, but especially so for Turkey. Thus, the end of the Ottoman period, and the rise of independence movements all across its former territories, raised in an acute way the question of the content of this new Turkish national identity. Not only was Turkey going have to make a transition from being the core of a once glittering empire to just another nation-state, but it was also going to have to sort out its affiliations with a global entity such as Islam, of which it had been, as seat of the caliphate, the international center. Adding to this problem of national identity was, as well, Turkey's attraction to the ideals and social institutions of Western Europe—an attraction that had been growing steadily since it began in the early decades of the nineteenth century. Literally, with one foot in Europe and Mediterranean Christian history, but the other in Asia and on the spiritual ground of Islam, Turkey was split astride a kind of spiritual Bosporus. The question of the balance of elements that might go into making up this new Turkish identity as a nation-state became ever more acute.

Part of Gökalp's efforts at addressing the matter of the Turkish national identity crisis was his part in articulating a vision with practical political consequences. This is what one may call a national *mythos*. Perhaps, recalling his youthful poetic and artistic life, a portion of Gökalp's response to this national identity crisis was his imaginative interpretation of Turkish history, partly within the larger context of what one might call a Turanian *mythos* (Gökalp 1968b, 5–7, 20f). Gökalp saw all Turkic peoples originating from a single source at the heart of Asia, and retaining, in however faint a form, the fundamental traits of the old Turks (Gökalp 1968b, 12–13). Now, however, Turks had dispersed into their various regional forms, identified by labels naming peoples inhabiting the vast extent of Asia Minor, through Central Asia, to the borders of China. But to Gökalp, they were all still Turks.

But Gökalp's thinking was not without its inner tensions. This tendency to trade on ethnic and geographic identifications of Turkishness rested somewhat uncomfortably with Gökalp's avowed wish to resist a strictly ethnic or territorial definition of Turkish identity. Indeed, he explicitly dismissed the unifying ideas of "ethnic purity" or geographical unity as definitively constituting the essence of the nation. In its place, he put the Durkheimian ideal of socialization by way of education as the defining element in Turkism (Strenski 1993, 189–92):

> What, then, is a nation? What sort of tie do we have that can be superior to, and take precedence over, racial, ethnic, geographic, political and volitional forces? Sociology asserts that this tie is a sharing of education and culture, that is, of sentiments. . . . one's pedigree is not to be sought in nationality but only in national education and ideals. . . .
>
> Here is a practical conclusion to be drawn from these considerations. There are fellow citizens in our country whose ancestors came from Albania or Arabia sometime in the past. If they have been educated as Turks and have become used to working for the Turkish ideal, we must not set them apart from other citizens. (Gökalp 1968b, 15–16)

Gökalp's role as scholar, educator, and sociologist was, accordingly, devoted to instilling a sense of what essential "Turkism" was, even if it may have been a potentially conflicted one.

Balancing Gökalp's adventures in the mytho-poetry of national identity was a program of practical reform. Gökalp's proposals for the reform of the language spoken in Turkey may serve as an example (Gökalp 1968b, ch. II). Gökalp argued that in Turkey two languages existed. One was Ottoman ("Ottoman Esperanto," Gökalp called it). This was a written language, used in Istanbul, but which was not spoken. It was an amalgam of Turkish, Arabic, and Persian. The other language was the popular argot of the people, that was spoken but not written. It was what one might call, simply, "Turkish" (Gökalp 1968b, ch II).

3.2 Reviving Turkish "Culture" and Entering Western "Civilization"

The basis for this division of languages illustrates a key distinction guiding Gökalp's practical political ideas and programs. On the one side was "culture"—the emotive, unpremeditated, and inherent element of the life of a people; on the other side was "civilization"—the international, intellectual, and conscious side of the life of nations (Gökalp 1968b, 29). Like Islam, modern science, technology, and such, the Ottoman language exemplifies "civilization," since it embodies the international aspect of a nation as well as the work of "conscious action and individual wills" (Gökalp 1968b, 22). For example, Arabic features of Ottoman reflect Turkey's deliberate links with the Islamic world. As such, "civilization" for Gökalp, "is the sum total of concepts and techniques created consciously and transmitted from one nation to another by imitation." Opposed to "civilization" is a principle rooted in the unpremeditated and emotive side of the life of nations, what Gökalp calls "culture." It "consists of sentiments which cannot be created artificially and cannot be borrowed from other nations through imitation" (Gökalp 1968b, 24). For Gökalp, language again presented an example of this side of his distinction.

> Just as plants and animals develop naturally and spontaneously, so too arise and mature the elements of a culture. Language, for example, is not something that has been consciously created by individuals. We cannot change the words of a language or replace them with newly coined ones, nor can we change a language's grammatical rules that have grown out of its nature. Words and grammatical rules change only by themselves, while we remain merely spectators. (Gökalp 1968b, 22)

Part of Gökalp's practical Turkist policy was, without diminishing Turkey's participation in "civilization," as we will see, to raise "culture" to a higher level of participation, status, and visibility in modern Turkey, a process that had already been begun by Ottoman reformers. Gökalp urged that the spoken language of Turkish, for example, should supplant Ottoman Esperanto, the old written one, and become itself the official written language suitable for facilitating international transactions between civilizations (Gökalp 1968b, 77).

While much of Gökalp's heart was in securing and bringing out the "cultural" aspects of Turkish life, he was no chauvinistic fool. He did not imagine that it was either desirable or possible for Turkey to isolate itself in its own self-contained world of pure "culture"—of a pure Turkishness (Gökalp 1968b, 77–84). No nation could thrive outside of intimate connections with others, and therefore, without participation in the "civilizational" part of the life of nations. A balance needed to be struck. For example, while Gökalp wished to minimize foreign loan words in the official language of Turkey, he resisted eliminating Persian and Arabic words. But, at the same time, Gökalp insisted that Persian and Arabic linguistic structures had to give way to Turkish ones (Gökalp 1968b, 8–9). Out of a delicate balance between Gökalp's "culture" and "civilization," in effect, a balance between mythopoetic visions and practical policies, Gökalp tried to condense the features of an essential Turkish identity into what was for him the essence of his nationalism—his "Turkism." This distinction likewise permitted Gökalp to theorize Turkey's adoption of Western "civilization," with its science, technology, democratic political structures, and such, without losing Turkish identity. Since Turkish identity was, for Gökalp, a matter of "culture," it occupied, in theory at least, another plane from "civilization," whether Western or not. The problem with the Ottoman reformers, dating from the early nineteenth century, was, in Gökalp's view, that they tried to merge two irreconcilable "civilizations"— "Western" and "Eastern." Putting his views starkly, Gökalp says that "Turkists wish to enter Western civilization completely and unreservedly, while remaining Turks and Muslims" (Gökalp 1968b, 33).

3.3 Nationalism, Statism, and Fascism

As an ardent nationalist, Gökalp has understandably been called the "official ideologue of the war and revolution" (Smith 1995, 48). Uriel Heyd even went so far as to say that Gökalp's real religion was not Islam, but Turkish nationalism, a result, thinks Heyd, of replacing "nation" with the "society" of Durkheim's alleged identification of god and society (Davison 1995, 192; Heyd 1950, 57f). Heyd argued that Gökalp saw Durkheim as promoting his Kemalist Turkish nationalism and corporatist statism by its emphasis on the agency of "'collective representations'" such as ideals, values, and even religion, specifically against the historical materialism of Marx (Gökalp 1968a, 52–53). This embrace of Durkheimian idealism likewise made it easier for Gökalp to write about the self-annihilation of the individual in society as a kind of "'Social Sufism.'" Here, there "are no individuals, there is (only) society" (Heyd 1950, 56). From his social neo-Sufism, Gökalp reinterpreted Allah as society, and society as the (Turkish) nation. Taking Durkheim further than even so fervent a nationalist as he would take it, Turkish nationalism for Gökalp becomes the religion of Turkey—at least in Heyd's view (Heyd 1950, 56–57).

Against readings such as Heyd's, David Norman Smith refuses Heyd's laying of equal blame upon Gökalp and Durkheim for legitimizing proto-fascist political tendencies. Smith says, in effect, that even if Heyd were right about linking Gökalp's thought to fascism in Turkey, Heyd had not read enough Durkheim to conclude the same about Durkheim in France. He had not, I would note, taken into account the very Durkheimian text that I have made the focus of this discussion, *Professional Ethics and Civic Morals*. Of course, Gökalp would not have been in a position to have read *Professional Ethics*, nor the words of Durkheim's dedication to the religion of humanity, the cult of the individual, that he puts into balance against his own collectivism found in *Professional Ethics*, since it was made available only decades after his death. These differences in reading Durkheim can be easily traced in part to the different Durkheims that emerged over the years, with the Durkheim emphasizing the individual emerging in great strength only after the Dreyfus Affair. At any rate, Gökalp was reading the Durkheim of *The Rules* and *The Division of Labor* in a way that suited his own corporatist program, which was taken over—with or without his approval—by the Kemalists (Gökalp 1968a; Gökalp 1968b, 49–54).

Yet, although Smith exonerates Durkheimian corporatism of fascistic tendencies in his article, he agrees with Heyd and others about Gökalp's political orientation toward the extreme right in Turkey. Davison, Parla, and others, as we will see, contest this characterization of Gökalp's thought and actual influence (Davison 1998; Parla & Davison 2004). For example, during the war, says Smith, Gökalp adopted an "ultra-nationalist perspective" which left no room for individual liberties and initiatives. In Smith's view, the authoritarianism of old was reborn in a corporatist 'Durkheimian' guise. Citing Robert Melson's study of the Armenian genocide, Smith also claims that Gökalp "defended the policy of 'deporting' the Armenians," and, in effect, approved a genocidal policy, since the deportees were often sent to virtually uninhabitable wastelands (Melson 1992, 164; Smith 1995, 48).

I am not prepared to evaluate the charges of excessive patriotism on the part of Gökalp, although it would seem only reasonable to situate Gökalp's nationalism in the objective political situation of the day, before passing final judgment. At any rate, Andrew Davison and Taha Parla have marshaled an impressive array of arguments and facts to refute at least the face value claims of Gökalp's detractors. A partial list would include such points as the denial that Gökalp was the source of Ataturk's "tutelary democracy" (Davison 1995, 192), or that he was a proto-fascist or fascist (Davison 1995, 13, 192), or that he sought to bring religion under the strict kinds of controls associated with Kemalism (Davison 1995, 217), or that he identified nationalism as his or Turkey's religion (Davison 1995, 194), or despite his role as advisor and social theorist, that he was a major operative in the Kemalist regime (Davison 1995, 194). For Davison and Parla, Gökalp was a democrat and pluralist (Davison 1995, 207), a variety of Muslim reformer, who sought to combat Quranic fundamentalism (Davison 1995, 195f), and someone who tried to articulate a formula by which Turkish Muslim religious cultural values and sensibilities could be respected while at the same time establishing Turkey as a novel kind of secular state.

What is clear is that the context of Ottoman collapse, Western occupation and dismemberment of the old empire, and the imposition of the humiliating conditions of the Treaty of Sèvres, need to be part of the context of this discussion. On 16 March 1920, for example, Istanbul was occupied by the Entente States, and Gökalp was arrested with a number of his fellow CUP parliamentary deputies (Tourism). Gökalp was then tried by the victorious British forces as a war criminal (Smith 1995, 48). Even in exile, Gökalp never ceased his intellectual activities. In prison, he set up what was a kind of informal barracks university-in-exile on Malta for men more accustomed to the life of political action than theoretical sociology. Nonetheless, Gökalp undertook to teach these men as best he could of the utility of Durkheimian social thought.

Thus, it is a certainty that Gökalp was a strong Turkish nationalist, and that he, at least, understood his patriotic orientations in light of opposition to Western colonial domination in the post-war situation. Thus, he says, "There is no way to end colonial life in the Islamic World also except by strengthening the national consciousness." But, Gökalp says further, religion can no longer be the "civilizational" horizon against which the Turkish future can be cast:

It was once believed that the ideal of Pan-Islamism would assure the attainment of independence by Muslim ethnic groups and the deliverance from colonial status of their territories. Political experience showed, however, that Pan-Islamism actually prevented the progress of Muslim peoples and hindered their attainment of independence, because it gave rise, on the one hand, to such reactionary movements as theocracy and clericalism and, on the other hand, was opposed to the awakening of national ideals and national consciousnesses in the Islamic World.

Thus, with the failure of Islam, Turkish nationalism is the only realistic recourse available to Turkey and other newly liberated entities of the old Ottoman dominions.

> This being the situation, what must be done? Above all, efforts must be made unceasingly to awaken and strengthen the national consciousness both in our country and in other Islamic lands, for national consciousness is not only the source of all progress but also the source and cornerstone of national independence. (Gökalp 1968b, 60–61)

These sentiments may then make more understandable the course of Gökalp's unsettled political and controversial life after the war.

3.4 Gökalp's Durkheimian "Idées-Forces"

In Malta, Gökalp used his enforced leisure to study newly available Durkheimian texts, and thus more thoroughly to increase his grasp of the French master. Prepared in this way, Gökalp then undertook to form the minds of his fellow prisoners—those who would become part of Turkey's future intellectual and political leadership. In this way, Gökalp spread Durkheimian ideas to his fellow exiles, many of whom returned to Turkey well exposed to, if not necessarily persuaded of, the virtues of Durkheimian social theory.

Foremost among these Durkheimian notions was that of the "conscience collective." Gökalp appealed to this idea in order to instill hopes for a national revival in his fellow exiles that despite their country's humiliation at the hands of the British and the attempts made by them to deny the reality of a distinctly Turkish national identity, Turkey was not destined to be the "sick man" of Europe. Gökalp made a deliberate link between the reality of "nationhood" and Durkheim's view that all forms of "society" required consciousness. Pointedly against historical materialism, Gökalp affirms a stoutly Durkheimian position:

> Collective representations are not, as Marx believed, ineffective epiphenomena in social life. On the contrary, all aspects of our social lives are shaped by the effects of these representations. For example, every aspect of our social lives will begin to change when the representation, "we belong to the Turkish nation, the Islamic community and Western civilization," begins to acquire standing as a definite concept in the common consciousness of us Turks. Once we say that "we belong to the Turkish nation," we will begin to show in our language, aesthetics, morals and law and even in theology and philosophy the originality and personality which befit Turkish culture, taste and consciousness. (Gökalp 1968b, 52)

Thrusting his argument directly into Marx's face, as it were, Gökalp in effect reinterprets Marx's notion of class consciousness in idealist Durkheimian terms as "collective consciousness":

> This term can be better explained by examples than by definition, so I will try to illustrate by a few examples precisely what this term means. There were workers in Turkey even before the 1908 Revolution, but their common consciousness held no such thought as "we constitute the working class." Since that thought did not exist neither did a working class. There were also many Turks in our country; but since there was, in their collective consciousness, no concept of "we are the Turkish nation," no Turkish nation then existed. In other words, a group is not a social group unless there is a conscious realization of that status in the common consciousness of its individual members. (Gökalp 1968b, 51)

Rallying his fellow prisoners in Malta from their gloom, Gökalp is reported to have said to them " 'You know well that each of us is made up of two parts—one part animal, the other, human. While the English may have carried the animal part of us off to Malta, nevertheless that other part of our individual being was left behind, and will once again dwell, in Istanbul' " (Findikoglu 1935, 25–26). In April of 1921, Gökalp returned from exile. When the 1923 nationalist revolution led by Mustafa Kemal—Atatürk—broke out,

Gökalp supported it, but did not live long enough to see it come to fruition. He died in 1924, shortly after publishing his main work on Turkish nationalism, *The Principles of Turkism* (1923) (Gökalp 1968b; Smith 1995, 48).

3.5 *Gökalp and Durkheim: Forerunners of Fascism?*

It is perhaps inevitable that a patriot such as Gökalp should be suspected of tending toward the further right end of the political spectrum, especially in light of his support for elements in Turkish politics that eventually directed fascist, or at least proto-fascist, policies in Turkey. While Gökalp's death in 1924 may mitigate the association with proto-fascism, since the Kemalists did not really take charge of Turkey until some years later, Davison and Parla also argue against linking Gökalp with Kemalism. In terms of corporatism, they argue that the Kemalists took the Durkheim/Gökalp ideas of solidarist corporatism and featured "certain protofascist corporatist tendencies" of it. After Gökalp's death, the Kemalists, in effect, "jettisoned other, more pluralistic dimensions of Gökalp's thought in the process" (Parla & Davison 2004, p. 13). The burden of the recent work of Davison and Parla, then, has been to counter the substance of the charges of Heyd and others, and to show Gökalp and Gökalp's use of Durkheim in an entirely different light than as a "scholarly forerunner of fascism" (Davison 1995; Davison 1998; Parla & Davison 2004). Of course, some years ago Steven Lukes, and, again, in the more recent cases cited, David Norman Smith and J. M. Hawkins, respectively, have made the case against the Ranulf argument (Hawkins 1994; Lukes 1972, 338–40). Durkheim never let go of the ideal of the sacredness of the individual, and thus always resisted assimilation into fascist thinking (Hawkins 1994, 480). But what of the case of Turkish uses of Durkheim, especially the Durkheimianism of Gökalp that has been made with such vehemence by Uriel Heyd, in particular? And, how might it be extended to Hüseyin Nail Kubali, particularly as evident in the thrust of the arguments embodied in *Professional Ethics and Civic Morals*?

The main specific point bearing on this issue would seem to be the nature of Gökalp's corporatism, its relation to Durkheim's corporatism, and their respective relation to fascist corporatism. This is to inquire about the related issues of Gökalp's nationalism and his attitudes to statism and the place religion might have in the new Turkish republic. First, to corporatism.

3.6 Durkheim and Gökalp on Statism

As early as his *The Division of Labor* (1893) and reiterated in its second edition (1902), Durkheim sketched the outlines of a vision of a future society organized around "corporations"—labor unions, professional and occupational groups, and other units of social organization active particularly in the economic realm. While always linked with economic activities, these corporations would also be englobing moral entities, saving individuals from anomie and the destructive atomization that modern mass society tends to produce among individuals. Durkheim saw the dangers inherent in leaving a vacuum between the unorganized individual and the powerful modern state, referring to such a state of affairs as a "veritable sociological monstrosity. . . . A nation cannot be maintained unless, between the state and individuals, a whole range of secondary groups are interposed" (Durkheim 1902, liv). Filling this gap, corporations would not only form the bases of local "moral authority . . . but also a source of life sui generis. From it there arises a warmth that quickens or gives fresh life to each individual, which makes him disposed to empathize, causing selfishness to melt away" (Durkheim 1902, lii). In Durkheim's view, society would then become a "vast system of national corporations" (Durkheim 1902, liii). So devoted to this concept was Durkheim that he imagined that voters might elect representatives to a national parliament from their particular occupational group, rather than from the geographic residential district in which they lived. Such corporations "should become the elemental division of the state, the basic political unit" (Durkheim 1902, liii).

Gökalp seemed completely in tune with Durkheim's conception of a solidarist corporatism—as opposed to a statist or fascist one. In Gökalp's exposition of the meaning of Turkism, he articulated a position identical to Durkheim's ambition of encouraging the existence of intermediary groups between the state and the rest of society: "A nation cannot be maintained unless, between the state and individuals, a whole range of secondary groups are interposed. These must be close enough to the individual to attract him strongly to their activities and, in so doing, to absorb him into the mainstream of social life" (Durkheim 1902, lv). In *Professional Ethics and Civic Morals*, Durkheim reaffirms this position: "The state must have a relation to the nation without being absorbed in it. . . . [It must] intercalate between the two some resistant bodies which will temper the action that has the greater force" (Durkheim 1957b, 101). Gökalp's words are practically identical, even as they emphasize the task before Turkey of solidifying its new identity as a republican nation-state:

> The first goal of legal Turkism, then, is to create a modern state. The second goal is to free occupational guardianships from the interference of public guardianship by establishing occupational autonomies based on the authority of specialists. Achievement of this goal will require the enactment, on the basis of this principle, of civil, commercial, industrial and agricultural codes, as well as laws relating to the occupational autonomies of such professional organizations as the university, bar, medical society, teachers' society, engineers' society, etc. (Gökalp 1968b, 118)

Indeed, like Durkheim and his allusions to the family and medieval European guilds, Gökalp hearkens back to the old "independent" Turkish "guild organizations" as a kind of model of what he means for the new solidarist corporatist social organization of the present day. Durkheim lamented the abolition of the European guilds by the French Revolution, or to be precise, lamented their abolition without the creation of some sort of updated institutions, such as labor unions, to fulfill the function the old medieval guilds had performed (Durkheim 1902, xxxvii–xxxviii). Without any mediating institutions between the individual and the state, Durkheim feared that the individual would be left unprotected from possible predations of the state. Durkheim was wary of the power of the state to crush such intermediary grassroots organizations, and noted that in ancient Rome, the system of artisan and workers' unions formed there was finally ruined by being subordinated to the state administration (Durkheim 1902, xxxvii–xxxviii).

Another benefit of the formation of such subgroups was their ability to corral the reckless "self-interest" of extreme individualism. The subgroups forced the individuals to take into account something beyond themselves, something of the general welfare of society. They gave individuals a "taste for altruism, for forgetfulness of self and sacrifice" (Durkheim 1902, xxxiv). It is in this context of national interest and nation-building that we should also see Gökalp's corporatism. But like Durkheim, Gökalp does not wish to resuscitate these medieval institutions. Instead, says Gökalp, "they must be abolished and replaced by national organizations having their centers in the national capital" (Gökalp 1968b, 106). He, like Durkheim, saw the "professional group" or "corporation" as the basis for his new project of social construction (Durkheim 1902, xxxv).

When compared to varieties of fascist corporatism, the Durkheimian and Gökalpian solidarist corporatisms show some prominent differences. Durkheim, for example, asserts that in his own day, the best examples of solidarist corporatism were labor unions (Durkheim 1902, xxxvi). Although some Marxist critics of Durkheim and Gökalp, like Taha Parla, try to elide the differences between Durkheimian thought and Kemalist statism, their charges lack substance. Parla, for example, claims that Durkheim sees "individuals [only] as components of occupational groups . . . not as beings with intrinsic value deserving equal respect" (Parla & Davison 2004, 284). As Steven Lukes, for one, showed decades ago, Durkheim has to his credit a representative body of publications on the sacredness of the individual, such as his "Individualism and the Intellectuals" (1898) (Durkheim 1975) as well as several chapters devoted to the relation of the individual to the state in the book edited by Hüseyin Nail Kubali, *Professional Ethics and Civic Morals*. There, for example, Durkheim rails against those who would "try to revive the cult of the City State in a new guise," (Durkheim 1957b, 54), and assigns to the state the duty of fostering individualism, by providing the "milieu in which the individual moves, so that he may develop his faculties in freedom." The part played by the state is "to ensure the most complete individuation that the state of society will allow" (Durkheim 1957b, 69). To Durkheim's writings, we need also to add the many activities in behalf of human rights undertaken by him throughout his life, beginning with early agitation in the defense of Dreyfus (Lukes 1972, 332–49).

More problematic in the minds of many is, however, the Kemalist picture of the corporate state, and its relation to Gökalp's thinking along these lines. After all, however activist and interventionist a state Durkheim's Third Republic may have been—a feature of the French central state, traceable back years, even centuries, *before* Durkheim to the ancien régime—it cannot be equated to the Kemalist regime of 1924 and beyond, that would claim Gökalp's thinking as part of its legitimizing ideology. Davison and Parla accordingly describe in detail the ways in which they see Kemalism as fascistic (Parla & Davison 2004, 263ff). They, for example, note unambiguously that Kemalism lacked an "emphasis on the autonomous status of the individual as such." Taking a classic statist position, the Kemalists see individual citizens as "means" to state goals (Parla & Davison 2004, 261). Gökalp, for his part, was no liberal, and opposed utilitarian and egoistic individualism—as indeed did Durkheim (Durkheim 1975). Gökalp sought a society that was "altruistic, tolerant and public-oriented" (Parla & Davison 2004, 193). But according to Davison and Parla, Gökalp did not divinize the nation—in no small part because he remained a pious, if progressive, Muslim (Parla & Davison 2004, 213–4, 217).

One final point needs to be made on this issue of the relation of individual to the state. It may well be true, as Robert W. Hefner argues, that the character of democracies developed in Muslim countries may take on a distinctive color of their own, that, in some eyes, they may not seem like "democracies" at all from the viewpoint of what Charles Taylor has called "Atlantic" societies (Taylor 2004). Adopting a similarly pluralistic viewpoint about the potential for innovative varieties of democratic political culture, Hefner reports of developments in Indonesian, and other Muslim, societies that would be all too recognizable to Durkheim and Gökalp, respectively. With clear echoes of Durkheim's and Gökalp's ideas of religious societies as mediating institutions, Hefner lays out how Muslim democracies might be more like those outlined in Durkheim's (or Gökalp's) solidarist corporatism.

> Muslim democrats, like those in Indonesia, tend to be more civil democratic or Tocquevillian than they are (Atlantic) liberal in spirit. They deny the need for an Islamic state. But they insist that society involves more than autonomous individuals, and democracy more than markets and the state. Democracy requires a non-coercive culture that encourages citizens to respect the rights of others as well as to cherish their own. This public culture depends on mediating institutions in which citizens develop habits of free speech, participation, and toleration. In all this, they say, there is nothing undemocratic about Muslim voluntary associations (as well as those of other religions) playing a role in the public life of civil society as well as in personal ethics (Hefner 2000, 13)

At least in his formal publications, this seems the way that the solidarist corporatism of Gökalp (and Durkheim) imagined Islam, as informing the social subgroups mediating relations between the individual and the state, playing a constructive role in a modern democratic nation-state.

3.7 Durkheim and Gökalp on Religion and Civil Society

At first, this inclusion of religion in the mix making up professional groups may seem out of place. Readers of *The Division of Labor* and *Professional Ethics* will recall how Durkheim insisted upon the primacy of the link of these intermediary groups with meaningful economic realities. "What past experience demonstrates above all is that the organizational framework of the professional group should always be related to that of economic life. It is because this condition was not fulfilled that the system of corporations disappeared" (Durkheim 1902, l–li). But, as a result of this economic emphasis, we tend to overlook the fact that both Durkheim and Gökalp assign a place to morals and religion among these social subgroupings. This fact accentuates the apparent evolution in Durkheim's thought from one of his earlier writings—the preface to first edition (1893) of Durkheim's *The Division of Labor*—to one toward the end of his life, the preface to the second edition (1902). This later preface is rightly singled out as one of the two places where Durkheim articulates his latter-day theory of the place of professional and occupational groups in the reconstruction that he imagined for a future society. The other locus classicus for such discussions is, of course, the work of Durkheim's that Hüseyin Nail Kubali saw to publication, *Professional Ethics and Civic Morals*. In his preface to the second edition of *The Division of Labor*, Durkheim brings out the place of religion in his conception of a future solidarist corporatist society. He does so by recalling the moral and religious character of the ancient Roman "corporation." Emphasizing that these corporations had far more than the dominant economic character of later European guilds, Durkheim notes that "Above all else, the [Roman] corporation was a collegiate religious body. Each one possessed its own particular god, who, when the means were available, was worshiped in a special temple" (Durkheim 1902, xl).

It is notable, as well, that Gökalp made a point of including religious groups among those that might count as "occupational" groups. One of Gökalp's earlier biographers and critics, A. Ziyaeddin Fahri Findikoglu, notes that Gökalp's view of occupational groups incorporates both their original economic and religious make-up: "Turkish towns have an economic life that is fundamentally corporate. The solidarity of the professions takes its origin in conceptions that have really nothing to do with economics, since these guilds are only religious confraternities" (My translation) (Findikoglu 1935, 41). In his own words, Gökalp says that "religious, political, scientific, aesthetic and economic groups are the specialized and professional groups that have been created by a division of labor" (Gökalp 1968b, 51).

But Gökalp argued, as well, that religion should be autonomous of political structures, and further that it could be useful to the nation only to the extent that it would "occupy its 'own sphere.' Its elites must give up their claims to politics, just as politicians should ensure the autonomy of religious practices and institutions" (Davison 1995, 213). But, this does not mean that religion should not influence the ethos of the nation. In his 1915 article, "The Social Functions of Religion," Gökalp argued, to an extent, like Durkheim, for the social value of religious groups in shaping individuals into social beings, but most notably to enrich the national ethos (Davison 1995, 211). Despite his personal Muslim piety, Gökalp, likewise, rejected both "theocracy" and "clericalism." True to Durkheim, Gökalp took the view that religion had "intrinsic value in human life and history." It is one of the "pillars of organic solidarity" and should "occupy a place in public life, (but) where public means something other than political" (Parla & Davison 2004, 217–8). This is what Gökalp meant by referring to religion in Turkey as " 'semi-public' "—as a "corporate subunit of the national culture" (Davison 1995, 213). Thus, in his own way, Gökalp adds to the data base of arguments made notably by Robert W. Hefner's *Civil Islam* about the potential for religion to contribute to civil society in Muslim countries (Hefner 2000).

3.8 Who Was Hüseyin Nail Kubali?

In light of the complex of moral, political, and religious issues conditioning the appearance and influential existence of Durkheimian social thought in modern Turkey, the shape of the story of the significance of Hüseyin Nail Kubali's publication of *Professional Ethics and Civic Morals* may now become somewhat clearer. This story is also something of an edifying one, especially to the extent that Kubali is linked to Gökalp's democratic values, and to the degree that Davison and Parla's interpretation of Gökalp as a democrat, albeit a distinctly *Turkish* one, can stand criticism. To conclude this chapter, it is not necessary to relate the entire life story of Kubali, but merely to draw together some of the themes already laid out. When we read Kubali in the light of what both Durkheim wrote in his works on solidarist corporatism and what Gökalp wrote on the same theme and on Turkism, we find further support for the theses of Davison and Parla. In the process, we find support, as well, for another argument against the "Ranulf thesis," as it might be applied to both Durkheim and Gökalp.

We already know some of the story of Kubali's history as student of law in Paris, as admirer of the work of Ziya Gökalp, and of his interest in Durkheimian materials, especially on the nature of the state, that formed the basis of his doctoral thesis in law. In touching on the content of that thesis, as well as of several other key writings by Kubali, we can at least begin plausibly to place him in relation to the issues of statism, the status of the individual, and democratic values in modern Turkey. What we know of Kubali's career likewise helps us see him—and his orientation to Durkheim's thinking about the rights of the individual over against the power of the state. The overwhelming weight of the evidence available in European languages—mostly in French—paints a picture of an impressive jurist and legal scholar, committed to the rule of law and the separation of judicial powers from those of the executive and legislative branches of government. In political terms, Kubali thus emerges as a Turkish democrat, committed to preserving individual rights against the predations of statism, while at the same time embodying the social sensibility of a Durkheim.

Witness to these characteristics of Kubali's vision are a number of articles and his doctoral thesis. In 1959, for example, Kubali authored a survey of the status of the rule of law in Turkey. "The Concept of the Rule of Law in Turkey." Published in the French-language journal of the faculty of law at the University of Istanbul, Kubali shows that he is willing to face up to the shortcomings of Turkey in respect to international democratic standards. Before a reading public he knew would come substantially from Western nations, Kubali frankly admitted that Turkey's *practice* of adherence to the rule of law fell short of the statutory guarantees of that principle in established law. "As in other countries, Turkish experience shows that the text of the Constitution is not effective by itself and that the legislator [legislature?] may sometimes be guided by practical aims, rather than by constitutional considerations" (Kubali 1959, 302–3).

One example of a legislative violation of the constitution occurred when the Turkish legislature passed "acts that are definitely restrictive in the field of freedom of association, public meetings and press" (Kubali 1959, 302). These included, apparently, references to a series of laws passed in 1953 "which the universities interpreted as unacceptable invasions of academic freedom" (Weiker 1963, 50). Among their provisions, Kubali himself notes, were "restrictive movement and penal provisions on libellious [sic] speeches and publication . . . Political gatherings outside the electoral period have been put under the discretionary authorization of administrative authorities, except for statutory meetings of political parties and associations" (Kubali 1959, 302).

Kubali came to learn something of the meaning of these laws from his own experience of the penalties meted out to those like him who were accused of violating these "violations" of the rule of law. Bringing these theoretical viewpoints down to the hard ground of practical political action, the historian of Turkey Walter F. Weiker reported that Kubali was one of four "important cases" of university professors dismissed from their posts under Law 6435, which the Menderes government had passed along with a series of similar laws to exert control over dissent emanating principally from the universities. Of Kubali, Weiker says further, "While attempting to be careful not to mix politics into his academic activities, he had nevertheless been a constant and outspoken commentator on national affairs." No right of appeal of Kubali's dismissal was possible (Weiker 1963, 51). Historian Howard Douglas elaborates further, telling us that "Kubali was suspended in 1958" (presumably from his post as dean of the law school at the University of Istanbul) for "denouncing press regulations" that had been ordered by the governing Democratic Party administration (Douglas 2001, 125). That is to say that Kubali was removed from his post precisely for defending the ideals of civil society formulated in Durkheim's *Professional Ethics and Civic Morals*. Kubali's civic activism in defense of the independence of the press is to affirm the rightness of the Durkheimian and Gökalpian ideals of the autonomy of professional groups. Kubali does nothing less than defend positions opposed to Turkish *étatisme* and, in effect, affirms Durkheimian and Gökalpian principles of civil society worked out in the book Kubali brought to light, which we know as *Professional Ethics and Civic Morals*.

It might also be noted that by Weiker's account, Kubali was a judicious "'legalistically' oriented" jurist, essentially a product, as indeed he was, "of the legal training of an earlier age, and of a conservative, legal orientation to the political process" (Weiker 1963, 68). The epithet "conservative" apparently means something close to what Americans understand in these days of controversy over US Supreme Court nominations, as a "strict constructionist." American readers might, however, be wise not to leap to conclusions about the politics of French legal conservatives, based on their feelings about those in the United States. One can infer this given Kubali's apparent admiration of the distinguished French legal conservative, the "textualist" Henri Capitant, who held forth while Kubali was still resident as a student in Paris (Collective 1974, 12). Claire M. Germain describes Capitant's legal philosophy, and thus I am assuming, something close to Kubali's, in terms that show their common fear of executive or legislative nullification of the judiciary. Says Germain,

> In 1935, a famous French law professor, Henri Capitant, wrote a piece against the use of legislative history in statutory interpretation, advocating the English position of not allowing it. Capitant argued that parliamentary discussions lead to the expression of personal views, rather than a general sense of the spirit of the law. His ideas may have been influenced by political considerations and the legislative process of that particular time period of the Fourth Republic. (Capitant 1935; Germain 2003, 199–200)

In sum, I believe that we can say that although Kubali was a conservative of the old sort, this would not make Kubali's politics regressive, and even less so, fascist. In addition, Henri's son, René, was a leader of the resistance in North Africa, founder of the publication *Combat*, and a major figure in the forces of Free France in World War II (Collective; Frenchwikipedia).

The dates of Kubali's suspension and of the publication of this treatment of Turkey's rule of law—1959—are additionally significant because they come in the midst of the unrest that culminated in the Revolution of 1960 against the regime of Prime Minister Adnan Menderes. Led by a "modernized" elite, based in the army, bureaucracies, and universities, the revolutionaries established a martial law regime with "very little opposition" (Shaw & Shaw 1977, 413–14). The National Unity Council government that ruled from 1960 to 1961 tried various members of the previous government, including the former Prime Minister Menderes. The Prime Minister was subsequent tried and executed (1961) for alleged violations of the then existing constitution. In this trial, Hüseyin Nail Kubali was counted among the academics who witnessed against Menderes, attesting to what he believed were the unconstitutional acts of the Menderes government (Kubali 2005).

One of the first acts of the revolutionary government was to restore autonomy to the universities, and to convene a constitutional committee to draft what would become what is now *mutatis mutandis*, the present constitution of the nation—the Constitution of 1961 (Shaw & Shaw 1977, 414–5). Initially seven law professors, making up the Onar Commission, were selected to begin the work on the new constitution. They represented the breadth of Turkish legal competences and philosophy, with Hüseyin Nail Kubali being among the four "'legalistically oriented'" figures selected, primarily for his mastery of the "elaborate legal framework for achieving both development and the preservation of basic political liberties" (Weiker 1963, 68). The work of the Onar Commission was often fraught with internal conflicts, attacked by its opponents, and finally greatly revised by political forces and a later constitutional committee. Nonetheless, it got the process of creating the new constitution of 1961 on its way. Kubali, thus, seems to have made a something of a mark in the creation of the new constitution, although the details of this are not clear (Kubali 2005).

At the very least, some of what Kubali stood for became part of the 1961 constitution. Judicial autonomy tops the list. An idea also favored early by Kubali—a Constitutional Court—was also adopted to insure judicial independence. Its aim was to balance the judiciary and rule of law against what had been until then sometimes arbitrary and unconstitutional uses of power by the executive and legislative branches of government. Anticipating this institutional innovation, one might recall the remarks of Kubali of few years earlier, cited from his article on the rule of law in Turkey. These already give us an idea of the dissatisfactions he had felt as the Menderes government came increasingly to abuse its power (Shaw & Shaw 1977, 410–14). Among the many democratizing provisions of the new constitution were its strengthening of the separation of powers among the various branches of government. It notably restored the ability of the judiciary to

. curb the government by ensuring its independence from both the legislature and government. Article 114 declares that no act of administration can be excluded from the control of the courts, including the Council of State, thus ending the practice of nullifying such authority by government decree. Article 140 assures its independence by having its members elected by an independent committee composed of members of the Constitutional Court, named both by the Council of Ministers and the General Council of the Council of State. (Shaw & Shaw 1977, 418)

The 1961 constitution also defined more clearly the basic rights of Turkish citizens, such as voting rights, universal and direct suffrage, something close to the full right of *habeas corpus*, and numerous welfare and economic rights, such as those to private property and inheritance, workers' rights to organize, and so on (Shaw & Shaw 1977, 421). It may be significant that in December 1964, the European Economic Cooperation Organization—the predecessor to the European Union—admitted Turkey to "associate" membership.

Although it is always treacherous to assume that the views of youth will survive into maturity, in the case of Hüseyin Nail Kubali we find continuity as well as a deepening understanding of what for him was the practical construction of a democratic culture. Thus, readers will not be surprised that Kubali's doctoral thesis of 1936 serves as a fair anticipation of what he would achieve in terms of his apparent part in the making of the Constitution of 1961.

The thesis, *L'Idée de l'état chez les précurseurs de l'école sociologique français* (1936), sought to compare the theories of the state of those thinkers commonly cited as "precursors" of Durkheimian sociological thought with what the Durkheimians really said. Given what we now know of the vogue for Durkheimian social thought—especially Durkheimian solidarist corporatism—among non-Marxist Turkish modernizers like Ziya Gökalp, and given the specter of fascism haunting both Western Europe and Kemalist Turkey, the political atmosphere of the time was certainly charged. Any Turkish intellectual, half-awake, writing at this time on the subject of the idea of the state, well knew what readers would be looking for. Would Kubali not only argue that many thinkers contributing to Durkheimian social thought were classic "statist" thinkers of the French "Right," such as Frédéric Le Play and Joseph De Maistre, but more importantly, that Durkheimian thought—and thus Gökalpian thought—was as well? In 1936, would Kubali be writing, therefore, to flatter his potential patrons, the fascist corporatists among the Kemalists, who had been firmly ensconced in power since 1924, and in so doing to further grant them intellectual legitimacy? Would Kubali have, in effect, aided the Kemalist assumption of Gökalp into their ideological camp, after the sociologist's death in 1923? Such are the questions to which we find answers in Kubali's doctoral thesis.

What we find there in Kubali's thesis is recognizably the work of the same man who stands up for the rule of law and for the independence of the social groups making up civil society, when such values were not altogether in favor by the regime. In then contemporary Turkey of the mid-1930's, Kubali laments the way the governmental administration takes "initiative" and exercises "extensive use of . . . general power" in political affairs, "where stability takes precedence over any other considerations" (Kubali 1936, 304, 305). Kubali also reveals something of his democratic pluralist politics by approving ideas of the balance of power. He celebrates Montesquieu's notion of what would become Durkheimian intermediating institutions—his "judicious conception of intermediary bodies—to which the Durkheimian School attaches such capital importance" (Kubali 1936, 256). Citing a contemporary French sociologist independent of the Durkheimian camp, Georges Gurvitch, Kubali affirms the "particular value and importance for today" of the St. Simonian ideas of "juridical pluralism" whereby "'different juridical orders limit themselves reciprocally in their independent collaboration on the basis of equality in national life as well as internationally'" (Gurvitch 1931, 14; Kubali 1936, 262).

As for statism, Kubali argues that the statisms of the eighteenth and nineteenth centuries must be distinguished—both from each other, and from Durkheimian thought, however indebted the Durkheimians may be to any of the thinkers one might call "statist." Kubali's analysis has the effect of defending the statist thinkers of the eighteenth century. He concludes that the statism of the Enlightenment is "conceived to safeguard the individual," much as were the interventionist actions of the US federal government in ending racial discrimination (Kubali 1936, 255). It was this kind of statism, Kubali asserts, that was "transmitted to the Durkheimian School" (Kubali 1936, 256). Of the nineteenth-century statists, Kubali paints a picture of irrationalism and mystagoguery. They were concerned with hierarchy and submission, seeking a return to a "static" order reminiscent of the European middle ages (Kubali 1936, 259). In the end, Kubali concludes that, despite the debts Durkheimian thought had to the nineteenth-century past, it "took an independent attitude" toward politics. Seeking to disengage Durkheimian thought from politics completely, Kubali takes a kind of pragmatist view of it. Durkheimian sociology should not be used to support any ultimate "metaphysical" or ideological "system," but should be seen to be "sociology and nothing but" (Kubali 1936, 265).

4. Afterword

In sum, then, the actual influence of Durkheimian corporatism in Turkey depends upon who, at a particular time, can be said to "own" and control it. Ziya Gökalp seems to have intended to use Durkheimian thought both to shore up Turkish national collective consciousness, and at the same time to create the theoretical basis for a regime of intermediary groups that would make up Turkish civil society. Hüseyin Nail Kubali, for his part, sympathized with this Gökalpian vision of Durkheimian civil society, and added to it his own reading of Durkheim as someone seeking to encourage a statism active in the interests of individual rights, not in their suppression. Of course, there might well have been little that one could have done to prevent Durkheim and Gökalp from being read as they were by the Turkish right wing. The best, perhaps, to be done in opposition to these fascist-tending attempts to "own" the thought of Gökalp and Durkheim was to do what Hüseyin Nail Kubali did. Both in his active political life and in his Turkish publication of the work I have sought to understand—his original edition of Durkheim's *Professional Ethics and Civic Morals*—Hüseyin Nail Kubali tried to reclaim a Durkheim and Gökalp he knew to be progressive thinkers.

Acknowledgments

I should like to thank Ilhan Citak, Andrew Davison, Joseph Esposito, Michael Feener, Emelie Olson, and Glenn Yocum for their advice and for directing me to some of the current sources and literature on Turkey. Particular thanks goes out to Hüseyin Nail Kubali's nephew, Ali N. Kubal, for providing me with biographical information on his uncle, as well as encouragement for my project and source materials from Turkish publications.

NOTES

1. In this sense, Stjepan G. Meštrovič's claim that Durkheim's thought is essentially Schopenhauerian not only falters straightaway for lack of textual support, but also never gains credibility because of its lack of strong cultural plausibility. Meštrovič rubs against the grain of received opinion: Durkheim, like Freud, was neither really Jewish nor a Neo-Kantian; he was nothing less than a Schopenhauerian pessimist. Durkheim's "representationalism," his way of posing the individual will against social constraint, his "renovated rationalism," are unambiguously supposed to require the direct influence of Schopenhauer. But simply because analogies exist between the thought of two thinkers is hardly sufficient evidence for hard historic claims. Schopenhauer may have been read by Durkheim, but does not seen to have penetrated the life and institutions within which Durkheim moved (Meštrovič 1988).

2. For a complete bibliography of Hamelin's work, see Turlot 1976, 435–44.

3. As we will see, it came against the background of a particularly French Hegelian renovation of the Neo-Kantian philosophy of Charles Renouvier (Turlot 1976).

4. Hamelin's renovations of Neo-Kantian rationalism fall into three areas: (1) the primacy of representations; (2) the primacy of "relation" as the "simplest law of things"; leading to (3) the dialectic resolution of oppositions.

5. There was even an attempt to reconcile the thought of Durkheim and Hamelin by René Hubert in his *Le sens du réel* (1925).

6. Durkheim taught at Bordeaux from 1886 to 1902, Hamelin from 1840 to 1903 (Turlot 1976).

7. Hamelin was also influenced by the neo-critical philosopher Jules Lachelier (Smith 1967, s.v. Octave Hamelin).

8. For concise accounts of Hamelin's thought, see Benrubi 1926; Gunn 1922; Lukes 1972.

9. Renouvier 1848; 1851; 1903; 1906; 1912; 1918; 1963.

10. Letter, Mauss to Hamelin, 1 January 1896. Bibliothèque Victor Cousin. Côte 346. In all, the Bibliothèque Victor Cousin has twenty-one of Mauss's letters to Hamelin and twenty-seven of Durkheim's (Turlot 1976).

11. Letter, Mauss to Hamelin, 2 July 1901. Bibliothèque Victor Cousin. Côte 356.

12. The first was for Victor Hommay (1877), the second for Hamelin (1907), the third for Robert Hertz (1916), the last for his son, André (1917). See Durkheim 1975. The task of writing such necrologies was typically left to his nephew, Marcel Mauss—as was the great work of editing the posthumous works of valued colleagues. Yet Durkheim took a large part in preparing Hamelin's *Le Système de Descartes*. For an account of Durkheim's part in editing Hamelin's papers, see Nabert 1957, 171. For the actual redaction of details of Durkheim's involvement, see the thirty-one letters sent Robin by Durkheim between 1914 and 1917 kept in the Bibliothèque Victor Cousin, Côte 356/2f.

13. Durkheim's French is rhetorically interesting in trading on sacrificial imagery. *Dévouement* is both "devotion" and "self-sacrifice." A stiffly literal English rendition of "mourait victime de son dévouement" as "died a victim of his devotion" eliminates heroism and substitutes "victimization" (Durkheim 1906).

14. See the correspondence between Charles Andler, Herr, and Hamelin in the Bibliothèque Victor Cousin, Côte 356/2a.

15. Herr merits special attention because he broke the silence in France over Hegel (and many other German subjects), which had prevailed since 1870. The best account of the fortunes of Hegel in France is Kelly 1981, 29–52.

16. Lucien Herr in *La Grande encylopedie*, s.v. "Hegel," speaks of a religious Hegel: "he sought an idealist formula of harmony and unity, in which feeling would be essential, modeled on a Greek religious and social conception."

17. Moreover, in Collins's judgment, Durkheim's talk of "the 'soul' of society, its sacred 'spiritual principle,'" amounts to the same thing. Society "can only be a reality through its instantiation in empirically, biologically individual beings." See Collins 1985, 79, n. 71. Collins cites *The Elementary Forms of the Religious Life*, 221, 347.

18. Although he lectured for years on moral philosophy, Hamelin never published an entire work of ethics or even a history of ethical theory. Like Durkheim, he was perhaps working toward a great work on the subject when he was cut short in his prime. Sections of his masterpiece, *Essai sur les éléments principaux de la répresentation*, several collections of reading and lecture notes from courses he taught at the lycée in Pau and later at Bordeaux from the early 1880s reveal the lines of his emergent thinking. See Hamelin 1907. The Hamelin manuscripts are kept in the Bibliothèque Victor Cousin, and include notes on Quatrefages's *Universality of Moral and Religious Sentiments* of October 1888 (Côte 352 C9), the undated notes entitled Études critiques sur la morale de Kant (Côte 352 C9), and thirteen lectures of his "Cours de Morale" (Côte 352E) which range from 1883–1884 to 1888.

19. See Durkheim's necrologie of Octave Hamelin in Durkheim 1907. There Durkheim singles out Hamelin's spirit of sacrifice in devoting himself unstintingly to his students (428). Hamelin died attempting to save his drowning niece; Durkheim puts him as having died "devoting himself for another" (429).

20. Readers should note that Durkheim never quite surrenders his altruism—if we restrict our view to the ideal level—even if he does force the ideal of altruism to cohabit with the reality and desirability of concrete individuality.

21. Now it should be granted that some of this can be found in Renouvier, too. But Hamelin is quick to point out that Renouvier's attempts to integrate his fundamentally individualist ethics with society do not make him a socialist (Hamelin 1927).

22. In apparent agreement, Louis Dumont notes cryptically that Hegel, not Marx, is the "'precursor' of sociology . . . just as Durkheim's 'collective consciousness' seemed dubious and mythical to many, so Hegel's indirect representation of society as the State was seen as a mere mystification" (Dumont 1970).

23. Hamelin's papers in the Bibliothèque Victor Cousin include discussions of moral philosophy such as Quatrefages's *Universality of Moral and Religious Sentiments* (October 1888) in Côte 352 C9. These undated notes are entitled "Études critiques sur la morale de Kant" (Côte 352 C9), and thirteen lectures of his "Cours de Morale" (Côte 352 E) which range from 1883–1884 to 1888.

CHAPTER 4   DURKHEIM, JUDAISM, AND THE AFTERLIFE

1. These lectures are taken from student lecture notes of Durkheim's course on philosophy in 1883–84 by the French philosopher André Lalande. For contemporary commentary on Durkheim's Spiritualism, see Céléstin Bouglé, "Le Spiritualisme d'Émile Durkheim," *Revue Bleue* (1924): 550–53 and Félix Pécaut, "Le Spiritualisme scientifique: la philosophie d'Émile Durkheim," *Revue de l'enseignement français hors de France* 2 (1920).

2. Cited in Kselman 1993, 127.

3. Durkheim's close friend and intellectual partner, the Protestant idealist Octave Hamelin, shared this view, as did Durkheim's intellectual opponent, the Jewish philosophical rationalist Léon Brunschvicg. Lukes tells us that Hamelin "held that in a rational morality God could not intervene as the source of obligation" (Lukes 1972, 358).

4. Pécaut was no rank and file Liberal Protestant, but one of the founders of the liberal Protestant movement itself. Along with Pécaut, we can also list other founders of the liberal movement, Edmond Schérer and Albert Réville—both of whom will figure in the discussion to follow.

5. Kselman 1993, 132–43.

6. Here Kselman seems to pass over the Catholic spirit of sacrifice, which had been resuscitated and put to work for nationalist ends during the Third Republic (Kselman 1993, 136). For discussion of Catholicism and civic sacrifice in France, see my book (in preparation), *Contesting Sacrifice: Religion, Nationalism and Social Thought in France.*

7. As Kselman points out, although Ferry's scientism won the day, he had in fact to compromise with the corps of teachers, who were by and large Spiritualists.

CHAPTER 5   ZIONISM, BRAHMINISM, AND THE EMBODIED
            SACRED

1. Marcel Mauss, review of *La Doctrine du sacrifice dans les brâhmanas*, by Sylvain Levi,
   Oeuvres. Volume 1. Les Fonctions sociales du sacré, ed. Victor Karady (Paris: Minuit,
   1968), 352 (First published in *L'Année sociologique* 3 [1900]: 293–95).

2. Major sources for the life and works of Sylvain Lévi are Filliozat 1964, 53; Level
   1935, 97–98; Mauss 1969, 535–47 and Mauss 1937. See also the *nécrologie* by
   Isidore Lévy, "Sylvain Lévi (1863–1935)," *Revue des études juives* 100 (1935): 1–3.

3. Sylvain Lévi was, along with Durkheim, Mauss, Lucien Herr, and about 500
   others, a member of the "gauchiste" association, the "Ligue républicaine
   d'Alsace et de Lorraine" (Andler 1932, 261). For biographical details, see also
   Level 1935: 97–98.

4. Compounding Lévi's concern was the fact that reactionary anti-Semitic Catholics
   in the France of his day were, like the Muslims, notorious for their desire to see
   religion and state fused into a seamless (of course, here Roman Catholic) unity.
   Making matters worse, intransigent Catholic propaganda routinely proclaimed
   the virtues of Islam in making the case for Catholic renewal. Given the fundamental fusion of politics and religion by Muslims and intransigent Catholics,
   and the relative vulnerability of Jews in the Muslim lands and (at least after
   Dreyfus) perhaps also in France, Sylvain Lévi's mind contemplated some very
   disturbing symbolic equivalences (Griffiths 1966, 244ff.).

5. Lévi reportedly asked the French foreign ministry to be sent on this mission
   (Level 1935, 98).

6. Sylvain Lévi in effect argued what Renou calls the "omnipotence" of ritual
   (Renou 1966, viii).

CHAPTER 6   THE RISE OF RITUAL AND THE HEGEMONY OF MYTH

1. Some would say that it came earlier with Robertson Smith. But Durkheim
   claimed to have been substantially influenced by Robertson Smith and by reference to the contents of Robertson Smith's classic work *Lectures on Religion of the
   Semites*.

2. But see Ranulf's criticism of the Durkheimians as precursors of fascism precisely
   on this point, as well as Mauss's implicit admission of unintended responsibility.

3. Remarkable to say in the light of those critics who attribute Durkheimian sociological ritualism to William Robertson Smith is Durkheim's view expressed in
   his 1887 review of Jean-Marie Guyau's *L'Irreligion de l'avenir*. It was not until April
   1887 that Robertson Smith had been invited to deliver his famous lectures; it
   was not until October 1888 that he began and October 1891 that he completed
   his commission. Durkheim reportedly had not read Robertson Smith's *Lectures
   on the Religion of the Semites*, earlier than the second edition, published
   in 1894.

4. See also Hubert, Preface to Czarnowski, *Le Culte des héros et ses conditions sociales. Saint Patrick, héros national de l'Irlande* (Hubert 1919). See especially Hubert's view that "it is myth which makes the hero, not his death" (lxxxix).

5. Now although Andrew Lang was probably the first vocal opponent of Max Müller's solarist mythology and mythophilia, we cannot materially link this eclectic virtuoso to any movement to take ritual more seriously than myth, and thus to our own ritualist movements in the study of religion.

6. Although he was more concerned about Max Müller's solarist interpretation of myths than his mythological reading of the Vedas, Salomon Reinach identifies our ritualists as the first critics of solarism—"Max Müllerism" as he calls it—as "Barth, Bergaigne and Darmesteter" (Reinach 1911, 423–41).

7. Interestingly, Sylvain Lévi's claim that the Brahmins practiced a violent rite conflicts with early German Romantic views, for example, Herder, that the Brahmins were actually remarkably gentle (Poliakov 1974). Albrecht Barth, however, is critical of Sylvain Lévi, saying he paints a "blacker" picture of the Brahmins than really was the case, indeed perhaps even a "caricature" (Barth, 60–98).

8. See also page 38, where sacrifice is identified as the life source of the gods, or page 54, where it is said to save the gods, and finally page 76, where the superiority of sacrifice to the gods, in particular, Indra, is asserted.

9. Friedrich Max Müller, too, felt that certain features of the narrative in the Vedas were "childish," even if he does not describe the language of the Vedas in this way (Müller 1882).

CHAPTER 7   DURKHEIM, HUBERT, AND THE CLERICAL
             MODERNIST DISCOURSE ON SYMBOLISM

1. This entire article, along with earlier presentations of Jones's historicist approach to Durkheim, outlines an approach to which I owe obvious debts.

2. Written by the mysterious "Agathon," the shared pseudonym for the Bergsonians, Henri Massis and Alfred de Tarde.

3. Reported in *La Petite Gironde* 24 May 1901.

4. In the *Année sociologique*, the arts fall under the rubric of "technology" or the "phenomenon of representation."

5. See especially *Bulletin critique* 6 (1900): 701–3; 7 (1901): 613–14; 9 (1903): 39–40; 11 (1905): 281–84 for reviews of current volumes of *L'Année sociologique*.

6. Here Hubert evinces some sympathy for Loisy's struggles with authoritarianism, noting that the Durkheimians "did not want to take sides" (290–91).

7. See Duchesne's letter of 12 October 1913, reproduced by Salomon Reinach (478f).

8. The representation of symbolic approaches to dogma as typical of religious modernists was common in the cultural and religious worlds of the day. Romain

Rolland's *Jean Christophe* speaks of the "clerical symbolists . . . who reproduced the ideas of Kant in allegorical pictures" (Rolland 1915, 51).

9. Letter of Henri Hubert to Marcel Mauss, n.d. 1898. I thank Marcel Fournier.

CHAPTER 8   DURKHEIM, DISCIPLINARITY, AND
THE "SCIENCES RELIGIEUSES"

1. Before the middle of the nineteenth century, there had also always been individual virtuosi of independent means who practiced what would later be declared by the state as the stuff of the "disciplines" right through the *fin-de-siècle*. The historian Jules Michelet at one time held a chair in the Collège de France as well as being *conservateur* of the National Archives. But neither Charles Renouvier, the most important and influential philosopher of the Third Republic, nor Henri Berr, one of the epoch's most original historians, ever had official posts as "historians" in the universities or in the various state-sponsored institutions.

2. Letter of Henri Hubert to Marcel Mauss, n.d. 1898. I thank Marcel Fournier for this citation.

3. On "orthodox" views favoring the atonement theory of Jesus's death, see Rivière 1912, 161–80 and 278–305.

4. Compare, for example, Mauss's rather soft criticism of Auguste Sabatier's work while he was still seeking appointment to the Fifth Section with his much more outspokenly critical attack on Sabatier after having been safely awarded his post in the Fifth Section. In 1898, before election to the Fifth Section, Mauss complimented Sabatier's *Esquisse d'une philosophie de la religion* for having put the "social and external character of dogma into bold relief" (Mauss, 1968, 535). He likewise passes over the theologian's treatment of primitive religion. But in his never completed PhD thesis, *La Prière* (1909), he calls Sabatier's treatment of primitive religions "cavalier" (535). Similarly, in 1898, Mauss politely notes about Sabatier that the "preoccupations of the soul sincerely burning with his religious faith compromises the uses of method here" (531). Yet, from the security of his post in 1909, Mauss damns Sabatier's entire discussion of prayer as "predetermined by the faith of the author" (375). In 1909, Mauss also notes that Sabatier's progressivist story of religious evolution is "broad and facile (536). . . . It is a matter less of analyzing facts than of demonstrating the superiority of the Christian religion" (375).

CHAPTER 9   LIBERAL PROTESTANT THEOLOGY AND/OR
"SCIENCE RELIGIEUSE"

1. We will soon see how the Révilles and Vernes parted ways. Quite unexpected from theological liberals, however, was the opposition of the otherwise undogmatic editor of the *Encyclopédie des sciences religieuses* and Vernes's superior in the Protestant Faculty of Theology, Frédéric Lichtenberger (Lichtenberger 1889).

Reminiscent of the recent conflict over academic freedom for Catholic theologians between the American, Father Joseph Curran, and the Vatican, Lichtenberger denied Vernes's demands for unlimited Lehrfreiheit, and thus forced Vernes to resign his post (Encrevé 1990, 97–100).

2. Albert Réville was later to translate a major work of Scholten's into French. This was J. H. Scholten, *Manuel d'histoire comparée de la philosophie et de la religion*, Albert Réville, trans. (Paris et Genève: Cherbuliez, 1861).

3. See along these lines, Don Wiebe's discussion of Tiele (1999, Ch. 3).

4. Goblet d'Alviella noted that the operation of "grouping things into a more general synthesis" as Albert Réville did in his *Prolegomena of the History of Religions* [1881], marked a decisive step beyond "analytic history." Goblet d'Alviella, review of Jean Réville, *Les Phases successives de l'histoire des religions* (Paris: Ernest Leroux, 1909), *Revue d'histoire des religions* 61 (1910): 351. For general and detailed information about Albert Réville's life and intellectual orientation, see Jacques Marty (1912).

CHAPTER 10   THE DURKHEIMIANS AND THE PROTESTANTS IN
             THE ÉCOLE PRATIQUE, FIFTH SECTION

1. Although close, as well, to Chantepie de la Saussaye in many of these same respects, the Révilles did not share his rather eclectic and somewhat more conservative Calvinism (Réville 1864, 275–77).

2. The Durkheimians did attack the liberal Protestant philosopher of religion, Auguste Sabatier, as Donald Nielsen has discussed at length. But it is also well to point out that their first review was not critical.

3. In intellectual terms there was, however, little to choose from between their views, especially Tiele's, and that of the Révilles. For a review of the history of religions in Holland near century's end, see Van Hamel 1880, 379–85.

4. Henri Hubert laments that Chantepie de la Saussaye had, however, excluded the taxonomic sections in the second edition. See Hubert 1904, vi.

CHAPTER 11   DURKHEIM SINGS: TEACHING
             THE "NEW DURKHEIM" ON RELIGION

1. The substance of this course now forms the basis of my recent book, *Thinking about Religion: An Historical Introduction to Theories of Religion* (Oxford: Blackwell, 2006) and its companion reader *Thinking about Religion: A Reader* (Oxford: Blackwell, 2006). Chapter 12, "Seeing the Sacred with the Social Eye: Émile Durkheim's 'Religious Sociology,'" develops the Durkheimian themes of this chapter in a fuller way.

2. In Muslim countries, the final disposition of physical versions of the Quran presents such a problem that some Muslim communities arrange for proper ritual burials of dilapidated texts, much as Americans dispose of old or damaged national flags.

3. An appendix listing Robertson Smith's citations of biblical sources' numbers shows as well that he was as much a master of the text as any student of the literature of the Bible. I count approximately 700 biblical entries for a book of about 400 total pages.

4. There, she notes that, from a "religious perspective, defilement is not merely a symbol of something else, or even the balance on which ideas of virtue and sin are weighed, but the basic condition of all reality." Yet, that this "idea is logical is," in Douglas's view, "difficult for modern readers of the Bible to appreciate" (21).

5. This current belief by some Muslims may well have been stimulated in part by attempts to compete against fundamentalist Christians and others holding that the Bible is just such a book of clear and unambiguous directives. This need, however misguided, to show the world that Islam is, after all, a genuine "religion" requires that it have a cognitively rich book capable of mapping out a clear path in life—with no ambiguities, conflicting passages or readings, or anything else that might weaken its prestige as a standard for living. Thus, the Quran must show that it is capable of being read as Christian fundamentalists read the Bible—cognitively—somewhat the way confused Western folk avidly consult their horoscopes.

CHAPTER 12   CHRISTIANS, DURKHEIMIANS,
AND OTHER ANIMALS

1. Cited in http://leo.jfredball.com/pipermail/oef-1/2002-June/001681.html.

2. Cited in http://leo.jfredball.com/pipermail/oef-1/2002-June/001681.html.

3. Fundamentalist Christians typically find biblical support for literal readings of scripture in passages like 2 Timothy 3:16: "All scripture is inspired by God and profitable for teaching, for reproof, for correction and for training in righteousness." However, this ignores the fact that for the writer (not Paul), "scripture" was almost certainly the Greek version of the Hebrew Bible, which did not include the New Testament. The literalist argument would be that if it is inspired, scripture must be literally the words and thoughts of God, and must be so interpreted. However, there was a rich tradition of interpreting the Hebrew scriptures allegorically among early Christians (e.g., Paul in Galatians 3–4), probably learned from Jews of the same time (e.g., Philo). There is no text comparable to 2 Tim. 3:16 in the New Testament, referring to the New Testament itself (which only came into existence years after the individual books were written). Jews, of course, did not need a particular text to tell them that Torah (the Pentateuch) was inspired. They had the canonizing tradition that these books had been written by Moses who was superior to all other prophets because he had seen God face to face (Numbers 12). In many places in Torah they are instructed to obey all the commandments (e.g. Deuteronomy 6). Literal obedience is commanded, but not literal interpretation (Professor Douglas Parrott, Department of Religious Studies, University of California, Riverside. Personal correspondence.).

CHAPTER 13   SACRIFICE, GIFT, AND THE SOCIAL LOGIC
OF MUSLIM "HUMAN BOMBERS"

1. Raphael Israeli occasionally speaks in social terms in passages where he addresses the matter of the communal "acceptance" and support of "human bombers," or in which he speaks of the role of the "human bombers" as "rescuing the *Umma*" (Israeli 2002, 37).

2. *http://abcnews.go.com/sections/world/DailyNews/aljazeeratape020415.html.* See also an interview with Al Qa'ida defector "Max": "MAX: 'Yeah, you know, each of them wanted to sacrifice on Usama bin Laden. They want to spend their money and their—everything—to sacrifice themselves on bin Laden. There was, you know, anyone that bin Laden asked them to do—to kill themselves, to sacrifice themselves on bin Laden. He won't say no. There are a thousand people; they want to sacrifice themselves on bin Laden.'" http://www.pastornet.net.au/jmm/aasi/aasi0496.htm.

3. See "Eid message to the Ummah from Shaikh Ahmad Yaseen on the struggle in Palestine": http://www.muslimedia.com/archives/movement02/hamas-eid.htm.

    Significance of Eid:
    These are the signs of our Ismail's. Let us search for them in ourselves and let us slaughter them to move towards Allah (swt) and to remove the real knife from the throat of oppressed Muslims from Bosnia to Kashmir, from Somalia to Palestine. Let us revolt against the heartless worshippers that we have become. Remember our Eid is not an Eid of victory. It is the Eid of sacrifice (adha). *http://www.guidedones.com/metapage/frq/eidadha10.htm.*

    Sacrifice and nationhood
    "We know what Palestine needs from us," said Reham. "Jihad. If Usama had chosen differently, he would have been living for himself, but failing Palestine. Everyone should choose sacrifice until we restore our rights. Israel is occupying our land and we have to get rid of it. Jihad is the only way." Then Reham turned to me: "I am sorry that I am not the shahid," she said. "Usama took my wish to be a martyr and preceded me. We were in a race and he beat me. It's what I've always wanted to do." Sandra Jordan, "The women who would die for Allah," *New Statesman* (Jan 14, 2002). *http://www.findarticles.com/cf_0/m0FQP/4570_131/82135394/p2/article.jhtml? term=%2B%22sacrifice%22+%2Bpalestine.*

4. In another comment by Bin Laden linking sacrifice and martyrdom: "Hani Hanjour, from Al-Ta'if, the destroyer of the centre of the US defence, the Pentagon. Clear purity and a splendid sacrifice. We beseech Allah to accept him as a martyr." *http://news.bbc.co.uk/1/hi/world/middle_east/2248894.stm.*

5. But see two recent articles that do pay attention to this religious rhetoric. John Kelsay, "Suicide Bombers: The 'Just War' Debate, Islamic Style," *Christian Century,* August 14, 2002; R. Scott Appleby, "Visions of Sacrifice. Roots of Terrorism," *Christian Century,* October 17, 2002.

6. Explicit links are made by Muslims to precedents for Islamic sacrifice in the Jewish Bible: *http://www.al-islam.org/islaminthebible/18.htm.*

7. Cowdrey cites the canonizations in the eleventh century of certain leaders of the Patarenes, a Milanese reform movement seeking a rule of clerical celibacy and the proscription of simony (Cowdrey 1985).

8. Pope Urban II, in addressing the religious of the congregation of Vallombrosa in 7 Oct. 1096, discouraged great shows of self-immolating martyrdom: "We have heard that some of you want to set out with the knights who are making for Jerusalem with the good intention of liberating Christianity. This is the right kind of sacrifice, but it is planned by the wrong kind of person. For we were stimulating the minds of knights to go on this expedition, since they might be able to restrain the savagery of the Saracens by their arms and restore the Christians to their former freedom: we do not want those who have abandoned the world and have vowed themselves to spiritual warfare either to bear arms or to go on this journey; we go so far as to forbid them to do so. And we forbid the religious—clerics or monks—to set out in this company without the permission of their bishops or abbots in accordance with the rule of the holy canons. The discretion of your religious profession must prevent you in this business from running the risk of either insulting the apostolic see or endangering your own souls. We have heard it said that your confrère, the abbot or the monastery of St. Reparata, is considering leaving the order shared by your congregation in common. And so in this present letter we send him an order, and by that we mean we forbid him to dare to rule the same monastery any longer without the permission of your common abbot, whom you call your major abbot. And if he does not obey, he or anyone else who perhaps dares to leave your congregation should be cut off with the sword of apostolic excommunication." (Pope Urban II, "Four Letters on Crusading from Pope Urban II," in Louise Riley-Smith and Jonathan Riley-Smith (eds.) *The Crusades: Idea and Reality 1095–1274* (London: Edward Arnold Ltd, 1981). I also thank Richard Hecht, University of California, Santa Barbara, for his advice on crusader martyrs.

9. *http://www.newadvent.org/cathen/04543c.htm.*

10. *http://www.newadvent.org/cathen/09736c.htm.*

11. *http://users.erols.com/saintpat/ss/1106.htm.*

12. *http://www.newadvent.org/cathen/09736b.htm.*

13. On "qurbani," see http://www.muslimindia.com/qurbani.htm. It is worth noting that the early tradition was divided as to whether this sacrifice involved Isaac—on Mount Moria, and his subsequent actual sacrificing of a goat provided by Allah instead of his son. My colleague, Michael Feener, informs me that in modern times, despite explicit Quranic passage to the contrary (Al-Saffat 37: 112–13), many Muslims hold that Ishmael, not Isaac, was the intended victim involved here. This, likewise, fits well the numerous departures from Muslim tradition described by Khaled M. Abou El Fadl. (Khaled M. Abou El Fadl, *And God Knows the Soldiers: The Authoritative and Authoritarian in Islamic Discourses* (Lanham, MD: University Press of America 2001).) Thus, in the article, "Khutba—Lessons from the Story of Ibrahim (AS)," 3 April 1998, the author states that "Ibrahim (as) was ordered

by Allah to sacrifice his own son for the sake of Allah and his son Ismael (Isaac) . . ." (my emphasis). http://www.shu.ac.uk/students/union/socs/Islamic/khtba-ibrahim(as).html). I cite here, as well, the Quranic passage from sura, "The Rangers" (Al-Saffat, 37: 112–13), where it concludes the account of Abraham's sparing of Isaac/Ishaq (37.112): And We gave him the good news of Ishaq, a prophet among the good ones (37.113). And We showered Our blessings on him and on Ishaq; and of their offspring are the doers of good, and (also) those who are clearly unjust to their own souls.

14. The terminology of sacrifice in Islam is particularly rich. In the primary instances, it refers to literal ritual sacrifice: "Udhiyah" refers to the animal (camel, cattle, or sheep) that is sacrificed as an act of worship to Allah. Note also "Id al'Adha" (or Eid Al-Adha) is the "Feast of the Sacrifice."

15. Here the author Malik ibn Anas in his *Ahadith al-Jami' al 'Saghir* in *Qira'a a fi Fiqh al-Shahada* (note 17), pp. 7–9, marks three cases where this self-sacrificial "giving up" is permitted. The first is the case where a chance to survive the risk to one's life is at least no less than that of losing it; the second is where Muslims are so outmatched that they must resort to audacious measures in order to equalize the struggle; the third is where such self-sacrificial acts cannot be avoided. Here, acts of self-sacrifice in jihad become martyrdoms by virtue of their being actions that save the entire umma (Israeli 2002, 33–34).

16. My thanks to my colleague, Michael Feener, for these points of Arabic meaning.

17. http://isgkc.org/udhiya.htm. See price list of proper sacrificial animals. Interpal, a relief effort for Palestinians, offers a special opportunity for Muslims to send corned or frozen lamb to Palestine, thus combining both their religious sacrificial duty and relief aid to the poor of Palestine. http://www.interpal.org/web/pdf/Qurbani99.pdf

18. *http://www.nooruddinonline.com/donation_centers.htm*

19. http://islamicity.com/mosque/Hajj/Udhiya.htm

20. In the article "Khutba—Lessons from the story of Ibrahim (AS)," 3 April 1998, the author argues that both father and son accept the command to sacrifice Ishmael. "Ibrahim (as) was ordered by Allah to sacrifice his own son for the sake of Allah and his son Ismael (as) willingly accepted because it was an order from Allah (SWT)." http://www.shu.ac.uk/students/union/socs/Islamic/khtba-ibrahim(as).html

21. Abraham's act of sacrifice in the Quran gives the following account:

   (Abraham prayed:) My Lord, grant me a doer of good deeds. So We gave him the good news of a forbearing son. But when he became of age to work with him, he said: O my son, I have seen in a dream that I should sacrifice you; so consider what is your view. He said: O my father, do as you are commanded; if Allah please you will find me patient. So when they had both submitted and he had thrown him down upon his forehead, and We called out to him saying, O Abraham, you have indeed fulfilled the vision. Thus do We reward the doers of good. Surely this is a manifest trial. And We ransomed him with a great sacrifice. (Surah Al-Saffat 37: 100–7)

There, however, is considerable dispute among Muslims as to whether Allah ordained it. *http://www.submission.org/Ismail.html.*

22. *http://www.youngmuslims.ca/publications/sacrifice.asp.*

23. *Significance of Eid:*
"These are the signs of our Ismail's. Let us search for them in ourselves and let us slaughter them to move towards Allah (swt) and to remove the real knife from the throat of oppressed Muslims from Bosnia to Kashmir, from Somalia to Palestine. Let us revolt against the heartless worshippers that we have become. Remember our Eid is not an Eid of victory. It is the Eid of sacrifice (adha)." *http://www.guidedones.com/metapage/frq/eidadha10.htm.*

24. There, however, is considerable dispute among Muslims as to whether Abraham actually willed Isaac's sacrifice or whether indeed Allah ordained it. *http://www.submission.org/Ismail.html.*

25. That the hijackers of 9–11 planned to kill flight attendants in deliberately sacrificial ways marks another departure from Muslim tradition (Lincoln 2003, 94).

26. http://www.youngmuslims.ca/publications/sacrifice.asp

27. See also an extended discussion of noble death in the Jewish and Christian traditions by Jan Willem van Henten and Friedrich Avemarie, *Martyrdom and Noble Death* (London: Routledge, 2002).

28. The transformation of the WTC and its site into a sacred site and holy ground is truly a remarkable feat, given that it was surely one of the least loved buildings in America until the moment of its demise. It went from saying everything that could possibly be said about America in terms of its arrogant, pushy projection of raw power onto the Manhattan skyline to being a tender embodiment of human hopes and dreams. See the WTC images from University of California, Riverside Spontaneous Shrines website *www.shrines.ucr.edu*

29. *http://www.biega.com/wwa-3.html.*

30. Levenson's otherwise powerful book regrettably makes no significant reference to Islamic traditions of commemoration of Abraham's sacrifice of Ishmael (Levenson 1994).

31. David C. Rapoport has made the identical point about Armenian terrorists performing their deeds of violence against the Turks, not primarily for the sake of the Turks, but to maintain the idea of a definite Armenian nation for the audience of the Armenian diaspora. In the case of bin Laden, it is the Caliphate of Islam that one wants to re-create in the world of globalized political and economic entities, but outside and above the nation-state—above the superimposition of that invention of godless *philosophes* and Jacobins upon the Muslim world.

REFERENCES

Abitbol, M. 1989. *Les Deux terres promises: Les Juifs de France et le sionisme*. Paris: Olivier Orban.

Alexander, J. C. 1982a. *Theoretical Logic in Sociology: Positivism, Presuppositions, and Current Controversies* (vol. 1). Berkeley: University of California Press.

——. 1982b. *Theoretical Logic in Sociology: The Antinomies of Classical Thought. Marx and Durkheim* (vol. 2). Berkeley: University of California Press.

——. 1983. *Theoretical Logic in Sociology: The Classical Attempt at Theoretical Synthesis* (vol. 3). Berkeley: University of California Press.

——. 1984a. *Theoretical Logic in Sociology: The Modern Reconstruction of Classical Thought. Talcott Parsons* (vol. 4). Berkeley: University of California Press.

——. 1984b. *Durkheim's Sociology of Religion: Themes and Theories*. London: Routledge.

——. (ed.) 1988. *Durkheimian Sociology: Cultural Studies*. Cambridge: Cambridge University Press.

Allen, N. J. 1985. "The Category of the Person: A Reading of Mauss's Last Essay." In *Category of the Person: Anthropology, Philosophy, History*. Cambridge: Cambridge University Press.

Allen, N. J., W.S.F. Pickering & W. Watts-Miller (eds.) 1998. *On Durkheim's Elementary Forms of Religious Life*. London: Routledge.

Alphandéry, P. 1906. "Albert Réville." *Revue de l'histoire des religions* 54, 401–23.

Anderson, B. 1991. *Imagined Communities*. London: Verso.

Andler, C. 1932. *La Vie de Lucien Herr*. Paris: Rieder.

Anon. 1901a. Procés Verbaux: Succéssion Sabatier, reporting the vote taken on 9 June 1901. Paris: École Pratique des Hautes Études, Fifth Section.

Anon. 1901b. Procés Verbaux, reporting the vote taken on 18 June 1901. École Pratique des Hautes Études, Fifth Section.

Anon. 1918. *Ecole Pratique des Hautes études, La vie univerisitaire à Paris*. Paris: Colin.

Anon. 1935. "Dans le troisième Reich." *L'Univers Israëlite* 03. 91, 103.

Antliff, M. 1993. *Inventing Bergson: Cultural Politics and the Parisian Avant-Garde*. Princeton: Princeton University Press.

Aron, R. 1961. *Introduction to the Philosophy of History* (trans.) G. J. Irwin. Boston: Beacon.

Ash, T. G. 1999. "Hail Ruthenia." *New York Review of Books*, 59. 22 April, 54–6.

Atran, S. 2003. "Who Wants to Be a Martyr?" In *Los Angeles Times*, 5 May 2003, A27.

Aulard, F. A. 1897. *La Société des Jacobins-Recueil des documents* (vol. 6). Paris.

Barth, A. 1899. "Bulletin des religions de l'Inde I: Vedisme et ancien Brahmanisme." *Revue d'histoire des religions* 39, 60–98.

Bediako, G. M. 1995. "To Capture the Modern Universe of Thought": *Religion of the Semites* as an Attempt at a Christian Comparative Religion. In *William Robertson Smith Essays in Reassessment* (ed.) W. Johnstone. Sheffield: Sheffield Academic Press, 118–31.

Bellah, R. N. 1959. "Durkheim and History." *American Sociological Review* 24, 447–61.

Benrubi, I. 1926. *Contemporary Thought in France* (trans.) E. B. Dicker. London: Williams and Norgate.

Bergaigne, A. 1978. *Abel Bergaigne's "Vedic Religion"* (trans.) (V.G. Paranjoti3). Delhi: Motilal Banarsidass.

Berger, G. 1968. "Experience and Transcendence." In *Philosophic Thought in France and the United States* (ed.) M. Farber. Albany: SUNY Press, 87–102.

Berr, H. 1906. "Les progrès de la sociologie religieuse." *Revue de synthèse historique* 12, 16–43.

Besnard, P. 1983a. "The 'Année sociologique' Team." In *The Sociological Domain* (ed.) P. Besnard. Cambridge: Cambridge University Press, 11–70.

———. (ed.) 1983b. *The Sociological Domain.* Cambridge: Cambridge University Press.

Besnard, P. & M. Fournier. 1998. *Emile Durkheim: Lettres à Marcel Mauss.* Paris: Presses Universitaire de France.

Besse, D. 1913. *Les religions laiques: un romanticisme religieux.* Paris: Nouvelle Librairie Nationale.

Birtek, F. 1991. The Turkish Adventures of the Durkheimian Paradigm: Does History Vindicate M. Labriola? *Il Politico* 56, 107–46.

Bloch, M. 1989. *The Royal Touch* (trans.) J. E. Anderson. New York City: Dorset.

Boer, P. d. 1998. *History as a Profession: The Study of History in France, 1818–1914.* Princeton: Princeton University Press.

Bossy, J. 1985. *Christianity in the West, 1400–1700.* Oxford: Oxford University Press.

Bouglé, C. 1938. *The French Conception of "Culture Générale" and Its Influences upon Institution.* New York: Teachers College, Columbia University.

Bourgin, H. 1938. *De Jaurès à Léon Blum.* Paris: Artheme Fayard.

Brooks, J. I. III. 1998. *The Eclectic Legacy: Academic Philosophy and the Human Sciences in Nineteenth-Century France.* Newark: University of Delaware.

Brown, P. 1981. *The Cult of the Saints: Its Rise and Function in Latin Christianity.* Chicago: University of Chicago.

Butler, J. 1834. *The Analogy of Religion, Natural and Revealed, to the Constitution and Course of Nature.* London: Longman & Co.

Byrne, P. 1989. *Natural Religion and the Nature of Religion.* London: Routledge.

Capitant, H. 1935. *L'Interprétation des lois d'après les travaux préparatoires.* N.p.: n.p.

Carbonell, C.-O. 1979. "Les historiens protestants dans le renouveau de l'historiographie française." In *Les Protestants dans les débuts de la Troisième Republique (1871–1885) Actes du colloque de Paris, 3–6 Octobre 1978* (eds.) A. Encrevé & M. Richard. Paris, 59–75.

Chantepie de la Saussaye, P. D. 1897. *Lehrbuch der Religionsgeschichte* 2 vols. Freiburg: np.
———. 1904. *Manuel d'histoire des religions* (trans.) H. Hubert & I. Lévy. Paris: Armand Colin.

Charlton, D. G. 1963. *The Secular Religions of France 1815–1870*. Oxford: Oxford University Press.

Chauduri, N. 1974. *Scholar Extraordinary*. London: Chatto and Windus.

Clifford, J. 1983. Power and Dialogue in Ethnography: Marcel Griaule's Initiation. In *Observers Observerd: Essays on Ethnographic Fieldwork*. (ed.) J. George W. Stocking. Wisconson: University of Wisconsin Press, 121–56.

———. 1988. "On Ethnographic Surrealism." In The Predicament of Culture (ed.) J. Clifford. Cambridge, MA: Harvard University, 117–51.

Cohen, E. 1986. "Law, Folklore and Animal Lore." *Past and Present* 110, 3–37.

Cohen-Sherbok, D. 1987. "Death and Immortality in the Jewish Tradition." In *Death and Immortality in the Religions of the World* (ed.) P. & L. Badlam. New York: Paragon, 24–35.

Collective. 1974. *Kubali ya Armagan. Mélanges Kubali* (new series, vol 8, no, 11). Istanbul: Institut de Droit Comparé de l'Université d'Istanbul.

Collective. Capitant, René (France). Paris: Charlesdegaulle.org.

Collins, S. 1985. "Categories, Concepts or Predicaments? Remarks on Mauss's Use of Philosophical Terminology." In *The Category of the Person: Anthropology, Philosophy, History*. Cambridge: Cambridge University Press, 46–82.

Collomp, P. 1912. "Les Phases succéssives de l'histoire des religions." *Annales de Philosophie Chrétienne*, 522–29.

Constable, G. 2001. "The Historiography of the Crusades." In *The Crusades from the Perspective of Byzantium and the Muslim World* (eds.) A. E. Laiou & R. P. Mottahedeh. Washington, DC: Dunbarton Oaks Research Library and Collection, 1–22.

Cornu, A. 1968. "Bergsonianism and Existentialism." In *Philosophic Thought in France and the United States* (ed.) M. Farber. Albany: SUNY Press, 151–68.

Coser, L. 1971. *Masters of Sociological Thought*. New York City: Harcourt, Brace.

Coulanges, N.D.F. d. 1980. *The Ancient City: A Study on the Religion, Laws and Institutions of Greece and Rome (1864)* (trans.) A. Momigliano & S. C. Humphreys. Baltimore and London: The Johns Hopkins University Press.

Cowdrey, H.E.J. 1985. "Martyrdom and the First Crusade." In *Crusade and Settlement* (ed.) P. Edbury. Cardiff: University of Wales, 46–56.

D'Hondt, J. 1971. "Hegel et les socialistes." *La pensée* 157, 1–25.

Dandieu, A. 1931. "Octave Hamelin, 1856–1907" in Arnaud Dandieu, ed., In *La philosphie contemporaine en France*. Paris: Sagittaire, 77–93.

Darmesteter, J. 1892. *Les Prophètes d'Israel*. Paris: Calmann Lévy.

Dauriac, L. 1909. "Les Sources néo-criticistes de la dialectique synthètique." *Revue de métaphysique et de morale* 17, 470–89.

Davie, G. 1986. "Protestants de droite et Action Française au temps de la condamnation." *Études maurrassiennes* 5, 169–80.

———. 1987. "The Changing Face of Protestantism in 20th Century France." *Proceedings of the Huguenot Society* 24, 378–89.

Davis, N. Z. 2000. *The Gift in Sixteenth-Century France.* Madison: University of Wisconsin Press.

Davison, A. 1995. "Secularization and Modernization in Turkey: The Ideas of Ziya Gökalp." *Economy and Society* 24, 189–224.

———. 1998. *Secularism and Revivalism in Turkey.* New Haven: Yale University Press.

Davy, G. 1919. "Emile Durkheim: l'homme." *Revue de métaphysique et de morale* 26, 181–98.

———. 1950. "Introduction." In *Professional Ethics and Civic Morals* (ed.) H. N. Kubali. Westport, CT: Greenwood, xii–xliv.

Derenbourg, H. 1886. "Le Science des religions et l'Islamisme." *Revue de l'histoire des religions* 13, 292–333.

Derrida, J. 1991. *Given Time:* I. *Counterfeit Money* (trans.) P. Kamuf. Chicago: University of Chicago Press.

———. 1995. *The Gift of Death* (trans.) D. Willis. Chicago: University of Chicago Press.

Devereux, R. 1968. "Preface." In *Ziya Gökalp, The Principles of Turkism* (ed.) R. Devereux. Leiden: E. J. Brill, ix–xi.

Douglas, H. 2001. *History of Turkey.* Westport, CT: Greenwood.

Douglas, M. 1970. *Purity and Danger.* London: Penguin.

———. 1973. *Natural Symbols.* New York City: Vintage.

———. 1993. *In the Wilderness: The Doctrine of Defilement in the Book of Numbers* (Journal for the Study of the Old Testament Supplement Series 158). Sheffield: JSOT Press.

Drouin, M. 1929. "Hubert (Henri)." *Annuaire. Association des Secours des Anciens Élèves de l'École Normale Supérieure,* 45–51.

Duchesne, L. 1903. *Christian Worship: Its Origin and Evolution* (trans.) M. L. McClure. London: SPCK.

———. 1906, 1907, 1910. *Histoire ancienne de l'Église.* Paris: Fontemoing.

———. 1920. *Les Origines du culte chrétien; étude sur la liturgie latine avant Charlemagne.* Paris: E. de Bocard.

Dumont, L. 1970. "The Individual as an Impediment to Sociological Comparison and Indian History." In *Religion/Politics and History of India. Paris:* Mouton, 133–51.

———. 1986. Marcel Mauss: A Science in Becoming. In *Essays on Individualism.* Chicago: University of Chicago Press.

Durkheim, É. 1884. *Cours de philosophie fait au Lycee de Sens.* Paris.

———. 1885. Review: "Fouillée, A., *La Propriété sociale et la démocratie.*" In *Revue philosophique* 19, 446–53.

———. 1887. "La Philosophie dans les universites allemandes." *Revue internationale de l'enseignement* 13, 313–38, 423–40.

———. 1898. "Individualism and the Intellectuals." In *Durkheim on Religion* (ed.) W.S.F. Pickering. London: Routledge, 59–73.

———. 1902. Preface to the Second Edition. In *The Division of Labour in Society* (ed.) L. Coser. London: Macmillan, xxxi–lix.

———. 1906. "Préface de la première édition." In Octave Hamelin, *Le Système de Descartes.* Paris: Alcan, v–xi.

———. 1907. Nécrologie d'Octave Hamelin in *Le Temps* 18 September. In Karady, V. (ed.) 1975. *Émile Durkheim.Textes: 1. Éléments d'une theorie sociale* (vol 1). Paris: Éditions de Minuit, 428–29.

———. 1915. *The Elementary Forms of the Religious Life* (trans.) J. W. Swain. New York: Free Press.

———. 1937. "Morale professionelle." *La Revue de métaphysique et morale* 38, 527–44, 711–38.

———. 1950. *Leçons de sociologie: physique des moeurs et du droit.* Istanbul: L'Université d'Istanbul, Publications de Université Faculté de Droit (vol. III).

———. 1951. *Suicide* (trans.) J. A. Spaulding & G. Simpson. New York City: Free Press.

———. 1957a. *Leçons de sociologie: physique des moeurs et du droit.* Paris: Presses Universitaire de France.

———. 1957b. *Professional Ethics and Civic Morals* (trans.) C. Brookfield. Westport: Greenwood Press.

———. 1960a. "The Dualism of Human Nature and Its Social Conditions." In *Essays on Sociology and Philosophy* (ed.) K. Wolff. New York: Harper and Row, 325–40.

———. 1960b. "Pragmatism and Sociology" (1914). In *Essays on Sociology and Philosophy by Emile Durkheim* (ed.) K. H. Wolff. New York: Harper, 386–436.

———. 1961. *Moral Education* (trans.) E. K. Wilson & H. Schnurer. New York: Free Press.

———. 1972. Letter to Xavier Léon dated 20 April 1916 cited in Steven Lukes, *Émile Durkheim: His Life and Work.* New York: Harper & Row, 1972, 556.

———. 1974. "Individual and Collective Representations." In *Sociology and Philosophy.* New York: Free Press, 1–34.

———. 1975. "Débat sur l'éxplication en histoire et en sociologie" In Karady, V. (ed.) 1975. *Émile Durkheim.Textes: 1. Éléments d'une theorie sociale* (vol. 1). Paris: Éditions de Minuit, 199–217.

———. 1975a. "Contribution to Discussion 'Religious Sentiment at the Present Time.'" In *Durkheim on Religion* (ed.) W. S. F. Pickering. London: Routledge, 181–89.

———. 1975b. "Review: Guyau, *L'Irreligion de l'avenir*" (1887). In *Durkheim on Religion.* London: Routledge and Kegan Paul, 24–38.

———. 1977. *The Evolution of Educational Thought: Lectures on the Formation and Secondary Education in France* (trans.) P. Collins. London: Routledge and Kegan Paul.

———. 1980. "Préface" to *L'Année sociologique.* In *Émile Durkheim: Contributions to L'Année Sociologique* (ed.) Y. Nandan. New York: Free Press, 47–58.

———. 1982. *The Rules of Sociological Method and Selected Texts on Sociology and its Method* (trans.) W. D. Halls. London: Macmillan.

———. 1982a. "The Contribution of Sociology to Psychology and Philosophy" (1909). In *The Rules of Sociological Method and Selected Texts on Sociology and Its Method.* London: Macmillan, 236–40.

Emirbayer, M. 1996a. "Durkheim's Contribution to the Sociological Analysis of History." *Sociological Forum* 11, 263–84.

———. 1996b. "Useful Durkheim." *Sociological Theory* 14, 109–30.

———. (ed.) 2003. *Emile Durkheim: Sociologist of Modernity.* Oxford: Blackwell.

Encrevé, A. 1979. "Les deux aspects de l'année 1876 pour L'Église réformée de France." In (ed.) A. Encrevé & M. Richard. Paris: Société de l'histoire du protestantisme français. *Actes du colloque: Les protestants dans les débuts de la Troisième République 1871–1885*, 371–410.

———. 1990. "La première crise de la Faculté de theologie de Paris: la démission de Maurice Vernes." *Bulletin de la Société de l'Histoire du Protestantisme Français.* 136, 77–101.

Encrevé, A., J. Bauberot & P. Bolle. 1977. "Les revéils et la vie interne du monde protestant." In *Histoire des Protestants en France* (eds.) R. Mandrou & J. Estebe. Toulouse: Edouard Privat, 263–336.

Fabiani, J.-L. 1988. *Les Philosophes de la république.* Paris: Éditions de Minuit.

Febvre, L. 1982. *The Problem of Unbelief in the Sixteenth Century: The Religion of Rabelais* (trans.) B. Gottlieb. Cambridge: Harvard University Press.

Félice, P. d. 1936. *Poisons sacrés. Ivresses divines: Essais sur quelques formes inférieures de la mystique.* Paris: Albin Michel.

Fern, M. 2002. *Nature, God and Humanity.* Cambridge: Cambridge University Press.

Filliozat, J. 1964. "Diversité d'oeuvre de Sylvain Lévi," in *Hommage à Sylvain Lévi: pour le centenaire de sa naissance (1963).* Paris: Bocard.

Findikoglu, A.Z.F. 1935. *Ziya Gökalp. Sa vie et sa sociologie: Essai sur l'influence de la sociologie française en Turquie.* Doctorat És Lettres: Université de Strasbourg.

Flori, J. 2001. *La Guerre Sainte: La formation de l'idée de croisade dans l'Occident chrétien.* Paris: Auber.

Flori, J. 1991. "Mort et martyre des guerriers vers 1100: L'exemple de la première croisade." *Cahiers de civilisation médievale* 34, 121–39.

Fournier, M. 1994. *Marcel Mauss.* Paris: Fayard.

Fournier, M. & C. D. Langle. 1991. "Autour du sacrifice: lettres d'Émile Durkheim, J. G. Frazer, M. Mauss et E. B. Tylor." *Études durkheimiennes/Durkheim Studies* 3, 2–9.

Frenchwikipedia. *Régime de Vichy en Afrique libérée (1942–43):* Wikipédia, l'encyclopédie libre et gratuite.

Germain, C. M. 2003. "Approaches to Statutory Interpretation and Legislative History in France." *Duke Journal of Comparative and International Law* 13, 195–206.

Goblet d'Alviella, C. E. 1885. "Maurice Vernes et la methode comparative." In *Revue de l'histoire des religions* 12, 170–78.

———. 1913. "La sociologie de M Durkheim." *Revue de l'histoire des religions.* 67, 192–221.

Gökalp, Z. 1968a. "Historical Materialism and Social Idealism." In *The Principles of Turkism* (ed.) R. Devereux. Leiden: E. J. Brill, 49–56.

———. 1968b. *The Principles of Turkism* (trans.) R. Devereux. Leiden: E. J. Brill.

Goodenough, E. R. 1965. *Jewish Symbols in the Greco-Roman Period: Summary and Conclusion* (vol. 12). New York City: Pantheon Books.

Grimsley, R. 1973. *The Philosophy of Rousseau.* Oxford: Oxford University Press.

Grogin, R. C. 1988. *The Bergsonian Controversy in France: 1900–1914.* Calgary: University of Calgary.

Gunn, J. A. 1922. *Modern French Philosophy.* New York: Dodd, Mead.

Gurvitch, G. 1931. *L'Idée du droit social.* Paris: Sirey.

Haizlip, S. T. 1999. "Living in Black History Today (Sigh)." *Los Angeles Times.* 21 February, M8.

Halbwachs, M. 1980. *The Collective Memory* (1950) (trans.) J. Francis J. Ditter & V. Y. Ditter. New York: Harper.

Halbwachs, M. 1930. *Les Causes du suicide*. Paris: Alcan.

Halls, W. D. 1996. "The Cultural and Educational Influence of Durkheim, 1900–1945." *Durkheimian Studies/Études Durkheimiennes* 2 ns, 122–32.

Halm, H. 1997. *Shi'a Islam: From Religion to Revolution*. Princeton: Markus Wiener.

Hamelin, O. n.d. Études critiques sur la morale de Kant. In *Collected Papers and Correspondence of Octave Hamelin*. *Bibliothèque Victor Cousin*. Paris.

——. 1907. *Essai sur les éléments principaux de la représentation*. Paris: Alcan.

——. 1927. *Le Système de Renouvier*. Paris: Alcan.

——. 1957. "Du Travail collectif en philosophie." In *Études philosophiques* (new series), 2/2, 151–57.

Harrison, P. 1998. *The Bible, Protestantism and the Rise of Natural Science*. Cambridge: Cambridge University Press.

Havet, L. 1918. "Section des Sciences Religieuses." In *La vie universitaire à Paris*. Paris: Colin.

Hawkins, M. J. 1994. "Durkheim on Occupational Corporations: An Exegesis and Interpretation." *Journal of the History of Ideas* 55, 461–81.

Hébert, M. 1909. "Review: Hubert and Mauss, *Mélanges d'histoire des religions*." *Revue d'histoire et de litterature religieuses* ns 1, 69–72.

Hefner, R. W. 2000. *Civil Islam: Muslims and Democratization in Indonesia*. Princeton: Princeton University Press.

Herr, L. 1885–1902. "Hegel." In *La Grande Encyclopedie*. Paris. H. Lamirault et Companie, 997–1003.

Hertz, R. 1909. "Review: Hubert and Mauss, *Mélanges d'histoire des religions*." *Revue de l'histoire des religions* 59, 218–20.

Hesse, A. & A. Gleyz. 1922. *Notions de sociologie appliquée à la morale et à l'éducation*. Paris: Alcan.

Heyd, U. 1950. *Foundations of Turkish Nationalism: The Life and Teachings of Ziya Gökalp*. London: Luzac.

Hofstadter, R. 1955. *Social Darwinism in American Thought*. Boston: Beacon Press.

Houtin, A. & F. Sartiaux. 1960. *Alfred Loisy: sa vie, son oeuvre*. Paris: Editions du CNRS.

Hubert, H. 1899. "Étude sur la formation des états de église." *Revue de l'histoire des religions* 69, 1–40, 241–72.

——. 1901. Review of J. Jüngst, *Kultus- und Geschichsreligion*. *Notes Critiques* 2, 226–27.

——. 1904a. "Introduction à la traduction française." In Pierre Daniel Chantepie de la Saussaye, *Manuel de l'histoire des religions* (eds) H. Hubert & I. Lévy. Paris: Colin, v–xlviii.

——. 1904b. "Systèmes religieuses." *L'Année sociologique* 7, 217–19.

——. 1905a. "Étude sommaire de la réprésentation du temps dans la religion et la magie." *Annuaire de l'École Pratique des Hautes Études, section sciences religieuses*, 1–39.

——. 1905b. "Review: A. Loisy, *L'Évangile et L'Église*." *L'Année sociologique* 8, 290–91.

——. 1919. "Préface" to Czarnowski, *Le Culte des héros et ses conditions sociales. Saint Patrick, héros national de l'Irlande*. In Czarnowski, *Le Culte des héros et ses conditions sociales. Saint Patrick, héros national de l'Irlande* (ed.) H. Hubert. Paris: Alcan, ii–xciv.

———. 1979. "Text autobiographique de Henri Hubert." *Revue française de sociologie* 20, 203–8.

Hubert, H. & M. Mauss. 1964. *Sacrifice: Its Nature and Functions* (trans.) W. D. Halls. Chicago: University of Chicago Press.

Hubert, H. & M. Mauss. 1968. "Introduction à l'analyse de quelques phénomènes religieux." In *Marcel Mauss, Oeuvres. Volume 1. Les Fonctions sociales du sacré* (ed.) V. Karady. Paris: Éditions de Minuit, 3–39.

Isambert, F.-A. 1983. "At the Frontier of Folklore and Sociology: Hubbert, Hertz and Czarnowski, Founders of a Sociology of Folk Religion." In *The Sociological Domain* (ed.) P. Besnard. Cambridge: Cambridge University Press, 152–76.

Israeli, R. 1997. "Islamikaze and their Significance." *Terrorism and Political Violence* 9, 96–112.

———. 2002. "A Manual of Islamic Fundamentalist Terrorism." *Terrorism and Political Violence* 14, 23–40.

Jennings, J. R. 1985. *Georges Sorel: The Character and Development of His Thought.* London: Macmillan.

Jones, R. A. 1975. "Durkheim in Context: A Reply to Perrin." *Sociological Quarterly* 15, 552–59.

———. 1977. "On Understanding a Sociological Classic." *American Journal of Sociology* 83, 279–319.

———. 1981a. "On Quentin Skinner." *American Journal of Sociology* 81, 453–67.

———. 1981b. "Robertson Smith, Durkheim and Sacrifice: An Historical Context for *The Elementary Forms.*" *Journal of the History of the Behavioral Sciences* 17, 184–205.

———. 1984. "Demythologizing Durkheim." In *Knowledge and Society: Studies in the Sociology of Culture Past and Present* (ed.) H. Kuklick. Greenwich, CT: JAI Press, 63–83.

———. 1999. *The Development of Durkheim's Social Realism.* Cambridge: Cambridge University Press.

Jones, R.A. & P.W. Vogt. 1984. "Durkheim's Defence of *Les formes élementaires de la vie religieuse.*" In *Knowledge and Society: Studies in the Sociology of Culture. Past and Present* (ed.) H. Kuklick. Greenwich, CT: JAI Press, 45–62.

Kaplan, M. M. 1956. *Questions Jews Ask.* New York City: Reconstructionist Press.

———. 1981. *Judaism as a Civilization* (1934). Philadelphia: Jewish Publication Society of America.

Karady, V. 1983. "The Durkheimians in Academe: A Reconsideration." In *The Sociological Domain* (ed.) P. Besnard. Cambridge: Cambridge University Press, 71–89.

———. (ed.) 1968. *Marcel Mauss, Oeuvres. Les Fonctions sociales du sacré* (vol. 1). Paris: Éditions de Minuit.

———. (ed.) 1975. *Émile Durkheim. Textes: 1. Éléments d'une theorie sociale* (vol. 1). Paris: Éditions de Minuit.

Kasprzycka, E. 2003. "Jewish Uprising's Heroes Honored in Warsaw." In *Los Angeles Times.* 1 May. A15.

Kelly, M. 1981. "Hegel in France to 1940: A Bibliographical Essay." *Journal of European Studies* 11, 29–52.

———. 1982. *Modern French Marxism*. Baltimore: Johns Hopkins University Press.

Keylor, W. R. 1975. *Academy and Community: The Foundation of the French Historical Profession*. Cambridge: Harvard University Press.

Kibbee, D. A. & Jones, R. A. 1993. "Durkheim, Language and History: A Pragmatist Perspective." *Sociological Theory* 11, 152–70.

Kolakowski, L. 1981. *Main Currents of Marxism. Volume 2. The Golden Age*. New York: Oxford University Press.

Kramer, M. 1996. "Sacrifice and 'Self-Martyrdom' in Shi'ite Lebanon." In *Arab Awakening and Islamic Revival* (ed.) M. Kramer. New Brunswick: Transaction Publishers, 231–43.

Kselman, T. 1993. *Death and the Afterlife in Modern France*. Princeton: Princeton University.

Kubali, H. N. 1936. *L'Idée de l'état chez les précurseurs de l'école sociologique français*. Paris: Les Éditions Domat-Montchrestien F. Loviton et Compagnie.

———. 1957. "Preface." In *Emile Durkheim, Professional Ethics and Civic Morals* (ed.) H. N. Kubali. Westport, CT: Greenwood Press, ix–xi.

———. 1959. "The Concept of the Rule of Law in Turkey." *Annales de la Faculté de Droit d'Istanbul* 9, 297–309.

———. 2005. electronic communication (ed.) I. Strenski. Los Angeles.

Kumar, K. 1993. "Civil Society: An Inquiry into the Usefulness of an Historical Term." *British Journal of Sociology* 44, 375–95.

Kurtz, L. R. 1986. *Politics of Heresy: The Modernist Crisis in Roman Catholicism*. Berkeley: University of California Press.

La Planche, F. (ed.) 1991. La méthode historique et l'histoire des religions; les orientations de la Revue de l'histoire de religions In *La Tradition française en sciences religieuses*. M. Despland, ed., Québec: Université Laval, 85–108.

Lalande, A. 1906. "Philosophy in France (1905)." *The Philosophical Review* 15, 252–62.

Langle, M. F. a. C. D. 1991. "Autour du sacrifice: lettres d'Emile Durkheim, J. G. Frazer, M. Mauss et E. B. Tylor." *Études durkheimiennes/Durkheim Studies* 3, 2–9.

Leach, E. 1968. "Ritual." In *International Encyclopedia of the Social Sciences*. D. L. Sills (ed.). New York: Macmillan, 520–26.

Legay, P. 1902. "Review: Hubert and Mauss, *Sacrifice: Its Nature and Functions*." *Revue d'histoire et de litterature religieuses* 7, 280–81.

Leroux, R. 1998. *Histoire et sociologie en France*. Paris.

Level, M. 1935. "Sylvain Lévi." *L'Univers Israelite* 91/7. 8 November, 97–98.

Levenson, J. D. 1994. *The Death and Resurrection of the Beloved Son*. New Haven: Yale University Press.

Lévi, S. 1898. *La Doctrine du sacrifice dans les Brahmanas*. Paris: Leroux.

———. 1900a. "La Régeneration Religieuse." *Archives israëlites* 61, 181.

———. 1900b. "Rituel du Judaisme." *Archives israëlites* 61, 62.

———. 1913. "Allocution to the General Assembly of the Société des Études Juives, seance of 24 January 1904." *Revue des études juives* 66, i–iii.

———. 1918. *Une Renaisssance juive en Judée* (Ligue des Maison du Sionisme, Tract No. 5. Paris: Driay-Cahen.

———. 1926a. "Civilisation bouddhique." In *L'Inde et le monde*. Paris: Honore Champion, ch 4.

———. 1926b. "Civilisation brahmanique." In *L'Inde et le monde*. Paris: Honore Champion, ch 3.

———. 1926c. "Eastern Humanism" (1922). In *L'Inde et le monde*. Paris: Honore Champion, ch 7.

———. 1926d. "Problemes indo-hebraiques." *Revue des études juives* 82, 49–54.

Lévi-Strauss, C. 1967. *The Scope of Anthropology*. London: Jonathan Cape.

Lévinas, E. 1977. "The Diary of Léon Brunschvicg." In *Difficult Freedom: Essays on Judaism*. Baltimore: The Johns Hopkins University Press, 38–45.

Lévy-Bruhl, L. 1966a. *How Natives Think* (trans.) L. A. Clare. New York: Washington Square Press.

———. 1966b. *Primitive Mentality* (trans.) L. A. Clare. Boston: Beacon.

Lichtenberger, F. 1889. "Sacrifice." In *Encyclopédie des sciences religieuses* (ed.) F. Lichtenberger. Paris: Sandoz et Fischbacher, vol. 8, 383–85.

Ligou, D. & P. Joutard. 1977. *Les Déserts (1685–1800). Histoire de Protestants en France*. Toulouse: Edouard Privat.

Linzey, A. 1998. *Animal Gospel*. Louisville, KY: Westminster John Knox Press.

Loisy, A. 1913. "Sociologie et religion." *Revue d'histoire et de litteratures religieuses* (new series) 4, 45–76.

———. 1920. *Essai historique sur le sacrifice*. Paris: Nourry.

———. 1930a. *Mémoires*. Paris: Nourry.

———. 1930b. *Memoires* (vol 2). Paris: Nourry.

———. 1968. *My Duel with the Vatican* (1925). New York City: Greenwood.

Lukes, S. 1972. *Emile Durkheim*. New York: Harper and Row.

Makiya, K. & H. Mneimneh. 2002. "Manual for a 'Raid.'" *New York Review of Books* 49, 18–21.

Malinowski, B. 1961. *Argonauts of the Western Pacific*. New York: E. P. Dutton.

Margalit, A. 2003. "The Suicide Bombers." In *The New York Review of Books* 16 January, 36–39.

Marrou, H.-I. 1973. "Mgr. Duchesne et l'histoire ancienne du christianisme." Paper presented to the *Monseigneur Louis Duchesne et son temps: Actes du colloque organisé par l'École Française de Rome*. 23–25 Mai 1973, Rome, 1973, 1–15.

Marshall, T. 2002. "Fighting Hard-Liners on Their Own Ground." *Los Angeles Times*. 20 October, A14.

Martin du Gard, R. 1949. *Jean Barois* (trans.) S. Gilbert. New York: Bobbs Merrill.

Martins, H. & W.S.F. Pickering (eds.) 1994. *Debating Durkheim*. London: Routledge.

Mathiez, A. 1973. *La Théophilanthropie et le culte décadaire* (1903). Geneva: Slatkine-Margolis Reprints.

Mauss, M. 1899. "Review: Cornelis P. Tiele *Inleiding tot de godsdientwetenschap* (Part 1)" in: *Marcel Mauss, Oeuvres. Volume 1. Les fonctions sociales du sacré* (ed.) V. Karady. Paris: Éditions de Minuit, 539–44.

———. 1902a. "Review: Frazer, *The Golden Bough. 3 volumes.*" *L'Année sociologique* 5, 205–13.

———. 1902b. "Review: Kraetschmar, *Prophet und Seher im alten Israel.*" *L'Année sociologique* 5, 312.

———. 1906. "Nomenclature." *L'Année sociologique* 9, 41–42.

———. 1908. "Review: Friedlander, *Jewish Religious Movements at the Time of Jesus.*" *L'Année sociologique* 10, 586–90.

———. 1913a. "Review: Duchesne, *Histoire ancienne de l'Église.*" *L'Année sociologique* 12, 310–13.

———. 1913b. "Review: Duchesne, *Les Premiers temps de l'État Pontifical. L'Année sociologique* 12, 319–20.

———. 1913c. "Review: P. Volz, *Der Geist und die verwandten Erscheinungen im Alten Testament und im anschliessenden Judentum.*" *L'Année sociologique* 12, 302–5.

———. 1967. *The Gift: The Form and Functions of Exchange in Archaic Societies* (trans.) I. Cunnison. New York: W. W. Norton.

———. 1968a. *La prière.* In Karady, V. (ed) *Marcel Mauss, Oeuvres 1. Les Fonctions sociales du sacré.* Paris: Éditions de Minuit, 357–548.

———. 1968b. "Review: Sylvain Lévi, *La Doctrine du sacrifice.*" In *Marcel Mauss. Vol. 1. Les fonctions sociales du sacré* (ed.) V. Karady. Paris: Éditions de Minuit, 352–54.

———. 1969a. "Cours scientifique (1925)." In *Marcel Mauss: Oeuvres. Volume 3. Cohesion sociale et divisions de la sociologie* (ed.) V. Karady. Paris: Éditions de Minuit, 477–82.

———. 1969b. "Introduction (1937)." In *Marcel Mauss: Oeuvres. Volume 3. Cohesion sociale et divisions de la sociologie* (ed.) V. Karady. Paris: Éditions de Minuit, 503–4.

———. 1969c. "Sylvain Lévi (1935)." In *Marcel Mauss. Oeuvres. Volume 3. Cohesion sociale et divisions de la sociologie* (ed.) V. Karady. Paris: Éditions de Minuit, 535–47.

———. 1983. "An Intellectual Self-Portrait." In *The Sociological Domain: The Durkheimians and the Founding of French Sociology* (ed.) P. Besnard. Cambridge: Cambridge University Press, 139–51.

———. 1990. *The Gift: The Form and Reason for Exchange in Archaic Societies* (trans.) W. D. Halls. New York: W. W. Norton.

Mayeur, J.-M. 1973. "Monseigneur Duchesne et l'Université." Paper presented to the *Monseigneur Louis Duchesne et son temps: actes du colloque organisé par l'École Française de Rome.* 23–25 Mai 1973, Rome, 1973, 329–49.

Melson, R. 1992. *Revolution and Genocide.* Chicago: University of Chicago Press.

Meštrovič, S. 1988. *Emile Durkheim and the Reformation of Sociology.* Totowa, NJ: Rowman and Littlefield.

Meyer, D. L. a. P. A. 1977. *Lucien Herr: Le socialisme et son destin.* Paris: Calmann Levy.

Milbank, J. 1990. *Theology and Social Theory: Beyond Secular Reason.* Oxford: Blackwell.

Mucchielli, L. 1998. "Les durkheimiens et la *Revue de l'histoire des religions*: (1896–1916) une zone d'influence méconnue." *Durkheimian Studies/Études Durkheimiennes* ns 4, 51–72.

Müller, F. M. 1891. *Physical Religion.* New York City: Longmans, Green and Company.

———. 1901. *An Autobiography: A Fragment.* London: Longmans, Green.

Mus, P. 1937. "La Mythologie primitive et la penseé." *Bulletin de la Societé Française de Philosophie* 37, 83–126.

Nabert, J. 1957. "Les manuscrits d'Hamelin a la Bibliothèque Victor-Cousin." *Études philosophiques* 2, 171.

Nandan, Y. 1977. *The Durkheimian School: A Systematic and Comprehensive Bibliography.* Westport, CT: Greenwood Press.

———. (ed.) 1980. *Émile Durkheim: Contributions to the L'Année Sociologique.* New York City: Free Press.

Newman, L. 2001. "Unmasking Descartes' Case for the Bête Machine Doctrine." *Canadian Journal of Philosophy* 31, 389–426.

Nielsen, D. A. 1986. "Robert Hertz and the Sociological Study of Sin, Expiation and Religion: A Neglected Chapter in the Durkheimian School." In *Structures of Knowing* (ed.) R. C. Monk. New York: University Press of America, 7–50.

———. 1987. "August Sabatier and the Durkheimians on the Scientific Study of Religion." *Sociological Analysis* 47, 283–301.

Nisbet, R. A. 1966. *The Sociological Tradition.* New York: Basic Books.

Nogent, G. o. 1997. *The Deeds of God through the Franks* (trans.) R. Levine. Woodbridge, Suffolk: Boydell and Brewer.

Novick, P. 1988. *That Noble Dream: The "Objectivity" Question and the American Historical Profession.* Cambridge: Cambridge University Press.

Ozouf, M. 1998. "The Pantheon: The Ecole Normale of the Dead." In *Realms of Memory: Symbols* (ed.) P. Nora. New York: Columbia University, 325–48.

Parla, T. & A. Davison. 2004. *Corporatist Ideology in Kemalist Turkey.* Syracuse: Syracuse University Press.

Parodi, D. 1913. "Le Problème religieux dans la pensée contemporaine." *Revue de Métaphysique et de Morale* 21, 511–25.

———. 1919a. "Émile Durkheim et l'école sociologigue." In *La philosophie contemporarine en France.* Paris: Alcan, 113–60.

———. 1919b. *La philosophie contemporarine en France.* Paris: Alcan.

———. 1922. "La Philosophie d'O. Hamelin." *Revue de Métaphysique et de morale*" 29, 187–88.

Parsons, T. 1937. *The Structure of Social Action.* New York: Free Press.

Partin, M. O. 1969. *Waldeck-Rousseau, Combes, and the Church: The Politics of Anti-Clericalism, 1899–1905.* Durham, NC: Duke University Press.

Peters, E. 1985. *Torture.* Oxford: Oxford University Press.

Pickering, W.S.F. 1975. *Durkheim on Religion.* London: Routledge.

———. 1984. *Durkheim's Sociology of Religion: Themes and Theories.* London: Routledge.

———. 1993. "Human Rights and the Cult of Individual: an Unholy Alliance Created by Durkheim?" In *Individualism and Human Rights in the Durkheimian Tradition* (eds.) W.S.F. Pickering & W. Watts-Miller. Oxford: British Centre for Durkheimian Studies, Ch 3.

———. 2000. "Review: Strenski, *Durkheim and the Jews of France*." *Religion* 30, 80.

———. (ed.) 2000. *Durkheim and Representations.* London: Routledge.

Plautt, W. G. 1965. *The Growth of Reform Judaism.* New York: World Union for Progressive Judaism.

Pocock, D. 1972. Foreword. In *A General Theory of Magic.* London: Routledge and Kegan Paul.

Poliakov, L. 1974. *The Aryan Myth*. New York: New American Library.

Poster, M. 1973. "The Hegel Renaissance." *Telos* 16, 110–24.

Poulat, É. 1979. *Histoire, dogme et critique dans la crise modemiste*. Paris: Casterman.

Preus, J. S. 1987. *Explaining Religion*. New Haven: Yale University Press.

Ranulf, S. 1939. "Scholarly Forerunners of Fascism." *Ethics* 50, 16–34.

Rapoport, D. C. 1984. "Fear and Trembling: Terrorism in Three Religious Traditions." *American Political Science Review* 78, 658–77.

———. 1992. "Some General Observations of Religion and Violence." In *Violence and the Sacred in the Modern World* (ed.) M. Juergensmeyer. London: Frank Cass.

Ravitch, N. 1990. *The Catholic Church and the French Nation, 1589–1989*. London: Routledge.

Rawlinson, G. C. 1917. *Recent French Tendencies*. London: Robert and Scott.

Reif, S. C. 1995. "William Robertson Smith in Relation to Hebraists and Jews at Christ's College, Cambridge." In *William Robertson Smith: Essays in Reassessment* (ed.) W. Johnstone. Sheffield: Sheffield Academic Press, 210–25.

Reinach, S. 1911. "The Growth of Mythological Study." *The Quarterly Review* 215, 423–41.

———. (ed.) 1923a. *Cultes, mythes et religions* (vol. 5). Paris: Ernest Leroux.

———. 1923b. "Monseigneur Louis Duchesne." In *Cultes mythes et religions* (vol. 5) (ed.) S. Reinach. Paris: Ernst Leroux, 392–413.

———. 1927. "Henri Hubert." *Revue archéologique* 26, 176–78.

———. 1930. *Orpheus* (trans.) F. Simmonds. New York: Liveright.

———. 1937. "Sylvain Lévi et son oeuvre scientifique." In *In Mémorial Sylvain Lévi* (ed.) J. Bacot. Paris: Hartmann, xi–li.

Renouvier, C. 1848. *Manuel républicain de l'Homme et du citoyen*. Paris: Pagnerre.

———. 1851. *Gouvernement direct et organisation communale et centrale de la République*. Paris.

———. 1863. *La Critique religieuse*. Paris: Ophyrs-Gap.

———. 1903. *Le Personnalisme*. Paris.

———. 1906. *Critique de la doctrine de Kant*. Paris: Alcan.

———. 1912. *Essais de critique générale*. Paris: A. Colin.

———. 1918. *Science de la morale*. Paris: Alcan.

Réville, A. 1858. "Review: De Rougemont, *Le Peuple primitif. Sa religion, son histoire et sa civilisation*." In *Le Lien*.9 October.

———. 1860. De la renaissance des études religieuses en France (1859). In *Essais de critique religieuse*. Paris: Cherbuliez, 361–415.

———. 1862. "Review: Pleyte, *De la religion primitif des Hébreaux*. In *Le Lien*. 12 July.

———. 1864. "Dutch Theology: Its Past and Present State." *Theological Review* 3, 275–77.

———. 1874. "Contemporary Materialism in Religion: the Sacred Heart." *Theological Review* 44, 138–56.

———. 1875. Evolution in Religion, and Its Results. *Theological Review* 12, 230–48.

———. 1883. *Les religions des peuples* non-civilisés (vol. 1). Paris: Fischbacher.

———. 1884. *Prolegomena of the History of Religions* (1881) (trans.) A. S. Squire. London: William and Norgate.

———. 1885. *Les Religions du Mexique, de l'Amerique centrale et du Perou*. Paris.

———. 1886b. *Religion chinoise*. Paris.

——. 1889. "Introduction: L'enseignement des sciences religieuses à l'école des hautes études." In *Bibliothèque de l'école des hautes études: Sciences religieuses.* Paris, i–xxx.

——. 1897. "Un essai de philosophie de l'histoire des religieuse." *Revue de l'histoire des religions* 36, 370–98.

——. 1902. Nécrologie of C. P. Tiele. *Revue de l'histoire des religions* 45, 70–75.

——. 1905. *Lectures on the ˙Origin and Growth of Religion* (1884) (trans.) P. H. Wicksteed. London: Williams and Norgate.

Réville, J. 1886a. "L'histoire des religions. Sa méthode et son rôle, d'après les travaux récents de MM. Maurice Vernes, Goblet d'Alviella, et du P. van den Gheyn." *Revue de l'histoire des religions* 14, 346–63.

——. 1892. "The Role of the History of Religions in Modern Religious Education." *The New World* I, 503–19.

——. 1899. "La Théologie partie integrante du cycle de l'enseignement universitaire et fondement indispensable de la Réformation." *Revue de l'histoire des religions* 39, 412–13.

——. 1900. "Congrès d'histoire des religions." *Revue de synthèse historique* I, 211–13.

——. 1901. "L'Histoire des religions et les facultés de théologie." *Revue de l'histoire des religions* 44, 423–37.

——. 1903. Leçon d'ouverture de M. Maurice Vernes. *Revue de l'histoire des religions* 47, 430–32.

——. 1905. "Review: Henri Hubert and Isidore Lévy, translation of Pierre Daniel Chantepie de la Saussaye, *Manuel de l'histoire des religions.*" *Revue de l'histoire des religions* 51, 75–82.

——. 1907. "Leçon d'ouverture du cours d'histoire des religions au Collège de France." *Revue de l'histoire des religions* 55, 189–207.

——. 1909. Les Phases succéssives de l'histoire des religions. *Revue de l'histoire des religions* 61, 100–25.

Ringer, F. 1992. *Fields of Knowledge: French Academic Culture in Comparative Perspective 1890–1920.* Cambridge: Cambridge University Press.

Rivière, J. 1912. "La redemption devant la pensée moderne." *Revue du clerge français* 70, 161–80, 278–305.

Robert, D. (ed.) 1978. *Les intellectuels d'origine non-protestante dans le protestantisme des débuts de la Troisième République* (Actes du colloque: Les protestants dans les débuts de la Troisième République 1871–1885). Paris.

Robertson, R. & Lechner, F. 1984. "On Swanson: An Appreciation and an Appraisal." *Sociological Analysis* 45/4, 185–204.

Sahlins, M. 1972. *Stone Age Economics.* Chicago: University of Chicago Press.

Savart, C. 1985. *Les Catholiques en France au XIXe siècle. Le temoinage du livre religieusex .* Paris: Beauchesne.

Schama, S. 1989. *Citizens: A Chronicle of the French Revolution.* New York: Knopf.

Schram, S. R. 1954. *Protestantism and Politics in France.* Alençon: Corbière et Jugan.

Scott, J. A. 1951. *Republican Ideas and the Liberal Tradition in France 1870–1914.* New York: Columbia University Press.

Senne, L. R. 1927. La Philosophie contemporaine en France. *Revue de métaphysique et de morale* 34, 105.

Shattuck, R. 1967. *The Banquet Years*. New York: Vintage.

Shaw, S. J. & E. K. Shaw. 1977. *History of the Ottoman Empire and Modern Turkey: Volume 2: Reform, Revolution, and Republic: The Rise of Modern Turkey, 1808–1975* (vol. 2). Cambridge: Cambridge University Press.

Simon-Nahum, P. 1990. "Émergence et spécificité d'une 'science du Judaisme' française (1840–1890)." In *Les Études juives en France* (eds) F. Alvarez-Pereyre & J. Baumgartner. Paris: Éditions CNRS, 24–32.

Singer, P. 1975. *Animal Liberation*. New York: New York Review of Books.

Skinner, Q. 1969. "Meaning and Understanding in the History of Ideas." *History and Theory* 8, 3–53.

Smart, N. 1984. *The Religious Experience of Mankind*. New York City: Charles Scribner's Sons.

Smend, R. 1995. "William Robertson Smith and Julius Wellhausen." In *William Robertson Smith Essays in Reassessment* (ed.) W. Johnstone. Sheffield: Sheffield Academic Press, 226–42.

Smith, C. 1967. "Octave Hamelin." In *Encyclopedia of Philosophy*. Vol. 3. New York: Macmillan, 408–9.

Smith, D. N. 1995. "Ziya Gökalp and Emile Durkheim: Sociology as an Apology for Chauvinism?" *Durkheimian Studies/Études Durkheimiennes* 1 ns, 45–50.

Smith, J. Z. 2004. *Relating Religion: Essays in the Study of Religion*. Chicago: University of Chicago Press.

Smith, R. J. 1982. *The École Normale Supèrieure and the Third Republic*. Albany: State University of New York.

Smith, W. R. 1912. "What History Teaches Us to Seek in the Bible." In *Lectures and Essays of William Robertson Smith* (eds.) J. S. Black & G. Chrystal. London: Adam and Charles Black, 207–34.

Sorel, G. 1902. "La Crise de la pensée catholique." *Revue d'histoire et de litterature religieuses* 10, 523–50.

———. 1908. "Modernisme dans la religion et dans le socialisme." *Revue critique des idées et des livres* 2, 177–204.

———. 1909. "La Religion d'aujourd'hui." *Revue d'histoire et de litterature religieuses* 17, 240–73, 413–47.

Staal, F. 1989. *Rules without Meaning: Ritual, Mantras and the Human Sciences*. New York: Peter Lang.

Stern, F. 1961. *The Politics of Cultural Despair*. Berkeley: University of California Press.

Storne, F. 1985. *Les Protestantisme liberale français au XIXème siècle a travers l'engagement des Révilles, pasteurs réformes*. Diplome d'études approfondies: Université de Reims.

Strenski, I. 1985. "What Structural Mythology Owes to Henri Hubert." *Journal of the History of the Behavioral Sciences* 21, 354–71.

———. 1987a. *Four Theories of Myth in Twentieth-Century History*. London/Iowa City: Macmillan/Iowa University Press.

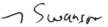

——. 1991. "L'apport des élèves de Durkheim." In *La tradition française en sciences religieuses* (ed.) M. Despland. Québec: Université Laval, 109–28.

——. 1993a. "Henri Hubert, Racial Science and Political Myth." In *Religion in Relation* (ed.) I. Strenski. London: Macmillan, 180–201.

——. 1993b. "Hubert, Mauss and the Comparative Social History of Religions." In *Religion in Relation.* (ed.) I. Strenski. London/Columbia, SC: Macmillan/University of South Carolina Press, 75–88.

——. 1993c. *Religion in Relation: Theory, Application and Moral Location.* London: Macmillan.

——. 1996. "Misreading Max Müller." *Method and Theory in the Study of Religion* 8, 291–96.

——. 1997. *Durkheim and the Jews of France.* Chicago: University of Chicago.

——. 2002. *Contesting Sacrifice: Religion, Nationalism and Social Thought in France.* Chicago: University of Chicago Press.

——. 2003. *Theology and the First Theory of Sacrifice.* Leiden: E. J. Brill.

——. 2006. *Thinking about Religion: An Historical Approach to Theories of Religion.* Oxford: Blackwell.

Tamir, Y. 1997. "Pro Patria Mori!: Death and the State." In *The Morality of Nationalism* (eds.) R. McKim & J. McMahan. New York: Oxford University Press, 227–44.

Taylor, C. 1975. *Hegel.* Cambridge: Cambridge University Press.

——. 2004. *Modern Social Imaginaries.* Durham, NC: Duke University Press.

Théau, J. 1977. *La Philosophie française dans la prémière moitié du vingtieme siècle.* Ottawa: University of Ottawa.

Thomas, K. 1996. *Man and the Natural World: Changing Attitudes in England, 1500–1800.* Oxford: Oxford University Press.

Tiele, C. P. 1877. *Outlines of the History of Religion to the Spread of the Universal Religions* (trans.) J. E. Carpenter. Boston: James R. Osgood.

——. 1896. *Elements of the Science of Religion. Part I: Morphological.* Edinburgh and London: W. Blackwood and Sons.

——. 1898. *Elements of the Science of Religion. Part 2: Ontological.* Edinburgh and London: W. Blackwood and Sons.

Tiryakian, E. 1979. "L'École durkheimienne à la recherche de la société perdue." *Cahiers internationaux de sociologie* 66, 97–114.

Titmuss, R. M. 1971. *The Gift Relationship.* New York: Vintage.

Toews, J. 1980. *Hegelianism.* Cambridge: Cambridge University Press.

Tourism, M. C. a. "Turkish Chronology": Turkish Ministry of Culture and Tourism.

Tresmontant, C. 1960. "La religion de Jaurès." *Ésprit* 28, 238–51.

Turlot, F. 1976. *Idéalisme dialectique et personnalisme: essai sur la philosophie d'Hamelin.* Paris: Vrin.

Turner, B. J. 1997. *The Social Origins of Academic Sociology*: Durkheim. PhD: Columbia University.

Turner, V. 1969. *The Ritual Process.* London: Routledge and Kegan Paul.

Van Hamel, M. 1880. "L'enseignement de l'histoire des religions en Hollande." *Revue de l'histoire des religions* 2, 379–85.

Van Kley, D. K. 1975. *The Jansenists and the Expulsion of the Jesuits from France, 1757–1765*. New Haven: Yale University Press.

Vernes, M. 1880/1881. "Introduction." *Revue de l'histoire des religions* 1, 10.

———. 1891. *Histoire Sainte. Première partie: Éléments d'histoire juive*. Paris: Ernest Leroux.

Vidler, A. 1970. *A Variety of Catholic Modernists*. Cambridge: Cambridge University Press.

Vigier, P. 1979. "Edmond Schérer, père fondateur de la Troisième République." In *Actes du colloque: Les protestants dans les débuts de la Troisième République (1871–1885)* (ed.) A.E.e.M. Richard. Paris: Société de l'histoire du protestantisme français, 183–97.

Vogt, W. P. 1983a. "Durkheimian Sociology versus Philosophical Rationalism: The Case of Celestin Bouglé." In *The Sociological Domain* (ed.) P. Besnard. Cambridge: Cambridge University Press, 231–47.

———. (ed.) 1983b. "Obligation and Right: the Durkheimians and the Sociology of Law." In *The Sociological Domain*. (ed.) P. Besnard. Cambridge: Cambridge University Press, 177–98.

Voigt, J. 1967. *Max-Müller: The Man and His Ideas*. Calcutta: Firma K. L. Mukhopadhyay.

Waldman, A. 2003. "Masters of Suicide Bombing: Tamil Guerrillas of Sri Lanka." *New York Times*. 14 January. A1, A8.

Wallwork, E. 1972. *Durkheim: Morality and Milieu*. Cambridge: Harvard University Press.

———. 1985. "Sentiment and Structure: A Durkheimian Critique of Kohlberg's Moral Theory." *Journal of Moral Education* 14, 87–101.

Webber, J. 1992. *The Future of Auschwitz*. Oxford: Oxford Centre for Postgraduate Hebrew Studies.

Weber, E. 1959. *The Nationalist Revival in France, 1905–1914* (vol. 60). Berkeley: University of California Publications in History.

Weiker, W. F. 1963. *The Turkish Revolution 1960–1961: Aspects of Military Politics*. Westport, CT: Greenwood Press.

Weisz, G. 1983. *The Emergence of Modern Universities in France, 1863–1914*. Princeton: Princeton University Press.

Westermarck, E. 1960. *Ethical Relativity*. Paterson, NJ: Littlefield, Adams.

Wimbush, V. L. & R. C. Rodman (eds.) 2000. *African Americans and the Bible: Sacred Texts and Social Textures*. New York City: Continuum.

Zeldin, T. 1979. *France 1848–1945: Politics and Anger*. Oxford: Oxford University Press.

INDEX

Abou El Fadl, Khaled M., 346–347n13
Abraham as model, 286–291
academic: culture, 184–191;
  philosophy, 34
adha (sacrifice), 286
afterlife, 89; in Durkheim, 108–110;
  Jewish beliefs about, 102
Agathon (jt. pseud.), *L'Esprit de la
  Nouvelle Sorbonne*, 160
al-Aqsa Intifada, 299
Alexander, Jeffrey C., *Theoretical Logic in
  Sociology*, 5
al-Islam wa-Filastin (handbook), 272
Allen, N. J., 39
Alliance Israëlite Universelle, 120, 122,
  123, 127
Al Qa'ida, 345n2
Altermann, Natan, "The Silver Platter"
  (poem), 297
altruism, 50–51, 339n20
"altruistic suicide" (Durkheim), 276
Amis du Judaïsme, Les, 128
Anderson, Benedict, 301
Andler, Charles, 45, 47
animal rights, 250; and Christianity,
  254–255, 257–258
animals: comity with humans, 250–251,
  267–268; symbolism, 262; temporal
  souls of, 255–256, 258; utility
  of, 259
Annalistes, 201
Année sociologique, L' (review annual), 14,
  79, 166, 183, 230, 313, 341nn4,5
"annihilationist" vs. "spiritualist"
  position on immortality, 100
Anselm of Canterbury, *Cur Deus Homo?*,
  264–265
anti-clericalism, 195–196
anti-propositionalism, 171
anti-ritualism, 119, 138–139
anti-Semitism, 99, 123, 145
Appleby, R. Scott, 345n5
Armenian terrorists, 348n31
art, 161–162, 341n4

"Aryan Bible," 156, 233
Aryanism, 121, 123–124, 144–146, 155, 156
Assassins, 273
Assumptionist order, 155
atheism, 80
authoritarianism, 46
avant garde, 160–162
Avemarie, Friedrich, 348n27

balance of power, 334
Barth, Albrecht, 341n7
beliefs, social context of, 242
Bellah, Robert, 8, 240
Benrubi, I., 337n8
Bergaigne, Abel, 130–131, 136, 152–153;
  La religion védique, 154
Bergson, Henri, 36, 160
Bernard of Clairvaux, Saint, 281
Berr, Henri, 68, 72, 193, 342n1
Besnard, Philippe, 5–6; *The Sociological
  Domain*, 5
Besse, Dom, *Les religions laiques*, 23
Bible, 145, 156, 244, 344nn3,5;
  345n6; literal and allegorical
  readings, 261–262; in Protestant
  Reformation, 262
biblical studies, 247
bin Laden, Usama, 278, 279, 296, 348n31
Birtek, Faruh, 307
Blake, William, *Jerusalem*, 251
Bloch, Marc, 201
Bordeaux, University of, 12, 13, 37, 303
Bossy, John, *Christianity in the West,
  1400–1700*, 263, 264, 265–266
Bouglé, Céléstin, 10, 339n1
Bourgin, Hubert, 163
Boutroux, Émile, 12
Brâhmanas, 132, 152
Brahmanism, 125
Brahmins, 341n7
British Centre for Durkheimian Studies,
  Oxford, 6
Brown, Peter, 103

Brunetière, Ferdinand, 239
Brunschwicg, Léon, 88–89, 90–91, 339n3
Buddhism, 123–124, 125–126, 253–254
Buisson, Ferdinand, 24, 112, 113
Bulletin critique de littérature, d'histoire et de théologie, 166
Butler, Bishop Joseph, 257

Caliphate of Islam, 348n31
Campbell, Joseph, 135
Capitant, Henri, 331
Cartesianism, 255
Cassirer, Ernst, 36
categories of inquiry, 74, 80
Catholicism, in France, 112, 113, 165, 197–200, 339n6, 340n4
causal ritualism, 154–155
Chantepie de la Saussaye, Pierre Daniel, 77, 219, 220–221, 343n1; *Lehrbuch der Religionsgeschichte,* 220
Christianity, 250; and animal rights, 254–255, 257–258; and historical research, 210; late medieval, 264–268; and nature, 250–254, 261; origins of, 163; pre-Reformation, 264–268; and ritual, 147; theology, and Durkheimian sociology, 249–251; values, 260, 263–269; and the Vedas, 145
christology, 264–266
civil rights, in Turkey, 333
civic morality, 112–113, 225
"civil religion" (Bellah), 240
civil society, in Turkey, 330
"civilization" and "culture," 315–317
classification, 78
clustered ritualisms, 138
cognitivism, scriptural, 244
Colani, Timothée, 187
"collective consciousness" (Durkheim), 321
collective representations and social morphology, 60–62
Collège de France, 202
Collège Libre des Sciences Sociales, 183
Collins, Steven, 37–38, 48, 52, 338n17
comity, in value systems, 264, 267
Committee of Union and Progress (Turkey), 312
community with animals, 269
Comte, Auguste, 22, 113, 114
concreteness, 53, 54, 174
"conscience collective" (Durkheim), 320–321
Constantine, Emperor, Edict of Milan, 283
Constitutional Court (Turkey), 332
continuity, historical and ideological, 96–99

contradictions, 55
corporations, Durkheimian, 323, 327–328
corporatism, for Durkheim and Gökalp, 322; Durkheimian and fascist, 306–311; influence of, 335; solidarist, 311, 322–328
Coulanges, Numa-Denis Fustel de, 12, 95–98; *La Cité Antique,* 96
Cousin, Victor, 111
Cowdrey, H.E.J., 346n7
cruelty to animals, 254–255
Crusades, 281–282, 346n8
cults of the dead, 103, 114
cultural distinctiveness, 125
cultural strategies, 151–152
"culture" and "civilization," 315–317
culture générale, post-Revolutionary, 182
culture philosophique (Durkheim), 34
Czarnowski, Stefan, 119

Darmesteter, James, *Prophets of Israel,* 157
Darwin, Charles, 259
Davison, Andrew, 306, 318, 322, 325–326
Davy, Georges, 37
dead: cults of, 103, 114; status of, 100–106
Deism, 111, 186, 192; and rationalism, 186–187, 188
De Maistre, Joseph, 334
democratic socialist movement, 41, 62
Derenbourg, Hartwig, 130
Derham, William, 263
Descartes, René, 59–60, 255
Deveraux, Robert, 310
disciplines, 181–191
Dorson, Richard, 139
Douglas, Howard, 330
Douglas, Mary, 18, 135, 246–247, 344n4; *Natural Symbols,* 119; *Purity and Danger,* 119, 246–247
Doumer, Paul, 174
Doyle, Arthur Conan, 105
Dreyfus, Alfred, 13
Dreyfus Affair, 21, 63, 163, 239
dualism, 59–60
Duchesne, Msgr. Louis, 163, 165–169
Dumont, Louis, 48, 201, 339n22
Durkheim, André, 338n12, 106, 338n12
Durkheim, Émile, 93–96, 139, 224; activism, 325; on afterlife, 108–113; anti-statist thought, 308; atheism, 20; bibliography, 4; biography, 4, 229–230; on continuity of past, 99; corporatist thought, 306–311; course on philosophy, 339n1; critics, 249; defense of Dreyfus, 230; on

education, 93–94; *équipe*, 183–184; essays on, 6; Hegelianism, 33, 36, 40, 47, 48, 59; historical intentions, 9; historical re-evaluation, 11, 230, 232; on history and sociology, 194; and human rights, 325; as idealist, identities, 116; influence of, 310; influences on, 12–13, 110; Jewishness, 11–12, 88, 89–92, 97–98, 112; and Kant, 50; lectures, 303, 305; liberalism, 13; on Müller, 141; "new" philosophy, 57–58; non-dualist perspective, 109; obituaries by, 39; plots against Protestants, 217–220, 343n2; as "positivist," 101; on the power of the state, 324–325; on religion, 169–171, 141, 233, 236–238, 239–240; on religion and society, 158–159, 240–241; on religion and sociology, 195; "religion of humanity," 21–26, 239–240; and religious modernists, 173, 176; Renouvierism, 37; and A. Réville, 211; on ritual, 139, 149; on science and religion, 161, 173, 174; sociology of religion, 175; on soul and body, 107–108; Spiritualism, 106; on suicide, 276; symbolism, 160, 161, 169
  Works: "Contribution to Discussion 'Religious Sentiment at the Present Time,'" 170; *Cours de philosophie*, 19; *The Division of Labor in Society*, 13, 15, 303, 323, 327; *The Elementary Forms of the Religious Life*, 14, 15–16, 61, 81, 139, 159, 173, 276; *The Evolution of Educational Thought*, 96, 97, 308; "Individual and Collective Representations," 61, 150; "Individualism and the Intellectuals" (essay), 23, 239, 325; *Leçons de sociologie physique des moeurs et du droit / Professional Ethics and Civic Morals* (set of lectures), 303, 305–310, 313; *Moral Education*, 158; *Professional Ethics and Civic Morals*, 303, 305–310, 325, 327; *The Rules of Sociological Method*, 13; *Suicide*, 13, 15, 276
Durkheimians, 74–83, 89–90, 160, 176, 184–191; on afterlife, 115; and anti-historicism, 78; and art, 161–162; conflicting views among, 77; cultural strategies, 151; on the dead, 104; and fascism, 340n2; in Fifth Section, 200–201; imperialism" of, 184–185; and modernism, 173–174; on myth and ritual, 150; partisan attacks, 184; political tendencies, 110, 189; and precursors, 333; and Protestants,

216–225; and religious studies, 194–195, 242; on ritual, 135–137, 150; ritualism of, 146, 148, 151; and *science religieuse*, 184–185; and social theory, in Turkey, 306–311, 320, 322, 328; and sociology, 34, 313; symbolism of, 159–165; thought of, and statism, 309, 310, 334–335; "weak" and "strong," 234–235
"Durkheim Pages, The" (website), 7

École des Hautes Études Sociales, 183
École Normale Supérieure, 12, 182
École Pratique des Hautes Études, history, 165, 182–183; Fifth Section, 118, 121, 129, 138, 163, 181, 184–191, 195–196, 199–200, 203, 205, 207–208, 216–225, 240, 241; Fourth Section, 166; Sixth Section, 201
écoles libres, 183
education, 93, 113–114, 183; law of 1882, 113. *See also* moral education
efficiency, in military operations, 273
Eid of sacrifice, 345n3
embodied religions, 119–120, 124–126
Emirbayer, Mustafa, 8–9, 308
empiricism, 73–74, 75; challenges to, 67, 76–77
Enlightenment, 186–187
Espinas, Alfred, 12
essays, 6
eternity of the past, 95
ethics, 49–52, 54
evangelical movement, 139, 186, 187
evolution, religious and historical, 71, 172, 207
evolutionism, 73–74, 78; liberal, 206
extremist ideologies, 285, 287

facts and theory, 75–76, 81–83
fascism in Turkey, 307
Febvre, Lucien, 201
Félice, Philippe de, 148–149; *Poisons sacrés: Ivresses divines*, 149
Ferry, Jules, 113, 339n7
Figaro, Le (newspaper), 160
Filliozat, Jean, 120n2
Findikoglu, A. Ziyaeddin Fahri, 327
Flori, Jean, 283
Fouillée, Alfred, 311
Fournier, Marcel, 6
France: Catholic culture, 197–198; national government, 239, 325; national and social values, 240; politics, 63–65, 176; religious studies, 196–197
French Protestants, 98, 185–186
French Revolution, 96–98, 111

fundamentalists, Christian and Muslim, 245, 344n5
Fustel de Coulanges. See Coulanges, Numa-Denis Fustel de

Gasparin, Comtesse de, L'Hégélien, 43
"gauchistes," 340n3
Germain, Claire M., 331
German cultural nationalism, 143
gift relation, in Spiritism, 105
gifts and obligation, 292–294
Girard, René, 253
"giving of" vs. "giving up," 287, 288–292, 347n15
Goblet d'Alviella, Eugène, le Comte, 71, 74, 207, 222, 343n4
god/society identity. See religion/society identity
Gökalp, Ziya, 307, 310, 311–329; The Principles of Turkism, 322; "The Social Functions of Religion," 328
Goldsmith, Oliver, 269
Grande Encyclopédie, La, 46
guilds, 324
Guinefort, Saint, 267
Gunn, J. A., 337n8
Gurvitch, Georges, 334
Guyau, Jean-Marie, L'Irreligion de l'avenir, 340n3

Hajj, 287–288
Halbwachs, Maurice, 109, 278; The Causes of Suicide, 277; Collective Memory, 90
Hamas, 272
Hamelin, Octave, 33, 35–42, 44, 47, 51, 53–57, 59–60, 63, 338nn12,18, 338–339n19, 339n21, 339n3; Essai sur les é1éments principaux de la représentation, 35, 36, 338n18; Le Système de Descartes, 338n12
Haram al Sharif/Har ha-bayit, 299
Harrison, Peter, 261–262
hau (Maori spirit), 105
Hawkins, J. M., 308, 322
Hébert, Abbé Marcel, 172, 173
Hefner, Robert W., 326
Hegel, Friedrich, 338nn15,16, 339n22; influence of, 35–36, 40–49, 63; and Kant, 51; and Prussian authoritarianism, 46; on morality, 52; The Philosophy of Right, 46
Hegelianism, 13, 33, 41, 43
Herder, Johann Gottfried von, 341n7
Herr, Lucien, 13, 39, 45–48, 338nn15,16
Hertz, Robert, 75, 76, 338n12
Heyd, Uriel, 307, 317
"Higher Criticism," 246
Hinduism and Judaism, 123, 124

histoire de synthèse (Berr), 72
histoire historisante, 67, 68–74
historians and sociologists, 9, 12
historical continuity, 96–99
historicism, 7, 67, 68, 200, 205
history: and empiricism, 68; and morality, 54; "philosophical constructs" in, 70; within sociology, 194; study of, 182; teaching of, 165–166; writing, 69. See also historicism; religion, history of
Hizballah, 272
Hommay, Victor, 338n12
Houtin, Albert, 164
Hubert, Henri, 10, 27–28, 61, 75–77, 135, 161–165, 167, 175–176, 189–190, 217, 218, 221–224, 241, 341n4, 343n4; "Étude sommaire de la représentation du temps . . . ," 119; Étude sur la formation des états de l'Église" (two-article series), 168; "Introduction," in Chantepie de la Saussaye, Manuel d'histoire des religions, 221, 343n4
Hubert, Henri, and Marcel Mauss, Sacrifice: Its Nature and Functions, 75, 76–77, 129, 132–133, 150, 173, 276
Hubert, René, Le sens du réel, 337n5
"human bombers," 270–302, 345n1
humanism, 23, 44, 124, 174, 186
human realm of existence, 108
human sacrifice, 348n25
humans and nature, in Christianity, 250–254
Husayn, Imam, 284–285

ibn Anas, Malik, 347n15
ideal and material, 61–62
idealism, 56, 59
identity, 16, 116, 118; national, 313–315
immortality, 100, 105, 109, 110, 114
Indian civilization, 124–125; religious traditions, 123, 152–153
Indianism, 143
individual: rights of, 239; sacredness of, 240; and society, 52, 62, 240; value of, 290
individualism, 13, 21, 22, 52, 235, 325–326
"influences," 95
Institut Catholique, 199
Institut d'Ethnologie, 201
International Association for the History of Religions, 208
International Congress of the History of Religions, Paris (1900), 193
Interpal, 347n17
Intifada, 299
Iran, revolution against Iraq, 285

Islam: extremist versions, 271, 284, 296; and the state, 326; values of, 290
"Islamikaze," 275
Israel: conflicts, 299; and Palestine, 297
Israeli, Raphael, 270–272, 274, 275, 278, 285, 287, 298, 345n1
Istanbul, 311–312, 319; University of, 303, 313, 329

Jacobus de Voragine, The Golden Legend, 265
Jaurès, Jean, 41, 44, 45, 56
Jesuits, 198, 263
Jesus, humanity of, 264–266
Jeunesse Laïque, La, 37
Jewish: community, in France, 99, 167; "influence," 94–99; religion, 126–127, 155–156; rituals, 103; theology, 102–104; tradition, 116–117. See also Judaism
jihad, 271–275, 286
Jones, Robert Alun, 6, 136, 173, 174
Jordan, Sandra, 345n3
Juan de Capistrano, Saint, 282
Judaism, 87, 116, 155–157, 234; aspects of, 126–127; history of, 120; "Mosaic," 127, 156; "prophetic," 126–127, 156; socially embodied, 126–128; Talmudic, 155
judicial autonomy, 332
"juridical pluralism" (Gurvitch), 334

Kant, Immanuel, 37, 49–50, 51–52
Karady, Victor, 5, 34
Kelly, Michael, 40–41, 338n15
Kelsay, John, 345n5
Kemalism, 306, 322, 325, 334
Keylor, William R., 69
Khomeini, Ayatollah, 285
kindness to animals, 257
Kolakowski, Leszek, 44, 56
Kramer, M., 272, 273
Kselman, Thomas A., 110, 111, 112, 114
Kubali, Hüseyin Nail, 303, 304–306, 309, 310, 329–336; "The Concept of the Rule of Law in Turkey" (survey), 329; L'Idée de l'état chez les précurseurs de l'école sociologique français (doctoral thesis), 333–335

labor unions, 324–325
Lachelier, Jules, 337n7
Lagarde, Paul, 147
Lalande, André, 339n1
Lang, Andrew, 341n5
language and concept, as weapons, 270, 274
language reform, 315
La Planche, François, 206

Legay, Paul, 173
Leonard of Reresby, Saint, 282
LePlay, Frédéric, 334
Le Roy, Edouard, 176
Level, M., 340nn2,3
Levenson, Jon D., 348n30
Lévi, Sylvain, 92, 95, 117, 120–133, 136, 152, 153–157, 340nn2,3,4,6, 341n7; La Doctrine du sacrifice dans les Brâhmanas, 120, 130, 132, 153–154; faith, 122, 341n8; influence of, 120, 129; political life, 122; "La Régéneration Religieuse," 122; "Le Rituel du Judaïsme," 122; teaching, 121, 129–130
Lévinas, Emmanuel, 88–89, 90–91
Lévi-Strauss, Claude, 105–106, 135, 201–202
Lévy, Isidore, 221, 340n2
Lévy-Bruhl, Lucien, 10, 201
Liber, Maurice, 124
liberal Catholicism, 162–166, 171
liberalism, in the Third Republic, 41
liberal Protestantism, 71–74, 112, 185–195, 197, 208, 223, 339n4
liberal Protestants, in Fifth Section, 191–193, 194–195, 205–208, 216–225
Lichtenberger, Frédéric, 74, 205, 342–343n1
Ligue républicaine d'Alsace et de Lorraine, 340n3
liturgy, 147
Loisy, Alfred, 80–83, 164, 167, 172, 173, 174, 175
Louis IX, Saint, 282
Lukes, Steven, Émile Durkheim: His Life and Work, 4–5, 37, 38, 230, 322, 337n8, 339n3

Maimonides, 102
Maison des Sciences de l'Homme, Paris, 5
Malinowski, Bronislaw, Argonauts of the Western Pacific, 293
Maori, "Spiritist" beliefs of, 105
Margalit, Avishai, 277–278
Martin, Richard, 259
Martin du Gard, Roger, Jean Barois, 172
Marty, Jacques, 343n4
martyrdom: in Islam and Christianity, 281–285; and sacrifice, 345n4; Shi'a notion of, 284–285
Marx, Karl, 25, 44
Marxism, 159
Massis, Henri, 341n2
materialism and spiritualism, 13
Mauss, Marcel, 10, 27–28, 38–39, 61, 75–77, 78, 105–106, 115, 120, 122,

Mauss, Marcel (*continued*)
129–130, 135, 154, 163, 167, 191,
201–202, 216–220, 234, 242, 292, 294,
305, 338n12, 340n2, 342n4; *The Gift*,
105; *La Prière* (PhD thesis), 219, 342n4;
review of Frazer, *The Golden Bough*,
245. *See also* Hubert, Henri, and
Marcel Mauss, *Sacrifice*
mechanism and nature, 255–256
Melson, Robert, 318
Menderes, Adnan, 332
Meštrovič, Stjepan G., 337n1
méthode historique, 69
"methodological Methodism"
(J. Réville), 194
Michelet, Jules, 342n1
Milbank, John, 249
modernism, 166, 169–177
Modernist Crisis, in Roman Catholic
Church, 172, 176
"modern theology" movement, 210
Monod, Gabriel, 12, 165, 222
moral education, 113–114, 158
morality, 50; and ethics, 54–55, and
history, 53–54; humanist, 174; and
religion, 113–114
moral judgment, autonomy of, 54, 59
moral relativism, 53
Moréas, Jean, 160
"morphology" of religions (Tiele),
78–79, 214
"Mosaic" Judaism, 127, 156
Mucchielli, Laurent, 223–224
Muhammad as model, 286
Müller, Friedrich Max, 131, 135, 136,
139–146, 153, 192, 233; "Comparative
Mythology," 139; on myth, 139–142,
341n9; religion, 140; spirituality, 142
Mus, Paul, 131, 153
Muslims: extremism dividing, 271;
humanists, 289–290; and martyrdom,
284; societies, 326; traditions, 348n25
myth, 139–142; and religion, 135,
140–142, 144; vs. ritual, 134–135; social
context, 245
mythophilia, in religious study, 156

Nabert, J., 39n12
Nandan, Yash, 4
nationalism, 195, 301; French, 88; as
religion, 301, 317; Turkish, 310, 313–320
National Unity Council, Turkey, 332
nation-state, 301–302
natural religion, 78–79, 141, 186, 192, 213
nature: Christian attitude to, 252;
exploitation of, 251–252, 256;
and scripture, study of, 261–263;
usefulness, 251–252, 262–263
nature worship, 140

naturism, 139
Neo-Kantian rationalism, 337n4
Newman, Lex, 256
Nielsen, Donald, 343n2
Nisbet, Robert, 5, 98
noble death, 348n27
Nogent, Guibert of, *The Deeds of God
Through the Franks,* 282, 283

"objective" and "subjective"
immortality, 100, 114
occasionalism, 62
occupational groups, 327–328
"ontology," 79
opposition, 55
oppositions, social, 62
orientalism, 258
Ottoman language, 315–316

Palestine: and bombers, 278, 295, 296,
297; dying for, 297, 299, 345n3; relief
program, 347n17
Pan-Islamism, 319
pantheism, 41–42, 43, 140
papacy, history of, 168
Paris, University of (Sorbonne), 14
Parla, Taha, 306, 318, 322, 325–326
Parodi, Dominique, 24, 170
Parsons, Talcott, *The Structure of Social
Action,* 5
particularism, 117
past: continuous, 95; Jewish and
French, 91, 112; nature of, 92, 97, 99;
and present, 88, 93, 114
Patarenes, 346n7
Paul, Saint, 258
Pécaut, Félix, 112, 188, 339nn1,4; *Le
Christ et la conscience,* 188
perennialism, 137
personal divinity, 172
personalism, 51–52
phenomenology, 78
"Philosophical Religion" (Müller), 140
philosophy, 33–65; autonomy of, 59;
and religion, 42; and ritual, 152–153;
and science, 56–59; and sociology,
10–11, 34
"Physical Religion" vs. "Philosophical
Religion" (Müller), 140
Pickering, W.S.F., 6, 303
pluralism, in Jewish theology, 102–104
Pocock, David, 77
Poincaré, Henri, 57
Poliakov, Léon, 145
political culture, in France, 63–65
politics and religion, 197–199, 340n4
polytheism and monotheism, 207
positive sciences, 188–189
positivism, 101, 110, 113–115, 188–190, 193

"possibilist" socialists, 49
potlatch giving, 294
practical ritualism, 137, 152
Prague, Hyppolite, 124
prayer, social contexts, 242–243
Preus, Samuel, 159
"primitive": religions, 119, 212–213, 219;
societies, 15–16
professional groups: autonomy, 330;
place in society, 327
"prophetic" Judaism, 156
prophets, 234
Protestants, in France, 72, 185–186,
194, 216
psychology, and religion, 221
public education, 224–225
public morality, 110–112

Quran, 244–245, 343n2, 344n5,
347–348n21; values, 289
qurbani (sacrifice of Isaac), 288,
346–347n13

Radhakrishnan, Sarvapalli, 260
Ranulf, Svend, 307, 340n2
Rapoport, David C., 273, 348n31
rationalism, 37, 49, 63, 186–187
rationalists and empiricists, 77
real and ideal, 59
reconciliation, 56–63
reductionism, "hard" and "soft," 16, 17–18
reform, religious, 174–176
reformations, Protestant and Catholic,
186, 262–263
Reform Judaism, 103–104
Reinach, Salomon, 165, 341n6
relation, 56
religion: autonomy of, 220, 328; embodied, 119–120, 124–126; evolutionary,
71, 73–74, 192; function in society,
196; in high middle ages, 266;
historical study and theology, 210;
history of, 66–83; and myth, 140–142;
national, 44–45; and nation-building,
301; "natural," 78–79, 141, 186, 192,
213; nature of, 132, 219, 220, 239, 246;
normative sense, 141; origins, 153;
place of, in nation-state, 305; place of
myth in, 140–142; political utility, 196;
and politics, 197–199; "problematized,"
232–234; problems about, 242,
246–248; public discourse about, 224;
in the public domain, 236–238;
reform of, 176; role in society, 25; role
of rituals, 136; and science, 161, 185,
203–213; separate from morality,
113–114; "semi-public," 328; as social
identity, 18–21; social nature of, 219,
222–223; social ontology of, 237;

socially embodied, 124, 127, 128; and
society, 15; sociological reduction,
17–18; and sociology, 161, 195, 237;
and the state, 124n4; study of, 75–76,
135, 184–195, 159, 174, 182, 184–195,
196, 199–200, 203–212, 214, 234, 241;
symbolic interpretation, 169–177;
totemic, 235. See also religions;
traditional religions
religion-as-such, 79, 141, 214
Religion of Humanity (Comte), 114
"religion of humanity" (Durkheim), 13,
21–26, 42, 239–240
religion/society identity, 15–17, 21–26,
237–238
religions: classification and ranking, 78,
214–215; history of, 70, 140–142, 165,
201, 203, 204, 343n3; "primitive," 119,
212–213, 219; ritualist, 146; and sciences, 174; as social institutions, 234
religious: cultural values, 319; evolution,
152, 206–208; experience, origins and
causes, 233, 235, 237–238; groups as
"occupational" groups, 327; groups,
social value, 328; liberalism, 175;
modernists, 171–177, 342n8; movements, transnational, 301; reality,
and social reality, 238–240;
reformism, 175–176; sects, and
synagogues, 234; societies, 326;
studies, 135, 231–232, 234, 238–242;
texts, 233, 241–248; traditions, 15–16,
97, 120, 123, 155–156; violence,
277–278
"religious materialism" (Réville), 138
Renan, Ernest, 114, 209; L'Avenir religieux
des sociétés modernes, 121
Renou, Louis, 131, 153
Renouvier, Charles, 10, 13, 37–38, 44–45,
49, 50–52, 54, 55, 63–64, 112, 337n3,
339n21, 342n1
resurrection of the body, 102, 103
réveils, 186
Réville, Albert, 98–99, 118, 138–139,
185–189, 191–192, 192–193, 203, 207,
208–213, 339n4, 343n4; Prolegomena
of the History of Religions, 206, 343n4;
"scientific" theology, 212
Réville, Jean, 67, 71–74, 99, 189, 192,
193–194, 197, 203, 207, 222;
"scientific theology," 224
Revue de la faculté de la droit d'Istanbul
(periodical), 305
Revue de l'histoire des religions (journal),
69, 185, 204, 206, 212, 222
Revue de métaphysique et de morale
(journal), 305
Revue des deux mondes (periodical), 209
Revue des études juives (periodical), 120

Revue de Strasbourg (periodical), 187
Revue de synthèse historique
  (periodical), 72
Revue de théologie et philosophie
  chrétienne (periodical), 187
Revue historique (journal), 165, 168, 185
Ringer, Fritz, 68, 181
Ritschl, Albrecht, 148
ritual, 132, 132n6; causal priority of,
  149–151; historical treatment, 138;
  and myth, 134–135, 149–151; need
  for, 148; and philosophy, 152–153; in
  religion, 134–135, 146–148
ritualism, 130–131, 135, 136–139, 152–157;
  causal/constitutive, 136, 154–155;
  clustering, 138; "methodological,"
  136–137; perennial, 137; practical,
  137, 152
rituals, 288; in Jewish practice, 102–103;
  in religious life, 135
ritual sacrifice, 132, 151, 154, 286, 288,
  294, 296, 347n14
Rivière, Jean, 186n3
Robespierre, Maximilian, 111
Roch, Saint, 267
Rolland, Romain, *Jean Christophe*,
  342n8
Roman Catholic Church, 112, 166–167,
  185, 199, 341n6; liberal movements
  in, 171; on martyrdom, 283; and
  politics, 197; study of religion, 209
Romantic movement, 143, 258
Rotterdam, 209–210
Royal Society for the Prevention of
  Cruelty to Animals, U.K., 258
rule of law, in Turkey, 329–336

Sabatier, Auguste, 172, 191, 218, 342n4,
  343n2; *Esquisse d'une philosophie de la*
  religion, 219
sacred: idea of the, 131–133, 303;
  material, 120; in space and time, 120
sacredness, 298–300; of the individual,
  22; of place, 119
sacrifice, 70–71, 79, 132–133, 271–302,
  341n8, 345n3; bombings, 294–302;
  in Christianity, 253, 291, 339n6;
  definitions, 80–81; as a gift, 288,
  292–302; history of, 130; in Islam,
  280, 288, 291, 292, 345n6, 347nn14,15,
  348n25; in Judaism, 291, 345n6; as
  "making sacred," 298–300; and
  martyrdom, 280, 345n4; misapplied,
  272; for nations, 302; religious
  resonances, 278; ritual, 132, 151, 154,
  286, 288, 294, 296, 347n14; and
  society, 278; in Sunni tradition,
  286–289; and suicide, 274–280;

terminology, 347n14; in the Third
  Republic, 339n6
saints, 266–267
Saint-Simon, Claude-Henri, 113
Saint-Simonians, 43
Saussaye, Chantepie de la. *See* Chantepie
  de la Saussaye, Pierre Daniel
Schelling, F.W.J., 143
Schérer, Edmond, 187, 339n4
Schleiermacher, Friedrich, 206
Scholastics, 256
Scholten, J. H., 210, 343n2
schools, in post-Revolutionary France,
  182–183
Schopenhauer, Arthur, 145, 337n1
science: empiricist and rationalist
  views, 76; and modernism, 171;
  origins, 263; and philosophy, 56–58;
  and religion, 161, 174, 203–213, 220
"science of religion" (Tiele), 191–192, 212
science religieuse, 181, 184–185, 195–197,
  199, 208; attacks on, 195, 222
"scientific history," 203–213
"scientific theology" (Réville & Réville),
  73, 212, 224
scripture: cognitivist readings, 244, 247;
  liberal readings, 261, 344n3; non-
  cognitive uses, 243; religious
  problems and, 247; variety of
  approaches to, 248
Seignebos, Charles, 194
self-immolation, and Islam, 296,
  347n15
self-sacrifice, 50; in jihad, 287, 347n15
Senne, René Le, 35
separation of powers, 333
Shi'a militants, 284
Singer, Peter, *Animal Liberation*, 250,
  253, 254, 256–257, 259–260
Sittlichkeit (Hegel), 52
Skinner, Quentin, 6
Smith, David Norman, 318, 322
Smith, Jonathan Z., 303
Smith, William Robertson, 76, 119, 136,
  146–148, 153, 246, 340n1, 344n3;
  Lectures on the Religion of the Semites,
  15, 246, 340n1, 344n3
"social individualism" (Durkheim), 13
socialism, 41, 43, 49
socialization by way of education, 315
social: morphology, 60–62; realism,
  101; vs. religious reality, 238–240;
  virtues, 267
Société des Études Juives, 92, 120
societism and individualism, 240
society: ideal and material factors,
  61–62; as judge, 277; "religiousness,"
  15, 19, 20, 158

society/religion identity, 15–17, 21–26, 237–238
sociobiology, 108
sociologie religieuse, 237
sociologists and historians, 9
sociology, 9; and Christian theology, 249–251; as a discipline, 183; function of, 58; and history, 9, 194; and philosophy, 10–11, 34; and religion, 161, 195; success of, 224
sociology of religion, 249
solarism, 341n6
Sorbonne, Protestant Faculty of Theology, 205
Sorel, Georges, 159, 174
soul: in Durkheim, 107–108; socially formed, 19; and spirit, 105–106
speciesism and Christianity, 254–255, 261
spirit: and matter, 107–108, 118; and soul, European belief in, 105–106
Spiritism, 105
Spiritualism, 105, 106, 111, 112
"spritualist" vs. "annihilationist" position on immortality, 100
state, role of, 304, 324–326
statism, 41, 304, 334–335
Stein, Edith, 283
Storne, Franck, 209
Strenski, Ivan, 89, 223, 339n6, 343n1
structuralism, 202
"subjective immortality," 100, 114
subjectivism, in religion, 219
suicide, 271; "altruistic," 276; and sacrifice, 274–280, 294–302
Sunni: extremists, 284, 285; tradition, 281, 287; views of sacrifice, 286–289
supernaturalism, 106
superstition, 138
symbol, in religion, 159–165, 175, 342n8
Symbolism, 160–163, 171
synagogue, role of, 234
syndicalism, 49

Tamil Tigers, 295
Tarde, Alfred de, 341n2
Taylor, Charles, 52, 60, 326
Temple Mount, 299
Temps, Le (newspaper), 187; and "sciences religieuses," 188–189
Terrorism and Political Violence (periodical), 270
texts as actions, 242–243. *See also* religious texts; scripture
thatkodai (self-giving), 295
theism, and morals, 111
theological symbolism, 162–163

theology: Christian pre-Reformation, 263–269; vs. historicism, 205; in history of religion, 71–72, 78, 210; Protestant, 223; and religion, 221
Theophilanthropy, 111
theory vs. facts, 81–83
Third Republic, 63–64, 110, 113–114, 198–200; moral system, 195
Thomas, Keith, 257–258
thought and substance, 60
Tiele, Cornelis P., 77–79, 118, 192, 210–215, 219; anti-positivist approach to religion, 214; *The Elements of the Science of Religion*, 79, 204, 214; *Inleiding tot Godsdienstwetenschap*, 242; psychological approach to religion, 220; on religious "morphology," 214
Tiryakian, Edward, 160
Tournier, Édouard, 165
traditional: religions, 176; societies, 15–16
transcendence, 149
Turkey, 306–336; Constitution of 1961, 329–330, 332–333; division of languages, 315; government, 332–333; independence movements, 314; National Unity Council government, 332; political revolutions, 312; Revolution of 1960, 331–332; right wing, 335; social life, 313; social reconstruction programs, 304;
Turkism, 313–315
Turks, ethnic identity, 313–314
Turlot, Fernand, 57, 337n2
Turner, Victor, 135

Union of Free Thinkers and Free Believers, 20, 169
unions, 324–325
Urban II, Pope, 346n8

values: Christian and Durkheimian, 260, 264; organic and dialogic, 252; of society, 240
Van Hamel, M., 204, 343n3
van Henten, Jan Willem, 348n27
Vedas, 140, 142, 143, 144, 152–157, 341n9; hymns, 131
Vedic religion, 155
vengeance, 278
Vernes, Maurice, 69–74, 189, 204–208
Vincent, Samuel, 187
Vogt, W. Paul, 6, 75

Wallwork, Ernest, 50
warrior martyr, 283

Warsaw Ghetto Rising, 297
Weber, E., 256
Weiker, Walter F., 330
Weil, Alexandre, 44
Wellhausen, Julius, 246
Westermarck, Edward, 52
Wiebe, Don, 343n3
Wimbush, Vincent, 243
Wood, John George, 257

World Trade Center site, 299, 348n28
World War I, 105

Yaseen, Ahmad, 345n3
Young Muslims, "Sacrifice: The Making of a Muslim" (Web page), 291
Young Turk Revolution, 312

Zionism, 127–128, 156

ABOUT THE AUTHOR

IVAN STRENSKI is Holstein Family Community Professor of Religious Studies at the University of California, Riverside, and the former editor of the journal *Religion.*